PENNSYLVANIA

KEYSTONE OF THE NEW MILLENNIUM

PENNSYLVANIA

KEYSTONE OF THE NEW MILLENNIUM

LORETT TREESE

CHERBO PUBLISHING GROUP, INC.

ENCINO, CALIF.

FROM THE AUTHOR

For my husband, Mat Treese, who introduced me to the quiet beauty of central Pennsylvania,
and for our grandparents, who came to share in Pennsylvania's promise.

ACKNOWLEDGMENTS

The author would like to thank the staffs at the Pennsylvania Department of Community
and Economic Development, the Pennsylvania Chamber of Business and Industry, the Pennsylvania Economy
League, and the State Library of Pennsylvania, as well as editors Tina G. Rubin and Margaret Martin.

CHERBO
PUBLISHING
GROUP, INC.

PRESIDENT **Jack C. Cherbo**

EXECUTIVE VICE PRESIDENT **Elaine Hoffman**

EDITORIAL DIRECTOR **Christina M. Beausang**

MANAGING FEATURE EDITOR **Margaret L. Martin**

FEATURE EDITOR **Tina G. Rubin**

ESSAY EDITORS **Sylvia Emrich-Toma, Margaret L. Martin**

SENIOR PROFILES EDITOR **J. Kelley Younger**

PROFILES EDITOR **Diane M. Ver Steeg**

SENIOR PROFILES WRITER **Brian K. Mitchell**

PROFILES WRITERS **Barbara Beckley, Maria A. Collis,
Linda Chase, Camilla Denton, Paul Lavenhar, Beth Mattson-Teig,
Felicia Molnar, Nancy Smith-Seigle, Paul Sonnenburg,
Diane M. Ver Steeg, and Stan Ziemba**

SENIOR PROOFREADER **Sylvia Emrich-Toma**

SENIOR DESIGNER **Mika T. Mingasson**

PROFILES DESIGNER **Mary C. Barnhill**

PHOTO EDITOR **Catherine A. Vandenberg**

SALES ADMINISTRATOR **Joan K. Baker**

ACQUISITIONS ADMINISTRATOR **Bonnie J. Aharoni**

PRODUCTION SERVICES MANAGER **Ellen T. Kettenbeil**

ADMINISTRATIVE COORDINATOR **Jahnna Biddle**

EASTERN REGIONAL MANAGER **Marcia Weiss**

EASTERN DEVELOPMENT DIRECTOR **Glen Edwards**

PROJECT DIRECTORS **Tim Hoover, William W. McAllister**

Cherbo Publishing Group, Inc., Encino, Calif. 91316
© 2000 by Cherbo Publishing Group, Inc.
All rights reserved. Published 2000
Printed in the United States of America

Visit CPG's Web site at www.cherbo-publishing.com.

Library of Congress Cataloging-in-Publication Data
Treese, Lorett
  A pictorial guide highlighting 20th- and 21st-century
  Pennsylvania lifestyle and economic history.
    00-103969
    ISBN 1-882933-31-1

CORPORATIONS/ORGANIZATIONS PROFILED

The following companies and organizations have made a valuable commitment to the quality of this publication. Cherbo Publishing Group gratefully acknowledges their participation in *Pennsylvania: Keystone of the New Millennium.*

The Benjamin Franklin Bridge and the Philadelphia skyline © John McGrail

CONTENTS

Harrisburg skyline © Blair Seitz

ESSAYISTS

STATE OF PENNSYLVANIA
OFFICE OF THE GOVERNOR

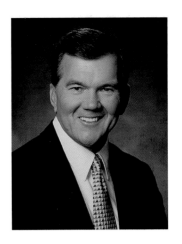

Dear Friends:

On behalf of 12 million Pennsylvanians, I am pleased to introduce *Pennsylvania: Keystone of the New Millennium.*

Throughout our nation's history, Pennsylvania has been a pioneer in new technology and a furnace of innovation. In our first century, Pennsylvania led the American Revolution—with the strength of our beliefs. In our second century, we led the Industrial Revolution—with the strength of our backs. In our third century, we are leading a new revolution—with the strength of our minds, the force of our will, and the fortitude of our souls.

To be Governor of "Penn's Woods" is to be custodian of a natural bounty that is unrivaled anywhere in the world. It is also to represent some of the finest, most decent, hardworking people you will ever meet.

From William Penn and Benjamin Franklin to the surging dynamism of Philadelphia and Pittsburgh to our verdant mountains and pastoral farmlands in between, Pennsylvania remains the keystone of this great nation.

As you read through the pages of *Pennsylvania: Keystone of the New Millennium,* you'll discover exactly what I mean.

Sincerely,

Tom Ridge

Tom Ridge

HISTORICAL HIGHLIGHTS

Offering freedom and boundless opportunity, Pennsylvania has proved a fertile ground for new ideas and big dreams—for more than three centuries. From statesmen like William Penn, who created the soundest government in the colonies, to humanitarians like Andrew Carnegie, Pennsylvanians leave a mighty imprint on this historic land.

PARAMOUNT PENNSYLVANIANS

ARTS & LETTERS

LOUISA MAY ALCOTT (1832–88)
One of the 19th century's greatest female writers, Alcott is remembered primarily for her novel *Little Women,* which captured middle-class life of the era. Since its first publication in 1868, the book has appeared in print continuously.

MARIAN ANDERSON (1897–1993)

Overcoming an impoverished childhood in Philadelphia, Anderson became a highly acclaimed contralto and the first black diva to sing with the Metropolitan Opera.

PEARL S. BUCK (1892–1973)
The daughter and wife of missionaries in China, Buck is famed for her novels about Chinese life—particularly *The Good Earth,* for which she won the Pulitzer Prize in 1931.

ALEXANDER CALDER (1898–1976)
Born in Lawnton, Calder made history as a pioneer of kinetic art. He is considered the father of the mobile and inventor of the stabile.

MARY CASSATT (1844–1926)
Cassatt, who was born in Allegheny, spent much of her life in Paris; she became the only American artist to exhibit with the late-19th-century French impressionists.

BILL COSBY (1937–)
Born in Philadelphia, Cosby became the first black star of a network TV series (*I Spy*) and later hosted the long-running *Cosby Show,* the nation's top-rated TV series in the 1980s.

THOMAS EAKINS (1844–1916)
Eakins, a Philadelphian, was one of 19th-century America's greatest artists. His enormous success in realist portraiture (capturing the personality) reflected his love of anatomy.

MARTHA GRAHAM (1894–1991)
Pittsburgh-born Graham redefined contemporary dance. Her style serves as the basis for teaching modern dance today.

GENE KELLY (1912–96)
Kelly's athletic approach to dancing resulted in his soaring success as a dancer and choreographer in such films as *Singin' in the Rain* and *An American in Paris.* He was born in Pittsburgh.

GRACE KELLY (1929–82)

An international cinema star from Philadelphia, Kelly was known for such films as *High Noon* and *The Country Girl.* She became a princess with her marriage in 1956 to Prince Rainier of Monaco.

CHARLES WILLSON PEALE (1741–1827)
Peale, who settled in Philadelphia in 1776, became the most renowned portrait painter in the colonies and was a founder of the Pennsylvania Academy of the Fine Arts.

HORACE PIPPIN (1888–1946)
The West Chester native was one of the country's great African American artists. Among his celebrated oil paintings is his *Cabin in the Cotton* series.

WILL SMITH (1968–)
The multitalented MTV and Grammy Award–winning rap star from Philadelphia (shown here with his wife, Jada Pinkett) is known not only for such megahits as "Miami" and

MEMORABLE MOMENTS OF THE

1716
In Oaklawn, Thomas Rutter produces the first iron in the New World, on a tributary of the Schuylkill River

1751
Pennsylvania Hospital, the first institution of its kind in the American colonies, opens in Philadelphia

1781
American banking begins in Philadelphia when Congress enacts the Charter for the Bank of North America; the first chartered commercial bank opens a year later

"Just the Two of Us" but also for films such as *Men in Black* and *Wild Wild West*.

GERTRUDE B. STEIN (1874–1946)

The legendary author's avant-garde literary works include her 1932 *The Autobiography of Alice B. Toklas*. Also a patron of the arts, the Allegheny-born writer helped support Picasso.

JAMES STEWART (1908–97)
The well-loved Indiana (PA)–born movie star is known as much for his own upright character as he is for his roles in such hit films as *It's a Wonderful Life* and *Vertigo*.

IDA M. TARBELL (1857–1944)
Born in Erie County, Tarbell defined investigative journalism. Her famous series of articles, "A History of the Standard Oil Company," led to the adoption of antitrust and monopoly legislation.

THE WYETH FAMILY
A beloved illustrator, N. C. Wyeth (1882–1945) settled in Chadds Ford, bringing vivid imagery to such books as *Treasure Island* and *The Yearling*. His son Andrew (1917–) gained international recognition for his paintings, many of which were set in rural Pennsylvania, and grandson Jamie Wyeth (1946–) became a well-known portrait artist.

BUSINESS & INDUSTRY
ANDREW CARNEGIE (1835–1919)
Carnegie (right) emigrated from Scotland to Pittsburgh, where he built the first steel plants in the nation to use the Bessemer process extensively. A philanthropist, he donated more than $350 million and endowed nearly 3,000 libraries.

HENRY CLAY FRICK (1849–1919)
Born in West Overton, Frick supplied Pittsburgh's iron and steel industries with coke and helped form the United States Steel Corporation with Carnegie. His Pittsburgh home and art collection are open to the public.

FOOD, GLORIOUS FOOD!

The Swedes and the Germans, who were the earliest to settle in the Delaware Valley, shared a tradition of making hash out of pork by-products. Sometime during the 18th century, they began adding American cornmeal, and a new delicacy was born. The dish caught on in the city and became known nationwide as Philadelphia scrapple. • In the early 1800s, settlers in the Lebanon Valley began making a thick, spiced beef sausage smoked in a traditional wooden smokehouse. Known locally as summer sausage, the treat eventually became Lebanon bologna, today manufactured by several food processing firms. The companies welcome visitors to taste free samples . . . but they'll never share their closely guarded recipes. • The famous Philadelphia cheesesteak started out as chipped steak seared on a grill, then piled into an Italian roll and topped with sautéed onions. Around the 1940s, short-order chefs began finishing the sandwich with melted cheese—the Cheez Whiz brand is considered traditional. • Philadelphians must have had the original sweet tooth, because they concocted treats that quickly became staples and remain so today. Root beer made its debut in Philly in 1866, followed (not soon enough, in the opinion of some) by the ice-cream soda in 1874. • It takes 50,000 cows to supply the milk used for one day's production of Hershey Kisses—roughly 33 million of the milk chocolate delights.

EIGHTEENTH CENTURY

1787
Federal leaders convene in Philadelphia to draw up a new frame of government; by the end of the year they ratify the U.S. Constitution

1787
John Fitch, of Bucks County, builds the country's first working steamboat and tests it on the Delaware River

1791
Philip Ginter accidentally discovers anthracite coal in Carbon County, but the populace regards it as a species of black stone for another 17 years

LANDMARKS OF LIBERTY

Philadelphia's Independence Hall, built in 1732, is where the nation began. Both the Declaration of Independence and U.S. Constitution were signed there, laying the framework for America's future. • The Liberty Bell, cast in 1752 to celebrate the 50th anniversary of William Penn's Charter of Liberties, carries the Biblical passage "Proclaim liberty throughout all the land. . ." Abolitionists rediscovered the bell a century later and claimed it as a symbol for their cause, giving it its popular name. • Sculptor Alexander Milne Calder's 37-foot statue of William Penn was 20 years in the making. The huge bronze was mounted atop Philadelphia's City Hall in 1894.

MORE PARAMOUNT PENNSYLVANIANS

ROBERT FULTON (1765–1815)
Born in Lancaster County, Fulton built America's first commercially successful steamboat, the *Clermont,* which he completed in 1807.

HENRY J. HEINZ (1844–1919)
The community-spirited Pittsburgh native founded the H. J. Heinz Company and coined the slogan "57 varieties" to advertise his ketchup and prepared foods.

MILTON S. HERSHEY (1857–1945)
Hershey, who was born near Hockersville, became nearly synonymous with chocolate. He began mass-producing the Hershey Bar in 1903, followed by foil-wrapped Hershey Kisses in 1907.

ANDREW W. MELLON (1855–1937)
Born in Pittsburgh, Mellon built a banking empire that provided financial backing to many of that city's firms.

A trusted and influential political figure as well, he served as U.S. Secretary of the Treasury from 1921 to 1932.

CHARLES M. SCHWAB (1862–1939)

In the early 20th century, Schwab, who was born in Williamsburg, Pennsylvania, led Bethlehem Steel to become one of the nation's greatest steel-producing firms.

POLITICS
DWIGHT D. EISENHOWER (1890–1969)
Eisenhower served as supreme commander of Allied forces in

western Europe during World War II and became the 34th president of the United States. He was born in Texas but retired to Gettysburg, where his farm is open to the public.

GEORGE C. MARSHALL (1880–1959)
Considered the greatest military mind of his time, the Uniontown native helped shape Allied strategy during World War II and authored the Marshall Plan for European recovery, winning the Nobel Peace Prize in 1953.

SCIENCE & RESEARCH
RACHEL CARSON (1907–64)

The Springdale-born scientist and author began the modern environmental movement. Her novel *Silent Spring,* warning of the dangers of pesticides, eventually resulted in the banning of DDT.

DANIEL HALE WILLIAMS (1858–1931)
A brilliant African American doctor, Williams performed the first open-heart surgery in 1893. His accomplishment opened the way for the training of many black doctors and nurses.

MEMORABLE MOMENTS OF THE

1805
The Pennsylvania Academy of the Fine Arts, America's first art school, is founded in Philadelphia to encourage Americans to create an art of their own, rather than mimic European art

1827
The first American railroad is constructed, running between Mauch Chunk (Jim Thorpe) and Summit Hill in Carbon County

1831
The first building and loan association in the United States, the Oxford Provident Building Association, is organized at a tavern in the Philadelphia suburb of Frankford

SPORTS

WILT CHAMBERLAIN (1936–99)

"Wilt the Stilt" was named one of the 50 Greatest Players in NBA history. The Philadelphian set myriad records playing for the Philadelphia 76ers and Los Angeles Lakers in the 1960s–70s.

STAN MUSIAL (1920–)

A baseball superstar, "Stan the Man" began playing for the

St. Louis Cardinals in 1941 and retired in 1963. Born in Donoroa, Musial won seven

batting crowns and held an amazing .331 lifetime average.

ARNOLD PALMER (1929–)

Palmer popularized golf as never before. The Latrobe native won nearly every major tournament and award in the 1950s–60s, becoming golf's first millionaire and first successful businessman.

TRAILBLAZING

GUION S. BLUFORD JR. (1942–)

Born in Philadelphia, Bluford was the first African American in space. His 1983 mission on the space shuttle *Challenger* was the first with a night launch and landing.

LUCRETIA MOTT (1793–1880)

A Quaker minister, Mott opened her Philadelphia home to runaway slaves. She founded the Philadelphia Female

Anti-Slavery Society and joined Elizabeth Cady Stanton in organizing the world's first women's rights convention.

BAYARD RUSTIN (1912–87)

Born in West Chester and raised as a Quaker, Rustin promoted nonviolence during the Civil Rights Movement of the 1950s–60s. He helped organize the 1963 March on Washington, D.C., in which 200,000 people participated.

DID YOU KNOW? . . .

The Pennsylvania Department of State Police, created in 1905, became a model studied the world over. • In 1937, Governor George E. Earle inaugurated a sweeping reform program, the Little New Deal, benefiting the Commonwealth's laborers. He also created the Pennsylvania Turnpike Commission. • In the 1950s, Pennsylvania began efforts to attract new industries and jobs and to continue its heritage of business and industry. By the 1990s the drive proved successful, positioning the Commonwealth to become a world leader in the 21st century. • The State Museum of Pennsylvania, across from the capitol in Harrisburg, was opened in 1905 as a repository of artifacts illustrating Pennsylvania history. Its 11 galleries/exhibits include a recreated 18th-century market square, a Delaware Indian village, the original entrance to the William Penn Memorial Museum (including a full-scale reproduction of the Pennsylvania charter), and much more.

NINETEENTH CENTURY

1859

The world's modern petroleum industry begins when Edwin Drake strikes oil in Titusville

1863

One of the bloodiest battles of the Civil War, sometimes considered its turning point, is fought in Gettysburg; President Lincoln memorializes the spot with his Gettysburg Address

1875

David Saylor, of Coplay, experiments successfully with a common rock, and America's portland cement industry is born

NOTEWORTHY NAMES

WILLIAM PENN (1644–1718)

The Quaker founder of Pennsylvania (shown at left) is remembered for his liberal frame of government. The Charter of Liberties, which he wrote in 1701, guaranteed self-government and religious freedom and established a standard of good relations with Native Americans.

BENJAMIN FRANKLIN (1706–90)

Originally from Boston, Franklin (shown at right) settled in Philadelphia at the age of 17. A printer, diplomat, scientist, philosopher, musician, and economist, he is perhaps best known for his inventions, such as bifocal lenses and the lightning rod.

FIRSTS AND INNOVATIONS

1682: William Penn's "Great Law" becomes one of the first documents to safeguard life, liberty, and property through trial by jury

1731: Benjamin Franklin founds America's first circulating library, in Philadelphia

1743: Christopher Sauer, of Germantown, prints the first Bible in the American colonies

1779: The University of Pennsylvania is the nation's first institution of higher learning to earn the title "university." Its first degrees were awarded in 1759

1782: The Lehigh Coal Mining Company becomes the first of its kind to surface-mine coal

1785: The Philadelphia Society for Promoting Agriculture becomes the first organization dedicated to the continuing scientific education of farmers

1791: The First Bank of the United States opens its main office in Philadelphia, becoming the prototype for a central banking system

1792: The Insurance Company of North America (INA) is formed in Philadelphia to underwrite marine casualties and offer fire and life insurance

1794: Construction is completed on the Philadelphia-Lancaster Turnpike, a toll road covered with crushed stone. The nation's first hard-surface highway gives Philadelphians a link to the Susquehanna River

1812: The Academy of Natural Sciences, the country's first science museum, is established in Philadelphia

1816: The Philadelphia Savings Fund Society (PSFS) becomes the first mutual savings bank designed to encourage the accumulation of capital and motivate workers—including servants—to save

1821: The Philadelphia College of Apothecaries becomes the first pharmacy college in the United States

1829: David G. Yuengling opens the Eagle Brewery in Pottsville. Eventually renamed Yuengling and Sons, it becomes the nation's oldest family-owned brewery in continuous operation

1829: The *Stourbridge Lion*, America's first locomotive, makes a trial run between Honesdale and Carbondale

1840: John Wagner, who has an eight-barrel kettle in his home in Philadelphia, manufactures the first lager beer and stores it in a cellar under the brewhouse

1841: Volney B. Palmer opens the nation's first advertising agency, in Philadelphia

1846: The first commercial telegraph line is run between Lancaster and Harrisburg

MEMORABLE MOMENTS OF THE

1903

The first modern World Series is played in Pittsburgh's Exposition Park between the Boston Pilgrims and the Pittsburgh Pirates; Boston wins

1905

The first all-motion movie theater, the Nickelodeon, is opened in Pittsburgh by John P. Harris and Harry Davis

1905

Milton S. Hershey opens the world's largest chocolate factory in the town bearing his name. The company town and factory represent a personal investment of about $2 million

1854: Lincoln University is chartered in Chester County, eventually becoming the oldest historically black institution of higher learning in the nation

1860s: The Cambria Iron Works in Johnstown and the Freedom Iron Works in Lewistown are among the first to employ the Bessemer process

1869: Philadelphia tailors found the first modern labor union, the Knights of Labor

1874: The first zoo in the nation opens in Philadelphia

1875–76: Philadelphia's Hale and Kilburn Manufacturing Company makes the first successful folding bed, inspired by the inception of apartment houses and the need for economy of space. The bed's flexible spring develops into the box spring in use today

1876: America celebrates its centennial with an exposition in Philadelphia. Among the innovations on display is the telephone, invented by Alexander Graham Bell in New York

1880: The first elevated railroad is built in Philadelphia

1883: In Sunbury, Thomas A. Edison is the first to successfully light an entire building with electricity. The building will become known as the Edison Hotel and will still be standing in the 20th century

1885: Bryn Mawr College opens in the town of the same name, the first institution of higher learning to offer graduate degrees to women

1886: An industry is born in Pittsburgh when Charles M. Hall and Arthur Vining Davis use the electrolytic process to produce aluminum cheaply

ON THE ROAD

The Conestoga Wagon, developed in 18th-century Pennsylvania to carry freight over deeply rutted roads, became the model for the covered wagons that took many pioneers west. • More than 200 covered bridges remain in the Keystone State from what may have been as many as 1,500 during their heyday between 1830 and 1880. One, built over the Schuylkill River in 1800, is among America's oldest. • The Lincoln Highway Association was established in 1913 to build a paved, toll-free road from New York to San Francisco in tribute to Abraham Lincoln. The portion of it that crosses southern Pennsylvania, known as Route 30, has always beckoned tourists and Sunday drivers with larger-than-life kitsch. Some of the items that still amuse passersby include a huge windmill east of Lancaster advertising Pennsylvania Dutch cooking, a giant shoe east of York built by a local entrepreneur known as the Shoe Wizard, and its most famous oddity, a steamboat on a mountaintop, representing the Grand View Ship Hotel at Grand View Point Lookout. • America's first high-speed train, the Acela Express (derived from the words *acceleration* and *excellence*), reaches speeds of up to 125 MPH along Amtrak's Northeast Corridor, reducing trip times by up to 20 percent.

TWENTIETH CENTURY

1911

John Wanamaker opens "a new kind of store" in what had been a freight shed. His Philadelphia department store covers a city block and has more than 45 acres of floor space

1920

Commercial radio broadcasting begins in Pittsburgh when radio station KDKA airs presidential election returns; the station is also first to offer regularly scheduled broadcasts of religious services

1940s

The world's first general-purpose electronic computer, ENIAC, is assembled at the University of Pennsylvania during World War II to compute shell trajectories

MORE FIRSTS AND INNOVATIONS

1886: The J. G. Brill Company, of Philadelphia, builds the first electric-powered trolley, making frequent and rapid transit practical and inexpensive within and between cities

1894: Pittsburgh's Schenley Park is the site of the first professional hockey game, played by the Pittsburgh Yellow Jackets and an unrecorded team

1895: The first professional football game is played in Latrobe, between the Latrobe YMCA and the Jeannette Athletic Club; the YMCA wins 12–0

1896: Henry J. Heinz gets the idea for his advertising slogan "57 varieties," even though his company makes more than 60 kinds of condiments. His pin, shaped like the green pickle of the Heinz logo, later becomes one of the most successful giveaways in advertising history

1900–11: Charles Duryea, sometimes called the Father of the American Car for arguably building the first gasoline-powered automobile, opens the Duryea Power Company in Reading to build automobiles

1903: In Easton, Binney & Smith manufactures and sells the first box of Crayola crayons. The five-cent box features eight different colors of crayons: brown, blue, red, purple, orange, yellow, green, and black. These are the very same colors that will be found in eight-count boxes far into the future

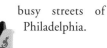

1903: The Sproul-Roberts Act creates the Pennsylvania State Department of Highways, and soon the Keystone State becomes a leader in the movement to improve America's roads

1910: Louis J. Bergdoll introduces the first automobiles that have been extensively road tested. They met the challenge of two years' wear and tear over the busy streets of Philadelphia.

1916: The Commonwealth opens its first, much-heralded chamber of commerce, in the capital city

1920s: The central Pennsylvania town of Bellefonte becomes one of the first refueling stops on the New York–Chicago route of the nation's airmail service

1921: Westinghouse markets the Aeriola Junior, the first home radio that is affordable and simple to operate

1926: The first scheduled commercial air passenger service in the United States connects Philadelphia and Washington, D.C., and later Norfolk, Virginia

MORE MEMORABLE MOMENTS

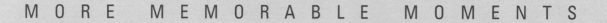

1940

The nation's first snow-making machines are introduced at Big Boulder Ski Area in the Poconos

1950s

During the administration of Governor John S. Fine, more than 6,000 miles of roads are improved and expressways are built for Philadelphia and Pittsburgh

1953

Working at the University of Pittsburgh, Dr. Jonas Salk develops the first successful polio vaccine

PIONEERING THE SUPERHIGHWAY

With the completion of the Pennsylvania Turnpike in 1956, the nation gained its first superhighway—and an excellent model for toll roads of the future. New hotels and motels quickly appeared along its route, and visitors poured into the state.

1932: Philadelphia gets its first international-style skyscraper in the PSFS Building, which also becomes the first completely air-conditioned building in America

1934: Pittsburgh's Central Air Lines is the first to hire a woman, Helen Ritchey, as a copilot on its Washington, D.C.–Pittsburgh–Detroit route

1939: Williamsport is the site of the first Little League World Series.

Playoffs begin in August with 30 players, establishing a tradition that eventually embraces 2.7 million players worldwide

1941–45: Thirty-two Pennsylvanians, more honorees than from any other state, win the Congressional Medal of Honor for valour during World War II

1941–45: The Philadelphia Naval Yard employs more than 70,000 people and builds 50 vessels, including two of the world's largest battleships, for use during World War II

1949: WDTV in Pittsburgh goes on the air and becomes the first television station to offer a serious local news program, "The Pitt Parade"

1963: The Bell System's Western Electric Manufacturing and Supply Unit places the nation's first Touch-Tone Telephone, with 10 push buttons, into commercial service between Carnegie and Greensburg

1967–68: A series of constitutional amendments culminates in a constitutional convention and what amounts to a new state constitution. Among the changes is a provision that prevents the denial to any person of his or her civil rights

1976: The Keystone State is among those hosting events to commemorate the nation's bicentennial and celebrate its stature as the oldest continuously surviving democratic republic in the world. Philadelphia's Parade of States draws more than two million onlookers

1982: The Philadelphia Stock Exchange invents exchange-traded currency options, putting it on the international map. To accommodate increasing foreign demand, in 1987 the exchange introduces the nation's first evening session, and in 1990 it becomes the first in the world to offer 24-hour trading

1999: Pennsylvania becomes the first state in the nation to establish a government-based school for information technology. The five-week residential program for gifted and talented high school juniors is taught at Drexel and Penn State Universities

DID YOU KNOW? . . .

Stephen Foster, one of the most popular composers of the 1800s, wrote the song "Camptown Races"—about a horse race that stretched for five miles between Camptown and Wyalusing—while visiting Towanda. • The Quakers were among the first Americans to stand up for the freedom of slaves, establishing an antislavery society in 1775. Five years later, Pennsylvania passed a law to end slavery in the state. It was another 70 years before the rest of the North joined the cause. • The oil industry started in America when oil was discovered at Titusville, Pennsylvania, on August 27, 1859, in a well drilled to a depth of only 69 feet.

OF THE TWENTIETH CENTURY

1957

The first atomic-powered plant for the production of electricity opens at Shippingport

1965

The Sylvania Electric Company, of Montoursville, revolutionizes photography by introducing the first multiple flashbulb device for cameras: Flashcubes

1989

The first heart-liver-kidney transplant is performed at Presbyterian University Hospital in Philadelphia

PART ONE

A REGIONAL PORTRAIT

In 1685, William Penn published a promotional pamphlet, *A Further Account of the Province of Pennsylvania,* to assure those coming to his province that they would find a government that nurtured virtue, the arts, and freedom of religion. Printed in English and Dutch, it attracted droves of immigrants from England, Ireland, Wales, and the Rhineland, who urged their friends and families to join them. Together they became the first of many millions to follow a dream to Pennsylvania. • Once there, they discovered not only fertile farmland, green mountains, and clean waterways, but Philadelphia, Penn's "intended Metropolis," a port designed for commerce and orderly expansion. In short, they found a place poised for growth and development. Philadelphia became British Colonial America's premier city. After the American Revolution, it was the birthplace of institutions that led to innovation and expansion during the following century on a scale the world had never seen. • Today's Pennsylvania is filled with monuments to a proud heritage, reminders of the kinds of opportunity the Commonwealth offers. And among its cosmopolitan cities large and small, convenient suburbs, and close-knit country communities, among its unspoiled open spaces, acres of farmland, and forested mountains, Pennsylvania ingenuity has wrought the ideal place to live and work. The words in Penn's 1685 pamphlet are as appropriate today as they were then: "I had in my view Society, Assistance, Busy Commerce, Instruction of Youth, Government of Peoples' manners, Conveniency of Religious Assembling, Encouragement of Mechanics, distinct and beaten Roads, and it has answered in all those respects, I think, to a Universal Contentment."

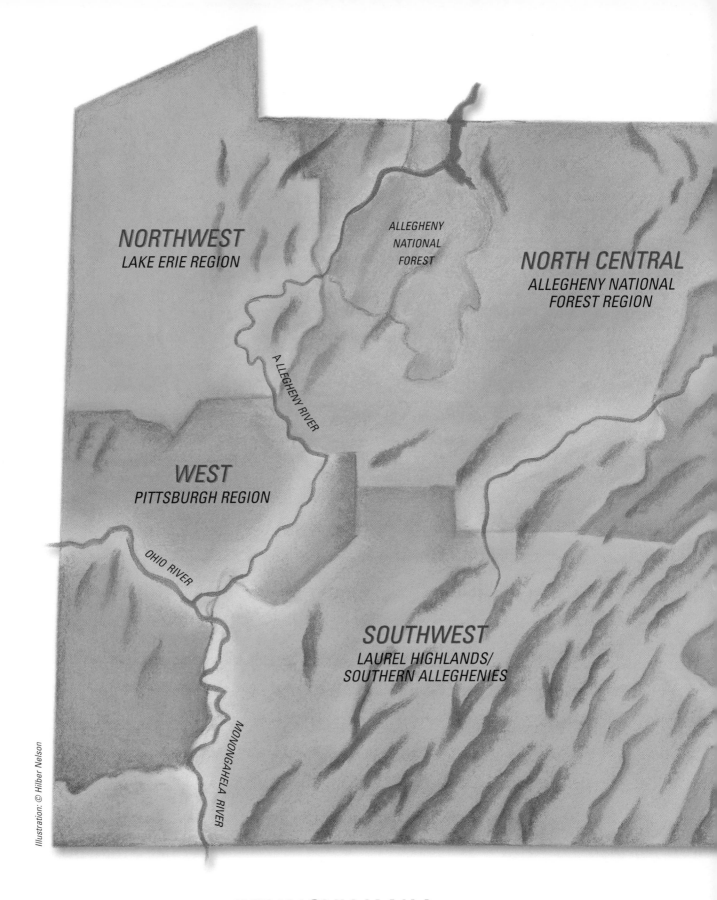

NORTHWEST
LAKE ERIE REGION

ALLEGHENY
NATIONAL
FOREST

NORTH CENTRAL
ALLEGHENY NATIONAL
FOREST REGION

A LLEGHENY RIVER

WEST
PITTSBURGH REGION

OHIO RIVER

SOUTHWEST
LAUREL HIGHLANDS/
SOUTHERN ALLEGHENIES

MONONGAHELA RIVER

Illustration: © Hilber Nelson

PENNSYLVANIA

AREA: 44,820 square miles
POPULATION: 12,096,000 (1994 est.)
CAPITAL: Harrisburg
MOTTO: "Virtue, Liberty, and Independence"

STATEHOOD: Second of the original 13 states to ratify
the Constitution, December 12, 1787
NICKNAME: Keystone State
BIRD/FLOWER: Ruffed grouse/Mountain laurel

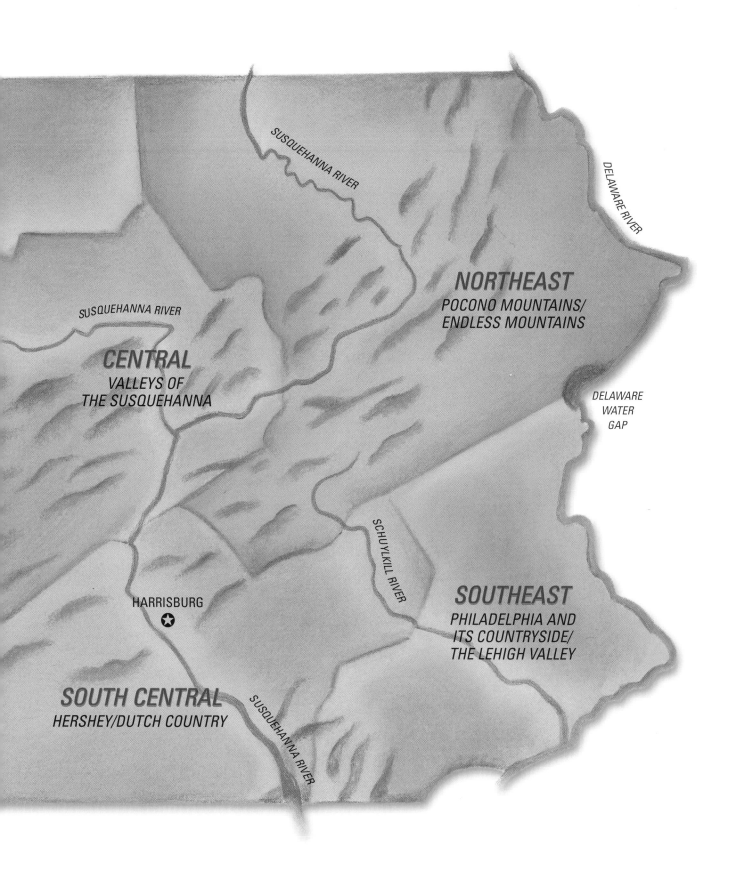

SUSQUEHANNA RIVER

DELAWARE RIVER

NORTHEAST
POCONO MOUNTAINS/
ENDLESS MOUNTAINS

SUSQUEHANNA RIVER

CENTRAL
VALLEYS OF
THE SUSQUEHANNA

DELAWARE
WATER
GAP

SCHUYLKILL RIVER

HARRISBURG

SOUTHEAST
PHILADELPHIA AND
ITS COUNTRYSIDE/
THE LEHIGH VALLEY

SOUTH CENTRAL
HERSHEY/DUTCH COUNTRY

SUSQUEHANNA RIVER

CHAPTER ONE

THE SOUTHEAST

PHILADELPHIA AND ITS COUNTRYSIDE/THE LEHIGH VALLEY

Philadelphia hosted America's first political convention in 1774, when the First Continental Congress met in Carpenters' Hall. Delegates to the Second Continental Congress made history on July 4, 1776, when they approved and adopted the Declaration of Independence, and so did the patriots who gathered in 1787 to craft the nation's constitution. In the meantime, a revolution was fought and won; some say its turning point came at nearby

Valley Forge, where George Washington's army battled and vanquished the enemies of disease and despair.

A new nation was born, and Philadelphia was its capital. Buildings that once housed the United States Senate, the House of Representatives, and the Supreme Court still stand, along with Independence Hall, in Independence National Historical Park, the city's venerated historic district. Here, as visitors from all over the world view the Liberty Bell and walk the streets of what was once called the Athens of America, the struggle of the patriots who risked their lives for freedom becomes almost palpable.

The 19th century brought busy factories and row house neighborhoods to the areas north and south of the city, where entrepreneurs manufactured textiles, shoes, paper, chemicals, and a host of other products. After the Civil War, burgeoning Philadelphia needed a bigger and better downtown. In 1870, citizens approved the construction of a magnificent new city hall, which stands today crowned with a statue of Pennsylvania's founder, William Penn, by sculptor Alexander Milne Calder.

Penn wanted Philadelphia to be a healthful, "green countrie town." When he laid it out in the 17th century, he chose a grid pattern that allowed room for open spaces such as Rittenhouse Square, today a genteel green common lined with pleasant cafes and shops. In 1867, the city created Fairmount Park, today one of the world's largest municipal parks at 8,900 acres—encompassing not only bike paths, hiking trails, and a profusion of spring cherry blossoms but also the Philadelphia Museum of Art, the Philadelphia Zoo (oldest in the United States), the historic Fairmount Waterworks, Boathouse Row on the Schuylkill River, the Mann Music Center (an amphitheater that doubles as the summer home of the Philadelphia Orchestra), historic homes, and much more.

Philadelphia's booming Victorian era ushered in many of the landmarks Pennsylvanians enjoy today, including the zoo and

ABOVE: *Philadelphia's century-old City Hall, one of the nation's finest examples of French Second Empire style, lights the night sky.*
OPPOSITE: *This topiary garden is part of 1,050-acre Longwood Gardens, on the former Pierre S. du Pont estate in Kennett Square.*

PHOTOS: BOTH PAGES, © *Jim McWilliams Photography*

The Benjamin Franklin Bridge links Philadelphia and Camden, New Jersey. Reaching 1,750 feet across the Delaware River, the bridge heralded an era of long spans after it opened in 1926.

Boathouse Row. But it also brought such cultural icons as the venerable Academy of Music, now home to the city orchestra; the Pennsylvania Academy of the Fine Arts, with its world-renowned collection of American art spanning three centuries; and the Academy of Natural Sciences, still a world leader in scientific research.

The Philadelphia Museum of Art was an outgrowth of the nation's Centennial Exposition of 1876, held in Philadelphia on the grounds of Fairmount Park. Built as an art gallery for the exposition, the original building

STEVEN H. KORMAN CEO, Korman Communities, Inc.

Not long ago, apartments were viewed as temporary places to live until one could afford a home. Today, thanks to the creative approach of Korman Communities, our apartments offer services and amenities similar to those of resort hotels.

We have maintained our market leadership through economic cycles by adhering to our vision and our operating basics. The Korman culture guides and defines each property and team, allowing us to anticipate change and grow while remaining true to our core values. It is not enough to merely operate apartments as others have in the past. We seek to redefine our industry to better meet the needs and wants of current and potential residents. Our mission is to make Korman Communities, along with home ownership, part of the new American dream.

© Ed Wheeler

WILLIAM F. MACDONALD JR. President and CEO, Houghton International Inc.

Houghton International Inc. was founded in Pennsylvania 135 years ago. Our mission has been to provide technical service and solutions to industry ever since. Over time, The Houghton Line of products has steadily expanded to cover a complete range of metal processing fluids and chemical management service.

While we have remained here to enjoy the history, culture, and beauty of our wonderful state, our company's business now extends to every corner of the industrial world. Our roots, however, remain in Pennsylvania, and happily so.

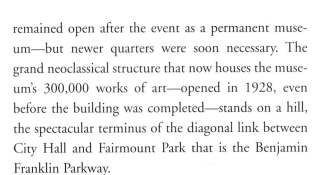

HOUGHTON

remained open after the event as a permanent museum—but newer quarters were soon necessary. The grand neoclassical structure that now houses the museum's 300,000 works of art—opened in 1928, even before the building was completed—stands on a hill, the spectacular terminus of the diagonal link between City Hall and Fairmount Park that is the Benjamin Franklin Parkway.

If the 19th century brought the city cultural sophistication and continued international renown, the last decade of the 20th gave it clout on the culinary scene. According to national surveys, by 1994 seven of the nation's top 50 restaurants were in Philadelphia, with the competition becoming ever more intense.

The city's latest urban improvement, the Avenue of the Arts, centers on the historic Academy of Music, built in 1857. A hit in a city where the arts are second only to breathing, this emerging performing arts district on Broad Street has added delightful new venues for opera, ballet, jazz, drama, musical theater, and more.

Sports fans find a haven here too, cheering for the Phillies in baseball season, the Eagles in football season, the Flyers in hockey season, and the 76ers in basketball season. South Philadelphia is the place to go for sports action, especially to the 21,000-seat Comcast-Spectacor First Union Center, built in 1996—considered one of the finest arenas in the nation.

Opportunity brought both immigrants and travelers to Philadelphia in the late 1800s, many on the

The 1921 Dentzel Carousel is one of the tamer rides at Allentown's Dorney Park & Wildwater Kingdom, which features more than 100 different rides—plus one of the nation's most visited water parks.

Delegates to the Second Continental Congress in Philadelphia signed the Declaration of Independence on July 4, 1776, after four months of deliberation. The document affirmed the right of the 13 American colonies to separate from Great Britain and announced the creation of the United States of America.

Reading Railroad. In 1892, the railroad built a market-place beneath its terminal. With 800 stalls, it wasn't long before the Reading Terminal Market was known throughout the world. Situated today near Philadelphia's new convention center, it still draws thousands of visitors a day to sample ethnic dishes that reflect Philadelphia's diversity, as well as regional favorites like scrapple and soft pretzels.

Pennsylvania's largest city celebrates its rich cultural heritage not only with culinary temptations from the Reading Terminal Market, the Italian Market, Chinatown, and other spots but also through cultural institutions and festivals. Ever since January 1, 1901, for example, Philadelphia has welcomed the new year by hosting the Mummers Parade, a lively event featuring costumed string bands, dancers, and comics, all of whom strut down Broad Street. The tradition grew out of European customs

MARVIN S. CADWELL President and CEO, Shared Medical Systems Corporation

From the entrepreneurial start-up days of Shared Medical Systems Corporation (SMS) more than 30 years ago to our position as a worldwide leader of health information solutions as the new millennium begins, technology continues to represent a critical component of this region's economy and infrastructure. Fostering economic growth and spurring innovative advancements remains an important priority among Pennsylvania's state and local officials, as well as its corporate leaders. As we recognize the extraordinary technological strides achieved during recent years—marked by the profound impact of the Internet on our daily lives—the future holds boundless opportunities for Pennsylvania, its corporate citizens, and its many residents.

A REGIONAL PORTRAIT

brought by the city's immigrants. Today, more than 10,000 Philadelphians participate in the annual event.

Around the turn of the century, electric streetcars, first used in the 1880s, opened up suburbs north and west of Philadelphia; the Pennsylvania Railroad carried executives and entrepreneurs to the stately western suburb known as the Main Line. When the Schuylkill Expressway was linked to the Pennsylvania Turnpike in 1954 at the village of King of Prussia (named for its colonial tavern), high-tech businesses began cropping up in the Valley Forge area to the west. Since the early 1970s, new science and

Washington Crossing Historic Park's 500 acres commemorate the spot where George Washington and his ragged troops crossed the frigid Delaware River in 1776, during the American Revolution.

technology companies have occupied the modern office and industrial parks in the area along State Route 202—the main artery just south of the turnpike, sometimes called eastern Pennsylvania's Medical Mile. King of Prussia also is known for one of the largest and most elegant retail shopping malls on the East Coast, the King of Prussia Plaza and the adjacent Court at King of Prussia.

E. S. BAGLEY JR. President, Amtrak Northeast Corridor

In many ways the words "railroad" and "Pennsylvania" are inextricably linked, from the chartering of the Pennsylvania Railroad in the 1840s to the introduction of high-speed rail at the dawn of the 21st century. Amtrak is honored to continue that tradition and is pleased to have a valued partner in the Commonwealth. From station improvements to track upgrades, Pennsylvania and Amtrak have worked together to improve rail transportation for Pennsylvania residents and visitors alike. With America's first high-speed service operated by Amtrak's Philadelphia–based Northeast Corridor business unit, and Amtrak and Pennsylvania collaborating on dramatic improvements to rail service throughout the Commonwealth, exciting new chapters in Pennsylvania's railroad heritage will be written for years to come.

Amtrak®

The Cunard cruise ship Queen Elizabeth 2 *departs Philadelphia via the* Port of Philadelphia and Camden *as the* Columbus America *cargo ship arrives. The port provides direct access to the Atlantic Ocean.*

In outlying Bucks County, people live and work among wooded hills and quiet farms. In the late 19th century, archaeologist, anthropologist, and ceramist Henry Chapman Mercer established a retreat in Doylestown, the county seat. He built museums and a studio, the Moravian Pottery and Tile Works, which became a major force in the Arts and Crafts movement. James A. Michener, prolific author of such works as *Hawaii* and *The Source,* was raised in Doylestown. He founded the James A. Michener Museum there, which features the works of regional artists along with a permanent exhibit on his legacy. The scenic village of New Hope, on the Delaware River, has long been a magnet for art lovers and antiques hunters, and lively Sesame Place, in Langhorne, captures the spirit of the popular preschool educational television program *Sesame Street* with rides, water slides, and life-size characters.

Bucolic Chester County has been the inspiration for many a painting by Andrew Wyeth. Born in

WARREN V. "PETE" MUSSER CEO, Safeguard Scientifics, Inc.
HARRY WALLAESA President and COO, Safeguard Scientifics, Inc.

The positively charged atmosphere at Safeguard Scientifics, Inc., starts at the top and sets the standard for an ideal workplace by promoting leadership, teamwork, and philanthropy. It is this culture of achievement and trust that keeps entrepreneurs and management talent flocking to Safeguard, making it one of the most desirable places to work in the area.

In addition to entrepreneurial support, Safeguard is extremely active in corporate philanthropy. Through the Musser and Safeguard Foundations, millions of dollars are donated each year to support both national and local charities, as well as local educational institutions.

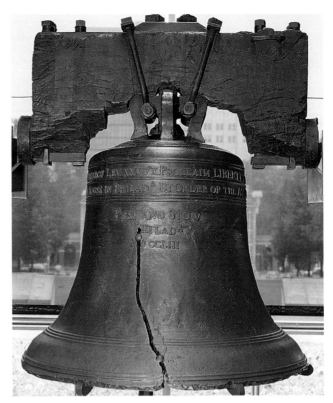

Chadds Ford, the artist is known worldwide for his realist images of rural America in such paintings as *Christina's World* and *The Trodden Weed*. Many of his original paintings are on exhibit at the Brandywine River Museum. Nearby Kennett Square is the home of Longwood Gardens, 1,050 acres of gardens and greenhouses created by industrialist Pierre S. du Pont beginning in 1907. In addition to the European-inspired gardens that the public has enjoyed since the 1950s, today Longwood offers concerts and theatrical performances as well.

The Liberty Bell, a symbol of freedom for more than 200 years, hangs in its pavilion at Philadelphia's Independence National Historical Park. Cast in England, it was first rung in America on July 4, 1776.

The Lehigh Valley, where the Lehigh River joins the Delaware, was settled by German immigrants in the 1730s. Industries in the area thrived thanks to abundant natural resources, and soon the valley's oldest city, Bethlehem (founded in 1741), was flanked by Allentown and Easton. The region has been home to Bethlehem Steel, Mack Trucks (of Allentown), and Binney & Smith (of Easton),

Boathouse Row, on the Schuylkill River in Philadelphia, was named for its string of Victorian boathouses. For generations, some of the world's finest rowers have trained here, including many Olympians.

makers of Crayola crayons, for more than 100 years. Today the region draws high-tech and agriculture-related firms to its modern business parks.

Bethlehem Steel recently joined with the Smithsonian Institute to plan a National Museum of Industrial History at the corporation's former headquarters. Lighter entertainment, of course, is still an option at such spots as Allentown's Dorney Park & Wildwater Kingdom, a 200-acre amusement/water park that began in 1884 as Dorney's Trout Ponds and Summer Resorts.

Since the 1940s, the Greater Philadelphia area has seen much redevelopment designed to support its businesses. The Southeastern Pennsylvania Transportation Authority (SEPTA), highways, the Port of Philadelphia and Camden, and the Philadelphia International Airport have all been improved. Employment has grown significantly, and the region, including the Lehigh Valley, now sustains one of the most diversified economies in the mid-Atlantic states.

RAJ L. GUPTA Chairman and CEO, Rohm and Haas Company

Rohm and Haas began as a Pennsylvania firm in 1909, when Otto Röhm opened his first office in Philadelphia. Today, more than 90 years later, Rohm and Haas is a $6.7 billion global chemical company that still calls Pennsylvania its home. We have been fortunate enough to benefit from Pennsylvania's favorable business environment and talented workforce for many years. With our worldwide headquarters, research laboratories, and a dozen other locations here, we hope to be a part of the Pennsylvania community for many years to come.

ROHM AND HAAS

Successful businesses in the area even compete with historic and cultural institutions as tourist attractions. Visitors come to watch Crayola crayons being made in Easton; sample potato chips at the visitor center of Herr Foods, in Nottingham, the third largest snack foods company in the nation; and tour QVC Studio Park, the West Chester TV studio of the famed home shopping channel.

Greater Philadelphia and the Lehigh Valley are known for the fine educational institutions located there. In addition to the giants in Philadelphia proper—the University of Pennsylvania, Temple University, and Drexel University—the suburbs house such institutions as Villanova University, Lincoln University, Bryn Mawr College, Chestnut Hill College, Beaver College, Swarthmore College, and dozens more. The Lehigh Valley is home to Lehigh University, Lafayette College, Muhlenberg College, and Cedar Crest College. The area's rich cultural and entertainment options enhance college life, and students and faculties return the favor by offering collegiate sports, campus concerts, and theater productions to the public.

LARRY COLANGELO President & CEO, SPD Technologies, Inc.

There was a time when SPD Technologies was one week away from closing its doors. As Cold War tensions thawed in the 1980s, big defense contractors like SPD saw their market evaporate overnight. By 1991, SPD's core business had dropped more than 70 percent and total liabilities were more than twice annual revenues.

Larry Colangelo, elected president and chief executive officer in 1992, obtained the capital to purchase SPD and, with a team of co-workers, implemented a growth strategy, built key relationships, and ultimately turned impending disaster into success. SPD has become one of the dominant providers of naval electrical power delivery systems in the world and the only fully integrated, full-line provider of these systems to the United States Navy.

communications
SPD Technologies, Inc.

A REGIONAL PORTRAIT

BERNARD POUSSOT President, Wyeth-Ayerst Pharmaceuticals

Pennsylvania has always been a leader in health care, and Wyeth-Ayerst Pharmaceuticals has been a part of that tradition. Beginning as a small Philadelphia drugstore in 1860, Wyeth-Ayerst has become a global leader in the pharmaceutical industry, serving the health care needs of people in more than 125 countries. From world-class medical centers and universities to a highly skilled workforce, the Commonwealth's resources have positively influenced our company's success. As we look to the 21st century, I am enthusiastic about the discoveries Wyeth-Ayerst will make in improving the health of people around the world and in knowing that Pennsylvania is helping to make this happen.

WYETH AYERST
® *Leading the Way for a Healthier World*®

OPPOSITE: *Designed by Helmut Jahn, 60-story One Liberty Place soars above the Arch Street Presbyterian Church in Philadelphia. Built in 1989, it was the first building granted approval to rise higher than the statue of William Penn atop City Hall (491 feet).*

BELOW: *The galleria of the Court and the Plaza at King of Prussia enhances the experience of the more than 16 million shoppers who visit the mall's nine department stores, 365 specialty shops, and 35 dining establishments annually.*

A feathered and bejeweled "fancy" participates in Philadelphia's annual New Year's Day Mummers Parade down Market Street. The tradition began officially in 1901, but its roots date back to the 1700s.

Centering around imaginative themes and elaborate costumes and floats, the parade features four divisions: comics, string bands, individual "fancies" (noted earlier), and fancy brigades.

J. RICHARD JONES Executive Managing Director, Insignia/ESG

Among the largest commercial real estate service firms in the United States, we enjoy a pre-eminent position in the Philadelphia metropolitan area and are considered to be a preferred provider of comprehensive commercial real estate brokerage and management services.

Insignia's dominant presence in Philadelphia is a result of the acquisition of Jackson-Cross Company, one of the nation's oldest commercial real estate services firms and a market leader in the region.

While we remain steadfast in our commitment to nurturing our traditional real estate services operations, we also are known as the high-tech real estate services provider of choice in Pennsylvania, New Jersey, and Delaware and, indeed, worldwide.

A powerful ally in a complex world

GENUARDI'S FAMILY MARKETS Norristown, Pennsylvania

At Genuardi's Family Markets, everything we believe in is a reflection of our "Family Pride." For 80 years we have based our decisions on what is best for the customer and the communities in which we do business. Our goal is simple—to provide a pleasant shopping experience by offering top quality, value, freshness, and clean, well-stocked, state-of-the-art stores staffed by friendly, caring employees. To ensure our customers' satisfaction, Genuardi's retains a team of excellent employees who are well trained, knowledgeable, and service-oriented. To our family of more than 7,000 employees we say "thank you." They are the secret to our success. It is because of them that Genuardi's was selected in 1999 as Pennsylvania's Family Business of the Year.

Kara Maureen Powers and Forrest Hedden play Sarah Brown and Sky Masterson in the Bucks County Playhouse 1999 production of Frank Loesser and Abe Burrows's Guys and Dolls.

Susan Keeth plays the narrator and Rick Hamilton is Joseph in the 1999 production of Tim Rice and Andrew Lloyd Webber's Joseph and the Amazing Technicolor Dreamcoat *at the New Hope playhouse.*

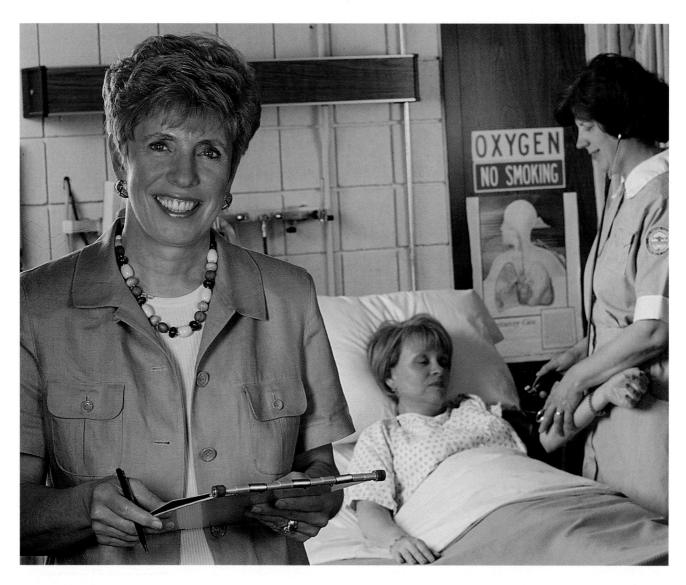

A student in Delaware County Community College's renowned nursing program attends to a patient while her instructor takes notes. Founded in 1967, the Philadelphia-area college is also known for its business and technology courses. Although the college is the ninth largest in the region, the individual attention its faculty, administrators, and staff members give each student is one of its hallmarks.

PETER LYDON Area President, North American Region, Pfizer Animal Health

Because "Community" is one of Pfizer Inc's core values, Pfizer Animal Health strives to be a good corporate citizen as well as a leader in the animal health industry. In fact, *The American Benefactor* has named Pfizer Inc one of America's Most Generous Companies. In 1999, Pfizer contributed to Pennsylvania in the following ways: Pfizer's Sharing the Care program provided more than $3.5 million in free pharmaceutical assistance for low-income, uninsured patients in Pennsylvania; more than $584,000 was donated to Pennsylvania nonprofit organizations by Pfizer employees and the Pfizer Foundation Matching Gifts program; more than $335,000 was donated by Pfizer and its employees to Pennsylvania community organizations through United Way; and the Pfizer Education Initiative supports three partner school districts in Chester County, including a fully equipped computer laboratory for science education.

A gorgeous spring day brings students on Widener University's main campus in Chester outside to enjoy the fresh air. A popular place to chat is in front of the Old Main building, whose cornerstone was laid in 1867. The university, opened in 1821, offers 147 programs of study, including liberal arts, nursing, business administration, law, and others. More than 7,000 students from 30 states and 39 countries attend class at the university's three campuses in Chester (the main campus) and Harrisburg, Pennsylvania, and Wilmington, Delaware.

ABOVE: *Art lovers pause outside the converted gristmill in Chadds Ford that houses the Brandywine River Museum, featuring regional and American art. The museum contains one of the world's largest collections of works by N. C., Andrew, and Jamie Wyeth.*

OPPOSITE: *At home on the Springton Horse Farm in Delaware County, these fine steeds are part of Pennsylvania's long equestrian tradition. More than 174,000 horses are raised in the state; Pennsylvanians spend upwards of $500 million a year on them.*

DR. RICHARD D. DECOSMO President, Delaware County Community College

Created with the purpose of providing affordable, accessible education for anyone who desires it, community colleges serve as unique and valuable resources for Pennsylvanians. Together, the Commonwealth's 15 community colleges provide opportunities for more than 350,000 residents and more than 1,200 employers annually.

Community colleges support and stimulate local economic development directly, by providing employment, and indirectly, by creating employee tax revenue and promoting the sales of goods and services in the community. Pennsylvania's community colleges are unique in that many graduates remain in the Commonwealth, contributing to the local economy in a number of different and meaningful ways.

Community colleges truly offer something for every Pennsylvanian.

CHAPTER TWO

SOUTH CENTRAL PENNSYLVANIA

HERSHEY/DUTCH COUNTRY

Before there was a U.S. Constitution, the Articles of Confederation governed the nation. They were drawn up in

York, in south central Pennsylvania, in 1777. Today people are more likely to associate York with the products

made there, such as Harley-Davidson motorcycles, Pfaltzgraff pottery—the nation's oldest pottery maker—and

York Peppermint Patties.

The fertile valleys of this region drew waves of German immigrants throughout the 18th century. Their descendants, including members of the Amish and Mennonite sects, still flourish there in Pennsylvania Dutch country—so named from a corruption of the original Pennsylvania Deutsch, or German—where life centers on traditions and time-honored values. Farms that operate just as they did over 200 years ago share the landscape with small, historic towns and diverse businesses, including many food processing companies such as Hanover Foods, in Hanover, and Nissin Foods (USA), in Lancaster. The rural life of a century past can be glimpsed in Lancaster at Wheatland, the Federal-style mansion James Buchanan purchased in 1848, where he lived the life of a country gentleman.

During the 19th century, several municipalities built elegant market houses and filled the stalls with locally grown, farm-fresh food. These huge markets can still be found in places like Lancaster and York, and they still do a thriving business—as do most farmers markets throughout the state. In addition to local produce, many markets offer specialty dishes like

shoofly pie (the name is of uncertain derivation), as well as quilts and other handcrafted items embellished with traditional folk art designs such as stars, hearts, flowers, birds, and geometric patterns. These symbols also appear on the colorful round "hex signs" hung on barns for good luck.

With a population of about 52,000, the state capital, Harrisburg, is the region's largest urban area, and the government is its largest employer. Named after founder John Harris Jr., Harrisburg became the state capital in 1812, when the seat of government was moved from Lancaster to a more central location. Governor Tom Ridge and the Pennsylvania Historical and Museum Commission recently designated the capitol a Commonwealth Treasure, a structure of outstanding historical significance. It resembles the

ABOVE: *An employee oversees the production of Hershey Kisses at the company factory in Hershey, circa 1937.* OPPOSITE: *A cannon at Gettysburg National Military Park bears mute tribute to the 51,000 men who died here during the 1863 Battle of Gettysburg. The battle lasted only three days, but it determined the outcome of the Civil War.*

A REGIONAL PORTRAIT

Renaissance buildings of Europe and incorporates features borrowed from the Paris Opera House and Saint Peter's Basilica in Rome. When it was completed in 1906, President Theodore Roosevelt proclaimed it the handsomest building he had ever seen. The state capitol is just a short walk from Riverfront Park and City Island, where families picnic on the bank of the Susquehanna and government employees find respite from their schedules. The Art Association of Harrisburg features invitational exhibitions and art classes, but Harrisburg's biggest event is the state farm show, an annual agricultural exhibition.

South central Pennsylvania is also home to the Commonwealth's best known historic site, Gettysburg National Military Park. In July 1863, more than 23,000 Union and 27,000 Confederate soldiers lost their lives on the fields at Gettysburg in one of the bloodiest battles of the Civil War. In November that year, President Abraham Lincoln attended the dedication of the Gettysburg

OPPOSITE: One lunchbox is big enough for these two Amish brothers on their way to school in Lancaster County. After eighth grade, they likely will return to the family farm, as do most Amish children.

This historic village in Lebanon County housed miners who worked the Cornwall Iron Furnace, which supplied cannons and ammunition to colonial troops from 1742 to 1883. The original furnace stack, open-pit mine, ironmaster's mansion, and other structures still stand.

National Cemetery and delivered his homage to the fallen, which became known as the Gettysburg Address. Today 1.5 million visitors a year, from every state and many foreign countries, relive the battle through walking tours of the grounds and frequently staged reenactments.

Almost as popular, but for entirely different reasons, is the town of Hershey, where the air itself is perfumed with the scent of chocolate. Sometimes called Chocolatetown U.S.A., Hershey is the namesake of Milton S. Hershey, who was the first to mass-produce the candy. He chose a rural area in south central Pennsylvania, near his birthplace, as his base of operations because of its numerous dairy farms with their ready supply of fresh milk. In 1903 he established the town, which he intended to become a utopia where his employees could enjoy every amenity. Hersheypark, an amusement park opened for their pleasure in 1907, today draws more than 2 million visitors a year.

That favorite pastime, shopping, attracts 10 million visitors annually to Reading and surrounding communities in Berks County. Formerly a center for textile manufacturing, by the 1920s Reading was known as the women's stocking capital of the world. Today Reading has traded that title for a new one: Outlet Capital of the World. Its ubiquitous outlet centers offer products by such well-known manufacturers as Lee, Vanity Fair, Black & Decker, Coach, and dozens of others. And thanks to Pennsylvania's tax-free shipping on clothing, bargains are always easy to find.

The area also abounds in historic sites, including the Daniel Boone Homestead in nearby Birdsboro, where the legendary American pioneer was born in 1734, and the Indian School in Carlisle, which was opened in 1879 to educate Native American youths. The rustic summer cottages of Mount Gretna reflect the town's resort fame during the late 19th and early 20th centuries, after its establishment in 1884 as a "picnic park" near the iron-making towns of Colebrook and Cornwall.

BELOW: *This Amish farm reflects a way of life that remains much as it was a century ago. Horses still pull the plows, there are no automobiles in the driveways, and the ponds have water-driven rather than electric pumps.* OPPOSITE: *A hex-sign maker displays his wares at the annual Kutztown Pennsylvania German Festival. The nine-day event is the nation's largest gathering of traditional craftsmen demonstrating their work.*

In the early part of the 20th century, many theater companies were established in the region, beginning what would soon become a tradition. The Allenberry Playhouse, in Boiling Springs, offers musical and dramatic productions each summer and fall as it has since 1949. Lancaster's new Millennium Theatre showcases sight-and-sound productions, while the annual Pennsylvania Renaissance Faire, near Manheim, features the creative improvisation of costumed knights and ladies in a recreation of a 16th-century English country fair.

QUINTIN F. FREY President, Turkey Hill Dairy

Pennsylvania was founded upon the precept of freedom in religious expression. William Penn advertised Pennsylvania throughout Europe as a place where people could live out their religious beliefs in freedom. That invitation brought to Pennsylvania people committed to their faith, families, hard work, and prosperous beginnings. That commitment, now called a "work ethic," is still very much a part of Pennsylvanians. Turkey Hill Dairy has been a grateful beneficiary of this great heritage. The spirit of those who work here has helped us to prosper through the challenges of 70 years, and leaves us poised for the future.

CHAPTER THREE

CENTRAL PENNSYLVANIA
VALLEYS OF THE SUSQUEHANNA

"I do not think there can be, in any part of the world, a more delightful situation than this," wrote Joseph Priestley, the pioneering chemist who discovered oxygen. He was talking about the central Pennsylvania countryside, where he had come to live in 1794 on the majestic Susquehanna River at Northumberland. Priestley built a country estate and took up the kind of life that can still be enjoyed in the region today. The least populated region of

the state, the Valleys of the Susquehanna contain not only the nation's largest outdoor recreational area—Susquehannock State Forest—but also a passel of reminders of the country's industrial past.

Native Americans called the Susquehanna the Long Reach river, and indeed, it unites the region's towns and farms, valleys and forested mountains. Its north and west branches meet at Sunbury, where the 444-mile river continues its long and winding journey south to the Chesapeake Bay.

Since the Susquehanna was never extensively navigable, today's network of highways linking central Pennsylvania with the East Coast, the Midwest, and Canada was a welcome addition. The region's successful traditional businesses, such as Pennsylvania House (maker of fine furniture), Woolrich (manufacturer of sportswear and outerwear), and Chef Boyardee (manufacturer of food products), are joined by leading-edge pharmaceutical firms such as Merck & Co.

Charming, revitalized river towns and cruises on paddle wheel riverboats conjure up the old days. The Victorian structures built by yesterday's coal and lumber tycoons now house restaurants and specialty retailers.

During the 1860s, Williamsport saw more millionaires created as a result of the lumber boom than any other town ever had before; today trolleys tour the eight blocks of their mansions on Millionaires' Row. Williamsport also gets international attention each year when it hosts the Little League World Series.

The historic structures of Boalsburg, settled in 1808, are maintained as shops and art galleries. The Boal Mansion, open to the public, has housed nine generations of the Boal family. David, the first Boal, who fought in the Revolutionary War, began building the present structure in 1789. His son built a tavern at a country crossroads, around which the present Boalsburg grew. The Columbus Chapel, once part of the Columbus family castle in Spain, was inherited by a Boal wife and brought to the estate in 1909. Also open to the public, it

ABOVE: *Sunset brings an ocher glow to the waters of the Susquehanna, referred to by artists as the "Currier and Ives" of rivers.* OPPOSITE: *One of the more than 40 illuminated rides adds sparkle to Knoebels Amusement Park, in Elysburg. Parking, admission, and live entertainment are free. Many families camp out or rent cabins in the surrounding woods.*

contains a collection of European art from the 15th through 18th centuries and the most important collection of Christopher Columbus artifacts in North America.

Even the name of the nearby town, State College, reflects the focus of the area. In 1855, Pennsylvania State University was chartered in State College as the Farmers High School, offering "the proper education of a farmer." Today thousands of sports fans converge on the town on autumn weekends for the Nittany Lions home football

OPPOSITE: *A couple in period dress add to the ambience of Millionaires' Row, in Williamsport. Formerly home to lumber barons, these architectural landmarks today are homes, offices, or B&Bs.*

The 1996 Little League World Series games filled the stands of South Williamsport's Lamade Stadium with die-hard fans, as it does every year. The city also takes pride in its Little League Baseball Museum.

games. Throughout the year, the Palmer Museum of Art, along with concerts, basketball games, and other events at the Bryce Jordan Center, draws a steady crowd. Some visitors come just to taste the latest creation at the Penn State Creamery, where students learn the fine art of commercially manufacturing ice cream.

Although much of this region's landscape may look largely as it did to Joseph Priestley, its towns offer more than he could have imagined.

ABOVE: *Candlelight services featuring the Rooke Chapel Choir are a 40-year-old Christmas tradition at Bucknell University in Lewisburg.*

BELOW: *The* Hiawatha *riverboat offers passengers a leisurely tour of the Williamsport area and a taste of life on the old Susquehanna.*

A REGIONAL PORTRAIT

BOALSBURG

CENTRE HALL 9
OLD FORT 8
POTTRS MILLS 7
TUSSY VILLE 5
LINDEN HALL 2

ABOVE: *Founded in 1808, Boalsburg still has a street plan and many buildings dating from colonial days. Boal Mansion, in the background, displays art and historical artifacts collected by nine generations of Boals.* RIGHT: *Razed and rebuilt between 1929 and 1930, Pennsylvania State University's Old Main building remains a landmark on the University Park campus.*

CHAPTER FOUR

THE SOUTHWEST
LAUREL HIGHLANDS/SOUTHERN ALLEGHENIES

Until the American Revolution, the Allegheny Mountains marked the beginning of Indian country, and Bedford, midway between Harrisburg and Pittsburgh, was the westernmost outpost of European civilization. Frontiersmen settled there to grow corn, oats, barley, and wheat. These intrepid 18th-century souls mounted the nation's first tax revolt—the Whiskey Rebellion—in 1794. George Washington took direct field command

of his army and marched on the rebels, but his show of federal strength was, fortunately, sufficient to make them back down.

During the 19th century, those who wanted to move farther west were challenged by "the ridge," a 1,200-foot obstacle looming above the Altoona-Hollidaysburg area with a grade far too steep for trains to scale. The ridge did, however, spark a great deal of technological ingenuity. Between 1831 and 1834, the Allegheny Portage Railroad was constructed as part of a transportation system to link Philadelphia and Pittsburgh. This engineering marvel placed canal boats on railroad cars and actually hauled them over the ridge on inclined planes.

In 1854, builders tackled the ridge in a more practical manner. The result of their efforts, Horseshoe Curve, utilized an enormous, gradually sloping loop that trains were able to climb. Scores of trains still use the curve, and visitors can watch them pass from an inclined plane at Horseshoe Curve National Historic Landmark. So renowned is this masterpiece of civil engineering that Altoona's new AA baseball team was named the Altoona Curve.

It also was during the 19th century that the Pennsylvania Railroad chose Altoona as a location for its repair facilities, and the town flourished as a gateway to the west. Its railroad heritage is honored today at the Altoona Railroaders Memorial Museum.

But Altoona has much more to offer than just its history; it competes with the top cities in the nation. A recent survey by *Money* magazine ranked Altoona among the 300 Best Places to Live in America for its low crime rate and excellent housing and schools, as well as several other factors.

Nearby Johnstown, one of the cities that rings the Laurel Highlands, was the scene of one of America's greatest tragedies. In 1889, a rainstorm overtaxed the South Fork Dam, and a 30-foot wall of water and debris rushed down Conemaugh Valley, engulfing the town—then one of the nation's most important steel centers. Thanks to the aid that poured in from all over the country, Johnstown was

ABOVE: *Governor Tom Ridge addresses employees at Cannondale's Bedford plant in 1998. Known as the bike industry's leading innovator, the company makes aluminum bicycles used by world-class cyclists.*

quickly rebuilt. The event is commemorated at the Johnstown Flood Museum. On a lighter note, the town also is renowned for its inclined plane. Cantilevered cars, mounted on tracks and powered by steam or electricity, were used in the late 19th century to haul miners, horses, and light freight up steep hillsides to the mines. At 1,693 feet and a grade of 71.9 degrees, the Johnstown inclined

A youngster leads her father down the slopes at Seven Springs Mountain Resort in Champion, about an hour's drive from Pittsburgh. The Southern Alleghenies are laced with cross-country trails, as well.

plane is considered the world's steepest. Today, it carries passengers and cars to a visitors center and observation deck overlooking the valley.

The Johnstown Flood National Memorial recalls the damage sustained when the South Fork Dam collapsed in 1862 and again in 1889. The site is 12 miles east of town on the Conemaugh River.

Railways and manufacturing are still important in the area, and companies in these sectors are among the region's leading employers—including those that produce heavy machine tools, paper, food products, and electronic parts.

The heart of the region is an emerging growth corridor along I-99/Route 220, the north-south roadway linking I-80 to the north and the Pennsylvania Turnpike to the south, the state's major east-west routes. The smooth flow of commerce and visitors has been attractive to developers, yet the area retains much of its original rural character. Farms dot the countryside, and Indiana County, birthplace of actor Jimmy Stewart, has long been known for the Christmas trees grown there.

Tourists have been attracted to the beauty of the Laurel Highlands for more than a century. President James Buchanan made Bedford Springs his summer White House during his term in office (1857 to 1861), and Charles M. Schwab, president of Bethlehem Steel in the early 1900s, built a summer estate in Loretto whose luxuriant gardens now are open to the public. The forests, mountains, and rushing streams of the area inspired Frank Lloyd Wright in designing one of his masterworks, Fallingwater, the house built on a waterfall in 1936 for Pittsburgh department store owner Edgar J. Kaufmann. Today, year-round mountain resorts and spas are a magnet for those who want to relax, while the Youghiogheny River draws whitewater rafting enthusiasts. There's even a place for those in between: Raystown Lake, Pennsylvania's largest lake wholly within its boundaries, is a center for boating, fishing, camping, hiking, and communing with nature.

OPPOSITE: *Fallingwater, Frank Lloyd Wright's 1936 architectural masterpiece, perches over a waterfall in Bear Run Nature Reserve. The governor recently approved $3.5 million toward its restoration.*

ABOVE: *Farms such as this are fixtures of the landscape in south-western Pennsylvania, where rapid economic growth and commercial development have not infringed on a way of life that has existed here since the original settlers tamed the land to plant their crops.*

OPPOSITE: *The mountain laurel, Pennsylvania's state flower, greets this family of hikers on Three-Mile Trail in Cowans Gap State Park. Nestled in the Tuscarora Mountain valley, the 1,085-acre park offers water sports, camping, skiing, and other pleasures of nature.*

DAVID G. ASSARD President and Chief Executive Officer, Elliott Company

At Elliott Company, employees have a long service record; many are second- and third-generation employees. They are extremely proud of their work and possess one of the strongest work ethics found anywhere. This is perhaps due to the history and cultural background of Western Pennsylvania.

Elliott is committed to being a good corporate citizen by supporting many charitable organizations in the community. The company is proud of its involvement in these programs and is especially pleased with its employees, who volunteer their time, energy, and money for these causes.

Elliott makes superior turbomachinery, but its most precious asset is the workforce that builds it.

CHAPTER FIVE

THE WEST
THE PITTSBURGH REGION

"Workshop of the World"—that's what Pittsburgh was called when it grew so dramatically between the Civil War and World War I from a small, industrial city to the steel-producing capital of the world. Andrew Carnegie contributed to Pittsburgh's success by introducing the Bessemer process, a method of converting pig iron into steel, on a large scale. As long as the best metallurgical coke was readily available from the fields of nearby

Connellsville, in Fayette County, no other place in the world could compete. Around the turn of the century, hundreds of firms were consolidated into giants like U.S. Steel Corporation.

The French were the first to establish a presence in the region when they captured a colonial fort, at the point where the Allegheny and Monongahela Rivers meet to form the Ohio, in the 1750s. After renaming it Fort Duquesne, they were forced to abandon it by the British during the French and Indian War (an alliance of the French and Huron Indians against the British). The British then rebuilt it as Fort Pitt, after William Pitt, the political leader responsible for their victory. From the late 1760s to the mid-1820s, the population rose as the frontier post became a commercial center in the nation's expansion westward. In 1793, the settlement's first iron foundry was established.

The story of Pittsburgh's growth can be seen in its historic buildings, monuments to the city's immense wealth. Downtown, the Romanesque Allegheny County Courthouse, designed by renowned architect H. H. Richardson and completed in 1888, is one of the nation's most impressive 19th-century buildings. In the city's east

end, the Frick Art & Historical Center is considered one of the best house museums in the country. Henry Clay Frick, who supplied Pittsburgh with the coke needed for its iron and steel industries in the 1870s, built the magnificent mansion—originally called Clayton—that today is part of the center.

Pittsburgh offered special challenges to those who wanted to relocate to its suburbs: beyond its rivers, the city was hemmed in by steep hills. The development of the inclined plane gave planners a way to conquer Mount Washington, to the south of the city, and a suburb sprang up there during the 1860s. Both the Duquesne and the Monongahela Inclines today offer breathtaking views of the city's distinctive Golden Triangle, the point of land at the rivers' confluence.

The first of Pittsburgh's many ethnic enclaves, known locally as Dutchtown, was settled by Germans. Irish Catholics also established their own neighborhoods, as did Poles, Italians, Jews, Greeks, Chinese, and African

ABOVE: *The River City Brass Band plays at Carnegie Music Hall in Pittsburgh. Modeled after New York's Carnegie Hall, the 788-seat auditorium is part of the Andrew Carnegie Free Library.*

Americans. Shops and restaurants full of the respective national character thrive in neighborhoods like Italian Bloomfield and the German North Side. The popular Nationality Rooms at the Cathedral of Learning on the University of Pittsburgh campus reflect the city's ethnic heritage, each room depicting a particular country through furnishings, artifacts, and information.

Pittsburgh shines as an American success story. Thanks to its legendary entrepreneurs and steely immigrants, the city went from a gritty, smoky industrial town to one of America's most livable cities, honored repeatedly as such by Rand McNally's *Places Rated Almanac.* Its renaissance started in the years following World War II, when business leaders such as financier Richard King Mellon and private and civic groups came together with government leaders to revitalize the central business district. In the decades-long collaboration, blue-collar Pittsburgh became a white-collar center of finance and services for the nation, and now ranks among the top U.S. cities for corporate headquarters. A strong spirit of cooperation between business and government endures.

There is more to downtown Pittsburgh, however, than corporate headquarters. The cultural district is a center for performances, especially classical, pop, or Broadway

The Pittsburgh Steelers go up against the Cincinnati Bengals in a 1997 game at Three Rivers Stadium. The four-time Super Bowl champs will soon move to their new home, Steelers Stadium, scheduled to open in August 2001.

concerts by the Pittsburgh Symphony Orchestra at Heinz Hall. Dining and sightseeing boats cruise the three rivers downtown. The annual Three Rivers Regatta held annually in July attracts over a million spectators.

The city's Carnegie Institutes and Museums, at three locations in the city, comprise a natural history museum, a science center, an architectural center, halls of sculpture and architecture, a library, a music hall for the performing arts, an Andy Warhol museum and an art museum. The latter was founded in 1896 by Andrew Carnegie himself, who created America's first museum of modern art through his determination to collect the "Old Masters of tomorrow." Carnegie believed that knowledge of the arts and sciences was the key to the betterment of the people, rather than charities, and devoted his fortune to philanthropy of this nature. The Andy Warhol Museum, the most comprehensive museum in the world devoted to a single artist, showcases the work of this renowned Pittsburgh native.

A REGIONAL PORTRAIT

FRED C. YOUNG CEO, Black Box Corporation

As Black Box rapidly approaches Fortune 1000 status in the highly competitive, global network services marketplace, we attribute much of our success to the commitment of our team members in Pittsburgh—and around the world.

We believe that Western Pennsylvania provides an excellent environment for the development of a technology business such as ours. From its people to the regional investment in technical education and training, to the support of local and state government, Pittsburgh and Pennsylvania have provided many of the necessary ingredients to help the company grow from a good idea to a multinational network services organization. (As you read this, we may now be a Fortune 1000 company!)

Black Box Corporation

OPPOSITE: *Heinz Hall in Pittsburgh, home of the Pittsburgh Symphony Orchestra, underwent a $6.5 million renovation in 1995. Many other groups also perform here, including the Pittsburgh Youth Symphony.*

BELOW: *The Duquesne Incline trolley takes passengers up to an observation deck, from which they have a spectacular view of downtown Pittsburgh's Golden Triangle.*

The Dinosaur Hall at Pittsburgh's Carnegie Museum of Natural History displays much of the museum's renowned paleontological collection.

The Pittsburgh Children's Museum now occupies the former Allegheny County post office. Its hands-on exhibits include the puppets from *Mister Rogers' Neighborhood,* the popular Pittsburgh-based public television program.

Pittsburgh's stature as the nation's largest inland port makes it a center for commerce. Contributing, too, to the fine reputation of the city and of southwestern Pennsylvania in general are a crime rate below the national average and outstanding educational institutions. The region is home to 29 colleges and universities, including the University of Pittsburgh, Carnegie Mellon University, and Duquesne University.

Pittsburgh and southwestern Pennsylvania are also associated with breakthroughs in modern medicine, such as Dr. Jonas Salk's announcement of the world's first

HELGE H. WEHMEIER President and Chief Executive Officer, Bayer Corporation

Make no mistake, the assets we manage at Bayer Corporation are entrusted to us by our parent company on behalf of investors who rightfully expect a worthwhile return.

But it matters that Bayer chooses to fulfill this duty by employing science to save lives; promote health; conserve energy; and add knowledge, convenience, and color to the world.

And it matters very much that in the workplace we praise and promote safety, environmental responsibility, honesty, personal initiative, and respect for all employees as individuals.

Bayer is a company in which all stakeholders can take great pride.

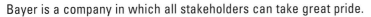

successful polio vaccine at the University of Pittsburgh in 1953. Today, Pittsburgh's health care community is known for pioneering research in organ transplant surgery, diabetes, and cardiology. In fact, the University of Pittsburgh Medical Center has the largest and busiest organ transplant program in the world.

A solid sports and recreation scene also enriches the area's livability. Despite Pittsburgh's many economic and cultural offerings, most Americans associate the city with Three Rivers Stadium, where the Pittsburgh Pirates play baseball and the Pittsburgh Steelers often begin an advance to football's Super Bowl. Excellent golf courses exist close to the metro area, as does Kennywood Park, the amusement park that has the distinction of being a National Historic Landmark. The park was built in 1905 by creative genius Frederick

The dining room at Clayton, the Italianate mansion of Henry Clay Frick that is part of the Frick Art & Historical Center in Pittsburgh, reflects the opulence of the Victorian era.

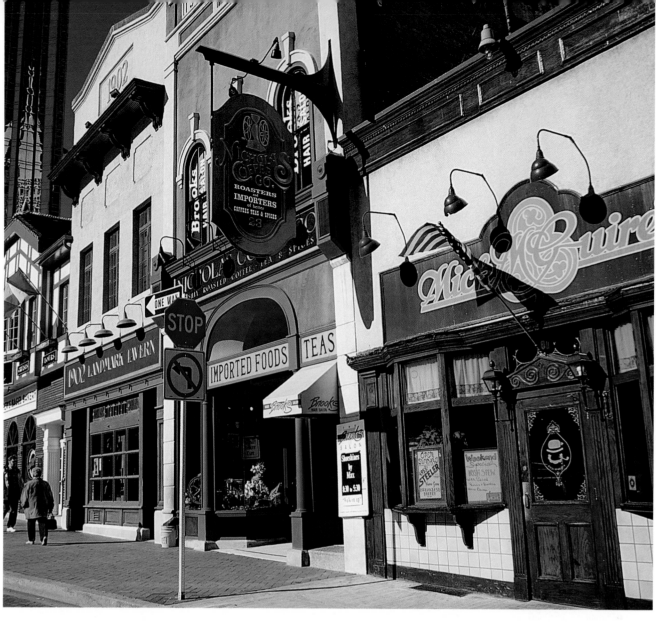

Ingersoll, who also built the world's first roller coaster there. Of nearly 50 similar amusement parks that went up at the time within a 100-mile radius, Kennywood is the only one still in operation.

As modern Pittsburgh enters the new millennium, it reflects the best of both worlds: it is more cosmopolitan than ever, yet retains the solid values of its community-oriented neighborhoods and industrious people.

PHOTOS: BOTH PAGES, © *Blair Seitz*

MARTIN G. MCGUINN Chairman and Chief Executive Officer, Mellon Financial Corporation

At Mellon Financial Corporation, we see Pennsylvania as not only the Keystone State, but also key to our long-term growth as we look toward the future with business and technology innovation clearly in mind. The elected leaders of our headquarters state are making the business climate even better by addressing critical business issues, including lower taxes. The state also is a leader in expanding its skilled workforce, including helping people move from welfare to the workplace, an initiative that Mellon continues to support. With an emphasis on emerging technologies, Pennsylvania is developing programs that will better prepare our young people for future employment opportunities. These programs will ensure not only that Mellon's future remains bright, but also that Pennsylvania will continue to enhance its reputation as a leading commercial center during the 21st century.

 Mellon

OPPOSITE: *Market Square, the commercial center of Pittsburgh in 1800, remains one of the city's most popular spots. It features shops and services, restaurants, an Irish pub, bakeries, and more.*

BELOW: *Women cyclists gear up for a race at Pittsburgh's Station Square. Characterized as sports devotees, Pittsburghers enjoy a bike route that links Highland, Mellon, Frick, and Schenley parks.*

ABOVE: *Union Station, a 1903 beaux arts masterpiece, is still in oper- ation on a limited schedule. The 10-story station building behind it has been converted to condominiums as part of an urban renewal effort.*

OPPOSITE: *Sunrise captures Pittsburgh's skyline—and the West End Bridge, which frames it—in silhouette. Completed in 1932, the 778-foot-long span is on the National Register of Historic Places.*

KENT G. GEORGE, A.A.E. Executive Director, Allegheny County Airport Authority, Pittsburgh International Airport

Recently voted the number one airport in America and number three in the world, Pittsburgh International Airport represents a significant economic resource for Pittsburgh and the region it serves. Along with its role as a passenger and cargo hub, Pittsburgh International serves as the gateway to Southwestern Pennsylvania and is a critical component in developing the region as a leader in the global marketplace.

Airports exist in a competitive environment. For more than 19 million travelers annually, Pittsburgh International Airport has become our most visible ambassador, presenting Pittsburgh as a viable multicultural region with abundant resources and opportunities to succeed in the world economy.

CHAPTER SIX

THE NORTHWEST
THE LAKE ERIE REGION

Life in America changed dramatically after 1859, when Edwin Drake struck oil in Titusville. His oil well, the country's first, launched the modern petroleum industry. Almost overnight, northwestern Pennsylvania was dominated by oil company agents and speculators. Oil wells soon lined Oil Creek and Pitthole Creek. Boomtowns appeared overnight—and some disappeared just as quickly. • Because of its high paraffin content,

Pennsylvania crude was—and still is—considered one of the best lubricating oils in the world, and the search was on for more and more oil sites. As vast new oil fields continued to be discovered in other areas, extensive drilling in this region faded. But the area's oil heritage is preserved at the Drake Well Museum, where a replica of Drake's original well still pumps "black gold," and aboard the Oil Creek and Titusville Railroad, which tours Oil Creek Valley between Titusville and Oil City.

Around the same time that oil was discovered, William Griffith, a farmer, began planting grapevines on his land on the south shore of Lake Erie. The rich soil of the Great Lakes Plain offered excellent support for the fruit, and soon Griffith opened the South Shore Wine Company. Today, vineyards line a scenic route between the Commonwealth's borders with New York and Ohio. A growing number of excellent wineries, such as Penn Shore Vineyards, Presque Isle Wine Cellars, and Mazza Vineyards, are open for tours and tastings of their renowned Cabernet Sauvignons, Catawbas, Chardonnays, Pinot Noirs, and other wines.

Situated in the heart of Pennsylvania's wine country is the Commonwealth's third largest city, Erie. Still just a small frontier town on Lake Erie at the turn of the 19th century, the city's destiny would change with the War of

1812. As the battle between Great Britain and America for control of the Great Lakes came to a head, a fleet of ships was constructed secretly in Erie's partially developed harbor and floated out to join the war effort. Commodore Oliver Hazard Perry (who gave America the phrase "We have met the enemy and they are ours" as well as the motto on his battle flag, Don't Give Up the Ship) sailed to victory against the British on one of the new vessels, the U.S. Brig *Niagara*. Now Pennsylvania's official flagship, a replica of the *Niagara* is berthed outside the new Erie Maritime Museum and tours the Great Lakes and Eastern Seaboard as an ambassador of friendship.

After the War of 1812, Erie flourished, both in shipbuilding and as a port. The Erie Extension Canal, built in 1844, facilitated lucrative business between Erie and Pittsburgh, Conneaut Lake, Franklin, and New Castle, but by the mid-19th century, railroads had rendered the canal obsolete. At the same time, however, commercial fishing increased and has been important to the economy ever since.

ABOVE: *Vineyards in the Lake Erie Viticultural Area, a 40,000-acre region between the Ohio and New York borders, produce a variety of fine wines.* OPPOSITE: *Wind fills the sails of the U.S. Brig* Niagara *on Lake Erie, a replica of the original that sailed in the War of 1812.*

PHOTOS: THIS PAGE, © Digital Stock; OPPOSITE PAGE, © Commonwealth Media Services

A few decades ago, Lake Erie began to deteriorate from agricultural runoff. Pennsylvanians rallied, as they have throughout history. Local manufacturers, colleges, and concerned individuals joined local and state governments in a massive effort to turn the situation around. Today, game fish are back, the ecology of the lake is constantly monitored, and Erie is once again a thriving port and commercial center.

Long known for tourism, Erie is seeing new popularity with its revitalized bay front, where shops and restaurants surround an observation tower that offers views of downtown Erie and Presque Isle Bay. Nearby are an art museum, a zoo, and a historical museum and planetarium housed in a brownstone mansion. The city's philharmonic orchestra and ballet company are among the groups that perform regularly.

Presque Isle State Park, "almost an island" as its French name implies, is a National Natural Landmark. Situated on a 3,200-acre peninsula that juts out into Lake Erie, the park has six distinct ecological zones and is visited by more than 320 species of migratory birds on their path along the Atlantic flyway. The historic Presque Isle Lighthouse, built

Presque Isle State Park in Erie offers year-round attractions: ice dunes in winter, wildflowers in summer, migrating birds and monarch butterflies in the fall. ABOVE: *Hopeful fishermen cast their lines at the Presque Isle Lighthouse, built in 1872.* OPPOSITE: *Strollers along one of the park's sandy beaches stop to enjoy the sunset.*

in 1872, stands as a reminder that the lake has been, and will always be, central to the character of this region.

On summer weekends, the towns of northwestern Pennsylvania empty and everybody heads for the beach. Besides marinas and numerous sandy beaches, Presque Isle State Park offers trails for hiking, biking, and in-line skating. Even in winter, the park contributes to the outstanding quality of life with opportunities for cross-country skiing and other winter sports.

Although more than four million people visit Presque Isle each year, the state park is never so crowded that visitors can't find a place to park or an empty stretch of beach. Coupled with the region's scenic wine country and historic attractions, the lakeshore and growing sophistication of Erie make northwestern Pennsylvania enticing in all seasons.

CHAPTER SEVEN

NORTH CENTRAL PENNSYLVANIA
ALLEGHENY NATIONAL FOREST REGION

The eyes of the nation have turned toward Gobbler's Knob on the second of February every year since 1887, when the groundhog known as Punxsutawney Phil is yanked from his burrow to predict the length of winter remaining. German farmers in Punxsutawney, a rural town northeast of Pittsburgh, brought the tradition with them, perhaps to call attention to their isolated community. And draw attention it does. Today Groundhog Day attracts about

20,000 tourists to daylong festivities that include parades, ice carving competitions, sleigh rides, music, and food.

Whether an early spring or an extended winter follows Phil's forecast is of no great consequence to lovers of the outdoors, for this thickly forested region abounds with recreational opportunities in every season. The Allegheny National Forest— the state's only national forest— alone covers more than half a million acres, all of it accessible by trail, river, stream, or road. The region's wealth of scenic beauty attracts visitors who like to hike, camp, ride horseback, fish, canoe, raft, tube, snowmobile, ice skate, sled, and cross-county ski. The Allegheny Reservoir, stretching 27 miles on the upper Allegheny River, features a number of recreation areas, and the Longhouse National Scenic Byway, a 29-mile drive along the Kinzua Dam side of the reservoir, yields spectacular views of the forest and river valley. (The name "Longhouse" honors the Seneca Indians, who lived in the valleys now blanketed by the reservoir.)

Nearly 9,000 acres of wilderness in the Allegheny National Forest have been designated as a nationally protected area. Another 23,000 acres, part of the Allegheny National Recreation Area, are protected under the Pennsylvania Wilderness Act. Some of the oldest and

largest tracts of virgin beech-hemlock forest in the eastern United States are preserved in the Tionesta and Hearts Content Scenic Areas of the forest.

During the 19th century, fortunes were made when trees were harvested and floated downriver to growing Pittsburgh. The town of Kane is known as the Black Cherry Capital of the World, thanks to the quality and quantity of the hardwood grown there. Kane was founded by Thomas L. Kane, who built the Kinzua railroad bridge in 1882 for use by his railroad, the Lake Erie & Western. Constructed by a 40-man crew in slightly more than three months, the bridge was the highest and longest in the world at the time. Reconstructed in 1900, it stands today 301 feet high, a National Historic Civil Engineering Landmark overlooking the spectacular natural beauty of the Kinzua Creek Valley Gorge.

U.S. Route 6, perhaps Pennsylvania's most scenic highway, goes right through Kane and other small towns in the region. Smethport, for example, is a former lumber

ABOVE: *A 40-foot-tall Zippo lighter marks the entrance to the Zippo/Case Visitors Center in Bradford.* OPPOSITE: *Rich autumn colors can be seen for miles in this forest of birch and hardwoods off Route 6 in McKean County, between Marvindale and Smethport.*

Water roars through the 179-foot-high Kinzua Dam into the Allegheny Reservoir, about eight miles north of Warren on the Allegheny River. The reservoir is a favorite spot for boating and trout fishing.

center and the seat of McKean County. Many fine Victorian homes, built here by 19th-century timber barons, have been converted to bed-and-breakfasts popular

HARRY R. HALLORAN JR. Chairman and CEO, American Refining Group, Inc.

As we enter the new millennium, addressing the enormous energy needs of the world will be a challenge with great opportunities. For decades, American Refining Group and its sister company, Energy Unlimited Incorporated, have been preparing, be it through conventional or renewable energy vehicles. All energy-related companies must understand, and as they do business today, develop a vision that incorporates strategic thinking that is far-reaching and maybe outside the box. The new millennium will provide an ample supply of anxiety to business. The start of anything new always brings uncertainty, but energy companies with vision will develop products and services that will lead the way.

AMERICAN REFINING GROUP

for weekend escapes or as bases from which to do business. Within driving distance of major metropolitan areas, the region hosts numerous businesses such as Chef Specialties, whose pepper mills have been manufactured in Smethport since 1940.

At the northeast edge of the forest near the New York border, Bradford, the "Oil Capital of the World" in 1875, today is the home of refineries, sawmills, and manufacturers such as Zippo Lighter and its subdivision, Case Cutlery. The beautiful Bradford campus of the University of Pittsburgh, just outside town, enriches the region, as does the Bradford Creative and Performing Arts Center.

In addition to Zippo/Case, manufacturers with a presence in the area include Pittsburgh Corning Corporation, in Port Allegany—one of the few glass-block makers in the United States—and Sealy Mattress Company, in Clarion.

The Allegheny National Forest region also includes Cook Forest State Park, Clear Creek State Forest and State

The Knox, Kane, Kinzua Railroad excursion train crosses the Kinzua Bridge on a 97-mile round-trip from Marienville to Kinzua Bridge State Park. The park offers 316 acres of fishing, hunting, and more.

Park, Cornplanter State Forest, Susquehannock State Forest, and Tioga State Forest. The Grand Canyon of Pennsylvania, one of the Commonwealth's most magnificent gorges, can be found in Tioga State Forest. Carved by glaciers, this National Natural Landmark in Pine Creek Gorge extends for 50 miles and is 1,000 feet deep. The two state parks on opposite sides of the canyon offer the best lookout points—and when autumn colors the trees, the view is particularly inspiring. Two hiking trails descend into the canyon for those who want a close-up look.

Seasonal homes of people who live and work as far as 200 miles away dot the region. Campgrounds, cabin parks, and rustic inns and lodges join the bed-and-breakfasts in welcoming visitors, some of whom invariably decide to sink roots here.

LEFT: *The handsome profile of an American bald eagle is one of the sights visitors may glimpse at the Allegheny Reservoir in Warren County. The area is also home to turkeys, pheasants, black bears, whitetail deer, and many other species.* BELOW: *Local hero Punxsutawney Phil and his handler, Bill Deeley, greet the nation on Groundhog Day, February 2nd, a popular tradition in the United States. On this day, the groundhog comes out of his hole after a long winter sleep to look for his shadow. If he sees it, he regards it as an omen of six more weeks of bad weather and returns to his hole. If the day is cloudy and, hence, shadowless, he takes it as a sign of spring and stays above ground. In 1997, Phil went on-line with the first live Web broadcast of his prognostication.* OPPOSITE: *The beauty of McGees Mill, in Clearfield County, can easily restore one's sense of well-being. One of America's few easy-to-reach mountain woodland areas, Clearfield County offers easy access to streams and hiking trails, snowmobiling, bicycling, skiing, and some of the best wilderness hunting and fishing in the East—not to mention a fine array of country inns and family restaurants.*

A REGIONAL PORTRAIT

CHAPTER EIGHT

THE NORTHEAST
POCONO MOUNTAINS/ENDLESS MOUNTAINS

Geology was destiny for Pennsylvania's Pocono Mountains and the region nicknamed "Endless Mountains." This section of the Appalachian Plateau sits on anthracite coalfields, the rarest geological phenomenon on the continent. Formed millions of years ago, anthracite coal fueled America's 19th-century industrial revolution and inspired a great deal of technology designed to get this valuable resource from the mountains to the cities. • The initial efforts were

made in the early 1800s by entrepreneurs who formed canal companies, and soon enough (in 1848) John Augustus Roebling had spanned the Delaware River with an aqueduct through which the coal boats of the Delaware and Hudson Canal Company could navigate. Roebling's aqueduct, an important forerunner of his masterpiece, the Brooklyn Bridge, stands today as the oldest wire suspension bridge in the country.

Canal boats were quickly replaced by anthracite railroads, some of the most lucrative enterprises in the nation. To get the trains across the steep valleys of the "endless mountains," Pennsylvania's railroad companies built towering viaducts with immense arches, such as the Starrucca and the Tunkhannock. The latter is the nation's largest steel-reinforced concrete railroad bridge.

Now that oil has largely replaced coal as a fuel, the few working coal towns that remain offer glimpses into this vanishing culture. An approximately 90-mile route from Centralia to Eckley passes through forested hill country and alongside piles of shiny black slag to the towns themselves. Eckley Miners Village in Eckley, the Pioneer Tunnel Coal Mine in Ashland, and the Lackawanna Coal Mine in

Scranton are among the sites that illuminate the risky business of coal and the brave lives the miners led.

And while the anthracite railroads, too, have all but disappeared, today's railroads continue to influence growth in the northeast. The region is preparing for Scranton, the state's fifth largest city, to become the terminus of a commuter rail line to New York. The area has seen growth in the transportation equipment and communications industries and has been chosen as a location for a number of telemarketing call centers and back-office operations.

Scranton's Steamtown National Historic Site explores steam railroading, another aspect of the region's railroading history. Located in the original yard of the Delaware, Lackawanna & Western Railroad (DL&W), this railroad museum is the only site in the national park system that illustrates the steam train era. Scenic rail excursions in the area carry passengers over the old anthracite routes.

ABOVE: *This daring snowboarder takes a wild ride at one of the popular ski resorts in the Pocono Mountains. The area boasts some of the East's longest and steepest ski runs.*

Another reminder of Scranton's railroad days is the Radisson Lackawanna Station hotel, on the National Registry of Historic Places. The hotel was converted in 1983 from the neoclassical Lackawanna train station, which was hailed as one of the most beautiful in the country when it was completed in 1908. The hotel lobby retains the station's original Siena marble walls, mosaic tile floor, faience tile murals, and barrel-vaulted, stained-glass atrium ceiling, shedding light on just how much wealth coal once created—and the meaning of the phrase "black diamonds."

It's no wonder the abundance of those days has been translated today into superb accommodations, from the opulent to the rustic. The Poconos have welcomed tourists since 1829, when Antoine Dutot opened what would become Kittatinny House at the Delaware Water Gap, a scenic break in the Kittatinny

Time seems to stand still in Hawley, located in Wayne County in the heart of the Poconos. Wayne County, home to nearly 40,000 people, was named for Revolutionary War hero General Anthony Wayne.

Ridge of the Appalachian Mountains threaded by the Delaware River.

In the years following the Civil War, the Delaware Water Gap drew wealthy summer visitors from New York and Philadelphia, who came to escape the heat of the city. Soon it rivaled Saratoga Springs as an inland resort town. Railroads and later modern highways encouraged the development of other Pocono resorts, and visitors began coming year-round. In 1926, the Pennsylvania Power and Light Company, in the process of building a dam east of Scranton, incidentally created Lake Wallenpaupack, the third largest lake in the state. Like many of the lakes and streams in the area, it's stocked for

The grand lobby of the Radisson Lackawanna Station hotel in Scranton, with marble walls and a Tiffany stained-glass ceiling, testifies to the wealth the railroads generated in the early 20th century.

excellent sport fishing. Anglers and other visitors stay at the cottages and country inns surrounding it.

The National Park Service protects the Delaware River through most of this corner of Pennsylvania. The scenic Delaware Water Gap National Recreation Area stretches for 40 miles along the river and encompasses more than 70,000 acres, providing opportunities for hiking, horseback riding, canoeing, river rafting, and more. The "Niagara of Pennsylvania," Bushkill Falls, also offers breathtaking scenery, much of it reachable via rustic bridges and easy trails.

Most of the state's alpine skiing areas are located in this region, and the mountains abound in resorts, the larger ones to the south. The Poconos are known for specializing in romance—newlywed couples eagerly seek out accommodations that include private indoor swimming pools and whirlpool baths shaped like hearts or champagne glasses. Farther north are bed and breakfasts, small hotels, and country inns offering fine dining.

The mountains also have towns that time forgot, such as Eagles Mere, where wealthy families once spent entire summers at the resorts surrounding the clear lake. In Jim Thorpe, not much has changed except the town's name, which since 1953 has honored the world-renowned American athlete interred there. Tourists have been coming to this well-preserved, pretty Victorian town for more than a century. Then it was known as Mauch Chunk or its nickname, the Switzerland of America—a place where one could take in the natural beauty, walk the narrow, winding streets, ride a scenic railroad, or step into the mysterious, alien world of coal with a visit to a mine.

OPPOSITE, TOP: *A spring day is perfect for a horseback ride in the Poconos, as this father and daughter discover.* BOTTOM: *Railcars roll through the town of Jim Thorpe, which thrived in the late 19th and early 20th centuries as a transport center for coal. Known for more than a century as the Switzerland of America, Jim Thorpe has attracted flocks of tourists, who come for the clean mountain air.*

PART TWO

A WORLD OF INNOVATION

Although Benjamin Franklin regularly advised "industry plus frugality" as the formula for success in business, he also recognized a paradigm shift when he saw one. In a 1764 letter to a friend, Franklin addressed Britain's attempt to manipulate the American economy in a way that would keep the colonists as consumers, rather than allowing them to become competing manufacturers. Writing with tongue in cheek of the discovery of "Button-mold Bay," he explained that the Americans had discovered "a Beach in a Bay several Miles round, the Pebbles of which are all in the Form of Buttons." This would be bad news for British button makers. Furthermore, "As we have now got Buttons, 'tis something towards our Clothing; and who knows but in time we may find out where to get Cloth?" • Pennsylvania is in the midst of another paradigm shift: from leadership in an industrial era to leadership in the new economy. Since the early 1980s, the state has enjoyed an almost steady creation of jobs in the new service industries or with manufacturers who produce highly sophisticated products in highly sophisticated ways. In the first year of the new century, Pennsylvania's small and mid-sized emerging technology manufacturers, for example, plan to expand their workforce by a combined total of 5.9 percent; more than 40 percent of these companies will increase jobs by 15.7 percent. For every business sector in the new economy, the Commonwealth is committed to providing the resources necessary for growth. For Pennsylvania, then, it appears that the sun—to paraphrase Benjamin Franklin's words during the final moments of the signing of the American Constitution—is a rising, not a setting one.

CHAPTER NINE

TOOLS OF MODERN MEDICINE
BIOTECHNOLOGY AND HEALTH CARE

In 1750, Dr. Thomas Bond arrived back home in colonial Philadelphia after his surgical training in England only to realize that, unlike London and Paris, America's most cultured city did not have hospitals. The wealthy were cared for at home when they were sick, while the poor were treated at the almshouse. If an epidemic threatened the city, patients were isolated at a facility known as a pesthouse. • Bond tried to spark interest in building a hospital,

eventually gaining the ear of Benjamin Franklin. Franklin lobbied the provincial legislature, arguing that the presence of such an institution would protect every citizen's health. In 1751 the Pennsylvania Assembly chartered the Pennsylvania Hospital, the first institution in the British colonies for the care of the physically or mentally ill.

The next hospital was more than a century in coming. The College of Philadelphia opened a hospital in 1874, long after it had already established America's first medical school, today's University of Pennsylvania School of Medicine, in 1765.

During the 19th century, Philadelphia became known as a center of health care training with the establishment of five other area medical schools: Thomas Jefferson University in 1824; Homeopathic College of Pennsylvania, which later became Hahnemann University, in 1848; the Female Medical College of Pennsylvania, which later was consolidated with Hahnemann and is now MCP Hahnemann University, in 1850; the Philadelphia College of Osteopathic Medicine in 1899; and the Temple University School of Medicine in 1901.

Meanwhile, in 1847, the Catholic Sisters of Mercy from Carlow, Ireland, established Mercy Hospital in Pittsburgh, western Pennsylvania's first health care institution. Mercy Hospital grew to become the Pittsburgh Mercy Health System, which today is part of the Catholic Health East System.

A number of other hospitals were established in and around Pittsburgh during the 19th century. The opening of Mercy Hospital was followed by that of Western Pennsylvania Hospital in 1848. In 1862, Western Pennsylvania Hospital responded to activist Dorothea Dix's report about Pittsburgh's deplorable treatment of the mentally ill by opening a special department for their care, which later became Dixmont Hospital. The Pittsburgh Infirmary, the oldest Protestant hospital in America, was originally established in Allegheny in 1849.

Today, Western Pennsylvania Hospital is the clinical campus for students at the Temple University School of

A medical technologist at Temple University Hospital puts bone marrow from a cancer patient into a tank of liquid nitrogen, where it will remain frozen for later evaluation by a team of specialists.

Medicine. The Western Pennsylvania Healthcare System airs an informative KDKA-TV series, *Ask the Doctor*, with material provided by Western Pennsylvania Hospital.

Dr. Jonas Salk, who developed the polio vaccine, displays it at its release in 1955. A doctor and epidemiologist, Salk began working on the vaccine in his University of Pittsburgh laboratory in 1947.

AN ABUNDANCE OF CHOICES

The Commonwealth is served by a variety of excellent hospitals and health systems, many affiliated with major universities. A 1999 study of the nation's best hospitals by *U.S. News & World Report* ranked Thomas Jefferson University Hospital the best in Philadelphia for cardiology, orthopedics, and rehabilitation. The Wills Eye Hospital, Jefferson's department of ophthalmology, was ranked third in the nation and first in Philadelphia for ophthalmology. Among Jefferson's "firsts" was the heart-lung machine, invented in the 1950s by John Gibbon, a surgical resident.

The University of Pennsylvania Health System includes several venerated Philadelphia health care institutions, among them the University of Pennsylvania Medical Center, Penn Medicine at Radnor, Pennsylvania Hospital, Phoenixville Hospital, and Presbyterian Medical Center. Over the past 30 years, a number of discoveries have been made and procedures developed by University of Pennsylvania physicians and scientists, including the first vaccine to fight pneumonia, magnetic resonance imaging, and the "Philadelphia chromosome" that established the connection between genetic abnormalities and cancer.

The UPMC Health System, affiliated with the University of Pittsburgh Schools of the Health Sciences, comprises a growing number of affiliated hospitals and specialized medical centers, including UPMC Presbyterian, UPMC Shadyside, Eye & Ear, McGee-Women's Hospital, the Western Psychiatric Institute and Clinic, Children's Hospital of Pittsburgh, and many more. The health system is known for specialty programs in transplantation, cardiology, neurosciences, occupational and environmental health, geriatrics, and genetics.

With grants from the Milton S. Hershey Foundation and the United States Public Health Service, the Pennsylvania State University in 1963 established a college of medicine in Hershey. The Penn State College of

A researcher at Glaxo SmithKline's Philadelphia laboratories checks the properties of a vaccine. The company's recent merger created one of the most extensive development pipelines in the industry.

Medicine, also an academic health center, provides some of the best medical care available today. Particular areas of scientific and clinical interest at the school include Alzheimer's Disease, AIDS treatment, artificial organs, cancer treatment, and genetic diseases.

The Tenet Healthcare Corporation, a nationwide provider of health care services, operates eight hospitals in the Philadelphia region. Its St. Christopher's Hospital for Children specializes in organ transplant, pediatric burns, and cystic fibrosis.

Since the best medical facilities still tend to cluster around urban centers, coalitions such as PA HealthNet bring quality health care to outlying areas through the use of computer-based telecommunications equipment that facilitates videoconferencing among doctors.

PIONEERING THE FUTURE

In addition to Pennsylvania's outstanding medical communities and university-based health organizations and research laboratories, the state's history of leadership in

PHOTOS: BOTH PAGES, © John McGrail

medicine and chemical production has made it an ideal location for today's biotechnology industry—the application of science and engineering to develop products that prolong life and enhance the environment.

By the early 19th century, Pennsylvania was on its way to becoming a world center for the manufacture of medical and pharmaceutical chemicals. It was in Philadelphia in 1792 that James Woodhouse, author of one of the first experimental guides for the study of chemistry—*The Young Chemist's Pocket Companion*—established America's first organization for the pursuit of chemical interests, the Chemical Society of Philadelphia. At the time, two Philadelphia firms, the Rosengarten Company and Powers & Weightman, were manufacturing important drugs such as sulfate of quinine, used for malaria and other fevers, and sulfate of morphia, a sedative and painkiller. These companies were merged to form the Powers-Weightman-Rosengarten Company, which in turn was consolidated in 1927 with Merck & Co., today a global, research-driven pharmaceuticals firm. Another Philadelphia company, Bullock & Crenshaw, sold wholesale chemicals and chemical wares from the mid-19th century to well into the 20th, supplying colleges and schools throughout the country.

Biotechnology has revolutionized modern health care. In America, formal biomedical research began at the Wistar Institute of Anatomy and Biology (today an institute of the University of Pennsylvania), opened in Philadelphia in 1892.

Pennsylvania ranks second in the nation for people employed in the biopharmaceutical industry and fifth in the number of small biotechnology firms. Biotechnological, pharmaceutical, and related industries account for 59,000 jobs in 1,100 Pennsylvania establishments. Most Pennsylvania pharmaceutical manufacturers are clustered in the southeastern corner of the state.

Working her way back to health, a Pittsburgh Mercy Health System patient participates in a cardiac rehabilitation program, pedaling at a slow, steady pace while the nurse checks her heart rate.

Pennsylvania's wealth of colleges, universities, and health care institutions makes for tremendous contributions in biotechnology research and testing. Pennsylvania State University's nationally prominent

THE RAT THAT MADE HISTORY

Among the developments and discoveries that can be attributed to Philadelphia's Wistar Institute of Anatomy and Biology is the famous WistaRat, the first standardized laboratory animal, bred by Helen Dean King in 1906. Many lab rats at work today can trace their ancestry to the WistaRat.

Philadelphia's Fox Chase Cancer Center ranked number one (again) for cancer care in Pennsylvania, Delaware, and New Jersey. Opened in 1904, the nation's first cancer hospital has had numerous firsts, including Baruch S. Blumberg's discovery of the virus that causes hepatitis B, for which he received the 1976 Nobel Prize.

Trade organizations such as the Pennsylvania Biotechnology Association lend support through business networking and cooperation with the state government to formulate industry strategy. Pennsylvania's biotech network comprises a team of biotechnology executives, government representatives, and university researchers dedicated to synergistic communication addressing issues of importance to this industry.

plant genetics and breeding laboratories, for example, have solved practical research problems for many a pharmaceuticals company. In one case, the university field-tested a bacteria developed by Langhorne-based Ecogen to kill crop-eating pests and fungi.

An infant receives comfort and care at the Newborn Infant Center of the Children's Hospital of Philadelphia, ranked the number two pediatric hospital in the country by U.S. News & World Report.

A STELLAR ROSTER

Glaxo SmithKline, one of the world's largest producers of vaccines—including the world's first hepatitis A vaccine and a hepatitis B vaccine—employs more than 8,000 in the state, many in the Philadelphia area where SmithKline Beecham's U.S. headquarters had been situated prior to the companies' merger. Wyeth-Ayerst's North American headquarters is in St. Davids, just outside Philadelphia, where the company employs 15,000 people. The Wyeth brothers began making drug

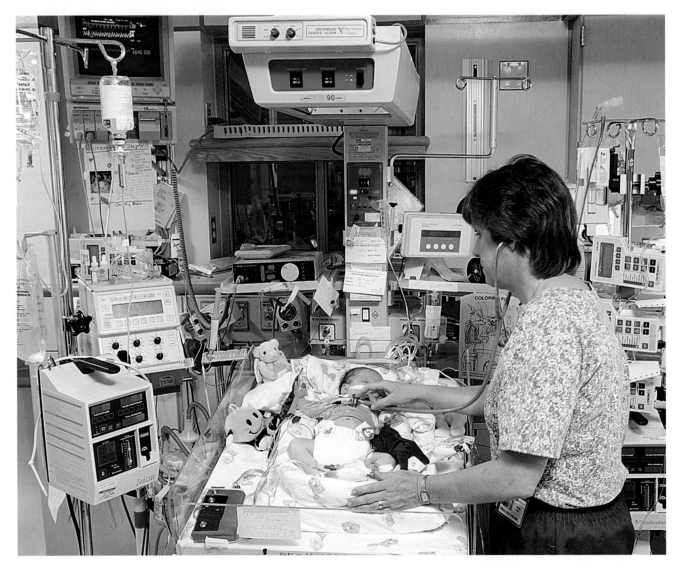

preparations in the area during the 1860s, later establishing the firm that produced both the first penicillin tablets and the first orally active estrogen. The aforementioned Merck, which employs about 11,000 people in the state, operates a major research facility in West Point (Pennsylvania), where many of its breakthrough medicines such as Fosamax, a treatment for osteoporosis, and Singulair, a preventative asthma medication, have been developed. The North American headquarters of Pfizer Animal Health, which operates one of the largest animal health businesses in the world, is farther west, in Exton.

The southeast may have the majority of Pennsylvania's pharmaceutical companies, but the west is not far behind. A 1999 article in *Chemical Week* stated that Pittsburgh and the Ohio River Valley are "gateways to one of the most dynamic chemical-producing regions of the United States."

Among the top companies in the region, Bayer, a household name in pharmaceuticals, is based in Pittsburgh, where it employs approximately 1,900 people. In addition to aspirin and both One-A-Day and Flintstones vitamins, Bayer introduced Kogenate for the treatment of hemophilia and Adalat CC for the treatment of hypertension. Calgon, another biotech leader in Pittsburgh, was founded in 1918 and grew to become a leader in specialty chemical

Temple University School of Pharmacy students measure the weight of chemical components in a medication. As part of Temple's extensive health sciences center, the school offers exceptional resources.

applications and water management technology. Two of the company's worldwide production facilities are situated in Ellwood City and Greentree. Degremont, a subsidiary of Paris, France–based Suez Lyonnaise des Eaux, acquired Calgon in 1999.

Other major firms are scattered throughout Pennsylvania. Lancaster Laboratories, for example, a subsidiary of Thermo TerraTech, a Thermo Electron Company and one of the largest analytical laboratories in the country, is based in Lancaster. The company employs

GOING THE DISTANCE

In 1991, Pfizer introduced Norvasc, the first calcium channel blocker for treating angina and hypertension that is safe for patients with congestive heart failure. Norvasc has since become one of the most successful drugs ever launched by a pharmaceuticals firm.

LIFE SAVERS

In 1998, for the third year in a row, the Greater Philadelphia area led the nation in organ donations, with 298 donors. As a result, the lives of 927 transplant patients were prolonged or improved.

vaccines, based in Swiftwater; and Respironics, a division of Masimo, which makes patient ventilation medical products at its Murrysville headquarters in Westmoreland County.

The life-extending products of the biotechnology industry have permitted a large percentage of health care delivery to be moved out of hospitals to clinics, doctors' offices, and even to patients' own homes, revolutionizing

At Bayer corporate headquarters west of Pittsburgh, new applications for Bayer products are developed—from pigments in automotive components to raw materials for polyurethane coatings.

more than 600 people to provide analytical research and consulting services in the chemical and biological sciences to various businesses and industries, both foreign and domestic. In the 1970s, Lancaster Laboratories pioneered computerized laboratory information management systems.

Top biotech companies in the state also include Warner-Lambert, best known for brands like Listerine, Trident, and Halls, which operates a major facility in Lititz, in central Pennsylvania; Connaught Laboratories, a manufacturer of pharmaceuticals, biological products, and

the industry. In Pennsylvania, as in the rest of the country, a number of hospitals have closed, downsized, or merged in efforts to reduce the number of patient beds and reposition themselves as efficient providers of highly technical and intensive care.

TECHNOLOGY KUDOS

In 1999, the UPMC Health System earned a national Innovation in Healthcare Information Technology Award from *Modern Healthcare*—a leading health care industry magazine—and Cisco Systems, for technology that speeds up the admissions process.

Pennsylvania's soaring biotechnology and health care sectors are on track to continue transforming not only medical care but other industries as well, giving every Pennsylvanian the opportunity for a longer, better, more enjoyable life in the new century.

A doctor at one of Pennsylvania's many university-affiliated medical centers examines a series of MRI scans as her assistant logs the information into a diagnostic computer program.

TOOLS OF MODERN MEDICINE

CENTOCOR, INC.

A leading biopharmaceutical company, Centocor, Inc., creates, acquires, and markets innovative medical therapies for acute vascular disease, autoimmune disorders, and cancer.

With close to 1,000 workers at its headquarters in Malvern, Pennsylvania, Centocor is one of the largest employers in the Greater Philadelphia area.

Founded in Philadelphia in 1979, Centocor, Inc., quickly established itself as a pioneer in monoclonal antibody technology; then it underwent a bold transformation. By the end of its second decade, the research-driven biotechnology boutique had become a fully commercialized biopharmaceutical company with a broad portfolio of innovative therapies. What began as a laboratory focused on developing diagnostic assays is now a high-growth manufacturer and marketer of cutting-edge products, supported by unparalleled clinical research, integrated sales and marketing capability, and strategic international alliances.

From its inception, Centocor has been a leader in the commercial development of monoclonal antibodies—highly specific natural proteins whose usefulness in diagnosing and monitoring disease initially came to light in the mid-1970s. Centocor's first product, a diagnostic test for rabies, was approved by the Food and Drug Administration (FDA) in 1982. That same year Centocor moved its operations to Malvern, Pennsylvania.

Today, with nearly 1,000 workers, Centocor is one of the biggest employers in the Greater Philadelphia area. The company's newly constructed Malvern plant, when fully operational, will be one of the largest antibody manufacturing facilities in the world, and will complement Centocor's other mammalian cell-culture pharmaceutical plant in the Netherlands.

Thanks in large part to intensive research and development done at Centocor, it is now known that monoclonal antibodies can be used successfully to treat as well as diagnose serious diseases. In the 1990s, Centocor began focusing on the creation, acquisition, manufacture, and marketing of new, cost-effective therapies based primarily on the monoclonal antibody platform. In 1998 the company sold its diagnostic division in order to concentrate on therapeutic products, an area with higher profitability and growth potential.

BREAKTHROUGH THERAPIES

At present, Centocor's five leading products offer treatment in three major disease areas: acute vascular syndromes, autoimmune disorders, and cancer. ReoPro® (abciximab) is an antiplatelet agent designed for patients undergoing percutaneous coronary intervention (PCI) such as angioplasty or stent placement. RETAVASE® (reteplase recombinant) is a fibrinolytic or "clot buster" used in the treatment of heart attacks to improve blood flow in the heart.

A pioneer in biotechnology, Centocor is one of the industry's true success stories, with five therapeutic products in the marketplace and nearly $500 million in revenues in 1999.

Fragmin® (dalteparin sodium injection) is comarketed with Pharmacia & Upjohn for treatment of unstable angina and non–Q wave myocardial infarction. ReoPro, RETAVASE, and Fragmin together address the full spectrum of chest-pain management, and strengthen Centocor's leadership position in the acute coronary care market.

REMICADE™ (infliximab), approved by the FDA in 1998 for treating the bowel disorder Crohn's disease, is the first new treatment approved for Crohn's in 30 years. In November 1999 the FDA also approved REMICADE, in combination with methotrexate, for treatment of refractory rheumatoid arthritis.

Panorex® (edrecolomab), used in the treatment of postoperative colorectal cancer, is currently sold only in Germany. Clinical trials in other markets, including the United States, are scheduled for completion in 2000.

The foregoing products represent milestones—all achieved within the last decade—for medical treatment as well as for Centocor. Panorex, cleared for marketing in Germany in 1994, was the first monoclonal antibody ever approved to treat cancer. European and U.S. approval of ReoPro, also granted in 1994, marked a turning point for Centocor, and led to the company's first full year of profitability in 1997. The March 1998 acquisition of U.S. product rights to RETAVASE brought with it an experienced cardiovascular sales force, and accelerated Centocor's emergence as a fully integrated biopharmaceutical company. By the end of 1999, RETAVASE had gained a 30 percent share of the market.

A FUTURE FILLED WITH POSSIBILITIES

Building on its current portfolio across multiple markets, Centocor continues to look for additional indications for existing products while identifying new candidates for clinical development. Key ongoing clinical or preclinical trials involve treatment for unstable angina and stroke; use of drugs in tandem for acute myocardial infarction; anticytokines for autoimmune and other diseases, including ulcerative colitis, asthma, and psoriasis; and a DNA-based antibody vaccine aimed at lung or breast cancer.

Centocor's products, which are developed primarily through monoclonal antibody technology, help physicians deliver innovative treatments to improve human health and restore patients' quality of life.

Centocor also pursues product acquisitions and copromotional agreements that open the door to innovative and complementary technology and therapies. Strategic partners such as Eli Lilly and Company, Glaxo Wellcome, Fujisawa Pharmaceutical Company, Schering-Plough Corporation, and Tanabe Seiyaku Company help market Centocor products to a growing number of global customers.

In October 1999, Centocor and Johnson & Johnson—one of the world's largest manufacturers of health care products—completed a $4.9 billion merger, the largest in Johnson & Johnson history. "The merger with Johnson & Johnson gives us the global reach we need to succeed in today's highly competitive marketplace," says David P. Holveck, company group chairman. "Additionally, it provides the resources that will allow us to continue to develop and bring to market innovative products that meet critical human health care needs."

With a strong portfolio of innovative products, promising new therapies, manufacturing and clinical research excellence, and a well-established commercial presence, Centocor has the tools to build on its record of success in the exciting and challenging decades ahead.

The world's largest producer of commercial-scale antibodies, Centocor has manufacturing facilities in the Netherlands and recently completed construction of a 116,000-square-foot, state-of-the-art plant in Malvern.

WEST PHARMACEUTICAL SERVICES

An innovator in pharmaceutical development technologies, West Pharmaceutical Services has made a name for itself in this rapidly growing industry.

Using sophisticated technology and rigorous attention to quality, West Pharmaceutical Services has positioned itself to meet the increasingly complex needs of its global customer base that includes the world's leading multinational pharmaceutical companies.

Headquartered in Lionville, Pennsylvania, West is a broad-based, global provider of products and services that support product development processes in the pharmaceutical, medical device, and packaging industries. West's capabilities include research and development of drug delivery systems; design and manufacture of delivery devices and packaging components for pharmaceutical, health care, and consumer products; contract laboratory services; clinical services; and contract manufacturing and packaging services. West serves its customers from sales, manufacturing, and research and development centers in North and South America, Europe, Asia, and Australia.

Founded in 1923 in Philadelphia as The West Company, the company's mission has been to enhance the delivery of pharmaceuticals through advances in packaging components and delivery systems. West once provided systems and components for packaging injectable drugs. It now reaches across the spectrum of pharmaceutical product development, beginning with technologies applicable to the earliest stages of product development and following through to provide support for products that are on the market.

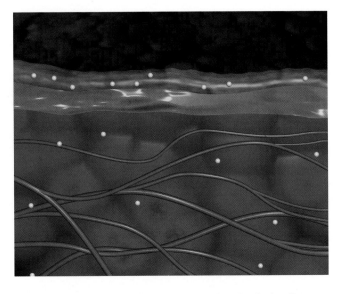

West scientists are developing advanced technologies for non-invasive delivery of drugs to the body, including formulations that enhance absorption of drugs through the nasal cavity.

By adopting the name West Pharmaceutical Services in 1999, the company sent a strong signal that it has a clearly defined sense of purpose and direction. In the process of making this transformation, West has invested more than $40 million in infrastructure, technologies, and people since 1994.

WEST'S MARKET POSITIONING

West's corporate strategy is grounded in a thorough understanding of the dynamics of the market. Because of the large investment needed for discovery, research, and commercialization, pharmaceutical companies are refining their product development processes by deploying their resources more efficiently. Rather than invest in all the technologies required to bring new compounds to market, they are forming partnerships and alliances with companies that can provide these technologies.

Bolstered by a solid financial foundation and a customer base that includes the world's leading pharmaceutical companies, West has built a platform of technologies that positions the company to become a significant participant in the growth of pharmaceutical outsourcing.

With a portfolio of more than 20 laboratory procedures that help customers expedite their product development process, West is successfully meeting the growing industry need for contract laboratory services.

WEST Pharmaceutical SERVICES ®

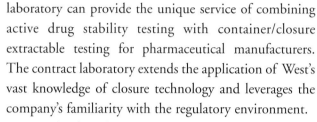

West processes Westar® ready-to-sterilize and ready-to-use pharmaceutical closures at its Jersey Shore, Pennsylvania, facility. Westar components are final-packed in a Class-100 clean room.

By becoming involved at the beginning of the development process, West can apply multiple technologies integrated throughout the life of a product, which expands commercial possibilities for West by creating opportunities to manage an entire project.

PRODUCTS AND SERVICES

West's core business is based on advanced technologies in the design and manufacture of elastomer, metal, plastic, and co-material products for the pharmaceutical, health care, and consumer markets. This segment of the business is focused primarily on the delivery of injectable pharmaceuticals.

West is creating additional opportunities for growth by adding capabilities that support its customers throughout the product development process. Since 1994, West has built its drug delivery technologies to create a strong platform for the development of delivery formulations and for the design and manufacture of delivery devices.

West took a major step in advancing its drug delivery technologies with the commencement in the first quarter of 2000 of Phase I clinical trials for the company's proprietary nasal morphine formulation. The development of the nasally delivered morphine product links West's technologies in drug delivery and clinical services into one product development stream. West has also filed an Investigational New Drug application for a nasal formulation for leuprolide acetate that will be tested to treat indications of endometriosis.

The company's contract laboratory can provide the unique service of combining active drug stability testing with container/closure extractable testing for pharmaceutical manufacturers. The contract laboratory extends the application of West's vast knowledge of closure technology and leverages the company's familiarity with the regulatory environment.

West's clinical services group includes a Phase I clinical research site that offers an 80-bed hospital unit for conducting first-time-in-human studies, a Phase II and III affiliated network of physicians and clinicians, and a consumer research facility for transitioning prescription products to over-the-counter status.

West's contract manufacturing and contract packaging services position the company to serve customers in the final step of introducing products into the market.

West will continue to add capabilities to support customers' product development by investing in current and new technologies and by initiating a disciplined acquisition strategy.

West also has improved profitability through gains in operational efficiencies. Plant expansions have added new capabilities and capacity for high-margin business and West has invested in world-class software and systems to improve manufacturing performance and upgrade product design capabilities.

West has attracted new talent into the organization globally and has made substantial investments in its corporate infrastructure. As the company expands its capabilities, it has strengthened its management team to lead the successful execution of growth strategies. In addition, West has added a wealth of talented people with scientific and pharmaceutical backgrounds whose knowledge and skills strengthen the company's ability to deliver needed technologies to customers.

West is meeting the increasing demand for precision injection molding of medical devices with clean room manufacturing at its Montgomery, Pennsylvania, facility.

WYETH-AYERST

Devoted to improving the health of people worldwide, Wyeth-Ayerst is an innovative international pharmaceutical company that researches, develops, manufactures, markets, and distributes health care products.

With facilities located worldwide, Wyeth-Ayerst maintains its global headquarters in St. Davids, Pennsylvania.

Millions of people around the world today are leading healthier lives thanks to the innovative pharmaceutical, vaccine, and nutritional products developed by Wyeth-Ayerst of St. Davids, Pennsylvania.

Dedicated to research and development, along with top quality manufacturing, marketing, education, and service to health care professionals, Wyeth-Ayerst is a global enterprise that has focused its efforts on technological innovation to meet today's health care challenges. It provides health care products to more than 145 countries and employs more than 40,000 people worldwide.

Wyeth-Ayerst is the pharmaceutical division of American Home Products Corporation (AHP), one of the world's largest research-based pharmaceutical and health care companies. AHP is a leading developer of prescription drugs, over-the-counter medications, and animal health care products. Wyeth-Ayerst is composed of several operating units involved in the research, development, manufacturing, marketing, and sales of ethical pharmaceuticals, biopharmaceuticals, vaccines, and nutritionals.

Wyeth-Ayerst provides a working environment that encourages new ideas and promotes scientific and technological innovation.

Wyeth-Ayerst traces its beginnings to the assimilation of four major companies:

- Wyeth Laboratories, Inc.—a drug-catalog business created by brothers John and Frank Wyeth in Philadelphia, Pennsylvania, in 1862;
- A.H. Robins—an apothecary and manufacturing chemist shop that eventually produced prescription medications founded in Richmond, Virginia, in 1866;
- Lederle Laboratories, Inc.—a company that was created to produce diphtheria antitoxin and was founded by Dr. Ernest Lederle in New York, New York, in 1906;
- Ayerst, McKenna & Harrison, Ltd.—a laboratory established with the production of a biologically tested cod liver oil in Montreal, Canada, in 1925.

More recently, Genetics Institute, a leading biotechnology company based in Cambridge, Massachusetts, became a wholly owned subsidiary of American Home Products in 1996 and a fully integrated operating unit of Wyeth-Ayerst in 1998. With the addition of Genetics Institute and its world-class team of scientists, Wyeth-Ayerst is considered a leader in the biopharmaceutical industry.

Today, the Wyeth-Ayerst organization is actively involved in research and development on several important medical fronts: the treatment of chronic diseases such as diabetes and Alzheimer's; the development of compounds in immunology and transplant therapy; and the testing of innovative new drugs and vaccines for infectious disease, cancer, respiratory illness, and sexually transmitted diseases.

ACHIEVEMENTS AND ADVANCES

From its early beginnings to its current innovations, Wyeth-Ayerst can count among its many achievements a wide array of pharmaceutical advances which include: the compressed pill, or tablet; the first soluble gelatin capsules; the first oral polio vaccine; the first penicillin tablets; a heat-stable, freeze-dried vaccine and bifurcated needle, which resulted in the worldwide eradication of smallpox; the first orally active estrogen, which became the pioneer product for estrogen replacement therapy; the first combination progestin-estrogen hormone therapy in a single-tablet format; and much more.

WYETH AYERST LABORATORIES

DIVERSE DIVISIONS

Headquartered in St. Davids, Pennsylvania, Wyeth-Ayerst produces and sells pharmaceutical and vaccine products worldwide. With more than 40,000 employees, the company provides the broadest, most diverse line of prescription products in the pharmaceutical industry. Among the largest manufacturers and suppliers of generic oral products, it is also a leading supplier of injectable products to U.S. hospitals.

Wyeth-Ayerst maintains a network of pharmaceutical, biological, and nutritional operations including 52 manufacturing facilities in North America, Europe, Asia, the Far East, Australia, and South America. In addition to its 10 overseas nutritional plants, the St. Davids-based company also maintains a state-of-the-art facility in Georgia, Vermont, that produces infant nutritional products for export to international markets.

Wyeth-Ayerst Research employs approximately 5,000 men and women in the development of new drugs

The Wyeth-Ayerst Women's Health Research Institute, located in Radnor, Pennsylvania, is a state-of-the-art research facility dedicated exclusively to women's health.

People around the world lead healthier, fuller lives because of the products developed by Wyeth-Ayerst.

designed to enhance the quality of health care for millions of people worldwide. While chemists and biologists devote their efforts to identifying new molecules with therapeutic potential, other scientists amass data in drug metabolism, toxicology, chemical processing, and pharmaceutical sciences in order to secure product approval. Clinical research and development activities are managed from the 230,000-square-foot facility in Radnor, Pennsylvania.

Also located in Radnor, the Wyeth-Ayerst Women's Health Research Institute exclusively researches and develops women's health care products, focusing on hormone replacement, contraception, and reproductive disorders. In addition to developing strategies for identifying and evaluating new treatments, the institute conducts a variety of educational programs. The goal of the institute is to develop a wide range of state-of-the-art products that will provide improved benefits while ensuring the highest levels of safety and efficacy.

Overall, Wyeth-Ayerst is involved in the development of a number of exciting new products that could improve significantly the health of countless numbers of people. Some of these new products include Sonata®, a novel insomnia treatment, and Rapamune®, an immunosuppressant that helps prevent organ rejection following kidney transplantation. Prevnar™, a new pneumoccal vaccine approved by the Food and Drug Administration, could prevent thousands of deaths from pneumonia, bacteremia, and sepsis.

With its dedication to research and development of innovative new products, Wyeth-Ayerst promises to be on the forefront of health care well into the 21st century.

PFIZER ANIMAL HEALTH

Serving the world's largest market for animal health products from its North America Region headquarters in

Exton, Pennsylvania, Pfizer Animal Health makes leading, innovative veterinary products for pets and livestock.

Pfizer Animal Health is a world leader in the development, production, and sale of veterinary medicines, with a comprehensive line of vaccines, anti-infective, antiparasitic, and anti-inflammatory products for companion animals and livestock. The North America Region of Pfizer Animal Health operates from its Exton, Pennsylvania, headquarters, from which it serves an area that constitutes the world's single largest market for animal health products.

Pfizer Animal Health is a major business group of Pfizer Inc, one of the world's most successful and respected health care companies. Pfizer Inc was named *Forbes* magazine's "Company of the Year" in 1999 and *Fortune* magazine's "most admired pharmaceutical company" in both 1998 and 1999. In 2000, *Fortune* also named Pfizer Inc as one of its coveted "100 Best Companies to Work for in America."

The North America Region headquarters for Pfizer Animal Health is strategically located in historic Chester County, Pennsylvania. Nearly half the U.S. population lives within a 500-mile radius.

Pfizer Inc's approach to business is grounded in the company's eight core values: *community, customer focus, innovation, integrity, leadership, performance, respect for people,* and *teamwork.* These principles have brought the company success throughout its history and will continue to guide its approach to business in the future.

Pfizer Inc is a research-based company. In 2000, Pfizer committed $3.2 billion to research and development, a significant part of which is devoted to research in animal health. It is this investment that sustains the company's pipeline of new and differentiated products that allow people and animals to live healthier lives.

Pfizer Animal Health has developed several products that improve the quality of life for many older dogs. At her veterinary hospital in Pottstown, Pennsylvania, Dr. Leslie Gall examines a patient treated with a Pfizer product for osteoarthritis.

A rancher uses Dectomax®, a broad-spectrum parasiticide developed by Pfizer Animal Health to control internal and external parasites in cattle.

PRODUCTS FOR PETS AND LIVESTOCK

Pfizer has one of the largest animal health businesses in the world. Pfizer Animal Health sells a portfolio of more than 240 livestock products and companion-animal products directly to veterinarians and distributors. Many of these are innovative products that lead their market categories.

The North America Region (NAR), composed of the United States and Canada, represents the single largest market for Pfizer Animal Health, accounting for half its worldwide revenue. From its Exton, Pennsylvania, headquarters in Chester County, NAR serves more than 30,000 U.S. customers. An office in London, Ontario, oversees Canadian operations and reports to NAR headquarters.

North America Region headquarters is the nerve center for its U.S. commercial operations—in effect, creating and fulfilling demand for Pfizer Animal Health products through sales, marketing, and related support services. A full-time field sales force of more than 300 territory managers promotes livestock and companion-animal products and programs for their respective commercial divisions.

PROVIDING CUSTOMER FOCUS

Innovative marketing is a hallmark of the Pfizer Animal Health approach to business. Product-related messages often are delivered in the context of marketing strategies that create new markets, help customers build their veterinary practices or livestock operations, emphasize customer and client education, strengthen the bond between pets and their owners, and provide solutions to animal health problems.

For example, Senior Care™ is a companion-animal marketing program that educates veterinarians and creates pet owner awareness about the special needs of older dogs and the role Pfizer products have in helping animals live longer, more productive lives. In livestock marketing, Pfizer's Select Supplier program adds value by providing herd management information and product knowledge for the entire cattle production life cycle. Similar programs represent a customer-focused, innovative, or technology-based approach to marketing that has made Pfizer Animal Health a preferred partner for copromotional alliances with industry partners.

The sales and marketing groups are complemented by the company's U.S. customer service center, located at NAR headquarters. Using state-of-the-art telecommunications technology, the center handles more than 600,000 customer calls annually, and has a 99.95 percent error-free order processing record. The customer service center has received an Award of Excellence from *Call Processing* magazine in 1993, and in a recent independent survey, it was ranked first in the animal health industry.

ASSURING CONTINUED SUCCESS

The year 1999 marked Pfizer's 150th year of operation. The company's exceptional combination of longevity and excellence is ultimately based on its outstanding people and their commitment to the Pfizer values. Pfizer Animal Health is proud to be part of Pfizer Inc and proud to be part of Pennsylvania.

UPMC HEALTH SYSTEM

Affiliated with the University of Pittsburgh, UPMC Health System focuses on high quality health care throughout western Pennsylvania, along with medical research, health education, and community support.

UPMC Health System, the western Pennsylvania region's premier health care system, provides health services ranging from comprehensive care for the most complex diseases, to primary health care and health-related services. Affiliated with the University of Pittsburgh, UPMC Health System includes an internationally recognized academic medical center, community hospitals, regionwide outpatient treatment centers, physician practices, and a range of health insurance plans. UPMC Health System is one of the largest nonprofit health care systems in the nation.

UPMC hospitals ranked among the nation's top 12 hospitals in a 1999 *U.S. News & World Report* survey of "The Best of the Best." UPMC Health System also is among the top 10 recipients of NIH research funding and sets a standard for health care and biomedical research in the region.

UPMC Health System, headquartered in Pittsburgh, includes 19 tertiary care, specialty, and community hospitals; offers the services of more than 5,000 physicians; and provides more

One of a select number of National Cancer Institute–designated comprehensive cancer centers, and the only one so designated in the region, the University of Pittsburgh Cancer Institute is a particularly bright jewel in UPMC's crown of medical care, research, and education.

UPMC Health System sets the standard for health care in the region: In a recent survey by U.S. News & World Report, *UPMC ranked among the top "Best of the Best" hospitals in the country—the only health care provider in the region ever to do so.*

than 400 primary care, surgery, rehabilitation, and other treatment centers. Ninety percent of the population of western Pennsylvania and eastern Ohio live within 30 minutes of UPMC treatment. But UPMC offers residents of the region much in addition to treatment: its services include health insurance, in-home services, retirement living options, a mail-order pharmacy, and durable medical devices.

INNOVATIVE HEALTH CARE, RESEARCH

At the heart of UPMC Health System is the western Pennsylvania region's only academic medical center. Through its affiliation with the University of Pittsburgh School of Medicine and other schools of the health sciences, UPMC shares in the academic mission of the university by funding a broad range of programs in education, biomedical research, training, health promotion, diagnosis, and treatment of human disease and disability. UPMC also supports continuing education programs for more than 15,000 local health care professionals each year.

UPMC Health System includes internationally renowned programs in a number of specialties, such as the region's only National Cancer Institute–designated comprehensive cancer center. UPMC's Department of Psychiatry leads the nation in NIH research funding. Pioneering research programs for organ transplantation are creating the next generation of transplantation procedures and developing artificial organs that some day may offer an alternative to donor

UPMC
HEALTH SYSTEM

organs. Revolutionary UPMC programs also are exploring medical applications of genetic science and minimally invasive approaches to surgery.

UPMC Health Plan, UPMC's innovative health insurance subsidiary, was established in the belief that the best people to reduce health care costs are the people who provide the care—health practitioners who share data and identify the best practices. UPMC Health Plan places coverage decisions in the hands of practicing physicians, rather than insurance executives. UPMC Health Plan also allows patients to seek specialist care without referrals.

To date, UPMC Health Plan has extended medical coverage to nearly 200,000 members. The plan offers insurance products for employees of small, medium, and large businesses and an HMO for Medicaid recipients, and is developing plans for Medicare recipients.

SUPPORT FOR THE GREATER COMMUNITY

With more than 30,000 employees, UPMC Health System is the largest employer in western Pennsylvania. A $3.6 billion enterprise, UPMC's nonsalary spending in the region's business community amounts to nearly $750 million yearly, helping to create, beyond direct employment, an additional 80,000 jobs.

As part of its commitment to the communities it serves, UPMC annually contributes uncompensated care, community services, and voluntary payments valued at more than $100 million.

Beyond its fundamental principles of providing affordable, accessible health care and charitable community support, UPMC Health System annually supports more than 2,000 community service initiatives to address the health and welfare of its neighbors. It sponsors approximately 500 initiatives to teach consumers, patients, and professionals about important health care issues through

A new computer program developed at UPMC Health System gives doctors the capability to access high quality radiographic images from personal computers located in remote sites throughout the region.

health fairs, free and low-cost lectures, and printed materials. UPMC is involved in nearly 750 initiatives to help prevent disease and disability. Almost 200 UPMC-involved programs support patients and their families with counseling, support groups, and subsidized services, such as housing and medical prescriptions. And about 200 UPMC Health System philanthropic initiatives contribute to the success of civic, advocacy, and charitable organizations through in-kind donations and leadership programs.

UPMC is using its resources to improve the community's health status by designing prevention and screening programs and preserving health care services in some of the region's most disadvantaged communities. UPMC also uses its financial means to transform its technological innovations into spin-off companies, bringing new products to market, while helping expand employment and spur the region's economy.

Above all, UPMC remains committed to its core mission of easing human suffering, discovering new medical breakthroughs, and educating tomorrow's health care professionals.

UPMC provides its services throughout western Pennsylvania's urban, suburban, and rural areas, providing outpatient treatment for everything from pre-birth counseling for pregnant women, to family-oriented community health centers, to 24-hour emergency care.

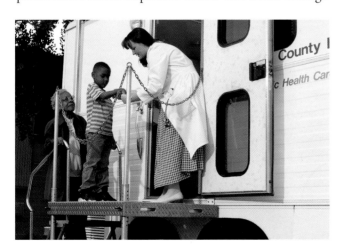

BAYER CORPORATION

As part of The Bayer Group, one of the largest health care and chemical companies in the world, Bayer Corporation

is dedicated to creating and developing a wide variety of products that improve, change, and even save lives.

In 1897 when Bayer scientist Felix Hoffmann developed acetylsalicylic acid (the active ingredient in Bayer Aspirin), no one imagined the phenomenal contribution he was making to health care. A full century after Hoffmann's discovery, aspirin's therapeutic powers continue to impress doctors all over the world. In the United States, the Food and Drug Administration (FDA) has recognized its potential to reduce the risk of heart attack and stroke, and it is currently the subject of research involving the prevention of migraine headaches, Alzheimer's disease, and even cancer.

The most profound discoveries often come from paying careful attention to detail. Bayer's ability to do so, along with the company's energy and integrity, are manifested in an amazing array of chemical and pharmaceutical products. Bayer's products help purify water; improve automobile durability and fuel efficiency; protect crops, homes, and pets from pests; and diagnose and treat disease.

More than 100 years ago, Bayer created a revolutionary breakthrough in pain management: aspirin. By continuing to mine its potential, Bayer has uncovered ways this ordinary, everyday drug can save lives in addition to relieving day-to-day aches and pains.

From a large electronic sign atop Pittsburgh's Mount Washington, the well-known Bayer cross shines on the city of the worldwide Bayer Group's U.S. headquarters. Bayer Corporation's operations extend to more than 50 locations across the United States.

A SOLID FOUNDATION

The history of Bayer Corporation in the United States started in 1865, when Friederich Bayer and Friederich Weskott purchased a stake in the first American coal tar dye factory in Albany, New York, just two years after founding "Friedr. Bayer et comp." in Elberfeld, West Germany. The two visionary Germans were convinced that their company would have a bright future in the United States. They were right. Today, Bayer ranks among the largest health care and chemical companies in the world. In the United States, it has approximately 22,000 employees. Sales are expected to exceed $10 billion in 2000, doubling from 1992, the first year Helge H. Wehmeier began serving as president and chief executive officer.

Bayer's presence in Pittsburgh began as a joint venture with Monsanto for the production of polyurethane raw materials. Called Mobay Chemical Company, after the first letters of the names of its parent companies, the operation was established in 1955.

The Bayer name is recognized throughout the world as a symbol of strength, integrity, and care.

Later, in 1964, Bayer acquired Monsanto's 50 percent holding in Mobay, and thereafter, expanded beyond its original activities as a polyurethane manufacturer to produce plastics and chemicals.

EXPANSIVE BUSINESS

Today, Bayer Corporation's business covers three main areas—health care, life sciences, and chemicals. These in turn are divided into nine operating divisions: pharmaceutical; diagnostics; consumer care; agriculture; plastics; polyurethanes; industrial chemicals; coatings and colorants; and fibers, additives, and rubber.

In all its concerns, Bayer remains a global leader in applying advanced science to worthy causes, such as saving lives; treating illnesses; sustaining good health, hygiene, and comfort; enlarging the world's supply of food and fiber through improved crop protection and animal health technologies; and advancing the accuracy, productivity, and personal convenience of medical diagnostic technology. Bayer is also an industry leader in developing, producing, and formulating high performance compounds as well as bulk and fine chemicals that push the boundaries of material performance, including corrosion resistance, impact absorbency, thermal insulation, and electrical conductivity.

To provide for continued growth well into the future, Bayer will invest $16 billion in its U.S. businesses in the form of capital projects and research and development over the 10-year period ending in 2004.

As an integral part of its business mission, Bayer seeks to continually lessen the impact of industrial production on the natural environment, and to improve safety practices in its plants, laboratories, and offices.

As the optical media industry and its products grow more sophisticated, so too does the Optical Media Lab at the Pittsburgh campus of Bayer Corporation. Bayer is expanding the lab to accommodate the addition of a full digital versatile disc (DVD) manufacturing line and is upgrading compact disc (CD) support as well.

The company is strongly dedicated to protecting and improving health and the environment. Its commitment goes beyond products to include safeguarding the health of employees, customers, business partners, community members, plant neighbors and the environment.

As another facet of its commitment to society, Bayer Corporation has long been committed to improving science education in the United States. In the early 1990s, the company formalized this commitment with the Making Science Make Sense program, an award-winning Bayer initiative advancing science literacy across the United States through hands-on, inquiry-based science learning, employee volunteerism, and public education.

Considering the thousands of beneficial products that emerge from Bayer's research and development activities, along with the company's sense of responsibility to good corporate citizenship, exemplified by environmental and safety initiatives, plus Making Science Make Sense and numerous other gestures of community support, it is understandable why people who know the company well say that Bayer is changing the world with great care.

Bayer's Making Science Make Sense education advocate Dr. Mae C. Jemison—physician, chemical engineer, educator, and former astronaut—visits Bayer site communities and major U.S. cities to bring home the science literacy message.

MERCK & CO., INC.

With longtime roots in the Commonwealth, noted pharmaceuticals maker Merck & Co., Inc., today employs nearly 10,000

people at its Pennsylvania research, manufacturing, and marketing sites and continues its strategic global growth.

Surrounded by today's excited commentary about the global economy, it is easy to forget that society's most important innovations currently stem from a fruitful blend of individual local effort combined with global resources. The Pennsylvania facilities of Merck & Co., Inc., exemplify such cooperation. Pennsylvanians have made many of the discoveries and produced many of the products that Merck has taken to the world. The Commonwealth has provided a business environment friendly to the pharmaceutical industry, and Merck, for its part, has brought to the state the leadership, the capital, and the market links needed to sustain innovation and growth in this vital industry.

A FOUNDATION FOR GROWTH

Merck traces its roots to 1668, when Friedrich Jacob Merck acquired an apothecary named "At the Sign of the Angel," in Darmstadt, Germany. His descendant, Emanuel Merck, took over the pharmacy in 1816 and began to manufacture bulk quantities of alkaloids and other chemicals. In 1891, George Merck, grandson of Emanuel Merck, became head of the company's New York offices and later began manufacturing his own chemicals in a new facility at Rahway, New Jersey. Although World War I forced Merck & Company to sever ties with its German parent, expansion continued under the guidance of George Merck's son, George W. Merck. Mergers in 1927 with chemical maker

Situated in Montour County on a bank of the Susquehanna River, Merck & Co., Inc.'s Cherokee plant in Danville celebrates its 50th anniversary in 2000. The Danville facility, recognized for its environmental stewardship, continues to be both an economic engine for central Pennsylvania and a key component of Merck & Co.'s success.

Powers-Weightman-Rosengarten and in 1953 with the pharmaceuticals firm Sharp & Dohme steered Merck & Company into the business of pharmaceuticals research.

Sharp & Dohme, which had a well-established network for distributing pharmaceutical products, helped launch Merck on one of the most exciting eras of its drive to preeminence as a global innovator. The merger enabled Merck to add to its facilities in New Jersey Sharpe & Dohme's manufacturing, warehousing, and research operations at West Point, Pennsylvania. Three years earlier, in 1950,

The main entrance to the Merck & Co. West Point campus is seen here from Sumneytown Pike in Upper Gywnedd Township, Pennsylvania. The campus has been the site of pharmaceutical discovery and manufacturing since 1947.

Merck had acquired another Pennsylvania manufacturing operation, the Cherokee Chemical Plant in Danville, which was producing synthetic vitamins and antibiotics. Both of these Pennsylvania sites have continued to play central roles in Merck's progress.

MANUFACTURING AND BREAKTHROUGH RESEARCH

Today the West Point plant is Merck's largest manufacturing site as well as a center for breakthrough research. The home of the Merck Vaccine Division, a hub of research activities through Merck Research Laboratories, and the headquarters for Merck's U.S. Human Health sales and marketing teams, the West Point facility has an impressive history. Scientists and researchers there have had a considerable impact on health care since the 1950s.

Merck researchers at the West Point plant revolutionized the treatment of high-blood pressure and congestive heart failure with the discovery of *Diuril* (chlorothiazide) in 1958. Vaccines researched, developed, and produced at Merck's West Point site have all but conquered many of the major childhood diseases, including measles, mumps, and rubella. In fact, since 1958 more than 20 vaccines have been developed at the site, and currently Merck's West Point scientists are continuing in their efforts to develop new vaccines to prevent such illnesses as rotavirus, human papillomavirus, and HIV/AIDS.

More than 9,000 Pennsylvanians are employed at the Merck West Point campus, a 400-acre site. According to *Fortune* and *Working Mother* magazines, Merck is one of the nation's best employers, and in 1998 *Working Mother* magazine recognized Merck's chairman and CEO,

Opened during the summer of 1999 on the campus at West Point, Building 97 houses the international headquarters for the Merck & Co. Vaccine Division.

Ray Gilmartin, with its Family Champion Award. Governor Tom Ridge also has given the West Point facility six Governor's Awards for Environmental Excellence.

Similar accolades have been given to Merck's Cherokee plant in Danville, which is celebrating its 50th anniversary in 2000. The plant's first assignment was to produce vitamin B_{12} and penicillin. Merck played a central role in researching the process that enabled the mass production of penicillin for the first time, and the company has continued to discover and produce significant antibiotics. Dr. Selman Waksman, who won the Nobel Prize for discovering streptomycin, said, "Without Merck, most, if not all, antibiotics that we have isolated would have remained bibliographic curiosities."

Over the years, the Cherokee plant's 500 employees have compiled outstanding records for productivity and a low rate of absenteeism. Merck has responded to this positive effort by investing nearly $400 million in capital improvements over the past six years. The plant employees' dedication to environmental stewardship was recognized in 1998 when the site received the Governor's Award for Energy Efficiency.

A STRONG GLOBAL FUTURE

Merck and Pennsylvania can reflect on 50 years of successful cooperation. Meanwhile, new developments in genomics and combinatorial chemistry have opened for the Merck research laboratories a vast new frontier of drug discovery. Working together, Merck and Pennsylvania can explore that exciting frontier to the immeasurable advantage of the state, the nation, and the world.

Recently opened research laboratories in West Point are a further example of Merck & Co.'s expanded operations in Pennsylvania and its history of growth through discovery.

CHAPTER TEN

REACHING NEW HEIGHTS
INFORMATION TECHNOLOGY

The age of information technology dawned in the mid-20th century, when scientists at Philadelphia's University

of Pennsylvania developed the Electrical Numerical Integrator and Calculator (ENIAC), the world's first digital

computer. The trouble with ENIAC was that it weighed 30 tons due to its tens of thousands of vacuum tubes.

Scientists just across the Delaware River solved that problem by inventing the transistor, which replaced the

tubes and allowed this important technology to be miniaturized. That crucial development led to the smaller, smarter products that people everywhere are using as the new millennium begins.

The information technology industry produces leading-edge computer technology, which in turn enables people to work more quickly, conveniently, and efficiently. It comprises makers of computer hardware and its components, developers of software, providers of computer services, and the networking and communications industries.

According to the U.S. Department of Commerce, the information technology sector is growing twice as fast as the overall economy. This is certainly the case in Pennsylvania, where at least 4,300 information technology companies constitute the third largest concentration in the country, employing a growing percentage of the population. The growth of this high-tech sector provides both a wealth of opportunities for Pennsylvanians and a promising information infrastructure for the growth of other industries.

The Commonwealth's information technology firms include businesses such as King of Prussia–based Lockheed Martin Management & Data Systems, part of Lockheed Martin, which employs about 6,000 people in systems engineering and integration, software development, information management, and systems operations. Another high-tech leader, Unisys Corporation, employs more than 4,000 people at both its Blue Bell headquarters and its Malvern facility. The company applies information-management technology to business problems through the use of computing equipment, programming, and software services. Malvern-based Systems and Computer Technology (SCT), which employs approximately 2,300 people, provides client/server software and long-term information and technology solutions for government, manufacturing and distribution, and higher education. The firm's 2,500 clients worldwide include nearly half of the educational institutions in the United States that have at least 2,000 students. The company also helps the courts streamline docket management.

Dr. J. P. Z. Eckert, chief engineer of ENIAC—the first general-purpose electronic digital computer—readies the unit for demonstration in 1946. Built at the University of Pennsylvania, the computer weighed about 60,000 pounds and contained nearly 18,000 vacuum tubes.

Another successful Pennsylvania company is DecisionOne, headquartered in Frazer. With more than 6,500 employees—including more than 5,000 technical personnel at 150 service locations—DecisionOne is the largest independent provider of multivendor computer maintenance and technology support services in North America, coordinating its assistance from among hundreds of sources. Yet another leading firm, Lucent Technologies Micro-electronics Group, based in Allentown, has more than 6,000 employees and ranks first in the world in the sales of modem chips for personal computers, standard-cell application-specific integrated circuits, and telecom optoelectronics. Its components can be found in many communications applications.

In 1998 and 1999, CB Technologies, of West Chester, was included in Deloitte & Touche's Fast 500, a list of the fastest growing technology companies in America; the company had previously been named one of the fastest growing privately held companies in America by *Inc.* magazine. CB Technologies delivers custom software development E-business solutions and consulting services to Fortune 500 and other leading companies. One of its key products, MetaTrial, an electronic data capture system, helps drug companies get new products on the market more quickly.

Shared Medical Systems (SMS), of Malvern, one of the world's two leading suppliers of information solutions for health care providers, serves 5,000 customers in 20 countries with clinical, financial, and administrative software applications, as well as consulting, network, desktop, and outsourcing services. The company, which provides jobs for 7,600 employees, was bought in 2000 by Siemens Medical Engineering Group, of Germany.

SAP America, a German company and a relative newcomer to the Commonwealth, is one of the fastest growing computer software companies in the world. SAP designers create business software systems that run on mainframe computers for the chemical, pharmaceutical, electronics, and oil and gas industries. SAP started its American operations in Tinicum in 1988 and is now

Repairmen work together to get this telecommunications system up and running. Among Pennsylvania's more than 43,000 information technology companies, service is an important part of the package.

in the process of building a $150 million facility in Newtown Square, where it will employ about 2,400 people at the building's completion in 2002.

A PERFECT HIGH-TECH INCUBATOR

Pennsylvania possesses all the features that business analysts consider important for the growth of technology "cities" or "cyberstates." These features include the presence of an educated workforce coming from local colleges and universities, good telecommunications capabilities, access to adequate venture capital for research and development, transportation connections to national and international markets, plus a physical environment that can attract and hold people who could work anywhere in the world.

The state is particularly fortunate to have universities that have long been associated with world-class technical education, such as Philadelphia's Drexel University and

Pennsylvania's Ben Franklin Partnership, an economic development program, is designed to make advanced technology more competitive internationally and to spin off new businesses. The partnership links business, industry, and educational resources, particularly research capabilities available at the state's universities.

Technology cities have already emerged in Pennsylvania, and not only in the southeast. In 1999, the California-based Milken Institute ranked the Harrisburg-Lebanon-Carlisle metropolitan area fifth among the top 50 metro regions in the nation for growth in high-tech output. In the same study, Lancaster was ranked 30th and Johnstown 45th.

Pittsburgh, which already has over 900 information technology firms employing about 24,000 people, may make world history as a technology city thanks to the Pittsburgh Digital Greenhouse. A partnership of international corporations, universities, and state government, the project is designed to make southwestern Pennsylvania a leader in the development of system-on-a-chip (SOC) technology, which literally places fully integrated, functional systems directly on a chip, eliminating the need for separate chips to accommodate functions such as memory or peripheral control. Pennsylvania universities now offer a special degree program for SOC engineers.

Just as real greenhouses are designed to promote growth, the digital greenhouse will provide capital, support, and expertise to promote the development of this relatively new SOC technology. Among the participants in the project are Sony, a leading developer of communications and information technology products as well as audio and video goods; Casio Computer; Cisco Systems; Cadence Design Systems; IBM; Carnegie Mellon University; the University of Pittsburgh; the Pennsylvania State University; and the Pittsburgh Regional Alliance, which includes the Allegheny Conference on Community Development and the Pittsburgh Technology Council.

Michael J. Kelly (left), a technical manager in the Product Analysis Laboratory of Lucent Technologies Microelectronics Group, discusses a silicon wafer with Gov. Tom Ridge. The governor visited the Allentown facility in 1998 to announce its $165 million expansion.

the University of Pennsylvania, Pittsburgh's Carnegie Mellon University and the University of Pittsburgh, and Bethlehem's Lehigh University. By 1995, more than $122 million worth of research had already been conducted at these institutions in such fields as artificial intelligence, computer visualization, and manufacturing and design. In 1999, Pennsylvania State University opened its School of Information Sciences and Technology, specifically designed to meet an anticipated need by 2005 for one million computer scientists, systems designers, and programmers who are also educated in communication and business skills, logic, and mathematics.

What could be better than a Web site that links businesses to hot leads from other businesses? PA SourceNet not only does just that, it also provides companies around the world with listings of potential Pennsylvania partners and suppliers. When businesses in the Commonwealth decide to go global or even just national, PA SourceNet connects and supports them.

PHOTOS: THIS PAGE, © Commonwealth of Pennsylvania/Courtesy, Department of Community and Economic Development; OPPOSITE PAGE, Courtesy, Swarthmore College

The Pittsburgh Digital Greenhouse will also encourage start-up companies to use the predesigned chips with their fully integrated systems. The end result for consumers will be next-generation products that are smaller and cheaper, do more, and work faster. The end result for the Pittsburgh region will be a thriving digital video and networking technology cluster.

INNOVATIVE INFOTECH USE

The Commonwealth has fostered growth in the information technology industry by eliminating the state tax on computer services, creating a research and development tax credit, and protecting electronic or digital signatures by law. But it also uses information technology to bring services to Pennsylvanians. The Pennsylvania Education Network, for example, connects public and private elementary, middle, and high schools, vocational technology schools, colleges, and universities with one another and the Internet. A related initiative, the Link-to-Learn program, provides teachers with training in the latest technology and classrooms with Internet-ready computers and connections to universities, businesses, and libraries. Together these programs have the potential to foster communication and cooperation among communities and regions.

The Commonwealth also designed JNET, the Justice Network, for public safety agencies. This telecommunications network makes criminal history files more widely available to state and local police, prisons, and probation officers, making it easier to track dangerous individuals and keep neighborhoods safe.

Information technology is proving useful in another way, as well: to get the story out on Pennsylvania. In early 2000, the Keystone State and Microsoft Corporation announced a partnership to power up Pennsylvania's award-winning Web site.

Swarthmore University engineering professor Bruce Maxwell (left front), computer science professor Lisa Meeden (right front), and a team of students flank Alfred, a penguinlike robot they created. Programmed with artificial intelligence, Alfred speaks, responds to voice commands and questions, and delivers all-important appetizers.

TECH ASSISTANCE

PENNTAP, or the Pennsylvania Technical Assistance Program, a federal, state, and university partnership, provides scientific and technological information and expertise through a statewide network of technical specialists to resolve problems for smaller businesses. PENNTAP has been serving Pennsylvania since 1965 and was one of the nation's first technical assistance programs.

BLACK BOX CORPORATION

Headquartered near Pittsburgh, Pennsylvania, Black Box Corporation is the market leader for high quality network services throughout the world. Black Box provides expert-level technical services for hundreds of thousands of customers who require high speed and very reliable communication networks. Black Box is playing an important role in the ever evolving communication age by designing, building, and maintaining the communication "roadways" required for the 21st century and beyond.

During the 1950s and 1960s, in the early days of the electronic computer, its potential applications unfolded in modest increments. From university and corporate research laboratories emerged the huge, self-contained mainframe machines known to the public as much for their flashing lights and spinning tape reels as for their actual output.

It was not until the development of the personal computer in the 1970s that people began to fully realize the computer's potential in fields as diverse as science, commerce, education, and business. Just when some eager engineers linked one computer to another is not precisely recorded, but it would be hard to overstate the impact. Networking lies at the heart of the computer revolution. From a simple office with a few linked PCs and a printer, to large multisite networks connecting thousands of PCs to mainframes and servers, to the vast World Wide Web, today's computing world means networks.

Connecting computers and related devices—making networking possible—has been the business of Black Box for nearly 25 years.

THE COMPANY

Headquartered in Lawrence, Pennsylvania, 20 minutes south of downtown Pittsburgh, Black Box Corporation is a leading worldwide provider of network services specializing in infrastructure—the cabling and related components that support electronic networks in a building or on a campus. The company operates subsidiaries on five continents and provides products and services to customers in more than 130 countries throughout the world.

Black Box was launched in April 1976 with one objective: to sell a range of connectivity products from a catalog while providing free technical assistance on the phone to customers needing help installing and operating data communications products. The first Black Box® Catalog, published in early 1977, offered just nine products in six pages and generated $170,000 in revenues in its first year.

Black Box remains solidly focused on delivering world-class technical services while providing the greatest range of networking products available. The Summer 2000 edition of its catalog contains more than 15,000 products in 1,344 pages and weighs nearly five pounds. The company's revenues for fiscal 2000 reached $500 million and are expected to quickly surpass this mark. Moreover, Black Box's technical experts are now available not only by phone but also on-site and on-line.

TECHNICAL SERVICES . . . ON THE PHONE

Black Box technicians are true experts in their field. They are trained and certified in a wide array of solutions and products. Each expert

Black Box Corporation's world headquarters is located in Lawrence, Pennsylvania, just 20 minutes south of downtown Pittsburgh. In 1999, Black Box Corporation was recognized by the Pittsburgh High Technology Council as one of the 50 fastest growing technology-oriented companies in southwestern Pennsylvania.

Black Box Corporation, "The World's Best Network Services Company," provides excellent technical support by highly trained experts on the phone (symbolized at left), on-site (as shown above), and on-line through its Web site (above left).

receives an average of 45 minutes of training per day and technical certifications are earned through programs offered by the industry's leading manufacturers and standards organizations and, most importantly, through Black Box's own programs.

Callers to the Black Box technical support hotline reach a technician in less than 20 seconds—the fastest response time in the industry and nearly 30 times faster than industry standards. Customers are given the assistance they need free of charge from experienced specialists in conversion, connectivity, communications, and networks, who are available around-the-clock. Black Box technicians are regarded as being among the best in the industry, capable of diagnosing customer problems and recommending solutions all in one phone call.

TECHNICAL SERVICES . . . ON-SITE

The telecommunications market in which Black Box operates has grown dramatically in recent years. Industry analysts project that with increasing worldwide demand, this market will grow from $830 billion in 2000 to $1,250 billion by 2003. It also is projected that business and government sectors combined are generating as much as 100 percent more data each year. Network administrators face a constant challenge to upgrade their networks to ensure that they have the capacity to handle such increases.

To serve this burgeoning market, Black Box is pursuing an expansion strategy based on mergers with well-established, on-site structured cabling and telephony companies in the United States and abroad. These organizations have excellent reputations and proven marketplace performance as well as an outstanding commitment to providing the highest quality service, a culture compatible with Black Box's own, a strong financial performance record, and a superior management team that is enthusiastic about future opportunities.

Black Box's on-site expansion began in January 1998 when it merged with a Pittsburgh-based company that provides installation services for premise cabling and related products to customers at their locations. By spring 2000, Black Box had merged with technical service companies that provide design, installation, maintenance, and ongoing support throughout the United States and the United Kingdom with combined annual revenues in excess of $300 million. The company is now one of the largest providers of structured cabling services in the world.

As are all its phone-based technicians, Black Box on-site professionals are highly trained and experienced. Every design produced by the Black Box Network Services team originates with engineers who are members of the Building Industry Consulting Service International organization. Each design is reviewed by a member of the Black Box team of Registered Communications Distribution Designers (RCDDs), one of the largest and most experienced RCDD staffs in the industry. Black Box on-site cabling designs meet or exceed standards set by the American National Standards Institute, the Telecommunications Industry/Electronic Industries Association, and National Electric Code (NEC).

The company continues to expand its on-site capabilities worldwide and expects revenue from this segment of the business to grow significantly.

ABOVE: *Black Box corporate officers include (from left): Francis Wertheimber, Vice President, Pacific Rim/Far East; Roger Croft, Vice President, Europe and Latin America; Anna M. Baird, Vice President and Chief Financial Officer; Kathleen Bullions, Vice President of Operations; and Fred C. Young, Chief Executive Officer.* BELOW: *In addition to the company's headquarters in Pennsylvania (shown here) and other locations across the United States, Black Box also operates subsidiaries throughout the world.*

TECHNICAL SERVICES . . . ON-LINE

In August 1999 Black Box significantly enhanced its World Wide Web site at www.blackbox.com. Complementing traditional telephone support services and the printed catalog, Black Box on-line support is another valuable resource for customers.

The site features technical information for all the company's products and includes graphics showing examples of product applications. The site extends phone support capabilities and has an efficient product-ordering mechanism. Black Box On-Line also includes a "Contact Tech Support" feature, which enables customers to click on a link to receive an immediate call from a Black Box hotline technical support expert. The site also includes information on the company's ever-growing family of on-site network service companies.

PRODUCTS

Black Box offers the industry's most extensive range of network infrastructure solutions and products—more than 45,000. The company markets these high quality products and services through many publications produced by its in-house team, as well as through its Web site, but the primary selling tool is its award-winning catalog. This comprehensive catalog includes personal computer communication components and accessories; cables and connectors; cabinets and racks; testers and tools; power and surge protection products; video and mass storage products; switches; printer devices; converters; line drivers; modems and multiplexors; local and wide area network products; technical information; and information on installation services.

Over the years, the catalog itself has become a model of its genre. For four years running, the U.S. version has won top honors for computer equipment catalogs in *Catalog Age* magazine's annual awards competition. In addition, for the last two of these years two of its international business-to-business catalogs also won top honors.

Dubbed by one industry reporter as "the bible of connectivity components," the catalog is printed in multiple languages. It not only includes detailed product descriptions, full-color photographs, and application diagrams, but also valuable comparative product specifications, compatibility charts, and recommended uses.

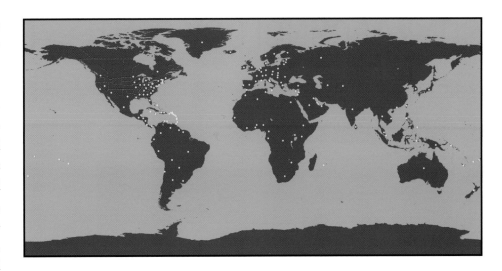

Spanning five continents, Black Box offers network services to over 130 countries around the world.

Using its extensive database of networking professionals, purchasers, and resellers, Black Box mails millions of catalogs and complementary publications, including new product supplements, specialty catalogs, and its monthly periodical *Connectivity news*.

Along with its off-the-shelf offerings (subjected to rigorous in-house testing, some 90 percent of the catalog's listed products have the Black Box label), the company designs and builds tens of thousands of custom-made products, ranging from modified standard items like cables and adapters to custom-designed equipment requiring sophisticated engineering.

SUPERIOR SERVICE, COMMITMENT

In addition to its unparalleled technical support and products, the entire Black Box team's dedication to quality customer service and satisfaction underlies the organization's worldwide reputation for service and quality. Customers have maintained a loyalty to Black Box for nearly a quarter of a century.

Black Box's service commitment begins with prompt customer response and timely follow-through. Like the phone-based technical support team, the customer service team is also committed to providing quick response. Calls requesting service are answered within 20 seconds. Black Box handles more than two million customer calls per year in its 365-day, 24-hour operation. Product delivery is fast as well. More than 95 percent of all items are shipped the day an order is received and same-day delivery is also available.

To provide complete customer satisfaction, Black Box offers an unsurpassed warranty program. It includes lifetime guarantees for many products, swift turnaround time for

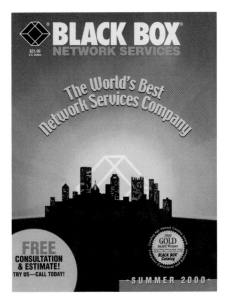

repairs, a product evaluation program, and protection against accident, surge, or water damage. The company's industry-leading warranties extend to its on-site network infrastructure services. When customers use Black Box products and the company's specialists to design, install, and maintain their structured cabling systems, the system's performance and products are guaranteed for life.

To ensure that the company will continue to meet its high goals for service, it invests heavily in people, as well as in its own internal systems, enabling team members to immediately access product availability; determine customer order status; track sales trends; and access, sort, and analyze relevant customer information—all in real time. A key element to the dramatic success of Black Box's dynamic merger strategy is the ability to find good leaders and swiftly assimilate the people, processes, and systems of the various operations.

An aggressive expansion of technical services, extensive product offerings and effective execution continue to strengthen Black Box's performance and profitability, yet the company's success remains firmly rooted in its original vision of quality and service.

Building on its solid record in an industry of seemingly unlimited potential and vital importance to the future, Black Box Corporation is uniquely positioned to continue its success.

The award-winning Black Box® Catalog offers network services and products backed by expert technical support and excellent warranties. The Summer 2000 catalog, with 1,344 pages, features more than 15,000 products.

SONY TECHNOLOGY CENTER–PITTSBURGH

Sony Corporation's commitment to quality, to community, and to the environment is alive and well at the Sony

Technology Center–Pittsburgh, where everything from high-definition televisions to bar code adhesives are made.

Sony Technology Center–Pittsburgh, located on a 650-acre campus in Mount Pleasant, features state-of-the-art color-television and picture-tube manufacturing facilities.

According to A. C. Nielsen Co. research, 98 percent of U.S. households have at least one television set, and the average American watches nearly four hours of TV a day. Yet, except when actually acquiring a new one, most of us pay scant attention to our television sets themselves. And fewer still know that the manufacture of today's most advanced television receivers is not only a fascinating and sometimes dramatic enterprise, but a powerful engine of community and prosperity for people throughout the regions where it occurs.

The model for state-of-the-art television manufacturing may be found some 35 miles east of Pittsburgh in Mount Pleasant, Pennsylvania. There, on a 650-acre campus established in 1990 on the site of a former Volkswagen assembly plant, thrives Sony Technology Center–Pittsburgh (STC-P). The center's drama unfolds around-the-clock as nearly one million pounds each day of silica sand, soda, lime, and recycled glass are continuously fed into American Video's huge melting furnaces. Fiercely glowing gobs of molten glass are dropped into molds and precision-pressed into the sturdy funnels and screen panels that will become cathode-ray picture tubes.

The center's immense contribution to the region's economic health and community strength begins with its direct employment of some 3,200 people and Sony's cumulative capital investment at Mount Pleasant of approximately $600 million.

The positive impact radiates throughout the region with the procurement of parts, materials, services, and equipment from more than 1,500 local suppliers in southwestern Pennsylvania.

AN OVERVIEW

Sony's decision to establish a major new U.S. color television and picture tube manufacturing facility resulted in the Sony Technology Center–Pittsburgh. Today, STC-P is home to three independent Sony business groups. Two of these business groups work in unified synergy. The divisions of Sony Electronics Inc. (SEL) make television receivers, aperture grilles, and cathode-ray tubes, while American Video Glass Company produces the television glass itself. The site is the world's first vertically integrated television manufacturing facility capable of going from sand to glass to television picture tube to finished receiver in one location.

Each Sony rear-projection television set is adjusted individually before being shipped to a retailer or customer.

Also located on the Sony Technology Center–Pittsburgh campus, the American Video Glass Company (AV) manufactures television glass exclusively for Sony.

The third core operation combines the worldwide management and coated thermal-transfer ribbon manufacturing activities of the Sony Chemicals Corporation of America (SCCA). In 1998, a fourth company, Display Systems Service Company–Pittsburgh (DSSC), inaugurated computer monitor refurbishing operations.

AMERICAN VIDEO GLASS COMPANY (AV)

At STC-P, American Video Glass Company (AV), a partnership between Sony Electronics and Corning Asahi Video Products, manufactures television glass exclusively for Sony. AV glass is used in the cathode-ray tubes (CRTs) not only for televisions built at Mount Pleasant, but for use by other Sony centers in North America and the United Kingdom. From AV's continuously fired furnaces, molten glass is press-molded into two primary shapes: the deep funnel that holds the CRT's electron guns and the front panel where the gun's precisely aimed electron streams form an image on the screen's inner phosphor coating. The lead-free front panels are then finished to meet rigorous optical standards.

Staffed by some 600 employees, AV's $300 million, 750,000-square-foot plant went on-line in 1997 and can produce more than four million pieces of television glass per year at costs among the industry's lowest.

SONY ELECTRONICS INC. (SEL)

Under the umbrella of Sony Electronics Inc., three groups are responsible for their respective contributions to the center's output of television sets.

At Display Device Pittsburgh (DDP), glass funnels and panels are combined with other components, then joined and vacuum-sealed to produce two kinds of CRTs: Sony's signature direct-view Trinitron® picture tubes (conventional and flat display) in sizes up to 36 inches.

At the heart of the Trinitron picture tube lies a sophisticated template made from thin sheet steel. Called an aperture grille, the template precisely guides each of three electron beams through the tube's vacuum onto the corresponding stripes of red, green, and blue phosphor on the inside of the front panel to produce an image of exceptional fidelity and brilliance. In 1995, STC-P inaugurated the company's first in-house aperture grille production capability; today, it makes this critical component not only for Mount Pleasant CRT assembly, but for Sony plants in San Diego, the United Kingdom, Spain, Singapore, China, and Japan.

Finished direct-view picture tubes move to the Color Television Assembly–Pittsburgh (CTV-P) group, where they are mated with their waiting chassis units; then electronic circuit boards, speakers, and cabinet housings are added. Sony's direct-view color televisions are assembled adjacent to the CRT production line, an arrangement (called the "Symphony" concept) that enhances feedback between work groups and minimizes costly inventories.

The most imposing televisions built at Mount Pleasant take form in the assembly bays of the Projection Television Group of America (PJA), Sony's global engineering center for large-screen, rear-projection televisions.

To this unit come DDP's seven-inch CRTs in sets of three, whose overlapped red, blue, and green images are projected from the rear onto the big

Seven-inch cathode-ray tubes (CRTs), shown here, are used in Sony's rear-projection Videoscope® televisions.

screens of Sony's rear-projection Videoscope® and High Scan® units—from the impressive 43-inch console to the 61-inch leviathan. In May 1999, production began on the biggest Sony consumer unit yet, a 65-inch, rear-projection, high-definition television (HDTV). Designed at STC-P, where the prototype was also made, this groundbreaking receiver launched Sony into the HDTV market and was also the first of its kind to be produced in the United States.

SONY CHEMICALS CORPORATION OF AMERICA (SCCA)

Although its operations are largely unrelated to television manufacture, Sony Chemicals Corporation of America (SCCA) relocated its headquarters to the STC-P site because of its ideal location, strong infrastructure, and diverse technological capabilities. The new headquarters—and SCCA's first North American manufacturing facility—opened in 1995. There, Sony Chemicals produces coated thermal transfer ribbon, used primarily for bar coding applications, and a range of adhesive products.

While most shoppers are familiar with the bar codes that speed supermarket checkout, most may not know that the clever little stripes are essential for almost every step of today's manufacturing, inventory control,

The Sony aperture grille production line creates sophisticated templates made of thin sheet steel that lie within Trinitron® picture tubes. These templates help produce exceptionally clear and brilliant images.

printing, materials handling, packaging, and shipping processes. At key points throughout the manufacturing and distribution of everything from jets to postage stamps, high-speed scanners read the codes affixed to objects in order to record their location and control their movement. Almost every manufactured or processed item (and each of its parts) needs a bar code affixed to it for much of its passage from origin to end user. Bar codes are big business indeed, and millions of feet of Sony's coated thermal transfer ribbon flow out of STC-P each month to keep the scanners glowing all over the planet.

SCCA also produces industrial adhesives for difficult bonding and protective coating applications for the consumer electronics, communications, automotive, and aeronautics industries, among many others. As one of the company's major operations, the center includes a comprehensive research and development lab, production areas, quality control, applications engineering, and sales and marketing functions.

At Sony Chemicals Corporation of America, employees produce coated thermal transfer ribbon, which is used primarily for bar coding applications, along with a range of adhesive products.

PEOPLE, MANAGEMENT, ORGANIZATION

Although STC-P's operations are comprised of independent businesses, strong common threads unite them. Among these are progressive management techniques in which self-directed teams plan their work to meet production targets, order parts, and staff the various functions; personnel policies in which promotion is based upon knowledge and performance, not seniority; and a dynamic program of technical training and education. SEL, for example, maintains a dedicated training staff of eight that conducts in-house classes in salient topics and skills; an apprentice program encourages job advancement; and a generous program of tuition reimbursement permits employees to take advantage of the Pittsburgh region's world-class college and university offerings.

ENVIRONMENTAL CONSCIOUSNESS, COMMUNITY IMMERSION

As with Sony operations worldwide, the men and women of STC-P are committed to conserving resources and energy, minimizing waste, and improving efficiency. For example, Sony's environmental experts determined that iron chloride waste produced in the making of aperture grilles could be used to control pollutants in wastewater. The iron chloride generated at STC-P is now safely managed and sold to a local wastewater treatment plant. In 1999, Sony Electronics and Waste Management Company formed a research and development project to identify ways to recycle post-consumer electronics products. Today, obsolete consumer electronic units—from TVs to copying machines—arrive at the on-site waste management facility

Employees at Sony's Display Systems Service Company refurbish computer monitors.

where they are broken into components. Much of the glass goes into the adjacent mixing hoppers at American Video for melting into new TV glass. Since 1998, parallel efficiencies have been accomplished by Sony's Display Systems Service Company (DSSC), which refurbishes computer monitors at the facility.

A major contributor to every positive aspect of the local and global communities in which it thrives, Sony Technology Center–Pittsburgh begins the millennium in a spirit of optimism and commitment to outstanding performance in all its diverse enterprises.

SONY CORPORATION OF AMERICA

Sony Corporation of America, based in New York City, is a subsidiary of publicly held Sony Corporation, headquartered in Tokyo, a leading manufacturer of audio, video, communications, and information technology products for the consumer and professional markets. Sony Electronics, with annual sales of over $12 billion, provides a wide range of consumer and professional electronics products and recording media. Worldwide, Sony and its 1,059 consolidated subsidiaries employ some 163,000 people, about 24,000 in the United States and Mexico; and generate annual sales of more than $56 billion, and U.S. sales of some $18 billion. Sony Electronics operates major research and development and manufacturing centers in eleven states and Mexico.

Sony Technology Center–Pittsburgh is the world's first vertically integrated television manufacturing facility capable of going from sand to glass to television picture tube to finished receiver in one location.

SCT

SCT, of Malvern, Pennsylvania, helps clients utilize valuable information technology and the Internet to leverage

relationships and create breakthrough results.

Headquartered in Malvern, Pennsylvania, SCT serves more than 2,500 organizations around the world. Its clients include process manufacturing and distribution enterprises; utility, energy, and communications companies; colleges and universities; local and state governments; and courts. SCT's 3,400 talented employees help clients enrich relationships with their customers—and ultimately achieve breakthrough results.

SCT's information management software and consulting services give clients valuable resources that in turn make an immediate impact on their businesses. Using SCT solutions, organizations can realign processes and information systems to better support relationships with customers, channels, constituents, suppliers, and other key partners. The end result for the client is loyal customers and higher profits.

THREE DECADES OF INDUSTRY IMMERSION

SCT was founded in 1968 to provide information technology services and custom-built software for higher education institutions. In its 30-year history, SCT has grown exponentially while maintaining its defining principle of industry immersion. This focus on select industries enables SCT to offer clients unmatched experience and know-how. SCT has achieved this goal by strategically choosing markets that needed solutions and then acquiring the expertise to make it happen.

After two successful decades of providing information technology services to colleges and universities, SCT began a series of acquisitions to enhance its software development capabilities and expand beyond the higher education industry. In 1990, with its acquisition of Moore Governmental Systems, SCT entered the local government market. The following year saw the acquisition of Mentor Systems and Digital Systems, Inc. (DSI), which added to SCT's government solutions and also introduced the company to the utility market.

Michael J. Emmi, chairman and CEO of SCT, has become a local leader for the information technology workforce.

In 1992, SCT acquired Information Associates—then a formidable competitor—to augment SCT's robust higher education solutions and give the company an unchallenged leadership position in that market.

Three years later, SCT decided to address the vast need for enterprise resource planning (ERP) in the process manufacturing and distribution industries. The company acquired Adage Systems, International in 1995 for its ERP application. Subsequent acquisitions of Fygir Advanced Planning in 1998 and Advanced Planning Systems, Inc., in 1999 made SCT a premier provider of supply chain solutions for the process industries.

All the while, SCT has continued to lead the higher education market. The first provider of Web-based applications for colleges and universities, SCT broadened its Internet offerings with a strategic investment in the Campus Pipeline enterprise information portal in 1998.

SCT's four-building campus is located just outside Philadelphia in Malvern, Pennsylvania, on the rapidly growing Route 202 tech corridor.

At an SCT workforce development forum, students, faculty, and employers focus on bringing Pennsylvania universities and businesses together to meet mutual needs.

DELIVERING BREAKTHROUGH RESULTS

Today, SCT helps clients realize greater benefits from their information technology. The key is SCT's commitment to helping clients leverage their relationships to achieve breakthrough results—results that solve long-standing business problems, dramatically increase revenues, or improve outcomes in an organization's key strategic areas. Relationship leverage means viewing events, tasks, and processes as a continuing series of interactions that define relationships over time. Done correctly, it provides greater benefits to all parties, while lowering costs and time needed to achieve those benefits.

Organizations of all types and sizes have awakened to the power of relationship leverage. Many are turning to SCT

SCT operates extensive training facilities for workforce development programs, offering employees the maximum number of opportunities to develop their business and technical skills.

to help them realize its benefits. SCT helps clients to understand their key relationships and to optimize tools such as the Internet, supply chain management, and connected learning to meet constituents' needs cost-effectively—building loyalty while increasing revenues.

SHARED MEDICAL SYSTEMS CORPORATION

Shared Medical Systems Corporation offers the health care industry a comprehensive suite of clinical, administrative, and financial information solutions to help maximize quality of care, productivity, and profits.

Providing information systems and services for the health care industry globally is the objective of Shared Medical Systems Corporation (SMS), a Malvern, Pennsylvania, health information technology firm. Drawing on its 30 years of experience and capitalizing on the power of the Internet, SMS helps its customers improve quality of care, productivity, and financial performance by integrating health care data into easily accessible, secure computer-based systems.

Cofounded in 1969 by a former IBM medical marketing manager, James Macaleer, SMS began as a provider of financial information systems, then added advanced clinical solutions. SMS provides integrated computer applications, technology, and services to more than 5,000 health care providers worldwide, including integrated delivery systems, clinics, physician groups, home health, and long-term care providers.

The full spectrum of SMS applications run the gamut from tracking billing and insurance information and scheduling appointments to managing clinical histories, storing medical images, and analyzing the results of managed care contracts.

In 1981, the company moved from King of Prussia, Pennsylvania, to its new headquarters on 116 acres in Malvern. It also began providing its services internationally, starting with customers in Europe. SMS

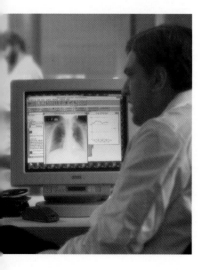

SMS health care applications give physicians and clinicians instant access to vital patient information at the touch of a button or the click of a mouse. Through a secure electronic medical record, patient histories, medical images, and results are readily accessible to all care providers, eliminating problems of missing or incomplete patient charts.

While the SMS corporate headquarters is located in Malvern, Pennsylvania, the company boasts an impressive global team of 7,000 health and technology professionals, with 60 offices worldwide.

became a publicly held company in 1976, moving from Nasdaq to the New York Stock Exchange in 1997.

Boosted by its own innovations and an industry trend toward outsourcing, the company's annual revenue in 1999 from customers in 20 countries and territories in North America, Europe, and Asia reached $1.2 billion.

EFFICIENT ACCESS TO HEALTH CARE INFORMATION

One primary SMS system, INVISION®, is installed in one out of every three university hospitals in the nation. A powerful updated version, INVISION.*e*, incorporates Internet capabilities, along with new clinical functions. Physicians using INVISION.*e* can access SMS clinical applications securely via the Internet to obtain patient information whenever and wherever they need it.

SMS is committed to providing innovative solutions to meet its customers' complex and ever-changing needs. In 1998 the company was instrumental in assisting its customer Tenet Healthcare Corporation of Santa Barbara, California, following Tenet's purchase of eight Allegheny Health Education Research Foundation East hospitals in the Philadelphia area. With SMS support,

a vast 1.3 terabytes of the customer's data was successfully transferred from a data center in Pittsburgh to the SMS Information Services Center (ISC) in Malvern. The industry-leading center provides a secure infrastructure for enabling electronic transactions of health care information; application hosting; enterprise systems management; and managed Internet services. As the premier application service provider (ASP) in health care, the SMS ISC operates health care applications for more than 1,000 health providers with connections to more than 400,000 customer workstations and processes nearly 80 million transactions per day.

SMS also partnered with Virtua Health of Camden, New Jersey, in launching one of the largest Internet-based disease management projects thus far, a project designed to help Virtua improve the medical management of its patients with diabetes.

The SMS Information Services Center (ISC) is one of the largest health care data processing centers in the world. The ISC is at the core of SMS's operations as a health care Application Service Provider. Through the ISC, SMS also helps its health care customers with a variety of technology needs, from managing complete networks of connected computers and servers, to cost-effectively outsourcing the full operations of information systems.

RESEARCH, DEVELOPMENT, AND OUTREACH

SMS invests in its customers by forming strategic alliances with world-class companies like Microsoft Corporation, IBM, Lawson Software, and Cisco Systems. The company also embarks on joint development relationships with leading physician information technology experts from prestigious facilities such as the Regenstrief Institute—a leader in health care informatics. These partnerships support SMS's efforts to develop better clinical products to help improve the practice of medicine. SMS recently expanded its alliance with Microsoft to create an application development and test laboratory on-site at Microsoft's headquarters in Redmond, Washington. "This joint laboratory is a true milestone in the alliance between SMS and Microsoft," says David E. Perri, SMS senior vice president of technology and customer services. SMS, which currently offers more than 30 applications developed with Microsoft technology, will use the laboratory to create a new generation of health care applications for the ASP delivery model.

SMS actively participates in its local communities and makes many charitable contributions. For example, through a local mentoring program, SMS employees meet with students from an area middle school to provide career awareness and personal support. The Sponsor-a-Child program, another SMS favorite, enables SMS employees to give holiday gifts to children in need.

SMS is preparing its customers to achieve compliance with the Health Insurance Portability and Accountability Act (HIPAA). While federal mandates designed to protect the confidentiality of electronically stored and transferred patient information do not go into effect until early 2002, SMS has made HIPAA a top priority for its customers today.

"Our success has been dependent on our meeting the changing needs of the health care industry over the past three decades," says Marvin S. Cadwell, SMS president and CEO. "Together with our customers, we have built relationships based on collaboration, performance, and results. Our ongoing ability to work effectively with our customer partners will continue to shape the future of information technology in health care settings around the world."

SMS solutions support physicians and other providers at the point of care, or anywhere, via Internet technology. By streamlining workflow, making it easier to capture and retrieve patient data, and providing on-line tools and knowledge bases, SMS systems help enable more informed clinical decision making and more efficient care delivery.

SAFEGUARD SCIENTIFICS, INC.

Committed to supporting high-tech entrepreneurs, Safeguard has thrived and prospered as a company that works as a partner and a long-term supporter.

Based in Wayne, Pennsylvania, Safeguard Scientifics, Inc., is a leader in incubating and operating premier technology-developing companies in the Internet infrastructure marked with a focus on three sectors: software, communications, and E-services.

With a history beginning in 1953, Safeguard first began investing in emerging technologies when it backed a fledgling cable TV company in 1956 that later became known as Comcast.

The technologies have changed dramatically over the decades, but Safeguard's commitment to supporting high-tech entrepreneurs has remained the same. "We started very small, with no great dream or vision," says Warren V. "Pete" Musser, founder, chairman, and CEO. The company that has emerged today has far surpassed Musser's wildest expectations. Safeguard has grown to approximately $9 billion in market capitalization and more than 45 company partnerships. The firm plans to invest in more than 30 business ventures in 2000.

A SIMPLE START

In 1953 Musser was working as a stockbroker when he and fellow broker Frank Diamond decided to start their own firm. Musser and his partner raised $300,000 and created Lancaster Corporation, a holding company for investments, which went public in 1967. Safeguard Business Systems emerged out of that holding company in 1968 and eventually became one of its most profitable endeavors. The company, which became known as

The Safeguard Scientifics headquarters building is located at 435 Devon Park Drive in Wayne, Pennsylvania.

Safeguard Industries in 1968, went public and was listed on the New York Stock Exchange in 1971. In 1981 Safeguard officially changed its name to Safeguard Scientifics, Inc., to emphasize its focus on high technology.

TARGETING INTERNET INFRASTRUCTURE

In the past, Safeguard has invested in a wide array of technologies. But in 1999, Safeguard announced its new Internet strategy and in early

The Safeguard campus is comprised of eight buildings with more than 150,000 square feet of office space.

2000 began focusing on a specific segment of the market—Internet infrastructure.

Such Internet firms are the primary targets due in large part to the opportunities to capture sizable returns. "The potential market for Internet infrastructure companies is being gauged at well over $1 trillion, so the market opportunity is huge," says Harry Wallaesa, president and COO. This infrastructure component is probably the least developed among the Internet universe according to Wallaesa.

Safeguard has uniquely positioned itself as a long-term equity participant, operator, and manager that is looking to generate maximum returns for both itself and its partner companies. Safeguard provides its partner companies with a full range of operational and management services that help launch them to success. Each partner is assigned a team of experienced professionals in the areas of operations, business development, finance, and legal matters. Backed by Safeguard's seasoned experience, its network, and its resources, this team works to foster the company's growth and management goals.

Safeguard recognizes that many entrepreneurs are very good at focusing on their ideas to produce new products or services, but often lack the experience to start or run a company. "We do as much as we can. We help them to design their business plans, hire the people they need, and give advice on legal and financial matters, Securities and Exchange Commission (SEC) guidelines, and all the skill sets they need to be a growth-oriented—as well as public—company," Musser says. Working as a partner, Safeguard helps to foster the entrepreneurial spirit that created the partnership company.

"Everything that has been constructed here at Safeguard has been to encourage entrepreneurs," Wallaesa says. As an entrepreneur who founded the information technology management-consulting firm aligne, Inc., Wallaesa speaks from experience. Safeguard offers a number of strategies for assisting fledgling companies, including incubating start-ups at its own 150,000-square-foot campus in Wayne. Additional support services for partners include human resources, marketing, strategic planning, investor relations, and even information technology support.

Above is the entrance foyer of the main building at Safeguard's headquarters. Safeguard provides its partner companies with operational and management services and resources.

PARTNERS IN SUCCESS

Safeguard partnerships include 12 public partner companies, more than 30 private partner companies, and seven venture funds. One of Safeguard's most successful partnerships, Internet Capital Group, was incubated on the Safeguard campus. An Internet holding company that acquires business-to-business E-commerce companies, the firm went public in August 1999 at $12 per share, and six months later was valued at $40 billion.

Safeguard is not only committed to supporting individual entrepreneurs, but also is nurturing a growing technology base throughout Pennsylvania. Safeguard was the founder of the Eastern Technology Council, an organization that promotes technology in the eastern part of the state. Also committed to strengthening the state's educational resources, Safeguard is building a $3 million conference center at Penn State Great Valley and a $1 million E-commerce center at Drexel University. Additionally it is sponsoring an excellence in leadership course at Temple University and a business plan contest at the University of Pennsylvania's Wharton College. "We want to do anything that makes it possible for entrepreneurs to follow their dreams, get funded, and start companies," Musser says.

TELESPECTRUM WORLDWIDE INC.

A pioneer and leader in its field, TeleSpectrum Worldwide Inc. helps companies manage and expand their customer contacts by making efficient use of the many electronic communication channels available today.

As industry around the world synthesizes traditional brick-and-mortar companies into diverse new alliances with E-commerce enterprises, a sophisticated new customer service industry has emerged to become indispensable in potentially every realm of global commerce. At the forefront of this new industry—enabling even the largest enterprise to offer customers competent, efficient, individual service via multiple communication channels—is TeleSpectrum Worldwide Inc., headquartered in King of Prussia, Pennsylvania. TeleSpectrum swiftly became a leader in providing companies with solutions for managing customer relationships. Its clients include Fortune 500 and other firms in many sectors, including finance, insurance, health care, automotive, consumer goods, utilities, technology, and government.

TeleSpectrum Worldwide Inc. provides the most experienced client services team to work with the client during all stages of a project to exceed all expectations.

MAXIMIZING CUSTOMER CONTACT

The 11,000 dedicated and uncommonly skilled and motivated associates of TeleSpectrum assist their firm's clients with all facets of managing customer contact, providing: inbound and outbound acquisition and retention services, leading-edge contact center technology, hiring and training, and customer experience measurement. This is accomplished via some 6,200 workstations in TeleSpectrum's 28 call centers in the United States and Canada.

At the core of TeleSpectrum's services are state-of-the-art technology platforms. Its pioneering interactive voice response (IVR) products give clients a full range of telephone and database functions for optimal customer relations. TeleSpectrum FX integrates proprietary IVR software and hardware to make maximum use of the latest interactive technology across diverse client applications.

TELESPECTRUM
WORLDWIDE INC.

TeleSpectrum's customer contact centers, like the one shown here, are equipped with cutting-edge technology and are strategically located throughout the United States and Canada.

TeleSpectrum's Channel Care division incorporates technology from two of the world's leading providers of call center technology: CTI (computer telephony integration) Framework and Internet Suite from Genesys Telecommunications Laboratories and Web-based Front Office Applications from Siebel Systems. These systems are tailored by TeleSpectrum's seasoned professionals for a client's unique business needs, integrating on-line sales and customer service; E-mail; and Web-based collaborative browsing, chat, telephone, and fax functions.

Sophisticated technology-driven services are only as effective as the people who implement them, and TeleSpectrum has become a leader in recruiting, profiling, and hiring customer sales and service associates. Its comprehensive Identify-Recruit-Select program emphasizes skills and characteristics to match client needs. TeleSpectrum also operates finely tuned programs for the training of telephone sales and service associates, and management training, as well.

EXPANDED TOOLS AND SOLUTIONS

Of course, the driver of today's business environment is innovation, and TeleSpectrum continues to expand through acquiring and investing in technologies that offer the best of proven and promising resources and ideas.

Typical of this thrust is its e-Satisfy business, created with the acquisition of Customer Insites (CI), an Internet satisfaction measurement company, which TeleSpectrum merged with its TARP subsidiary. e-Satisfy provides dynamic cross-channel customer-satisfaction measurement services that focus on both large brick-and-mortar companies and emerging E-commerce enterprises. The combination of CI's proprietary tracking software with TARP's proven measurement capability allows unprecedented flexibility and power in solutions for clients.

TeleSpectrum has built its solutions components to address the needs of clients in businesses of all kinds.

- For customer relationship management (CRM) in the telecommunications sector, TeleSpectrum's TelCRM Solutions package has achieved superior results for five of the nation's seven regional Bell operating companies, the three leading long-distance carriers, and other communications providers worldwide. TelCRM programs couple

With its ChannelCare and Acquisitions divisions, Telespectrum provides multichannel electronic commerce solutions. It manages customer life cycles for its clients as it acquires, retains, cares for, and increases business with the customer. It also is equipped to measure customer experience along the way with its e-Satisfy.

inbound, outbound, and interactive call center technology with relational database and computer telephony integration capabilities to ensure that customer contacts and results are maximal.

- In the utilities sector, deregulation and restructuring has meant companies must redefine business methods to remain competitive. TeleSpectrum has provided its uCRM Solutions package—including communications programs, education, and innovative, comprehensive product and service offerings—to leading gas and electricity utility firms nationwide to help them effectively manage existing customer relationships while continuing to gain new market share.

A world leader in customer-service systems, TeleSpectrum today possesses the dedicated professional staff, the scale, the communications options, and the technological infrastructure necessary to deliver superbly effective customer services solutions to its partners around the globe.

TeleSpectrum's sales representatives and electronic commerce representatives are among the best in the industry. Through the firm's rigorous recruiting, hiring, and training practices, it ensures that its clients are represented by the most professional associates.

UNISYS CORPORATION

Backed by a team of creative, tenacious, technically excellent people, Unisys Corporation provides electronic business solutions that enable clients worldwide to succeed in the Internet economy.

With 36,000 talented employees delivering electronic-business solutions to customers in more than 100 countries, Unisys Corporation, headquartered in Blue Bell, Pennsylvania, is helping to drive the Internet economy forward.

The $8 billion company offers a rich portfolio of Unisys e-@ction Solutions that address business needs and opportunities in the financial services, government, communications, transportation, publishing, and commercial sectors. Unisys combines solutions, services, network infrastructure, technology, and people resources to help its clients become more competitive and successful.

A HISTORY OF INNOVATION

Unisys was formed in 1986 as a merger between two leading technology companies, Burroughs and Sperry. But the innovation that propels Unisys today began long before then. In 1873, E. Remington & Sons, a Sperry predecessor

that later became Remington Rand, introduced the first commercially marketable typewriter. In 1886, American Arithmometer Co. began manufacturing the first commercially successful adding and listing machine. The company was later renamed Burroughs after the machine's inventor, William Seward Burroughs.

"Our in-depth knowledge of business processes in our strategic market segments enables us to help customers define and then implement world-class, industry-specific, electronic-business solutions," says Lawrence A. Weinbach, chairman, president, and CEO.

One of several network outsourcing facilities worldwide, the state-of-the-art Unisys Network Command Center in Blue Bell, Pennsylvania, helps clients keep their business-critical networks up and running around the clock.

Similar innovation spawned ENIAC in 1946, the world's first large-scale, general-purpose digital computer, developed at the University of Pennsylvania by John Mauchly and J. Presper Eckert, who later became Remington Rand executives. From ENIAC came UNIVAC, the world's first large-scale commercial computer, which Remington Rand provided to the U.S. Census Bureau in 1951. The following year, UNIVAC proved its vast capabilities by predicting Dwight D. Eisenhower as the winner of the 1952 presidential election—before the polls closed. In 1955, Sperry merged with Remington Rand, forming Sperry Rand.

A THRIVING ORGANIZATION

Today, Unisys has parlayed its foundation of high-tech expertise into a thriving organization that provides information services and products relevant to today's economy. To help make businesses and governments more efficient and effective, Unisys provides consulting, systems integration, outsourcing, networking, and maintenance services. It also offers sophisticated software and hardware, including mainframe-class technologies that run on standard Microsoft and Intel platforms.

The company's knowledge of business processes in strategic markets is key to helping its clients become more successful. In fact, Unisys serves 2,200 financial services clients worldwide, provides solutions for 1,500 public-sector agencies, and manages more than 200 U.S. federal contracts. In addition, 90 of the world's leading telecommunications firms rely on Unisys solutions, as do more than 200 airlines and more than 180 newspapers.

COMMITMENT TO CLIENTS

"We are committed to working closely with our clients to help them address the challenges and opportunities of the Internet economy," says Lawrence A. Weinbach, chairman, president, and chief executive officer of Unisys. "We are also committed to winning in the marketplace and delivering significant value to our shareholders."

Bringing high-tech talent to the Keystone State, Unisys recruits from top universities worldwide.

Unisys also serves its communities through numerous sponsorships, many incorporating the company's technology expertise. One such sponsorship is the Science Learning Network, an Internet education project that involves museums and schools working together interactively through the World Wide Web.

Still headquartered in Blue Bell, Unisys maintains major offices in other Pennsylvania locations as well, including Harrisburg, Kennett Square, Malvern, and Tredyffrin. In addition, Unisys has locations in more than 100 countries worldwide.

Unisys employees are proud to serve their communities. In Pennsylvania, Unisys employees regularly visit area schools and demonstrate the latest technology to help local students gain skills in using computers.

UNISYS PEOPLE MAKE THE DIFFERENCE

Unisys employees are known for their creativity, tenacity, and technical excellence. In fact, Unisys people are what customers cite most often as the main reason for choosing Unisys services and products.

The company's successful "monitor-head" advertising campaign describes how Unisys people "eat, sleep, and drink this stuff." Such dedication has brought Unisys an average of 100 U.S. patent grants per year over the past three years, as well as product and service contracts with organizations that range from the Commonwealth of Pennsylvania to Hong Kong's Cathay Pacific Airways.

Because employees are the most important Unisys asset, the company invests in them by providing continuing education programs for all employees through Unisys University. To attract top talent, Unisys has committed resources to Web recruiting, employee referrals, and university relationships.

In Pennsylvania, Unisys participates in the SciTech Scholars program, through which the company provides internships for high-tech students and job opportunities for high-tech graduates.

CABLE DESIGN TECHNOLOGIES

Conducting industry-leading research, Cable Design Technologies provides high-speed fiber optics and connective technology for networking and communications.

Cable Design Technologies (CDT), working at the forefront of connective technology, is a global leader in the design and manufacture of high-bandwidth networking products, fiber-optic cables, connectors, and assemblies. CDT (www.cdtc.com) also manufactures specialty electronic products for wireless communications, "smart-house" residential applications, commercial aviation, and robotics.

CDT products are hard at work in industries demanding high-speed access with maximum reliability. People working on computer networks, accessing the Internet, using cellular telephones, or tuning in to airplane entertainment systems are likely to be benefiting from a CDT product.

CDT products routinely set industry benchmarks in an environment of continual change. Typically, this translates to approximately 15,000 CDT products being designed, developed, or manufactured, to meet the ever-expanding needs of an international marketplace. "There are probably more than 80,000 original specifications on the various products we offer," says Paul M. Olson, president and chief executive officer of Cable Design Technologies. "Normally, about one-third of our products were new within the past 36 months."

CDT's strong commitment to research and development in today's fast-paced technological climate keeps the company in the forefront of the industry. For example, in order to meet the demands of some particularly challenging environments, CDT engineers developed insulated cable that is at once fire resistant, highly flexible, and lightweight. The cable will fill special needs for electronic instrumentation, robotics, medical equipment, and internal-engine monitoring systems.

In response to the opportunities of high-bandwidth connectivity and the ongoing growth of wireless communication, electronic commerce, and multimedia transmission, CDT is emphasizing its development of fiber-optic

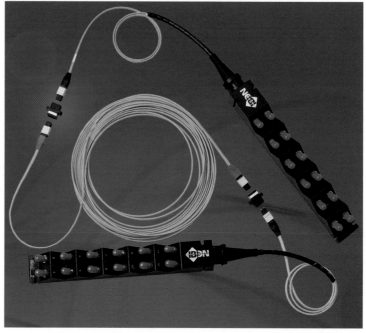

CDT's modular FiberExpress™ Bar has revolutionized the way fiber systems can be deployed throughout a building, bringing the high performance of optical fiber directly to the desktop.

products. It also is designing a sophisticated "fiber management system" that will bring together the main fiber-optic cable and fiber-to-copper conversion products for electronic media, to help companies maximize their use of broadband technologies as the global market builds its high-speed communication infrastructure.

CDT is the 17th largest wire and cable producer in the world, according to CRU International, Ltd., and among the top three specialty electronics producers in the United States. Publicly traded since 1993 (NYSE: CDT), the company projects fiscal year 2000 sales of approximately $800 million. CDT employs 4,500 people throughout its 22 business units worldwide.

"We have the best people in the industry—most with more than 20 years of experience—making our vision of becoming the best specialty electronic connectivity company in the world a reality," Olson says.

CDT
CABLE DESIGN TECHNOLOGIES

AMERIQUEST TECHNOLOGIES, INC.

With its Silent Partner™ program, AmeriQuest Technologies, Inc., provides not only products but also full system

design and installation services to its clients—value-added resellers and systems integrators.

Just how fast is the new high-tech segment of the economy growing in Pennsylvania? One indication is the dramatic growth of AmeriQuest Technologies, Inc., of Willow Grove, Pennsylvania, which provides information technology products, services, and expertise to value-added computer resellers (VARs) and systems integrators. AmeriQuest began as a computer product distributor, but as businesses' needs for the latest information technology intensified, the company expanded its role to become a complete solutions partner for its clients. AmeriQuest's behind-the-scenes, product-specific technical expertise helps resellers deal with the exponential growth of electronic commerce and other information-based business issues.

"AmeriQuest is a technology management company focused on providing vision for our client's technology needs and reacting to the dynamic nature of cyberspace business in the new millennium," says Howard Reid, the company's director of business development.

In 1999 Philadelphia Business Journal ranked AmeriQuest number eight out of the top-10 information technology companies in the Philadelphia area. AmeriQuest has developed a special niche, offering clients its Silent Partner™ program, which includes systems planning, hardware and software selection, bid preparation, installation, full testing, training, and financial and marketing services. As a distributor, AmeriQuest also provides the brand-name hardware and software that resellers and integrators need for their clients, including servers and

AmeriQuest provides technology-based solutions to assist its clients with computer systems design and installation.

desktop computers, system software and selected applications, network components, and peripheral equipment. In all, more than 13,000 products are available. AmeriQuest's net sales for 1999 reached $57 million. AmeriQuest also provides E-commerce expertise and experience, coordinating all components, services, and World Wide Web site creation. This single-source effort is easy and efficient for resellers to present to their targeted clients.

The spacious, 42,640-square-foot headquarters of AmeriQuest is in Willow Grove, Pennsylvania, just a half-hour's drive from downtown Philadelphia. With 75 employees, AmeriQuest is one of the few distributors with engineers working both off-site and on-site alongside computer resellers, assisting in all steps of managing computer technology. Operations of this scale can be costly for independent resellers and systems integrators; outsourcing such functions to AmeriQuest, on a project basis, mitigates the financial burden and risks of performing the work themselves. In effect, AmeriQuest allows resellers to provide the capabilities of a larger, more multifaceted organization while the role of AmeriQuest is performed in the background. Providing "the highest business-partner satisfaction" is AmeriQuest's mission.

AmeriQuest's corporate headquarters is located in Willow Grove, Pennsylvania, just a half-hour's drive to Philadelphia.

MARCONI

One of the world's fastest growing broadband communications companies, Marconi helps its customers gain speed, power, and momentum in the marketplace.

Real people. Passion and pride. Promises kept and potential fulfilled. That is what Marconi is all about.

Headquartered in Pittsburgh, Pennsylvania, Marconi Communications creates world-class technology solutions that help businesses gain speed, power, and momentum in the marketplace. Marconi Communications is the largest subsidiary of Marconi plc, which has 45,000 employees worldwide and sales in more than 100 countries.

With its pedigree firmly established in the pioneering work of Guglielmo Marconi, the Nobel Prize–winning inventor of the wireless telegraph, Marconi has a long history of innovation. Today, Marconi is a leader in the technology of global communication and a market leader in providing high-performance networking products and services.

As one of the world's fastest growing broadband communications companies, Marconi empowers customer networks and the overall Internet with greater capacity and speed through innovative *Netfrastructure*© solutions, e.g., technologies and services for corporate networks, service providers (telecommunications companies), and the global Internet infrastructure.

Marconi Communications employees are encouraged to think "outside the box"—an approach applied even to the deliberately quirky design of some of the buildings on the company's headquarters campus near Pittsburgh. Both photos © William J. Boyd

CUSTOMER FOCUS

Marconi has customers in education, government, health

care, and virtually all industries around the world. Companies use Marconi's Intelligent Broadband Networking Solutions to gain:

- **Speed** for quickly penetrating new markets and supporting emerging applications.
- **Power** for integrating innovative technology that delivers "smart services" and fast broadband connectivity.
- **Momentum** for growing business and seizing new opportunities in the marketplace.

THE BACKBONE OF TODAY'S GLOBAL NETFRASTRUCTURE

As a world leader in high performance optical networking, for example, Marconi empowers its service provider customers with the ability to support a variety of traditional and new services. And, by providing a reliable network foundation underpinning the Internet infrastructure core, Marconi supplies the multiservice transport switching architecture for 70 percent of all Internet backbone traffic, including voice, video, and data.

Many global companies turn to Marconi not just for world-class technology, but also for turnkey solutions. Marconi's professional services team addresses this rapidly growing area by applying a "Plan, Build, Operate" approach to support network implementation and facilitate customer success. The team leverages Marconi's state-of-the-art Network Operations Centers (NOCs) and Technical Assistance Centers (TACs), including those at its Pittsburgh headquarters, to provide total network management and support for customers—enabling them to focus on the things they do best. For additional information, visit the company's World Wide Web site at www.marconi.com.

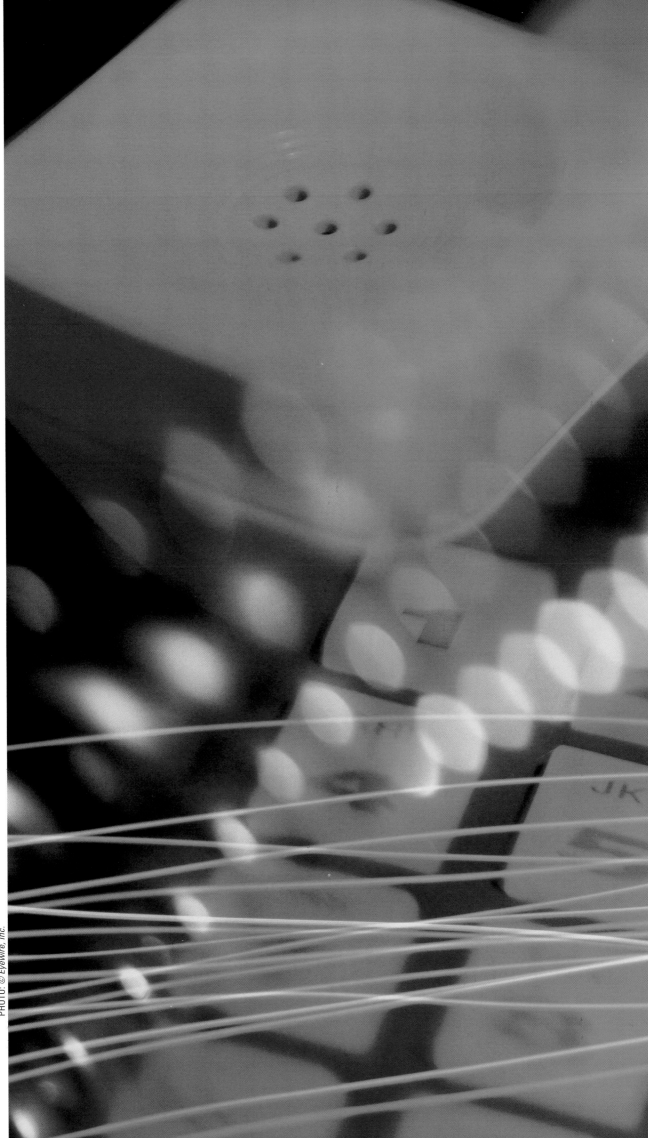

CHAPTER ELEVEN

PRESERVING THE NATURAL STATE

ENVIRONMENTAL TECHNOLOGY

At the beginning of a new millennium, Pennsylvania is emerging as a leader in a new industrial revolution that is some-times called the "green revolution," meaning the development of products and services designed to protect the earth's environment. Just as technological advances are important to the Commonwealth's economic growth potential, so, too, are its natural resources—clean air, land, and water. • Pennsylvania's environmental technology industry ranks fourth

in the nation in generated revenue, accounting for more than $10 billion annually. The Commonwealth leads the nation in the export of air pollution control equipment, with revenues that exceed $1.2 billion.

Companies in the environmental technology industry make products and equipment or provide the know-how to clean up the environment and prevent pollution. These companies include water treatment works services, solid waste management services, hazardous waste management services, remediation/industrial services, water utilities, and the makers of equipment for air pollution control and waste management.

The Roy F. Weston Company, for example, provides commercial, industrial, and government clients worldwide with consulting, engineering, design, construction, remediation, and redevelopment services to bring resources back to productive use. With two Pennsylvania facilities, in Exton and West Chester, and 60 offices throughout the United States and abroad, this leading infrastructure redevelopment services firm counts as clients such companies as the Aberdeen Proving Ground, in Maryland, where the soil and groundwater had become contaminated with lead, arsenic, and PCBs (toxic hydrocarbons used in

commercial applications such as paints, batteries, and lubricants). Weston also developed a method to safely excavate glass vials containing chemical warfare material.

Microbac Laboratories, a full-service testing lab and consulting group, has seven Pennsylvania facilities in New Castle, Pittsburgh, Warrendale, Erie, Bradford, Altoona, and Camp Hill. Microbac performs microbiological testing on water and wastewater, indoor air, and building systems; and chemical analyses of water and wastewater, hazardous waste, soil, air, petroleum products, coal, and natural gas.

Medical Waste Corp. of America's Sterile Technology Industries, based in West Chester, developed the first system for treating regulated medical waste without incineration. Its innovative Chem-Clav system, which utilizes a steam, air filtration, and chemical process, handles on-site treatment and disposal of regulated medical waste for hospitals. Other top companies include Hazleton Environmental, an equipment- and product-based system supplier providing engineered solutions for environmental

Personnel are on call 24 hours a day, seven days a week as part of the Emergency Response Program run by the Department of Environmental Protection (DEP) for emergencies such as oil spills.

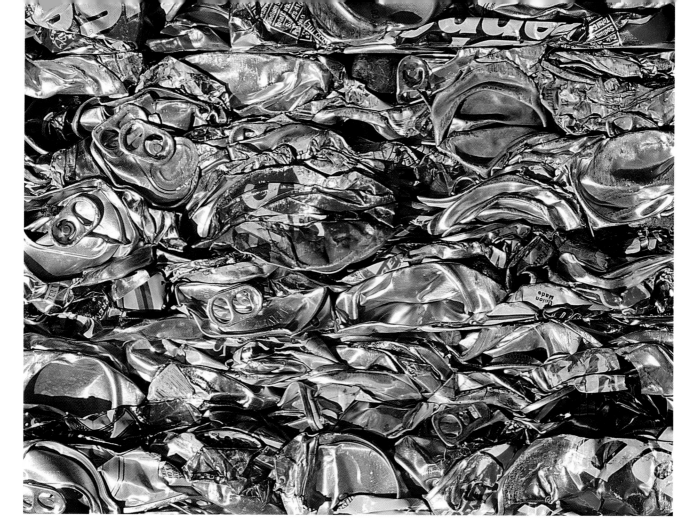

and industrial wastewater problems, and GAI Consultants, headquartered in Pittsburgh with other Pennsylvania offices in Monroeville and King of Prussia. GAI's staff of 400, including engineers, scientists, planners, and environmental specialists, provides consulting services in all areas of civil and environmental engineering. In 1998, the GAI group of companies was listed among the nation's top 500 engineering and environmental firms by *Engineering News Record* and *Environment Today* magazines.

The National Gypsum Company technically may not be in the environmental technology industry, but it has one of the largest single-line gypsum wallboard plants in the world. Situated in Shippingport, the plant cleanses sludge (produced in cleaning up emissions from coal-burning power plants) of pollutants and turns it into wallboard for the construction of homes and buildings.

Pennsylvania's traditional manufacturers, too, routinely take the environment into account. Pittsburgh-based Alcoa, the world's leading producer of aluminum, states in its environmental health and safety (EHS) policy its intention to operate in a manner that respects the environment and the health of its employees, customers, and the 250 communities in 30 countries where the company operates. Alcoa's recent 10-year initiative to plant one million trees and its EHS Achievement Award

Crushed aluminum cans such as these are a typical scene at Pennsylvania's numerous recycling companies. The DEP's Green Pages help firms locate the appropriate environmental assistance.

demonstrate its commitment. Alcoa has won several awards for environmental health and safety, including the Pennsylvania Governor's Award for Environmental Excellence and the Western Pennsylvania Safety Council Outstanding Achievement Award.

GOVERNMENT LENDS A HAND

The Commonwealth has supported its environmental technology firms with trade missions to Canada, Mexico, Poland, and South Korea. The economic and environmental alliances that have resulted are expected to help Pennsylvania businesses increase their revenues worldwide. For example, Concurrent Technologies Corporation (CTC), in Johnstown, signed a memorandum of understanding with Canada's Laboratoire des Technologies Electrochimiques et Electrotechnologies to develop and perfect environmentally safe and affordable methods for nutrient management and disposal of hog waste. The Commonwealth now has an agreement with Lucky Goldstar, of South Korea, that gives Pennsylvania firms an entrée into the country's environmental

Professor Terry Collins and his coworkers at Carnegie Mellon University were honored with the 1999 Presidential Green Chemistry Challenge Award for their development of iron-based catalysts that enhance the action of hydrogen peroxide to eliminate by-products such as dioxin, generated in the traditional chlorine bleaching process.

technology market. The Commonwealth also has participated in Globe 96, Globe 98, and Globe 2000, the world's foremost environmental technology trade show held every two years in Canada.

In addition, Pennsylvania has partnerships with five other states to facilitate approvals and issuing of permits across state lines to simplify the introduction of new environmental technologies.

Pennsylvania's former Department of Environmental Resources has been reengineered as the Department of Environmental Protection (DEP), with the mandate of balancing environmental protection and economic growth, helping industries comply with environmental regulations, and facilitating their permit-issuing processes—rather than merely levying fines for noncompliance. With the goal of promoting business in the United States and abroad, the

DEP developed the environmental Green Pages, listing all the environmental companies in the state and the products and services they provide. The DEP's County Environmental Notebooks provide information on environmental issues on a local level, while the agency's Citizens Advisory Council ensures public participation in the development of regulations and policies. The DEP also founded the Small Business Assistance Program to help companies comply with regulations and provide them with information that can save money through pollution prevention. A loan program, the Small Business Pollution Prevention Assistance Account, helps businesses use raw materials and energy more efficiently and eliminate toxic substances from their production processes, resulting in additional savings.

In addition, a government small-business ombudsman is available to serve as an advocate for these businesses in their dealings with the DEP. Mid-sized businesses have access to the Electrotechnology Applications Center for help in achieving and maintaining compliance with air quality regulations. The center provides technological assessment, laboratory analysis and evaluation, process analysis and auditing, as well as technical training.

Taking notes as he goes, an employee at a waste management pumping station checks the company's equipment. Since community growth means increased consumption, waste management systems such as this one provide a vital service to the state.

The DEP works with the Department of Conservation and Natural Resources (DCNR) to provide grants for environmental education. Pennsylvania takes part in the National Environmental Education Advancement Project, which funds initiatives to improve the delivery of environmental education programs at the state and local levels.

The Rachel Carson Environmental Education and Information Center operates in the lobby of the DEP's headquarters in Harrisburg. The center was named for the Pennsylvania biologist whose 1962 book *Silent Spring* stimulated reappraisal of the use of chemicals and pesticides such as DDT and called for a change in the way people treated the environment.

Pennsylvania's first Green Team was formed in response to the 1996 challenge of James Seif, DEP secretary, for the agency's south central regional office to be housed in a "green" building that would serve as a model for future facilities. Representatives from academia, industry, and government, together with the architect and developers, selected appropriate product manufacturers, contractors, and consultants. The resulting 73,000-square-foot building in Harrisburg was accordingly designed to improve the health and productivity of its tenants while utilizing high-performance technology to reduce energy consumption and operational costs.

IN TOUCH WITH NATURE

When people want to experience firsthand Pennsylvania's forests, rivers, streams, and fresh air, they head for one of 116 state parks. Pennsylvania established its first state park in 1893, preserving the hallowed ground of the Valley Forge encampment outside Philadelphia. The turn of the century was a time when many Americans were focused on

Autumn comes to Fayette County's Ohiopyle State Park, whose 18,719 acres of white-water rapids, waterfalls, and some of the East's most spectacular scenery are enjoyed by 1.5 million visitors each year.

saving the country's most scenic and historic sites from commercial development. Also at the time, a number of camps in state forest reservations became refuges for patients suffering from tuberculosis.

The use of Pennsylvania's state parks increased sharply throughout the 20th century. Today, the DCNR is committed to improving and restoring the infrastructure of the Commonwealth's state parks and forests, protecting their ecosystems, and generally serving in a position of stewardship for these areas. A new tourism strategy focusing on ecotourism hopes to ensure that these precious public areas will remain an asset in the new millennium.

ON TRACK

Pennsylvania was the first state to implement an on-line system to track environmental compliance and to make that information available to the public by means of the Department of Environmental Protection's Web site.

MEDICAL WASTE CORP. OF AMERICA, INC.

Medical Waste Corp. of America, Inc.'s Sterile Technology Industries has developed the innovative, nonincineration

STI Chem-Clav system for efficient, reliable, and environmentally protective disposal of regulated medical waste.

Medical Waste Corp. of America, Inc.'s Sterile Technology Industries (STI), based in West Chester, Pennsylvania, develops machinery for the treatment and disposal of regulated medical waste (RMW). STI, which was founded in March 1995 with the express mission of creating an environmentally compliant alternative to the incineration of medical waste, is at the forefront of change and innovation in its field.

STI's pioneering prototype system, designed to treat RMW with a steam, air filtration, and chemical process, was installed at Bridgeview, Inc., of Morgantown, Pennsylvania, in September 1995. Bridgeview serves the RMW treatment and disposal needs for southeastern Pennsylvania, central New Jersey, and northern Delaware.

The partnership with Bridgeview gave STI the research and development platform it needed to rapidly test and refine its equipment. Bridgeview presented both the quantity and breadth of materials challenges required to ensure that STI's equipment could handle any medical, infectious, and clinical waste stream.

STI currently has three process patents for its system, which is known as the STI Chem-Clav. The name reflects the several technologies that were combined to create the system: autoclave technology for the steam sterilization of the RMW; air filtration technology to control airborne pathogens; and chemical technology to disinfect the operating machinery. The system is free of combustion, microwaves, and radiation and its sterile residue is compacted and ready for landfill.

In 1996, after completing its development phase with Bridgeview,

Protection for the hydraulic lift portion of the STI Chem-Clav at left is ensured by the yellow cage surrounding it. This system is at Milton S. Hershey Medical Center, in Hershey, Pennsylvania.

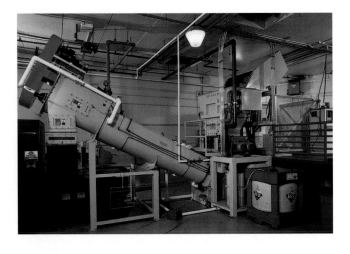

The pioneering, nonincineration STI Chem-Clav system by Sterile Technology Industries of West Chester, Pennsylvania, provides medical waste treatment that is environmentally compliant.

STI established its manufacturing plant in West Chester. In 1998 STI received a grant from the state of Pennsylvania to expand the application of the Chem-Clav to handle the on-site treatment and disposal needs of hospitals. The first such installations were made at the Holy Redeemer Medical Center in Philadelphia and the Milton S. Hershey Medical Center in Hershey, Pennsylvania. STI's systems for hospitals and laboratories are now available in 600- and 1,000-pound-per-hour capacities.

STI, while developing systems for hospitals, concurrently expanded the scope of its commercial business. In conjunction with a client in Ireland, STI will provide the systems and machinery required to build three plants to serve the Republic of Ireland and Northern Ireland. These facilities will replace 11 medical waste incinerators.

STI's commercial units are available in sizes from 1,000 to 4,000 pounds per hour in processing capacity, and larger units are being designed. There now are demonstrated capital and operating cost profiles for the Chem-Clav, which are making STI one of the industry leaders in the disposal and treatment of regulated medical waste.

STI Chem-Clav®

CHAPTER TWELVE

BUILDING BLOCKS OF CIVILIZATION
MANUFACTURING AND ADVANCED MATERIALS

Settlers in Colonial Pennsylvania would have looked upon the rushing waters of the colony's many rivers and streams and thought of . . . business and industry. The water cascading from the mountains and hills was precisely what was needed to power mills, forges, and furnaces in the 18th century. During the 19th century, another of the Commonwealth's abundant natural resources—coal—would usher Pennsylvania into the age of heavy industry.

Prior to the Civil War, factories producing textiles, iron, steel, and railroad equipment opened and expanded rapidly in Philadelphia and Pittsburgh, as well as in smaller cities such as Lancaster, Reading, and Pottstown. After the war, Pennsylvania's nickname, the Keystone State, took on new meaning as the state became the foundation of America's industrial economy. In fact, the period between the Civil War and World War I (1865–1914) has come to be known as Pennsylvania's golden age of heavy industry—a time when big businesses became even bigger through vertical integration, in which a single entity might gain control over a product's raw materials *and* distribution systems.

Industry in the state entered a long decline around 1920 and suffered especially during the depression. Although World War II brought temporary economic recovery and full employment, the Commonwealth's rate of industrial employment resumed its slide after the war. Job loss was particularly devastating in industrial cities like Philadelphia and Pittsburgh as employment shifted away from large urban plants, due in part to the development of highways. The coal industry, which had created boomtowns in a swath of central

Pennsylvania from Carbondale to Shamokin, virtually disappeared after World War II as the nation's industries increasingly turned to other sources of fuel.

Job losses in manufacturing took another plunge throughout the Rust Belt during the recession of the late 1980s and early 1990s. Finally, during the mid-1990s, this alarming trend began to slow down and finally turn around. As 2000 approached, jobs were increasing in Pennsylvania's manufacturing sector.

ON THE LEADING EDGE

The iron and steel products that were so important to Pennsylvania's economy during the 19th century were the advanced materials of their day. Today's advanced materials, from powdered metals to ceramics and plastics, have highly specialized properties and are used to manufacture new generations of products, from medical devices to electronics and transportation equipment. Economists use the term *advanced manufacturing* to refer to the use of

A driver has exactly what he needs in this 1915 Mack Trucks AC model. During World War I, British soldiers dubbed the AC "the bulldog" for its pugnacious, blunt-nosed hood and incredible durability.

PHOTOS: THIS PAGE, *Courtesy of Mack Trucks, Inc.;* OPPOSITE PAGE, *Courtesy, Rose Plastic USA, L.P.*

information, high technology, equipment, and human and physical resources to create high-quality products profitably. Today's advanced manufacturing is by definition increasingly dynamic and synergistic. Manufacturers must respond rapidly to the fluid demands of the marketplace and depend on the relationships they form with suppliers, consumers, and even competitors.

Examples of successful advanced manufacturing companies are Keystone Powdered Metal and Norton Pakco Industrial Ceramics. Keystone, whose manufacturing facilities are in St. Marys and Lewis Run, ships 650,000,000 parts per year, including their popular Selflube bearings, to customers in the automotive, home appliance, outdoor power equipment, and power tool markets. Latrobe-based Norton Pakco—a division of Saint-Gobain Industrial Ceramics, of France—distributes preengineered wear-resistant ceramic components and manufacturing abrasives.

A Rose Plastic USA technician marks the production status on each piece of equipment. Rose's plastic packaging systems add to Pennsylvania's stature as fourth in the nation for plastics shipments.

Mathias Baldwin built one of America's earliest steam locomotives, Old Ironsides, in Philadelphia in 1832. The Philadelphia & Germantown Railroad tested the engine and gave it the thumbs up. By the early 20th century, Pennsylvania led the nation in the production of steam locomotives.

Like powdered metals and ceramics, plastics are a good example of advanced materials. Laptop computers, microwave ovens, cell phones, cars, and airplanes are all "advanced products" that incorporate many components made of Pennsylvania plastics. Pennsylvania is the nation's sixth largest employer in the plastics industry; nearly 1,000 companies provide jobs for more than 70,000 people. The state ranks seventh in the nation in plastics shipments, sending out more than $15 billion worth of products.

The plastics industry has become one of the fastest growing in the state as companies continue to open or relocate there. Topcraft Precision Molders, for example, a leading plastics injection-molding company that makes industrial parts for manufacturers such as General Electric, recently opened in Warminster. Germany-based Rose Plastic, a maker of plastic packaging systems, set up its new American operations in California, in Washington County.

To retain plastics manufacturers and expand this industry, the Commonwealth established a statewide group of companies, Plastics Pennsylvania, to deal with issues important to the sector. The plastics industry also benefits from a number of innovative programs and centers associated with Pennsylvania colleges and universities. The Plastics Technology Deployment Center in Erie, for example, a program of Penn State Erie–the Behrend College, provides technical and educational services to help companies become more competitive. The Plastics Manufacturing Center at the Pennsylvania College of Technology in Williamsport helps meet industry needs for prototyping, testing, and evaluating new processes and products.

Large-diameter steel pipes get the final okay before being shipped from the Pennsylvania Steel Technologies mill (a subsidiary of Bethlehem Steel) to a pipeline construction project.

Slinky toys bring a smile to this foreman's face as they roll off the James Corporation production line with every detail correct. Invented by Richard James in 1945, the Slinky is as popular as ever.

Polymer research at the Penn State main campus has established the university as second only to the Massachusetts Institute of Technology for breakthrough technology in this arena.

ROARING INTO THE NEW MILLENNIUM

While the advanced manufacturing sector soars, diversified manufacturing holds its own as the third largest private-sector employer in the state, providing jobs for more than 950,000 people in nearly 19,000 companies. Pennsylvania is competitive thanks to its location within a well-established network of manufacturing suppliers and production centers, as well as its ready access to the kind of educated workforce that can only come from premier universities and the resources they are willing to devote to relevant research. Leading the way are manufacturers of metals, petroleum products, chemicals, machinery, trucks, home furnishings, and much more.

Bethlehem Steel, for example, one of the giants of Pennsylvania's industrial heritage, is still one of the largest steel producers in the nation. Headquartered in Bethlehem since 1857, the company ships 8.6 million tons of steel annually and employs more than 16,000

HANDS OFF! In the old days, putting coins into a newspaper vending machine would unlock the whole compartment, and a dishonest buyer could grab as many copies as he or she wanted. That changed in 1954, when United Sound and Signal Company in Columbia manufactured NewsVend—the first machine to dispense only a single copy at a time and even give change. The *Philadelphia Bulletin* was among the first papers to lease the new machines.

THE MODERN
CORPORATION

In the mid-19th century, the Pennsylvania Railroad pioneered a decentralized form of corporate organization in which staff executives set the standards and division managers took responsibility for the workers. Many other large corporations adopted this successful structure in the late 19th and early 20th centuries.

While loading Crayolas headed for the collating machine, a Binney & Smith employee gathers the fuschia-colored crayons into a heart. The company manufactures an average of 12 million crayons daily.

people nationwide. Allegheny Technologies, of Pittsburgh, a product of the mergers of the 1990s, is one of the world's largest and most diversified producers of specialty metals. The company maintains a staff of 11,500 to operate production facilities, service centers, and offices throughout the nation and sale of mining and construction tooling, employing 14,000 people worldwide.

Also contributing to Pennsylvania's manufacturing success is Philadelphia-based Sunoco, whose roots, like Bethlehem Steel's, date to the 19th century. One of the largest independent U.S. petroleum refiner-marketers in the United States, the company produces and sells a full

Using a power tool, a worker smooths the corners of metal parts at a truck factory. Producing top quality axles, brakes, wheel ends, clutches, and other parts requires much skill and a steady hand.

in 17 countries around the globe. Also on the list of top manufacturers is Kennametal, the market leader for metalworking products in North America. Latrobe metallurgist Philip M. McKenna founded the company in 1938, when he created a tungsten-titanium carbide alloy, "Kennametal," for cutting tools used in machining steel. Today, the company is a global leader in the

range of products, from fuels and lubricants to petrochemicals, employing more than 11,000 people. Air Products and Chemicals, based near Allentown, supplies industrial gases and related equipment as well as specialty and intermediate chemicals to a global market. A Fortune 500 company, Air Products provides more than 17,000 jobs and has operations in more than 30 countries.

FORGING AHEAD

The iron industry was one of Pennsylvania's earliest. During the 18th century, iron was produced at isolated "plantations" in the countryside where timber was available to make the charcoal for the furnaces and a stream flowed that could be dammed for water power. At the time of the American Revolution, a village outside Philadelphia was one such plantation. Its name? Valley Forge.

Another venerated name in manufacturing, also based in Allentown, is Mack Trucks, one of North America's largest producers of heavy-duty trucks and components since the 1890s. Now a wholly owned subsidiary of French-owned Renault V. I., the company employs about 5,700 people worldwide. Jeannette, in the Pittsburgh region, is home to the headquarters of the Elliott Company, a high-tech supplier of turbomachinery for the global energy market. Employing more than 2,000 people in its combined manufacturing, service, and sales offices around the world, the company has been a premium supplier to the refining, chemical, petrochemical, oil and gas, and industrial market segments for nearly a century.

Proving its vitality every day, Easton-based Binney & Smith has been producing art products, including its famed Crayola crayons, since 1903. The company employs more than 2,000 people and turns out at least 2 billion crayons, markers, chalk, and modeling compounds per year. Historic in its own right, Zippo Manufacturing Company, in Bradford, has been making lighters ever since George G. Blaisdell invented the Zippo model (a rectangular case with the lid attached by a welded hinge; a wind hood surrounds the wick) in 1932. That adds up to more than 325 million lighters produced since the company's inception, each one carrying Zippo's famed lifetime guarantee.

At Edgecomb Metals' Bensalem plant, a production chief marks stainless steel for shipment. The state's metal industry is thriving thanks to a solid network of suppliers and production centers.

A wide range of home furnishings companies also leads the diversified manufacturing sector. Established in 1811, York-based Pfaltzgraff is America's oldest and one of its most successful manufacturers of casual dinnerware. The company built its reputation early on with distinctive salt-glazed stoneware. W. Atlee Burpee, founded in Philadelphia in 1876, developed the Big Boy tomato and iceberg lettuce; today the Warminster company markets vegetable and herb seed varieties, bulbs, plants, and garden supplies. Pennsylvania House, a Ladd Furniture company based in Lewisburg, has been known for its solid cherry, oak, pine, and maple wood furniture since 1933. Companies such as these reflect the state of the manufacturing sector in Pennsylvania today: high-tech, highly diversified, and growing.

HARNESSING THE INTERNET

The number of virtual corporations in the state is rising thanks to Lightning Manufacturing, an initiative launched by Governor Tom Ridge and several leading industrial and technology companies in autumn of 1999. Using the Virtual Corporation Management System, a cutting-edge, Internet-based business model, companies now can collaborate via the Internet and jointly bid on manufacturing and design contracts that would be out of their reach individually. Three Pennsylvania universities, Lehigh, Pennsylvania State, and Carnegie Mellon, have joined the Commonwealth in piloting this innovative business model. Forming a strategic alliance to initiate the project along with the Commonwealth are industry leaders from across the nation, including Ingersoll-Rand, Cadence Design Systems, Lockheed Martin, and IBM. The first beta fest involves the powdered metals industry and St. Marys, in Elk County, known as the Powdered Metals Capital of the World. The companies expect Lightning Manufacturing to increase the purchase of Pennsylvania products by an estimated 10 percent annually.

With seemingly magic fingers, an artisan shapes stoneware at the Pfaltzgraff plant in York. Quality, craftsmanship, and service have been the company's hallmarks since its inception in 1811.

A SKILLED LOT

One factor that contributed greatly to Pennsylvania's growth in manufacturing during the 19th and early 20th centuries was the availability of skilled workers, many of whom were immigrants from southern or eastern Europe. By 1920, 16 percent of the Commonwealth's population was foreign born.

ELLIOTT COMPANY

Dedicated to total quality and the complete satisfaction of customers, the Elliott Company is working toward a

new century of excellence in the turbomachinery products and services industry.

A leading supplier of turbomachinery, the Elliott Company is known for building air and gas compressors, steam turbines, power recovery expanders, turbochargers, and power generation equipment.

The Elliott Company's tradition as a recognized supplier of turbomachinery and engineering and maintenance services to companies around the world can be traced back to 1895. For more than 100 years the people of Elliott have greeted clients in virtually every major spoken language.

The Elliott heritage goes back to the turn of the century and the original Elliott family business. This enterprise was sold in 1957 to the Carrier Corporation which, in turn, was acquired by United Technologies Corporation in 1979. In 1987, Elliott again became a private company through a management buyout. In 2000, Ebara Corporation, a public corporation in Tokyo, Japan, and a producer of turbomachinery, environmental engineering, and precision machinery, purchased Elliott.

Elliott, which employs 2,000 people, has earned its worldwide reputation as a foremost supplier of superior quality turbomachinery for the refining, chemical, petrochemical, oil and gas, and industrial market segments. It is best known for building air and gas compressors, steam turbines, power recovery expanders, turbochargers, and power generation equipment.

The Elliott corporate headquarters and main manufacturing site is located in Jeannette, Pennsylvania. Elliott also has two other manufacturing facilities and several shop locations in the United States (one of which is located in Donora, Pennsylvania), plus five international service shop locations (England, Italy, Taiwan, and two in Canada).

Elliott's apparatus and global service sales and marketing organization is also headquartered in Jeannette, Pennsylvania. Elliott maintains 26 sales offices, (15 of which also serve as service locations) including 18 in the United States, three in Europe, two in Canada, one in Asia, one in the Middle East, and one in Mexico.

MULTIPLE CAPABILITIES

To satisfy its customers' needs, Elliott offers a wide range of capabilities that includes research and development, design engineering, machining, fabrication, project management, and total field expertise.

This aerial view shows the Elliott Company's expansive Jeannette, Pennsylvania, headquarters and manufacturing facility.

The compressor/gas turbine string test facility at the Jeannette plant can accommodate loads of up to 105,000 hp (78,300 kW).

Elliott also offers total installation services, ranging from site preparation to erection, and start-up to maintenance. Each step is carefully supervised by a trained technical field staff that completes the installation and provides equipment start-up training. Elliott also rerates and upgrades existing equipment.

In today's business equipment, change is essential in achieving and maintaining a competitive edge. Elliott Company continues to develop new methods and technologies to better serve its customers during the new millennium. But one thing that hasn't changed is Elliott's commitment to the traditional values and high quality that its customers have come to know and trust.

RELIABILITY, EFFICIENCY, DELIVERY

What makes a world-class turbomachinery manufacturer? Reliability, efficiency, and delivery—attributes that the Elliott Company possesses.

- Reliability: The Elliott Company always strives for this honor. Its machinery is generally considered to be the most robust design in the industry. Elliott's engineering philosophy has always had a conservative, "bullet-proof" approach to design, which is exactly what customers need.
- Efficiency: In this industry, if an OEM (original equipment manufacturer) stands still for even a moment, it is left behind. At Elliott, research and development funding is provided to constantly develop and evolve its aero technology. Elliott has and will maintain its place among the top-tier manufacturers.
- Delivery: Over the last decade, shorter lead-time delivery has become increasingly more important for customers in the process industries to enable them to get their plants into production sooner. At Elliott, shortening product lead times is a continuing process.

Throughout its history, Elliott has lived on the cutting edge of technological advancement. Elliott engineers have consistently offered advanced technology in aerodynamics, rotor dynamics, computerized equipment selection, process simulation, and metallurgy. During the past 50 years, some examples of Elliott innovation include the pioneering of fabricated casing technology, high pressure casing technology, and impeller welding techniques.

Recently, Elliott provided the world's first "oil-less" process gas compressor/steam turbine string to a Middle Eastern petrochemical plant. This string was designed to incorporate magnetic bearings and dry gas seals, thus eliminating the need for lubrication or seal oil.

CUTTING-EDGE TECHNOLOGY

Elliott has always been at the forefront of ethylene plant technology. Elliott's cracked-gas and refrigeration compressors are world renowned; and Elliott has installed nearly 50 percent of the entire world supply of ethylene plant compressors. As process technology advances and ethylene plant sizes increase, the demand for larger and higher-pressure steam turbines increases. Elliott has met this challenge with the development of a 2,000 psi double-shell steam turbine and recently shipped a mechanical-drive steam turbine rated at over 71,000 hp. This turbine configuration can be utilized to drive Elliott compressors in ethylene plant service and is capable of up to 100,000 hp.

Other product advances include the Elliott Oil-Free Centrifugal Air Compressor Package, a simple, yet reliable, alternative to dry screw compressors. Elliott is

The interior of Elliott's Jeannette manufacturing operation shows the latest leading-edge technology for manufacturing compressor diaphragms and seal housings (end walls).

ABOVE: *Some of Elliott's employees stand atop an Elliott power recovery string that consists of an Elliott power recovery turbine (largest in the world at 42,200 hp), an Elliott axial compressor (34,400 hp), an Elliott steam turbine (17,100 hp), and an electric machinery synchronous motor/generator (15,000 hp). This string will operate at 3,600 rpm in a large refinery on the West Coast of the United States.* BELOW: *A worker checks out the Elliott all-inclusive centrifugal air compressor package for plant air requirements of 800-2000 cfm (200-450 hp). This compressor provides economical oil-free air for process or instrument use.*

the world leader for centrifugal oil-free air compressors in the refinery and petrochemical business. Units are installed in every continent and nearly every developing country of the world. New designs have also increased share in the widely diversified industrial air market. Smaller frames now compete directly with oil-free rotary screw compressors in the 200 hp range. Applications include air separation, electronic clean rooms, synthetic textiles, painting systems, and pneumatic conveying. Elliott is also proud of its shipment of three compressors to Salt Lake City, Utah, for snowmaking service in support of the 2002 Winter Olympics.

NEW DESIGNS

In March 1999, Elliott introduced a newly designed, horizontally-split, single-stage steam turbine that increases the product coverage into the lower end of the range. Typical powers for this machine are in the 50 to 200 hp range.

Elliott Company, dedicated to total quality and complete satisfaction of its customers, is constantly developing better processes and technologies to improve reliability in new and existing rotating equipment. Through its innovative engineering, modern repair techniques, and advanced materials, Elliott is well-positioned to provide the top-caliber, high quality, and reliable turbomachinery products and services that its reputation is built upon.

Elliott's executive management group voices optimism for the company's growth in the new millennium. "Elliott Company is totally committed to the future and setting world standards for rotating equipment and service. Our main objectives in meeting these goals are that we continue to supply our customers with the most efficient and reliable turbomachinery products—and that we give our customers prompt service throughout the world whenever they need us. We expect and demand another century of excellence."

THE BOEING COMPANY

With an impressive legacy that includes Pennsylvania's pioneering Piasecki Helicopter designs, The Boeing Company's Rotorcraft Program Management Center produces the world's most advanced rotorcraft.

The Boeing Company's vertical flight heritage spans six decades and 10,000 rotorcraft. Boeing continues this tradition at facilities in Philadelphia and in Mesa, Arizona.

The Boeing Company in Philadelphia has its own impressive history. Frank Piasecki, who designed and flew the second successful U.S. helicopter, founded the company in 1943, and soon designed tandem-rotor helicopters with two large counter-rotating rotors. The tandem-rotor design neutralizes torque, improves balance, and enables helicopters to use full power for lifting heavy loads. The company, renamed Vertol Aircraft Corporation, designed and built several tandem-rotor helicopters for civil and military missions, including the Vertol 107 and derivative CH-46, still a U.S. Navy and Marine Corps transport helicopter.

Boeing acquired Vertol in 1960 and began building the CH-47 Chinook, which is still in production today. U.S. Army Chinooks entered service in 1962 and through modernization will fly at least until 2033, an unprecedented 71-year service life. Many other nations fly Chinooks, and Boeing is producing the new CH-47SD, with advanced avionics, for the international market.

Boeing teamed with Bell Helicopter Textron in the 1980s to build the V-22 Osprey tilt-rotor aircraft. This remarkable design combines a helicopter's vertical takeoff, landing, and hover capabilities with a turboprop airplane's speed and range. Bell Boeing delivered the first production V-22 to the U.S. Marines in 1999 and will build more than 500 of these innovative aircraft for the U.S. Armed Forces.

The Bell Boeing V-22 Osprey is now in production for the U.S. Marine Corps. Boeing Philadelphia manufactures the fuselage of this innovative tilt-rotor aircraft.

The Boeing Company and Sikorsky Aircraft are developing the RAH-66 Comanche armed reconnaissance helicopter for the U.S. Army. Prototypes are in use during a successful flight test program. When it enters service in 2006, the Comanche will be the world's only stealth helicopter.

Boeing also is developing, with Sikorsky Aircraft, the Boeing Sikorsky RAH-66 Comanche armed reconnaissance helicopter for the U.S. Army. The Comanche is the world's most advanced combat helicopter, with a fully integrated digital navigation, communication, and targeting system and an all-composite airframe. Comanches will begin service in 2006.

After Boeing merged with McDonnell Douglas, in 1997, The Boeing Company in Philadelphia became the Rotorcraft Program Management Center, responsible for all Boeing helicopter production, including the AH-64 Apache, which is assembled in Mesa. Boeing Philadelphia currently manufactures AH-64D Apache Longbow fuselages for international customers. The company also has produced wing-fixed leading edge assemblies and other structures for Boeing commercial jetliners.

Boeing Philadelphia also is a state and community leader. With more than 5,000 employees, Boeing is Pennsylvania's largest manufacturer. Its Pennsylvania suppliers number in the thousands, and the company supports many community organizations and charities. Boeing Philadelphia truly is world-class in every respect and an asset to Pennsylvania.

HOUGHTON INTERNATIONAL INC.

Providing chemical management services as well as a full line of metalworking fluids and lubricants, Houghton

International Inc. has provided consistent customer satisfaction for more than 135 years.

Headquartered in Valley Forge, Pennsylvania, Houghton International Inc. processes and manufactures a variety of specialty chemicals, oils, and lubricants; provides chemical management services; and offers application consultation for the metalworking, automotive, and steel industries.

Successful in its business for more than 135 years, Houghton has a new corporate vision—to supply chemical management services and technology. "We want to

move away from selling products and providing services to selling services and providing products," says Bill Pearcy, president of the metalworking division of Houghton. Three key acquisitions in the chemical management area in 1998–99 have established the company as an industry leader.

Houghton's mission is "to supply high quality specialty processing products and services to industries throughout the world." It accomplishes this goal by meeting and exceeding customer expectations and by keeping its products in "strict compliance with all health, safety, and environmental regulations." The company consistently works at improving products and service.

As such, the company developed its original FLUIDCARE® program, a total fluid management service for manufacturers, to maximize the performance and efficiency of highly sophisticated manufacturing processes. Through this program, Houghton offers varying levels of involvement depending on customers' needs, including anything or everything from product supply to maintenance to disposal. Based on the idea of preventing excess—such as waste, downtime, or costs—this unique program can be customized to fit customers' requests. It can incorporate product and application advisement, inventory

Houghton International Inc. maintains its headquarters and a modern technical center in Valley Forge, Pennsylvania. © Ed Wheeler

control, technical support, employee training, and fluid disposal and recycling.

The many benefits of the FLUIDCARE program include increased plant productivity, optimized process performance, enhanced product application, maximized efficiency, and minimized environmental problems.

A LONG HISTORY OF SUCCESS

The origins of Houghton began in 1865 in Philadelphia, when Edwin F. Houghton started a fluid manufacturing business for the metalworking industry. The goals of the founder were simple: To study the industry and provide the oils and chemicals to keep it running. In 1867, the company introduced its first commercial product, a rust preventive called the Cosmic Counter Corrodent. Throughout the next decade, the company expanded its operations in petroleum refining, receiving medals for its achievements in the manufacturing of greases and oils. In 1910, the company was incorporated as E. F. Houghton & Co. In 1950, William F. MacDonald,

Edwin F. Houghton, founder, had a vision for his company that is still alive today in Houghton International's FLUID-CARE program.

treasurer of the company since 1927, became president and led the company in unprecedented growth. Son Bill MacDonald Jr. took over as president and CEO in 1978. Under his leadership, Houghton has continued to grow and prosper. It moved its headquarters to a suburban location in Valley Forge in 1981 and officially changed its name to Houghton International Inc. in 1993.

Today, the privately held company employs 350 people nationwide and comprises three divisions in the United States: FLUIDCARE, Houghton Metal Finishing Company, and Houghton U.S. Metalworking Division.

It is the metalworking division that manufactures the company's best-known product, Cosmoline, a rust preventive primarily used by the military. Houghton is also well-known for its fire-resistant hydraulic fluids used in the steel and automotive industries. These products, as well as the company's quench oils used in heat treating, have contributed to the worldwide success of Houghton.

UNIQUE SOLUTIONS

Also known for delivering its own unique solutions, Houghton has continued to stay abreast of technology. Its Houghto-Safe® water-glycol hydraulic fluids, developed more than 50 years ago, have set an industry standard for fire-resistant fluids. Other alternative fluids offered by Houghton include anhydrous synthetics, phosphate and polyol esters, water additives, and thickened, high water-based fluids.

To uphold its industry-leading reputation, Houghton has instituted its teamwork approach called the Total Quality Management Program. As part of this

Houghton International Inc.'s products and services are important to industries ranging from primary metals producers, such as this steel mill, to aerospace and electronics.

program, employees are trained in all aspects of product safety, chemical hazard, emergency response, and statistical process control with the goal of enhancing quality consciousness. With the motto "On Time and In Specification," Houghton is committed to delivering premium products and services to meet customers' exacting standards. Houghton's ISO-9002 plant certifications are a testament to its commitment to world-class quality.

In the last 10 to 15 years, Houghton has moved from a domestic company with international affiliates to a global corporation with controlling interests in numerous companies worldwide. Involved in exporting since the beginning of the century, Houghton has consistently worked to strengthen its international network. Today, the company has sales offices and plants in Carrollton, Georgia; Chicago, Illinois; Detroit, Michigan; Fogelsville, Pennsylvania; Houston, Texas (warehouse); and Longview, Washington; as well as subsidiaries and affiliates in 30 countries.

Houghton's goal for the future is to focus on enhancing the services and products that have put it at the forefront of the international fluid and lubricant manufacturing industry. Houghton looks to become a leader in providing chemical management services and technology. It also plans to continue changing and adapting its products to meet the needs of the environment by incorporating natural, renewable resources, higher performance additives, longer-lasting fluids, bio-resistant fluids, and compatible fluids.

Waste treatable products and fluids with minimal environmental impact are being developed to meet today's regulatory requirements and customer demands.

ROHM AND HAAS COMPANY

Since its founding in 1909, Rohm and Haas Company, one of the world's foremost specialty polymer and chemical

companies, has stayed true to its mission of "Quietly Improving the Quality of Life."

Amid today's numerous high-tech start-ups long promising their first profitable quarter, there's something reassuring about a strong and growing company that has successfully developed and applied superbly imaginative technology for nearly a century. Rohm and Haas Company of Philadelphia, Pennsylvania, is such a company.

From the tiny, one-product partnership launched by scientist Otto Röhm and businessman Otto Haas in 1909 and following its 1999 merger with Morton International, Rohm and Haas has grown to become one of the world's foremost specialty polymer and chemical companies. With annual sales exceeding $6.5 billion, nearly 150 manufacturing and research locations, and more than 20,000 employees in 25 countries, Rohm and Haas is more than ready for the 21st century. Though largely invisible to consumers, the output of Rohm and Haas contributes to the quality and performance of countless end products and finished goods. Its products are vital to diverse applications across an immense spectrum of manufacturing and other industrial processes. The company's innovative chemistry—marketed through

The Morton Salt family of products and the famous "Umbrella Girl" joined Rohm and Haas in 1999 as part of the company's acquisition of Morton International.

two dozen major product lines—provides touchstone components in paint and coatings, adhesives and sealants, household cleaning and personal care products, computers and electronic components, inks and paper coatings, water treatment and agriculture, construction materials and plastics and salt, and thousands of other everyday products.

A HERITAGE OF BREAKTHROUGHS

The Rohm and Haas heritage includes an intriguing list of firsts and breakthroughs, some of which proved to be the basis of success for entire industries. One such breakthrough was the introduction of cast polymethyl methacrylate, marketed on both sides of the Atlantic under the Plexiglas™ trademark. From the mid-1930s, the versatile acrylic's optical clarity, light weight, formability, and shatter resistance instituted its wide use as a replacement for conventional glass in aircraft. It was then used in applications such as signage, vehicle taillights, architectural components, and safety glazing. Other breakthroughs included acrylic polymers as oil additives; solvent-borne resins for coatings and plasticizers, the first synthetic organic fungicide; and ion exchange resins for practical high volume in water purification.

Rohm and Haas also pioneered acrylic emulsions for use as paint binders. The ease of use, rapid drying, and

Rohm and Haas technology was used to help create this multistory message board in the heart of New York City.

soap-and-water cleanup of acrylics soon made them dominant in the industry and led to the primacy of modern latex paints. Acrylic polymers also are used extensively

in building products, adhesives, plastics, textiles, paper, and nonwoven coatings; in leather finishes; in oil additives; and for water treatment programs. In fact, the firm's two dozen product lines touch every aspect of modern life, from graphics arts (paper coatings and ink) to DNA research (chromatographic columns for protein purification).

SUCCESS IN THE ELECTRONIC CHEMICALS INDUSTRY

Recognizing significant potential in the emerging industry, Rohm and Haas entered the electronic chemicals business in 1982 with partial acquisition of the Shipley Company, a leading supplier of specialty chemicals used in printed circuit fabrication, metal finishing, shielding, and plating on plastics and photoresists (used to make microelectronic devices such as semiconductors, thin film heads and flat-panel displays). In 1992 Rohm and Haas made a full purchase of Shipley. Rohm and Haas solidified its commanding presence in the field by its 1997 affiliation with Rodel, Inc., a maker of chemical slurries and polishing pads; and by its 1999 acquisition of LeaRonal, Inc., a manufacturer of specialty chemical additives used in electronic and metal finishing and the creator of patented precious metal electroplating

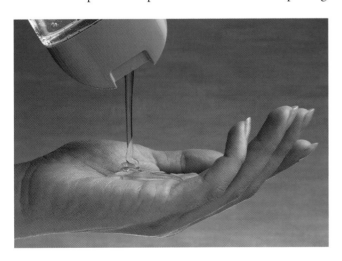

Purity also is essential for everyday products. Rohm and Haas chemistry keeps shampoos, toiletries, and other personal care products free from contamination.

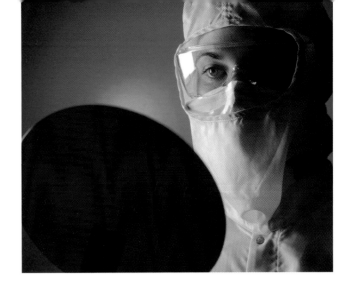

Ultra-high purity products from Rohm and Haas provide the enabling technology needed to make today's state-of-the-art integrated circuits.

processes for production of semiconductors, printed circuit boards, and electrical contacts.

COMMITMENT TO HIGH STANDARDS

The sustained dedication of Rohm and Haas management and employees to a corporate culture grounded in high ethical standards has been integral to its technological and financial success. The company has long recognized its responsibility to employees, stockholders, and the general public to be a major goal. In the process it has achieved long-term corporate success. Rohm and Haas also remains firmly committed to environmental protection. In 1966, Rohm and Haas issued its first environmental policy statement that described how the firm intended to operate its business with regard to its employees and neighbors. The company has aggressively pursued not only internal programs to ensure that its operations and products are as environmentally safe as possible, but also has worked closely with other companies, trade associations, and government agencies to promote such practices throughout the chemical industry.

Similar high standards and practices have been pursued with energetic determination in the policies and procedures affecting employee relations, as well as health and safety, to ensure that Rohm and Haas not only protects and cares for its employees, but consistently performs as a valued corporate citizen and a good neighbor.

Rohm and Haas Company, one of the nation's most innovative and consistently productive industrial enterprises for nearly a century, continues its leadership in research, manufacturing, and financial progress on an ever-broadening base of technical excellence and sound management.

L-3 COMMUNICATIONS SPD TECHNOLOGIES, INC.

A leading supplier of electronics and electrical power products and systems to the U.S. Navy, SPD Technologies,

Inc., also provides electrical power delivery systems to a wide range of commercial customers.

The secure and efficient operation of the world's most advanced fleet of ships depends on products and systems from a company that got its start in Philadelphia over a century ago. SPD Technologies, Inc., today is the largest designer and manufacturer of military-specification circuit breakers and switchgear for the U.S. Navy (USN), and a leader in the development of advanced shipboard monitoring systems. Virtually every conventional and nuclear-powered vessel in the navy's active fleet is equipped with SPD systems.

SPD also brings proven American-made technologies to power challenges in transportation, utilities, and other nonmilitary applications. In addition to circuit breakers and switchgear, key product lines include power panels, control panels, protective relays, operating control systems, and related components.

A TRADITION OF INNOVATION AND RELIABILITY

SPD traces its history back to Cutter Electrical Manufacturing Company, founded in Philadelphia in 1888 by Henry B. Cutter. The inventor of a unique "double-push" wall switch for household use, Cutter worked with Walter E. Harrington, chief engineer of the Camden Railroad, to develop the first inverse-time-element

SPD's Actron circuit breaker, "ACB-1606HRC", was developed for naval applications. These air circuit breakers are available in rating from 600 amperes to 4,000 amperes, and offer state monitoring of the electric system that they protect. State monitoring provides necessary information on such things as ground-fault types, phase current, and remote opening and closing of the circuit breaker.

The headquarters for L-3 Communications SPD Technologies is this 165,000-square-foot facility located in northeast Philadelphia.

(ITE) circuit breaker, which the company began manufacturing in a small factory in Center City, Philadelphia. The ITE principle that Cutter introduced became the basis for almost all air circuit breaker development after 1890. William M. Scott and A. Edward Newton purchased the company in 1900, joining Cutter and Harrington as the driving force behind its early growth.

In 1917 the company produced the first shock-hardened circuit breaker for the U.S. Navy, beginning a long, illustrious business relationship with the military. Although the company changed its name in 1928 to I-T-E Circuit Breaker Company, its tradition of innovation and reliability continued unbroken as it proceeded to acquire other businesses and to add and develop new product lines. During the Second World War, I-T-E made a number of landmark technical breakthroughs, and received two "E for Excellence" awards for an outstanding record of supplying circuit breakers to the U.S. Navy.

communications
SPD Technologies, Inc.

By the mid-1950s, the company was one of the largest manufacturing firms in Philadelphia, with operations across Canada and the United States.

In 1968, I-T-E merged with Imperial Eastman Company of Chicago to form I-T-E Imperial Corporation, and in 1976, Gould Inc. acquired I-T-E Imperial. In order to consolidate navy products under one roof, with renewed focus on military circuit breakers, Gould formed the Systems Protection Division as part of its defense group, and moved operations to a new 165,000-square-foot facility in northeast Philadelphia.

STRATEGY FOR THE TWENTY-FIRST CENTURY

In 1987, supported by employees, their union, and city leaders, a management team purchased the Systems Protection Division from Gould, and created SPD Technologies. The newly independent company faced one of its biggest challenges yet as Cold War tensions began to wind down. Under the leadership of Larry A. Colangelo, SPD met the challenge of repositioning itself for continued success in the 21st century.

Colangelo held several manufacturing and financial positions with the company before he was named president and chief executive officer in 1992. His knowledgeable and insightful strategy called for greater emphasis on product development, competitiveness, and aggressive growth, as well as the establishment of long-term agreements with organized labor and an effective program of acquisition and consolidation. In 1998, L-3 Communications merged with SPD and its subsidiaries. The following year, Colangelo, who remains at SPD's helm, was the recipient of the Greater Philadelphia Entrepreneur of the Year Award in manufacturing and was also named a national finalist for Entrepreneur of the Year in manufacturing.

Headquartered in New York City, L-3 is a leading merchant supplier of secure communications systems and products, avionics and ocean systems, microwave components and telemetry, instrumentation, and space and wireless products. Its customers include the Department of Defense, select U.S. government intelligence agencies, and commercial telecommunications and cellular companies.

SPD's Actron molded case circuit breaker was developed for naval applications and is available in ratings from 15 amperes to 1,600 amperes.

SPD Technologies, Inc.'s subsidiaries include:
- SPD Electrical Systems—specialists in circuit breaker design, engineering, manufacturing, and testing for the world's most demanding applications—headquartered in Philadelphia, Pennsylvania;
- SPD Switchgear—the most reliable line of electrical power control and distribution products for commercial, industrial, and military applications—headquartered in Philadelphia, Pennsylvania;
- Power Paragon, Inc.—specialists in power conversion/inversion technology and advanced electrical power delivery systems integration and design for mission-critical applications worldwide—headquartered in Anaheim, California;
- Henschel Inc.—one of the nation's premier producers of ship control and interior communications systems—headquartered in Newburyport, Massachusetts; and
- PacOrd, Inc.—one of the most respected names in combat systems repair and overhaul—headquartered in National City, California.

For more than 100 years, SPD products have been built to the most rigorous specifications, meeting the demands of highly critical installations and applications, from ships at sea to on-shore power plants. While SPD has evolved into a completely integrated company, providing a full line of turnkey products, systems, and technical skills across a broad range of industries, its century-old commitment to innovation, excellence, and dependability remains as strong as ever.

SPD's high speed circuit breaker has been specifically designed for use on a variety of mass transit vehicles including subway, commuter, and light-rail systems.

SKF USA INC.

As the world's leading ball and roller bearing manufacturer, SKF continues to set the global standard of excellence in bearing research, design, manufacture, and maintenance.

SKF founder Sven Winquist's invention, the double row, self-aligning ball bearing, earned its place in the New York Museum of Modern Art for its beauty, form, and function.

With a seldom seen product that literally makes the wheels of life go around, SKF is a company that has grown to become the world's largest manufacturer of rolling bearings, supplying a fifth of the global requirement.

SKF was launched in 1907 in Gothenburg, Sweden, when company founder Sven Winquist, a young maintenance engineer for a textile mill, invented the double row, self-aligning ball bearing to solve misalignment problems in the mill's overhead lineshafts. New products and patents soon followed and by 1912, demand for SKF products began to exceed supply. Rapid growth ensued as new factories and subsidiaries were established around the world.

SKF's American operations, now known as SKF USA Inc., began in 1909 with the establishment of a New York City sales subsidiary. In 1916, the SKF Administration Company was formed to headquarter the growing U.S. business. Within two years a plant was built in Hartford, Connecticut, and two plants were acquired in Philadelphia, Pennsylvania: Hess-Bright Manufacturing Company and Atlas Ball Company. In 1919, the company took the name SKF Industries, Inc., and expanded its operations with the construction of a new facility at Front and Erie Streets in Philadelphia. This site remained the U.S. headquarters

until the company moved it to the King of Prussia area in 1978. Another Philadelphia plant was constructed at Tulip Street and Aramingo Avenue in 1940 with other locations soon following, including two Pennsylvania plants that are still operating in Hanover and Altoona.

In recent years, SKF expansion in the United States included the purchases of TRW's MRC Bearings, leader in aero-engine bearings, in 1986 and Chicago-Rawhide, the world's leading supplier of fluid sealing devices, in 1990. The year 1990 also saw the acquisition of two instrumentation companies that would later become SKF Condition Monitoring, a leader in state-of-the-art instrumentation and software for monitoring and analyzing machine reliability.

Today the company employs some 41,000 people worldwide with an annual turnover of more than $4 billion. Of the 80 SKF factories in 22 countries, 16 are located in the United States. SKF USA accounts for approximately 25 percent of the annual sales and employs more than 6,000 people.

SKF recently gained significant recognition for its environmental efforts worldwide. It became the first major bearing manufacturer to receive ISO-14001 certification, the international standard for environmental

Global manufacturing processes and standards in SKF's 80 factories around the world assure customers get world-class quality.

SKF manufactures all ball and rolling bearing types in sizes weighing from just ounces to several tons.

management systems. This certification is the most comprehensive of its kind and quite often goes further than the measures stipulated in national legislation. It is the environmental equivalent of ISO-9000, the international quality management standard to which all SKF manufacturing units are certified.

A CRUCIAL COMPONENT

The importance of machinery in today's world confirms the significance of rolling bearings. They are the critical component to carry loads and reduce friction in rotating parts. SKF produces more than 22,000 variants covering all principal bearing types. From the smallest bearing weighing mere ounces to the largest over 7 tons, SKF has a solution for almost every application.

The list of applications is as diverse as SKF's product line and includes: aircraft and aero-engines, automobiles and trucks, electric motors and appliances, fluid machinery, industrial transmissions, material handling, office machinery, power tools, printing machinery, pulp and papermaking, railway, metalworking and mining.

RESEARCH, DEVELOPMENT, AND INVENTION

As with all successful high-technology enterprises, aggressive research and development has driven SKF from its outset. Indeed, the company leads the industry in pioneering inventions of rolling bearing technology, leadership verified by the SKF roster of some 2,200 patents. The SKF Engineering Research Centre in the Netherlands, and the North American Technology Center in Plymouth, Michigan, house extensive on-site product development and testing facilities. Complemented with manufacturing technology centers around

the globe, emerge the remarkable advancements upon which SKF's demanding customers have come to depend. Some recent developments include:

- Sensorized bearings incorporate the microchip technology into the heart of the bearing. SKF leads sensorized bearing development with units fitted in cars, trains, forklifts, escalators, papermaking machines, and electric motors;
- Chicago Rawhide Scotseal® Longlife provides superior sealing of the oil in truck wheel hubs. The new EP-2000™ from CR is the first seal development in several years specifically designed for demanding mill applications;
- Unitized wheel hub for automobiles and heavy-duty trucks integrate bearings, seals, wheel hubs, bolts, and sensors into a single unit that dramatically reduces assembly and extends service life;
- The toroidal roller bearing, a completely new bearing type patented by SKF, accommodates shaft misalignment and axial expansion. Called CARB®, this new bearing offers customers greater productivity and reduced costs;
- MARLIN® data management system streamlines the collection and recording of plant process data and enables maintenance, operations, reliability, and management to share the information they need to boost plant productivity; and
- The Explorer Series, a new generation of spherical roller bearings based upon engineering and manufacturing improvements made at the micro and molecular levels, has set a new world standard for bearing performance and reliability.

From the determined Swedish inventor's original double row, self-aligning ball bearing of 1907 to the sensorized and unitized state-of-the-art products of today, SKF has set the global standard of excellence in rolling bearing research, design, manufacture, and maintenance.

SKF is the leading producer of unitized wheel hubs for automobiles and heavy-duty trucks. They incorporate the bearings, seals, hubs, and other components. Pre-assembled and greased for life, many include built-in sensors for ABS systems.

BETHLEHEM STEEL CORPORATION

As one of the nation's largest steel producers, Bethlehem Steel Corporation strives to increase stockholder value, meet customers' needs, partner with employees, and demonstrate good corporate citizenship.

For nearly 100 years, Bethlehem Steel Corporation has provided steel products that have helped build, defend, and transport America.

The corporation traces its roots to 1857 when it was known as the Saucona Iron Company. In 1861 the company changed its name to Bethlehem Iron Company and began producing rails for the nation's rapidly expanding railroads. By 1904 Charles M. Schwab, formerly the president of U.S. Steel Corporation, bought Bethlehem Steel Company and then formed and incorporated Bethlehem Steel Corporation with headquarters in Bethlehem, Pennsylvania. Through a series of acquisitions, the corporation became the nation's second largest integrated steel producer by the 1920s—a position it continues to hold today. In addition, the corporation has been a major shipbuilder, coal and iron ore mine operator, and supplier of the structural steel that was used to build such landmarks as the Golden Gate Bridge, Madison Square Garden, and the U.S. Supreme Court Building.

Today, Bethlehem Steel is focused on providing superior flat-rolled products from facilities in Burns Harbor, Indiana, and Sparrows Point, Maryland, for a wide range of customers. Burns Harbor, Bethlehem's largest division, is a major supplier to the automotive industry. Burns Harbor also operates a galvanized sheet mill in Lackawanna, New York. In Sparrows Point, flat-rolled production is targeted at the construction and service center markets. The division is

Bethlehem acquired Lukens Inc. in May 1998, in order to add to its full range of plate products. Plates, such as those rolled on the sophisticated Steckel mill in Conshohocken, are used by the transportation, construction, machinery, and equipment industries.

also an important producer of tin mill products for the container industry.

A PROFITABLE GROWTH STRATEGY

As part of its profitable growth strategy, Bethlehem Steel acquired Lukens Inc. and its steel plate operations in Coatesville and Conshohocken, Pennsylvania, in 1998. The acquisition made Bethlehem Steel the largest supplier of plate products with the widest range of offerings in North America. The former Lukens' mill in Coatesville is the oldest continuously operating steel plant in North America. The Pennsylvania-produced plate products that come out of these facilities are marketed combining the well-known and well-respected names of Bethlehem Steel and Lukens.

Pennsylvania Steel Technologies, a division of Bethlehem Steel, is the nation's largest railroad rail production facility. Located in Steelton, Pennsylvania,

Bethlehem Steel's Pennsylvania Steel Technologies division in Steelton features a continuous bloom caster that produces a steel bloom that is rolled into rails for the nation's railroads. Steelton is the country's leading supplier of rails.

the company also supplies products such as blooms, bars, and large-diameter pipe to the transportation, forging, and energy markets.

The company's Homer Research Laboratories, located in Bethlehem, offer the largest research and development staff in the North American steel industry and play a key role in Bethlehem Steel's business and product development. The work at Homer Labs helps Bethlehem's customers obtain the maximum value from the corporation's steel products.

COMMITMENT TO CITIZENSHIP

One of Bethlehem's corporate objectives is to be a good citizen. Corporate citizenship is demonstrated by the firm's commitment to environmental performance, which is summarized in its corporate environmental policy: "We will comply with all environmental laws and regulations applicable to the conduct of our business." In recent years, state and federal environmental agencies have recognized Bethlehem Steel for achieving environmental excellence.

Another prominent Pennsylvania initiative that supports the company's citizenship objective is the Bethlehem Works project. The project, involving 163 acres of Bethlehem Steel property, will feature a mixed-use development of entertainment, cultural, retail, and recreational venues anchored by the National Museum of Industrial History in association with the Smithsonian Institution. Another adjoining 1,600 acres of former plant land are being used for the new Bethlehem Commerce Center. The center will include distribution, transportation, and industrial businesses, as well as the BethIntermodal yard, which opened in August 1999 to service customers such as Norfolk Southern. Upon completion, the projects are expected to create about 10,000 new jobs through private developer investment of approximately $1 billion resulting in $70 million in annual local and state tax revenue.

CONSISTENT QUALITY, CONSTANT INNOVATION

Across its product lines, Bethlehem Steel has entered into a number of joint ventures to enhance the corporation's overall market share, service to customers, and value to shareholders. These include additional coating capacity to provide superior corrosion-resistant sheet with different coatings for different end-uses. Another venture uses

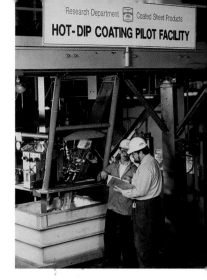

Bethlehem Steel's Homer Research Laboratories in Bethlehem, Pennsylvania, house the largest research and development staff in the North American steel industry. Researchers constantly seek ways to improve process and product quality, particularly for such high-value products as coated sheets used by the world's leading automakers.

Bethlehem coated sheet steel in the construction of metal residential and light commercial buildings.

As the corporation ends its first 100 years, Bethlehem Steel continues to leverage E-commerce as an integral and rapidly expanding business tool. In addition to its own Web site (www.bethsteel.com), the corporation has an equity interest in MetalSite, a neutral Web site for the sale of steel, where companies can buy or sell metal products and services.

In 2004, Bethlehem will celebrate its 100th year of providing premium quality products to its customers. It will enter its second century of operations with the same values as its first—produce innovative steel products of superior quality, provide outstanding technical support, and offer exceptional customer service—in order to become the premier steel production, services, and solutions company.

Bethlehem Works, located on the site of the company's former plant, covers 163 acres that are being transformed into a mixed-use complex of recreational, cultural, and entertainment venues, which will include the National Museum of Industrial History in association with the Smithsonian Institution. This artist's rendering depicts the main entrance to the complex, featuring industrial buildings from the late 1800s complemented by new building construction.

AIR PRODUCTS AND CHEMICALS, INC.

One of the world's largest producers of industrial gases, which are used in nearly every realm of manufacturing, Air

Products and Chemicals, Inc., supplies gases and equipment and selected chemicals to 100,000 customers worldwide.

Air Products was founded in Detroit, Michigan, in 1940 by the late Leonard P. Pool on the strength of a simple, but then revolutionary, idea: the "on-site" concept of producing and selling industrial gases, primarily oxygen.

Air Products and Chemicals, Inc., was founded in 1940 in Detroit, Michigan, by the late Leonard P. Pool. The company was built on the strength of a simple, but then revolutionary, idea: the "on-site" concept of producing and selling industrial gases, primarily oxygen.

At the time, most oxygen was sold as a highly compressed gas in cylinders that weighed five times more than the gas product. Air Products proposed building oxygen gas generating facilities adjacent to large-volume gas users, thereby reducing distribution costs. The concept of piping the gas directly from the generator to the point of use proved possible, and profitable.

In the intervening years, the company has expanded its business through internal development and acquisitions. Today Air Products is one of the world's largest industrial gas producers. The firm supplies a broad range of industrial gases—chiefly oxygen, nitrogen, argon, hydrogen, and helium, as well as related equipment for their production, distribution, and use—to 100,000

customers throughout the world. These gases are used in most industries, including food and metal processing, semiconductor manufacturing, medicine, aerospace, and chemical production.

In addition to industrial gases, Air Products also produces polymers, polyurethane intermediates and additives, amines, and specialty and epoxy additives used in applications such as adhesives, coatings, polyurethane foams, textiles, herbicides, pesticides, water treatment chemicals, reinforced composites, and inks.

INVESTING IN GROWTH

In its first 60 years, Air Products has grown from a company with annual sales of $8,300 to an international corporation with sales of $5 billion. The company and its affiliates have operations in more than 30 countries and employ 17,000 people. Corporate headquarters for Air Products is located on 600 acres in eastern Pennsylvania's Lehigh Valley, near Allentown. The company settled there in 1946 to take advantage of the area's high quality workforce and its proximity to the industrial markets of the Northeast.

Air Products and Chemicals, Inc.'s 600-acre corporate headquarters is located in eastern Pennsylvania's Lehigh Valley, near Allentown.

AIR PRODUCTS

Air Products supplies all of NASA's liquid hydrogen and liquid helium requirements at the Kennedy Space Center.

Air Products has invested approximately $1 billion in Pennsylvania. More than 5,000 of the company's employees work in Pennsylvania, staffing 13 manufacturing plants, administrative offices, and research and development facilities located throughout the Commonwealth. In eastern Pennsylvania, Air Products operates a state-of-the-art semiconductor equipment manufacturing center in Allentown that supports the rapidly growing electronics industry. That industry also is served by specialty gas products manufactured at company facilities in Hometown and Morrisville, Pennsylvania.

Near company headquarters, in Bethlehem, the company runs a helium and hydrogen distribution equipment manufacturing facility, and, through a joint venture with The BOC Group, it is constructing an air separation plant. At the Air Products facility in Wilkes-Barre, the company has designed, manufactured, and exported more than 60 heat exchangers—which typically reach more than 200 feet in length, more than 14 feet in diameter, and weigh more than 250 tons—used for liquefying natural gas. Air Products also operates an industrial gas production and distribution facility in Lancaster.

In the western portion of Pennsylvania, Air Products has an industrial gas production and distribution facility, located in Creighton, and a waste coal–fired cogeneration plant, in Cambria County. The Cambria plant produces 85 megawatts of electricity for a local electric company and steam for a nearby nursing home. The Cambria plant received the Pennsylvania Governor's Award for Environmental Excellence in 1996 for its superior emission-reduction control system and for beneficially using ash to reclaim more than 500 acres of abandoned mine beds, as well as decreasing acid drainage from mines in two major watersheds in western Pennsylvania.

SUPPORT FOR THE COMMONWEALTH

Air Products is a global company with a local commitment. The company and its employees donate more than $3 million annually to numerous educational, human services, and cultural organizations throughout the Commonwealth. These contributions are used to teach inner city elementary students about science and math; renovate homes for low-income families; sponsor a top-rated developmental cycling program for children and adults; build a community conservation and science center; and support theater, arts, and numerous other community programs.

Well over one-third of the company's charitable contributions are directed by current and retired employees and their spouses through a matching gifts program. An energetic group of employee volunteers supplements the various financial donations by collectively donating approximately 150,000 hours of their time each year to the communities in which they live and work.

Air Products is an active participant in many industry organizations and wholly supports Responsible Care®, an industry initiative aimed at improving environmental, health, and safety performance and increasing dialogue between manufacturers and their neighbors. The company also is a recognized leader in safety and received the Pennsylvania Governor's Award for Safety Excellence in January 2000.

Carburos Metalicos, a wholly owned subsidiary of Air Products, is Spain's leading supplier of industrial and medical gases.

ALLEGHENY TECHNOLOGIES INCORPORATED

One of the world's most diversified specialty metals producers, Allegheny Technologies Incorporated of Pennsylvania

provides seasoned expertise and innovative solutions to serve growing international markets.

Pennsylvania has been home to Allegheny Technologies Incorporated since the very beginning of the 20th century. The company started out in the early 1900s as a metals producer with a single factory in Pittsburgh and grew to become one of the largest and most diversified specialty materials producers in the world.

Today, from its Pittsburgh base, Allegheny Technologies maintains manufacturing and distribution operations and sales offices across the United States and in 17 other countries. Allegheny Technologies, formerly Allegheny Teledyne, was created in 1999 through a strategic transformation.

Allegheny Technologies provides global markets with specialty materials, which include stainless steel, nickel- and cobalt-based alloys and superalloys, titanium and titanium alloys, specialty steel alloys, zirconium and related alloys, and tungsten-based materials, as well as precision forgings and large gray-iron and ductile-iron castings. Product forms include flat-rolled sheet, strip, plate, and foil, and long products ingot, billet, bar, rod, wire, coil, tubing, and shapes.

From the beginning, the company has believed that its employees are its most important asset. Now 11,500 strong, its workforce is highly educated and talented. Allegheny Technologies recognizes that each employee's creativity and involvement makes a competitive difference for the company.

At the Vandergrift, Pennsylvania, plant of Allegheny Ludlum, a company of Allegheny Technologies, a new Sendzimir mill that produces 60-inch-wide stainless steel sheet is equipped with next-generation systems (shown above) for process control and shape control. One of the most productive stainless steel cold rolling mills in the world, the Sendzimir mill is designed to provide high quality across Allegheny Ludlum's broad product range.

A HISTORY OF INNOVATION

Since the early days of its ancestor firms, Allegheny Technologies has been a pioneer in making stainless steel for commercial use. The material itself was invented in 1912 at the firm's facility in Sheffield, England. Trademarked Allegheny Metal, it was the most widely used stainless steel of the day. In the late 1920s, it was chosen for one of the first uses of stainless steel over a large exposed building surface—the facing for the top of the Chrysler Building, which still shines as an icon of the New York City skyline. Maintained since 1929 with only one

As an experiment to demonstrate the durability and beauty of the material, Allegheny Ludlum and the Ford Motor Company used stainless steel to build a Ford 1936 deluxe sedan and a 1960 Thunderbird.

cleaning, the top of the Chrysler Building is a testament to the durability of the company's stainless steel.

Allegheny Technologies was the first company to make vacuum-melted nickel-based superalloys for commercial use, creating a technology that now is key to making the high performance materials needed for jet engines. The company also was the first to introduce plasma-cold-hearth melt technology (which uses plasma torches to melt and refine titanium alloys on a cold hearth) for titanium alloys, now the melt technology of choice for making the premium titanium alloys used in jet engines.

In addition, Allegheny Technologies built the first large-scale plant for manufacturing zirconium and related materials, which were instrumental in creating a nuclear-powered submarine program for the U.S. and developing the nation's nuclear-powered electricity generation industry.

In a joint venture with Shanghai No. 10 Steel Company Limited, Allegheny Technologies also built the first facility in China for manufacturing precision rolled stainless steel. The plant was created through the joint venture Shanghai Precision Stainless Steel Company Limited (STAL), of which Allegheny Technologies owns 60 percent.

TODAY'S INNOVATIONS

Innovation at Allegheny Technologies continues. Today the company's diverse products and technical and production capabilities enable it to respond to an extensive variety of needs. Allegheny Technologies supplies specialty materials and engineered solutions to industries including aerospace, automotive, and transportation, and for such demanding contemporary applications as chemical processing, oil and gas exploration and production, food processing, medical implants, and advanced technological processes such as fusion and superconductivity.

When a producer of land-based gas turbines decided to significantly improve product efficiency, the firm turned to Allegheny Technologies for technical assistance. When builders of new housing wanted a better way to pipe natural gas in homes, Allegheny Technologies helped create the solution—corrugated flexible hose made of Precision Rolled Strip® stainless steel, which can be made in a range of thinness from 0.015 inches to less than 0.0015 inches. When a large chemical producer wanted to develop a

Among the major strategic capital investments of Allegheny Technologies is an installation of sophisticated systems (shown above) for its Wah Chang new electron beam furnace in Richland, Washington. With a fiber-optic network, a beam guidance system, and the digital multiplexing of more than 20 cameras, systems like these help operators achieve an unparalleled level of productivity control in making low cost, high quality titanium ingots and slabs.

cost-effective alloy that could be used in its processing plants worldwide, it, too, turned to Allegheny Technologies.

THE FUTURE

Allegheny Technologies looks to the future with a vision toward becoming the world's preeminent specialty materials company. Recognizing that its markets are constantly changing, the firm is committed to not only adapting to change, but also to proactively using change to its own competitive advantage.

Allegheny Technologies intends to strengthen its customer focus and enhance its communications with customers. One initiative is to become involved earlier in the customer's product development cycle—the point in the process when problem solving can be of superior value.

The company also is implementing electronic commerce strategies, adding value for customers and increasing cost competitiveness. With E-business, it can advantageously present to markets worldwide its broad range of products, network of manufacturing and distribution, and prowess at creating innovative solutions. In addition, Allegheny Technologies will selectively pursue global alliances and joint ventures, as well as acquisitions, to build its specialty materials businesses and expand its capabilities.

Never satisfied with the way things are, Allegheny Technologies is committed to continued innovation and growth. That commitment benefits the company's employees and its home, Pennsylvania.

For additional information, visit the Allegheny Technologies Web site at www.alleghenytechnologies.com.

Allegheny Technologies

Specialty Materials That Make Our World

TIGHE INDUSTRIES, INC.

Backed by a history of growth and prosperity, Tighe Industries, Inc., continues to build on its reputation as an industry leading designer and manufacturer of dance costumes and gymnastics apparel.

Dance recitals, gymnastics schools, cheerleaders, and drill teams—all are as American as apple pie. Yet many of the garments for each are designed, manufactured, and marketed by a York County, Pennsylvania, company with a truly global focus.

With sales representatives in Japan, the United Kingdom, and Australia, that York County company—Tighe Industries—has become a world leader in producing dance costumes and gymnastics apparel. Olympic teams from around the world continue to compete in garments designed and produced by Tighe associates. In 1996, millions of Americans witnessed the dramatic gold medal efforts of the U.S. National Team as well as Russian gymnasts in uniforms produced by Tighe Industries through a strategic partnership with Reebok.

Tighe Industries stands out in what traditionally has been a cottage industry. Started in York in 1946 as one of the first ready-made dance recital costume companies, Curtain Call Costumes established a reputation for high quality ballet costumes. In the following two decades, the company's growth was modest, employing 13 people and servicing a small regional market.

Leroy A. King Jr. had other—bigger—ideas for the company. Fresh from a distinguished tour in Vietnam, decorated pilot King and his parents purchased Curtain Call's assets and equipment in 1969 and moved the entire operation into their sewing contracting company, King's Sportswear, in East Prospect, Pennsylvania. It was at this location that the company, incorporated in 1972 as Curtain Call Costumes, Inc., began its 30-year run of growth and prosperity.

Curtain Call Costumes, a division of Tighe Industries, has outfitted millions of dancers around the world.

Tighe Industries' Curtain Call Spirit division has made inroads into professional sports, outfitting cheerleading squads for teams such as the NBA's Dallas Mavericks.

GROWTH AND DIVERSIFICATION

By 1975, Curtain Call moved into its own manufacturing facility in Yorkana, Pennsylvania. King then diversified, founding Alpha Factor Gymnastics to produce and distribute competitive gymnastics apparel in 1978 and purchasing Gantner Swimwear in 1979. Tighe Industries, Inc., was soon formed as the parent company for the gymnastics, swimwear, and costume divisions.

In 1981, Tighe Industries built the 74,000-square-foot East Prospect manufacturing facility that still serves as the company's primary production facility. The purchase of another facility in Emigsville, Pennsylvania, and a 122,000-square-foot warehousing/distribution center in York that also houses Tighe Industries' corporate headquarters, soon followed.

IMPLEMENTING NEW STRATEGIES

First certified as a Class A manufacturing company in 1996, Tighe Industries continues to search for and implement new strategic initiatives to keep the company competitive in a global marketplace. State-of-the-art production, inventory, and delivery systems are continually improved through an associate input and feedback program that places an emphasis on the experience and expertise of every highly valued employee.

Tighe Industries has also entered the electronic marketplace with an Internet site showcasing its varied product line. Soon, a business-to-business E-commerce system will allow dance teachers and gymnastics coaches around the world to search, view, and purchase garments on-line at www.tighe.com, a natural step for a direct marketing company famous for comprehensive customer service.

BRIGHT FUTURE AHEAD

The future for Tighe Industries is as bright as its past successes. International sales continue to rise and beat projections. Specialized lines like Curtain Call Spirit have made tremendous inroads into the world of professional sports, outfitting cheerleading squads for teams like the NBA's Dallas Mavericks and Cleveland Cavaliers and the NFL's Philadelphia Eagles and

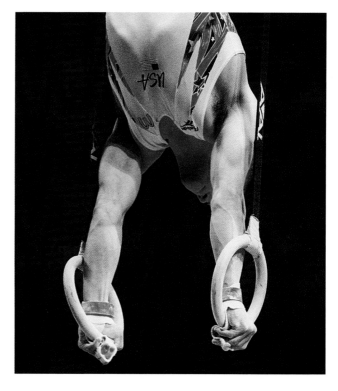

Olympic teams from around the world have competed in garments designed and produced by Tighe Industries' Alpha Factor Gymnastics division.

Buffalo Bills. Tighe Industries has also provided the costumes for the extravagant Orange and Sugar Bowl halftime shows.

New technologies and services are regularly being added to make Tighe Industries even more responsive to the ever-changing requirements of a fast-paced global market. Recently, embroidery and imprinting services were brought in-house to reduce lead time and maintain stringent quality control standards.

Ultimately, every innovation, new production process, or delivery system is designed to meet and exceed the demands of a growing customer base. Each Tighe Industries associate is up to the constant challenge of maintaining his or her status as a superior employee in a world-class company in a worldwide marketplace.

Tighe's Gantner Swimwear line has been featured in Seventeen, Cosmopolitan, *and* Good Housekeeping *magazines.*

LUCENT TECHNOLOGIES

A world leader in the research, design, and manufacturing of components for communications and computing networks, Lucent Technologies operates three major facilities in Pennsylvania, in Lehigh and Berks Counties.

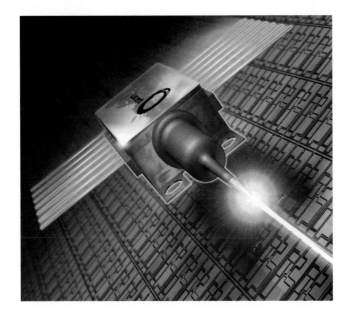

Lasers such as this one from Lucent Technologies Optoelectronics generate the light that carries voice and data through fiber-optic systems.

Lucent Technologies is North America's leader in designing, developing, and manufacturing communications systems, software, and other products used by most of the world's public and private communications network enterprises and service providers.

A spin-off of AT&T in 1996, Lucent Technologies is backed by the research and development of former AT&T arm Bell Laboratories. Lucent focuses its efforts primarily on such high-growth areas as optical and wireless communications networks, Internet infrastructure, communications software, communications semiconductors and optoelectronics (the electronics of emitting, transmitting, and sensing light), Web-based enterprise solutions that link private and public networks, and professional network design and consulting services. Lucent's customers include electronics and communications firms worldwide.

Within Pennsylvania, the Murray Hill, New Jersey–based company operates three major design and manufacturing facilities in the Lehigh Valley and in Berks County for its Microelectronics Group.

The Microelectronics Group, part of Lucent's Microelectronics and Communications Technologies business, includes, in Lehigh County, an integrated circuits (IC) division, headquartered in Allentown, and an optoelectronics division—the Optoelectronics Center —headquartered in Breinigsville. The Berks County facility, in Reading, houses segments of both divisions.

ALLENTOWN: INTEGRATED CIRCUITS AND SILICON

Lucent and its predecessors AT&T and Western Electric have been a fixture in Allentown since 1947, when Western Electric opened a plant to manufacture electron tubes and, shortly thereafter, the newly invented transistor. Today Lucent's Allentown plant, a virtual city-within-a-city with nearly 4,600 employees on a 108-acre campus and more than 1.5 million square feet of buildings, is a prime supplier of the transistor's successor, the integrated circuit. The Allentown plant today manufactures products for Lucent's global customers, including application-specific integrated circuits (ICs)

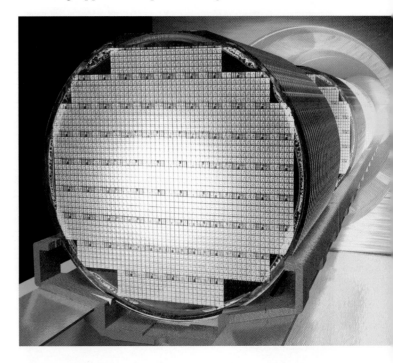

Silicon wafers, which will ultimately be cut into many integrated circuit chips, leave a furnace during processing in a Lucent clean room.

In an optoelectronics clean room, Lucent employees monitor a molecular-beam epitaxial (crystalline) growth system. The system is used to grow laser structures.

A Manufacturing Realization Center to produce optoelectronic devices was created in 1997, and the construction of a $24 million addition to expand capacity was completed in Spring of 2000. This new addition quadruples the amount of manufacturing space on the Breinigsville campus.

Now known as Lucent's Optoelectronics Center, Breinigsville houses engineers and manufacturing associates dedicated to fiber-optics discovery and innovation. Among the products it has developed, manufactures, and delivers worldwide are transmitters and receivers, integrated laser modules, photo diodes, and a variety of other electronic components.

and hybrid circuits, digital signal processors, transmission ICs, line card ICs, and read channel ICs. In addition, the Allentown facility is one of the few companies in the nation that manufactures silicon, the foundation of integrated circuits.

Besides facilities for manufacturing, Lucent also maintains office sites in Allentown for some of its engineering and design personnel. These offices are being consolidated near the company's existing campus in a new $165 million office building scheduled for completion in early 2002.

BREINIGSVILLE: OPTOELECTRONICS

In Breinigsville, Lucent's 200-acre campus employs more than 1,400 people. The site opened in 1988 and is known for its work in solid-state technology and optoelectronics. It is a key Lucent facility for creating and delivering innovative solutions for communications and computing in the United States and around the world.

Structurally, the Breinigsville plant is one of the most unique research, development, and manufacturing facilities in the world. Because ongoing laboratory research taking place at the facility must be free of any vibrations from natural geological movements, or even motor vehicle traffic, its skeletal system is constructed of oversize steel beams, and its foundation is anchored in the bedrock beneath the town.

READING: IC AND OPTOELECTRONICS

Lucent's Reading site is a 133-acre campus in Muhlenberg Township just outside the city of Reading. The facility, which today consists of 1.5 million square feet of manufacturing and office space, was established in a former knitting mill in 1952 by Western Electric to produce a variety of devices for government defense systems. A building for manufacturing was constructed in 1962, and an office building followed in 1982.

At Reading, both integrated circuit and optoelectronic components are manufactured. Major renovations have been made to the manufacturing areas to increase capacity to meet additional customer demand.

Lucent may, in fact, be a young company, but it is founded on more than a half-century of technological growth, research, and constant innovation at its Pennsylvania facilities, as well as at its other facilities worldwide.

Lucent has a strong commitment to its local community and encourages employees to be involved. Here, members of the Lucent Pioneers, a group of current and retired employee volunteers, have built a much-needed ramp.

Lucent Technologies
Bell Labs Innovations

FOAMEX INTERNATIONAL INC.

Foamex International Inc. is a world leader in producing foam cushioning products for the home furnishings and automotive markets and high-performance polymers for specialized, technical industrial applications.

Foamex polyurethane products protect passengers, cushion dashboards, make interiors more elegant, make seats more comfortable, and reduce noise and vibration. In fact, they are used in more than 20 different applications in today's motor vehicles. Foamex debuted its proprietary CPC^{SM} carpet underlay in the 2001 Pontiac Aztek (shown here).

Foamex International Inc., headquartered in Linwood, Pennsylvania, is the world's leading producer of comfort cushioning for the bedding, furniture, carpet cushion, and automotive markets. It also manufactures high-performance polymers for diverse applications in the aerospace, electronics, and computer industries, as well as filtration and acoustical applications for the home.

In addition to its corporate offices in Linwood, the company's Pennsylvania operations, which employ a total of 800 people, include facilities in Eddystone, Philadelphia, Fairless Hills, Stockertown, Williamsport, Corry, and Derry. In all, Foamex has 70 facilities at 50 sites across the United States and in Canada, Mexico, and Asia.

Foamex operates in four major market segments: automotive products; cushioning products, which also encompasses consumer products; carpet cushion; and technical products.

In the automotive industry, Foamex polyurethane products are used for more than 20 different applications in automobiles, minivans, sport utility vehicles, and pickup trucks. Foamex polyurethane protects passengers, cushions dashboards, makes interiors more elegant, makes seats more comfortable, and reduces noise and vibration. Foamex serves nearly every major automaker through suppliers such as Lear, Johnson Controls, Visteon, and Collins & Aikman.

Foamex is one of the leading suppliers of cushioning products to the bedding and furniture industries, where cushioning is an intrinsic component of the end product. Foamex provides bedding manufacturers such as Sealy, Simmons, Spring Air, and Serta with an extensive range of mattress-cushioning products, which vary in density, thickness, and firmness, and can be custom-contoured. Furniture makers such as Berkline, Action, Ethan Allen, and La-Z-Boy use Foamex products to enhance the appearance, comfort, and overall quality of their designs.

Consumer products by Foamex include Anatomic and Eggcrate® bedding brands, which are featured at Wal-Mart, Target, and Bed, Bath & Beyond. Foamex's Baseline Design™ division produces futon, bean-bag, and foam-based casual furniture, which is popular among

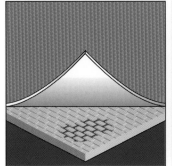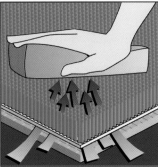

Foamex's ComfortGard™ carpet cushion with SpillTrap™ technology protects carpets and floors by containing spills and speeding drying while also reducing odors.

Foamex
Shaping things to come®

college students, the juvenile set, and young-at-heart adults of all ages.

Foamex is the world's largest producer of carpet cushion, offering consumers more product choices than any other manufacturer. The broad Foamex line includes proprietary carpet cushion, such as ComfortWear®, which contains five times more supporting cells than other carpet cushion, and Berber-Mate®, created especially to enhance the luxury, comfort, and durability of Berber carpeting. Foamex carpet cushion is available through major retailers, including Sears, Home Depot, Carpet One, Abbey Carpet, and Flooring America.

GROUNDBREAKING TECHNOLOGY

Foamex's skilled research and development team in Eddystone, Pennsylvania, creates proprietary products designed to provide improved safety and performance for customers in a wide variety of industries. Foamex technical foams are used in filters, dispensers, gaskets, and seals for industries including aerospace, communications, computers, industrial electronics, medical, and household. For example, Foamex researchers developed a special foam for use in heart-lung bypass machines; the foam is designed to ensure that blood removed during an operation is properly filtered and oxygenated before being replaced in the patient's body.

In addition to its proprietary products, Foamex has created several groundbreaking processes. Variable Pressure Foam (VPF^{SM}) technology is an environmentally friendly process that produces high-performance polymers in a fully enclosed chamber, eliminating the use of toxic blowing agents.

Surface Modification Technology (SMT^{SM}) is a process that can modify the foam

Foamex foams are used in filters, dispensers, gaskets, and seals in everything from color disk drives to blood oxygenators (shown here). In oxygenators, the foam helps ensure that blood removed during an operation is properly filtered and oxygenated before being replaced in the patient's body.

Foamex's Baseline Design™ division produces fun, comfortable, functional KidzLine furniture for kids.

surface in six ways—pattern type, position, size, spacing, depth of cut, and level—enabling bedding manufacturers to provide a nearly unlimited selection of contours and finishes.

CPC^{SM} Technology is an innovation that improves the automotive floor carpet underlay process, while adding softness, diminishing road noise, and reducing weight.

GLOBAL EXPANSION, CREATIVE INNOVATION

Foamex was founded in 1983, and since then has grown primarily through acquisition. The company's goal, according to its president, Jack Johnson, is, "To be recognized as the premier supplier of polyurethane foam and related products in the markets we serve.

"In 1999 we were a billion dollar company," says Johnson. "Through a combination of internal growth and acquisition, we plan to double that size in the first three to five years of this new century.

"We already create proprietary products for a wide range of industries," Johnson says. "Our challenge is to identify other areas where we can apply the creative thinking and innovation that have become Foamex trademarks." The company's focus is quite simple, he adds. "Customers, employees, and growth. Employees are the key to customer satisfaction, and satisfying our customers is the key to growth."

HARLEY-DAVIDSON MOTOR COMPANY

The Harley-Davidson Motor Company's plant in York, Pennsylvania—the firm's premier manufacturing center and one of

its two final-assembly sites—produces more than 600 motorcycles per day, eagerly awaited by customers worldwide.

At the Harley-Davidson plant in York, Pennsylvania, employees manufacture components and perform final assembly of motorcycles destined for customers all over the world. Courtesy, York County Convention and Visitors Bureau

Few states in the nation can brag about having an American icon manufactured within their borders. One of the few is Pennsylvania, and the icon made within the Commonwealth is the most recognized and revered of the world's big bikes—the Harley-Davidson motorcycle.

In fact, since the early 1970s southeastern Pennsylvania has been a second home for Harley-Davidson Motor Company, which is based in Milwaukee, Wisconsin.

In need of more manufacturing space to meet the booming demand for its venerable heavyweight

motorcycles, in 1972 Harley-Davidson production moved to a former naval ordnance plant in the Susquehanna Valley about 100 miles west of Philadelphia.

PREMIER MANUFACTURING AND FINAL ASSEMBLY

The Pennsylvania plant, just outside the city of York, is a sprawling 232-acre complex. It has become the focal point of chassis-making, fabrication, paint, and final assembly for Harley-Davidson bikes, while the company's headquarters and engine and transmission operations remain in Milwaukee.

Today, the York plant continues to be Harley's premier center for manufacturing and one of its two sites for final assembly. Here, in nearly one million square feet of manufacturing-related space, some of the best known models in the motorcycle industry are made.

The distinctive Harleys produced by the plant include the Softail, Dyna Glide, and Touring models. In addition, the York plant is headquarters for the Harley-Davidson operation that assembles limited-production, highly customized motorcycles.

Altogether, more than 600 gleaming Harley-Davidsons come rolling off the plant's four assembly lines each day. And each day, hundreds of those bikes, with their distinctive deep-rumbling engines, leave York for eagerly awaiting customers around the globe.

The plant in York, which employees 2,800 people—about half of whom are themselves motorcycle riders—manufactures more than half the parts that are used in putting a Harley together.

AN AMERICAN LEGEND

The York facility also is home to the Harley-Davidson Tour Center, where visitors can view, through the historic displays, the evolution of

At left is the Harley-Davidson 2000 FXSTD Softail Deuce.

the motorcycle and the sport of motorcycling. Among other things, the tour experience covers Harley-Davidson's history, including its founding in 1903 in a backyard shed in Milwaukee. The Davidson brothers, William D., Walter, and Arthur, and William S. Harley crafted their first motorcycle using the best available tools they had, mostly their hands and their ingenuity. In 1903, three motorcycles were built, and the Harley-Davidson Motor Company began its journey.

Visitors also learn about Harley-Davidson's role in World Wars I and II, when the company's entire motorcycle output was earmarked for the war effort; the emergence of a motorcycle culture in

America in the 1950s and 1960s, when owning a Harley and a black Harley-Davidson leather jacket became not just a fad and a fashion statement, but also a lifestyle; and

the transformation of motorcycling in America in recent years from what had been a fringe obsession into a weekend hobby for baby boomers.

COMMUNITY SPIRIT

With a workforce approaching 3,000 and likely to continue to grow, Harley-Davidson's York plant is, without question, a key part of southeastern Pennsylvania's economy. In fact, the company is one of the top three employers within York County. Besides being a major jobs provider, however, it also is a major contributor to the betterment of its community.

Each year in September, the plant holds a three-day-long open house to which the public is invited to see firsthand how Harleys are made. The event draws 40,000 visitors each year and raises money for the Muscular Dystrophy Association. The plant also is the host site for Ride for Life each spring, where bikers from throughout Pennsylvania and nearby states gather to raise additional funds to combat muscular dystrophy.

Employees of Harley-Davidson's York Operations build quality into every aspect of production. The facility manufactures chassis; fabricates, paints, and chrome-finishes metal parts; and produces many of the other components used in its final assembly process. Courtesy, York County Convention and Visitors Bureau

In addition, the plant and its employees actively contribute to such local causes as the United Way, the Salvation Army, the Byrnes Health Education Center, York College, the Easter Seal Society, and the York County Literacy Council.

York Harley-Davidson also prides itself on being a good neighbor, having been recognized by the state of Pennsylvania and local agencies for its exemplary employee safety measures and the steps it has taken to minimize the impact of its plant operations on the environment.

Harley-Davidson's mission has always been to fulfill people's dreams. Its York operation has certainly done much to accomplish that and more for the people of Pennsylvania for more than a quarter-century.

The local and rider communities come together to enjoy Harley's annual Open House, which showcases production at the plant, and offers shopping, entertainment, and a chance to ride the company's newest models at the York Expo Center.

BERWIND GROUP

Berwind Group of Philadelphia began in coal mining in the 19th century and diversified broadly in the 20th century,

resulting in vast industrial product, pharmaceutical, real estate, finance, and energy holdings in this new millennium.

Berwind Group was founded in 1874 as an old-line Appalachian coal mining company. But after nearly a century in business, the firm made a pivotal strategic decision that reshaped its future.

A new corporate strategy in 1962 shifted the firm's focus from coal mining to leasing the coal reserves, thus creating the cash flow necessary to begin a major diversification process. Berwind Group flourished as it expanded into new industries. Today the fourth-generation, family-owned enterprise has more than 7,500 employees and more than $1.3 billion in annual sales. Berwind Group, based in Philadelphia, is composed of four autonomous groups—natural resources, industrial products and pharmaceutical services, real estate investment, and financial services.

Berwind Natural Resources Corporation, one of the largest independent owners of Appalachian coal lands, leases its reserves to other energy-producing companies. The company is active in oil and gas production, timber production, and the development of its vast real estate holdings. Berwind Operating Companies combines industrial products and pharmaceutical products and services in one operating unit. An international holding company, it has interests in many diverse, freestanding businesses. Its subsidiary companies manufacture a variety of products, from wheel weights to security systems.

A symbol of long-term growth through diversification, Berwind Group is composed of four autonomous groups—contemporary industrial products and pharmaceutical services; financial services; real estate investment; and its founding business of natural resources (starting with coal mining, as depicted in its 1924 medallion, shown below).

Berwind Property Group is an entrepreneurial real estate investment management firm. The company's capabilities extend to active participation in every phase of a real estate project, including acquisition, financial analysis, and predevelopment services, as well as marketing, asset management, and disposition. Berwind Financial Group is a private investment banking, merchant banking, and money management firm organized to serve midsize to large corporations.

Each of the four groups has an independent board of directors and conducts business with its own operating philosophy and style. "We maintain an environment in which entrepreneurial management teams can thrive, giving them full responsibility for conceiving and implementing the strategic plans necessary to maximize their businesses," says C. G. Berwind Jr., Berwind Group chairman. "This entrepreneurial spirit is teamed with sound management and a culture that binds imaginative and energetic individuals together with common goals."

This 1924 medallion was created in celebration of Berwind's 50th anniversary.

BEN FRANKLIN TECHNOLOGY PARTNERS

A unique statewide network, Ben Franklin Technology Partners contributes to Pennsylvania's economy by helping technology companies secure the resources they need to be successful.

Ben Franklin
Technology PArtners

Truly ahead of its time, Ben Franklin Technology Partners is a nonprofit, state-sponsored organization that promotes technological innovation in order to spur economic growth and prosperity in Pennsylvania.

Established in 1983, Ben Franklin Technology Partners has made a significant impact on the Common-wealth by providing knowledge and capital to new and established companies. It also partners with a variety of businesses and organizations to offer these companies support. As a result, Pennsylvania has become a national leader in innovation and high technology and Ben Franklin has become an international model for fostering technology-based companies.

From 1989 to 1996, the Ben Franklin organization boosted the Pennsylvania economy by $2.9 billion and generated a sound 14-to-one return on state invest-ment. It has helped create and retain 50,000 high value jobs, establish and build more than 1,400 high-tech companies, and develop and commercialize more than 1,500 new products and processes.

Ben Franklin operates regionally from four strategi-cally located centers, working in collaboration with the Commonwealth's Department of Community and Economic Development. The organization partners with educators, investors, service providers, and community, government, industry, and labor leaders to provide three key services:

- Direct investment—critical seed and risk capital for company formation and growth.
- Business and technical support —quickly connecting com-panies to the resources they need to succeed.
- Regional infrastructure building for technology growth—univer-sity-based centers of excellence,

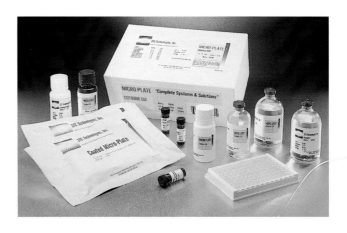

STC Technologies' successful growth and its array of diagnostic tests and medical devices highlight the value of Ben Franklin's business incubator support, university connections, and catalytic funding.

high-tech business incubator space, and venture capital funds.

"Ben Franklin plays a key role in making Penn-sylvania a leader in the new economy," says Governor Tom Ridge. "Working as partners to nurture and prepare the Commonwealth's technology-based enterprises will keep Pennsylvania at the forefront as we head into the new millennium."

Ben Franklin's leadership in technology includes a role in implementing Ridge's new Pennsylvania Technology Investment Authority (PTIA). PTIA pro-vides custom-made financing tools for high-tech firms.

As the new millennium dawns, Ben Franklin Technology Partners is poised to increase Pennsylvania's competitive edge through the building of advanced tech-nology companies. For additional information, visit the organization's Web site at www.benfranklin.org.

With assistance from Ben Franklin, a research scientist applied MRI technology to the oil and gas industry, building NUMAR Corporation—pictured in action at left evaluating the potential in an oil well—into a multimillion dollar international company.

CHAPTER THIRTEEN

LAND OF PLENTY

AGRIBUSINESS, FOOD PROCESSING, AND FORESTRY

In colonial times, Pennsylvania was called America's Breadbasket, an acknowledgment of the province's leadership in agriculture. Today, Pennsylvania remains a leader in agriculture and related businesses, which together account for one out of five jobs in the Commonwealth. • The province's earliest known water-driven grist mill for processing grain was built on Cobb's Creek in southeastern Pennsylvania in 1647. By the 1760s, there were more

than 100 mills operating in Philadelphia and surrounding counties, and Pennsylvania farmers and merchants were exporting grain and agricultural products worth hundreds of thousands of British pounds. A Philadelphian named Oliver Evans contributed to the technological advance of food processing with his publication in 1795 of the first of many editions of *The Young Mill-wright and Miller's Guide* containing descriptions for building improved and increasingly automated mills.

A CORNUCOPIA OF RICHES

Pennsylvania is the nation's number one producer of mushrooms. This industry, which got its start in the 1890s, is a good example of the kinds of challenges that today's agribusiness leaders face. Through most of the 20th century, Pennsylvania mushroom growers harvested button mushrooms to be processed and packed in cans and jars. One of the state's largest growers and packers of mushrooms, the Mushroom Canning Company, began as a cooperative in 1926. During the mid-1980s, international competitors began growing and packing the mushrooms less expensively. Many Pennsylvania growers switched to the production of fresh specialty mushrooms, such as the cremini, shiitake, and portobello varieties, which proved to be extremely popular with baby boomers

seeking fresh, wholesome, low-calorie foods. Mushroom growing thus remained profitable in Pennsylvania as families obtained access to quality ingredients that previously had been available only to urban restaurant chefs. Today, Pennsylvania leads the nation in the production of mushrooms. Pennsylvania growers produce 355 million pounds of them, roughly half the fresh mushrooms sold in the United States.

Animal agriculture is the largest sector of the Commonwealth's agricultural industry, with dairying of particular importance. The nation's fourth largest milk-producing state, Pennsylvania produces more than 10 billion pounds annually, or 6.9 percent of the country's milk. There are approximately 176,000 cows in southeastern Pennsylvania and another 106,000 cows in south central Pennsylvania.

The Pennsylvania Department of Agriculture is committed to the expansion of agribusiness in the global marketplace and has helped small specialty-food companies with marketing activities, such as by attendance at trade shows. The department's veterinary laboratory is

An employee makes a quality control check on Hershey's Kisses at the company's factory in Hershey. More than 12 billion Kisses are produced annually here and at the company's California facility.

PHOTOS: THIS PAGE, © Corbis/Richard T. Nowitz; OPPOSITE PAGE, © Corbis/Bettmann

170

part of the Pennsylvania Diagnostic Laboratory System, a cooperative agreement between the department, Pennsylvania State University, and the University of Pennsylvania. The Commonwealth should soon have a new meat-animal evaluation center for testing and recording animal genetic traits and a new Pennsylvania Equine Center.

Today, the industries of agriculture and food processing have been united and reborn as agribusiness, the application of agriculture to produce food products, including their processing, packaging, and distribution. Achievements in biotechnology, advanced manufacturing, and advanced materials are closely linked to the growth of agribusiness.

ALWAYS IN GOOD TASTE

For the food-processing industry, the same abundant, clean water supply that was so crucial to all industry during the 18th century today provides water for washing, cooling, and packing food products.

The largest food-processing state in the Northeast in terms of numbers, Pennsylvania is America's capital for such snack foods as chocolate, potato chips, and pretzels. It ranks second in the nation in the production of ice cream and in the number of breweries and is home to more bakeries than any other state.

During the 19th century, Milton S. Hershey became a wealthy man by mass-producing chocolate, which had formerly been a luxury item made by hand and sold in specialty shops. Henry J. Heinz, too, built a major business: he produced ketchup and other high-quality condiments that greatly livened up the typical winter diet of meat, potatoes, root vegetables, and bread.

The Heinz Hitch was used to deliver H. J. Heinz Company products at the turn of the last century. Today, a replica of the hitch logs 57,000 miles a year in goodwill tours in the United States and Canada.

Hershey and Heinz were both revolutionaries when it came to ensuring a desirable quality of life for their employees. Hershey built a company town unlike any other, a model village equipped with the latest amenities where workers would be happy to raise their families. Heinz was known in his era as the Prince of Paternalism because he provided his workers with benefits like free medical and dental care, a library, a gymnasium, and even free lectures and lessons in the complex he built near Pittsburgh.

Today, Hershey Foods is the market leader in the nation's candy business. Over 16,000 employees produce its famous candy brands and baking chocolate, chocolate syrup, cocoa, and ice-cream toppings, sold by more than two million retailers. The H. J. Heinz Company still makes ketchup, but it also makes Ore-Ida frozen potatoes, StarKist tuna, and Weight Watchers brands for dieters. Heinz employs more than 38,000 people worldwide.

Another Pennsylvania company whose fame extends beyond the state's borders is the Tasty Baking Company in Philadelphia, whose Tastykake's cakes and pies were once available only in the immediate area. Philadelphians who moved away would ask their friends to mail a carton or two of their favorites, such as Butterscotch Krimpets or the

NO MAD COWS In 1999, a new initiative made Pennsylvania one of the nation's leaders in having an emergency response protocol for foreign and exotic diseases in the realm of animal health.

Pennsylvania has been known for beer and breweries since the days of William Penn, who instructed his agents to include a brew house on his country estate at Pennsbury. Commercial breweries opened in Philadelphia before the 18th century dawned. Today, the Commonwealth is known for its many independent commercial breweries and their distinctive brews.

top-selling chocolate cupcakes. The products are now available in 47 states, Puerto Rico, and Canada. Since its founding in 1914, Tasty Baking has grown to employ over 1,200 people, and now bakes more than 3.5 million cakes and pies each day.

Another top food processor in the state, Peach Glen–based Knouse Foods Cooperative, is one of the largest apple-processing companies in the world. Owned by more than 150 fruit growers in the Appalachian region, it is best known to consumers through such brands as Lucky Leaf and Musselman's. In 1993, the company received the Pennsylvania State Agribusiness Achievement Award for its contribution to agribusiness and its production of high-quality products.

Three more food-processing companies top the list of achievers. The family-owned Turkey Hill Dairy, of Conestoga, markets its products—labeled "Imported from Lancaster County"—up and down the East Coast. Since its ice-cream flavors are changed on a regular basis, consumers are always eager to try the latest one. Hatfield Quality Meats, of Hatfield, a pork processor that employs 1,200 people, supplies fresh pork, ham, sausage, and bacon to supermarkets and restaurants. D. G. Yuengling & Son has been brewing beer in Pottsville since 1829. The

The Pennsylvania Department of Agriculture hosts an annual Farm-City Day to introduce urban and suburban elementary school children to the importance of agriculture when it comes to feeding and clothing their own families as well as people around the world. The Pennsylvania Farm-City Program was created in 1955.

company manufactures more than 500,000 barrels of beer annually, which are sold throughout Pennsylvania, New Jersey, Delaware, New York, and Virginia.

RESEARCHING THE POSSIBILITIES

Agribusiness and food processing, like many other Pennsylvania industries, also draw support from the research and development programs of Pennsylvania's schools and universities. In State College, the University Creamery, part of Penn State's department of food science, is renowned for its technical short courses on the manufacturing of ice cream and chocolate as well as other aspects of food processing. The university's Center for Food Manufacturing helps companies achieve higher processing efficiency. The food industry has access to Penn State's research and educational resources through an alliance, the Food Industry Initiative in Pennsylvania, comprising representatives from industry, academe, and government. In Philadelphia, Drexel University has a well-respected food science and nutrition program, and St. Joseph's University has long been known for its executive food-marketing program.

It is no secret that farmers are relying more and more on computers for efficient operations and increased profitability. In 1997, over 250 Pennsylvania farmers—up from 65 in 1990—used Penn State's

PHOTO: © John McGrail

computer-based Crop Information Management System. The field of biotechnology has already joined information technology in revolutionizing agribusiness, as breakthroughs make it possible to improve both crops and herds.

INTO THE WOODS

In colonial days, William Penn's colony abounded in forests that provided a harvest of materials for shipbuilding. During the 19th century, the demands of a growing and industrializing nation made Pennsylvania America's leader in the production of sawed and planed lumber. By 1850, thousands of logs could be seen on any given day floating in enormous log booms from lumber towns of the Susquehanna River Valley, such as Williamsport, Lock Haven, and Jersey Shore. Today, Pennsylvania produces more hardwood lumber than any other state in the nation. From 1976 to 1989, the removal of timber increased from 800 million to nearly 1.2 billion board feet per year, according to James Finley, associate professor of forest resources at the Pennsylvania State University. In 1996, professional natural resource managers, forestland owners, scientists, and environmentalists teamed up to develop official management practices for Pennsylvania forests, since only sustainable methods can ensure a continued harvest.

The lumber and wood products industry provides jobs for 34,000 people in more than 1,300 companies. A separate sector, wood furniture, employs more than 17,000. Based in Kreamer, Wood-Mode, one of America's premier manufacturers of custom cabinetry, produces cabinets of oak, cherry, maple, and pine, employing 1,300 people. Eastern Wood Products, of Williamsport, manufactures kiln-dried hardwoods for molding, furniture, and the mill-working industry. Allegheny Particleboard, of Kane, manufactures particleboard for the cabinet and furniture industry. Its plant in Mount Jewett, where the composite wood product is made from whole logs and sawmill and wood waste, is one of the largest of its kind in the world.

Dwight Taylor, one of many farmers throughout the state, prepares for a day of work on his farm in Brogue, in York County. The county leads the state in the production of winter wheat and soybeans and is number two in both hogs and corn for grain.

MUSHROOM CANNING COMPANY

Mushroom Canning Company of Kennett Square, Pennsylvania—the nation's primary mushroom-producing region—processes popular types of mushrooms, continually striving to create ever-finer products.

The origins of Mushroom Canning Company date back to 1926, when the Mushroom Growers Cooperative Association formed to market mushrooms more effectively. A mushroom-processing plant was established in 1931 and the association became known as Mushroom Cooperative Canning Company. Over the years, new members joined and some members retired. The four family farms that own the cooperative today had become members by 1973.

The primary function of the cooperative was to market the mushrooms grown on its members' farms. As the farms grew in size, the cooperative grew with them. But the cooperative was not as focused and progressive as it needed to be. To gain that focus, in 1991 the members converted Mushroom Cooperative Canning Company from a cooperative to a corporation, and the name of the business was officially changed to Mushroom Canning Company (MCC). Instead of serving as the marketing arm for the family farms, Mushroom Canning Company became a separate entity with the sole purpose of becoming the nation's best mushroom processor.

MAKING WORLD-CLASS PRODUCTS

Mushroom Canning Company's focus is to meet and exceed the needs of its customers by increasing productivity and investing in the new technologies and the state-of-the-art equipment required of a world-class mushroom processor.

As with other agricultural products, an important step in separating an excellent processor from an adequate processor is procuring the fresh fruits or vegetables needed to make its food products. "We believe herein lies the true strength of MCC," says Dennis Newhard, company president. Mushroom Canning Company procures most of its high quality mushrooms from its four family farms. These families have all been in the mushroom industry for three and four generations. And because sales continually increase, Mushroom Canning Company also procures mushrooms from more than 25 other farms with which the company has long-term relationships. "We treat our suppliers fairly and honestly, which means that even in periods of short supply we get the mushrooms we need to manufacture high quality products," Newhard says. "Processed mushrooms can only be as good as the raw mushrooms used to make them."

THE NATION'S MUSHROOM CAPITAL

Nearly 50 percent of all the mushrooms grown in the United States are grown in Pennsylvania. Mushroom Canning Company is located in southeastern Pennsylvania's Kennett Square—the heart of the state's mushroom-growing area—and thus the Mushroom Canning Company has an ample supply of fresh mushrooms. Within hours of being harvested, mushrooms reach the processor's loading dock. The fresher the mushroom, the better the processed product.

A solid basic structure is a key to any company's success, and each family farm owner is part of MCC's solidity. "They each are independently successful and contribute to the strength that is MCC," Newhard says.

The popular white button mushroom (Agaricus bisporus) is just one of numerous varieties of mushrooms processed by Mushroom Canning Company.

ALL IN THE FAMILY

All four family-owned farms that make up Mushroom Canning Company grow the mushrooms used by the company, and each farm adds its own special touch to MCC's products and processes.

Guizzetti Farms is operated by Guildo Guizzetti and his three sons: Victor, Michael, and Guildo Jr. The family grows white button mushrooms. It also manufactures the substrate that mushrooms grow in, to supply its own farm and to sell to other mushroom growers. Guildo Guizzetti was instrumental in the development of a Mushroom Canning Company–patented infusion technique that helps retain the color and flavor of mushrooms during processing.

Basciani Farms has been in business since 1925. It is run by Mario Basciani and his three sons: Michael, Mario, and Richard. Basciani Farms is one of Pennsylvania's largest growers of white button mushrooms. It also grows specialty mushrooms, such as crimini, shiitake, and portabello. Basciani Foods, the fresh-mushroom marketing arm of Basciani Farms, sells fresh mushrooms throughout the eastern United States.

Needham Mushroom Farms is run by Donald "Buster" Needham and sons Arthur and Donald. The Needhams are growers of white button mushrooms as well as one of the largest growers of crimini and portabello mushrooms in the nation. The Needhams also manufacture the substrate that mushrooms are grown in and sell it to other mushroom farms. They recently

installed the first automated fabrication line for mushroom substrate production.

The Yeatman family began growing mushrooms in 1921, and today C. P. Yeatman and Sons is run by descendants of the founder, brothers C. James Yeatman and Robert Yeatman and C. James's son Jerry Yeatman, and Robert's son-in-law Timothy Hihn. C. P. Yeatman and Sons grows organic white button and oyster mushrooms and is one of the largest growers of organic mushrooms in the nation. Mushroom Canning Company is the certified organic processor for C. P. Yeatman and Sons organic mushrooms, which are marketed by both Mushroom Canning Company and Mushroom Specialties, the fresh-mushroom marketing arm of C. P. Yeatman and Sons.

This vibrant group of family farm owners supplies Mushroom Canning Company with their many different types and sizes of mushrooms. "MCC processes only mushrooms, and we are completely focused on the very best practices needed to process mushrooms effectively," says Newhard. Other factors that contribute to MCC's success include its patented infusion process for retaining mushroom color and flavor and its varied product line that includes retail- and institutional-size cans of mushrooms, frozen mushrooms, quick-blanched mushrooms, and mushroom sauces.

"Our mission is to consistently exceed the expectations of all our customers in quality, service, and value," Newhard says, "while also continuing to increase our financial strength and be a rewarding company to be involved in."

In preparation for canning, blanched mushrooms are divided into precise portions in a volumetric filler.

TURKEY HILL DAIRY

From a "shy little dairy to a shy medium-size dairy," Turkey Hill Dairy continues to grow and prosper as a family-run business dedicated to delivering the finest products at prices that everyone can afford.

AT LEFT: *In 1935, Turkey Hill Dairy was only a small block building standing in the same place as the current plant resides.* BELOW: *This northern view of the current manufacturing facility shows just how much the dairy has grown.*

Today, Turkey Hill Dairy has grown into a major food business with annual sales of more than $200 million. Each year, the company sells an average of 35 million quarts of milk, 75 million quarts of teas and drinks, and 25 million gallons of frozen products. Turkey Hill Dairy employs over 500 associates and sells its products in 13 states through the mid-Atlantic and New England areas.

The history of Turkey Hill Dairy began in 1931, when Armor Frey started selling and delivering extra milk from his farm as a means to survive the Great Depression. Each morning, Frey would watch the sunrise from Turkey Hill then put bottles of fresh milk on ice in the back of his touring sedan, and sell the milk door-to-door to families near his farm. Gradually the delivery route grew and became his major source of business. He named his dairy Turkey Hill after its Lancaster County location.

KEY TO SUCCESS

A key ingredient to Turkey Hill's success has been the expansion and innovation initiated by the second generation of Freys. In 1947, Frey's sons Glenn, Emerson, and Charles bought the business their father had developed. While other small dairies struggled, Turkey Hill embarked on an aggressive expansion campaign to boost business. The dairy increased its home-delivery line in the 1950s and 1960s to include soda, bread, soup, and ice cream.

POPULAR PRODUCTS

Turkey Hill ice cream was introduced in the 1950s with much success. The firm's frozen line features seven product varieties ranging from premium ice cream to fat-free frozen yogurt. The popular ice-cream products are available in 20 feature flavors and 55 regular flavors ranging from Peanut Butter Ripple and Death by Chocolate to Strawberries 'n' Cream and Colombian Coffee. Other new additions include ice-cream sandwiches and sundae cones.

The Turkey Hill Giant Cow is transported along the East Coast, from Vermont to Virginia, highlighting new store openings and other special events.

Another innovation that spurred the growth at Turkey Hill was the vision to sell Turkey Hill products beyond the neighborhood routes. In 1967, the company created the Turkey Hill Minit Markets to retail its products more efficiently and profitably. Later, in the 1970s, Turkey Hill began selling to local wholesale accounts to widen its growth. More dramatic growth occurred when Turkey Hill entered metropolis areas such as Philadelphia and New York. These new markets and their grocery store outlets put Turkey Hill on the map.

CATERING TO CUSTOMERS

Turkey Hill also was one of the first ice-cream makers to bring a premium ice milk to the market with the launch of Gourmet Lite in 1986. Five years later, Turkey Hill introduced its premium frozen yogurt as well as a nonfat frozen yogurt. In addition Turkey Hill has continued to expand its line of teas and drinks, producing a wide variety of flavored iced teas and lemonades.

Frey's grandson, Quintin, represents the third generation of the Frey family to run Turkey Hill Dairy. Quintin serves the company as president and manages the business for Ohio–based Kroger Companies, which is the largest supermarket chain in the United States. Kroger purchased Turkey Hill Dairy in 1985.

Quintin is committed to maintaining the same philosophies that his grandfather, father, and uncles brought to the company. Those enduring principles include a commitment to customers, and the recognition that good employees are the foundation of the firm's success. Community involvement is another priority of the Freys that has extended to the Turkey Hill family. The company supports a variety of charities and nonprofit groups ranging from the Special Olympics to local libraries, fire departments, and conservancy groups.

A PROMISING FUTURE

Turkey Hill Dairy believes that no person or company can continue its success by resting on past accomplishments. That is why Turkey Hill Dairy continues to set goals for the future to constantly challenge itself to be the best in an increasingly competitive market.

Turkey Hill introduced its new package design for ice cream in early 2000. The new half gallon container features an easy-to-scoop design and space-efficient shape for the home freezer.

FURMAN FOODS INC.

Family-operated since 1921, Furman Foods Inc. sells tomatoes and other produce grown on their farmland in Northumberland and Lancaster, Pennsylvania, and in parts of Maryland, preserving high quality and ecological integrity.

A bumper crop of tomatoes was responsible for launching one of the largest tomato processors in the northeastern United States.

During the summer of 1921, a Pennsylvania farmer was left with a surplus of fresh tomatoes after making his usual rounds selling to local merchants. J. W. Furman, along with the help of his family, processed the extra tomatoes on their kitchen stove. The family preserved 30 dozen glass jars of tomatoes, which were sold to merchants later that winter.

More than 75 years later, the family business is still processing tomatoes at Furman Foods Inc. in Northumberland, Pennsylvania, and in Rhodesdale, Maryland. The company has come a long way since J. W. Furman used a home canner to seal two cans of tomatoes per minute. Today, 79 years after the company's inception, Furman Foods is one of the largest family-owned tomato processors on the East Coast. More than seven million cases of canned goods are produced by the company's two modern processing plants. One plant, consisting of 450,000 square feet, is in Northumberland, and the other plant, consisting of 55,000 square feet, is in Rhodesdale, Maryland.

Furman Foods sells its products through its consumer products unit to customers that include retail grocery

Furman Foods Inc. founder, J. W. Furman, believed in the biblical concept of stewardship, that he was personally responsible for taking care of the portion of the earth that was given to him.

distributors, supermarket chain stores, mass merchandisers, and drugstores. Its food service unit sells to restaurant chains, food service distributors, and manufacturing accounts. The company also exports its product line to Latin America, Europe, and the Middle East.

The best-known Furman Foods brands are Furmano's and DeCecco Italian tomato products and Furman's vegetable products. Furman Foods seasonally grown vegetables are packed at the peak of freshness and include a wide variety of tomatoes and tomato products, as well as peas and green beans. Other products include the company's customized formulas for tomato and bean products, such as pork and beans, kidney beans, chick peas, black beans, peas, butter beans, great northern beans, and three-bean salad.

Furman Foods also packs a number of private-label brands that are sold under 1,500 different labels. The company works with leading food service customers to create custom-formulated products to meet their special needs.

Furman Foods products are made from the finest quality ingredients.

CONSISTENTLY HIGH QUALITY

Furman Foods has cultivated a reputation for providing exceptional quality. In addition to the firm's continual quality-assurance product inspections, its top management team meets daily to evaluate the day's production. Furman Foods farm ownership enables greater control of product quality and ongoing research and development. The company supplements the output of its own farms by contracting with farmers in the region who are willing to grow their crops to meet the standards set by Furman Foods.

The firm's manufacturing philosophy is to integrate the use of cutting-edge technology with human workmanship. One example of this philosophy is seen in Furman's processing of whole peeled tomatoes. Tomatoes are delivered fresh from the fields and processing begins with a thorough washing and proceeds through mechanical color sorting and grading. The tomatoes are then visually inspected to spot any problems the machines may have missed. Next is a sophisticated peeling process during which the tomato skins are removed and the peeled tomatoes rinsed and finally rechecked by inspectors. None of the Furman Foods product lines operate without the human touch. In addition to providing quality products, Furman Foods implements the latest technology to improve efficiency and produce cost savings it can pass along to consumers.

PRESERVING THE ENVIRONMENT

Furman Foods also recognizes that the key to growing vegetables is clean soil, water, and air. As a result, the company is dedicated to maintaining a healthy environment

Franklin G. Furman, fourth-generation member of the Furman family, with his daughter, Lindsey Furman, inspects the quality of tomatoes in the field for Furman Foods.

through every step of its growing and canning processes. Furman Foods is working closely with Pennsylvania State University on an emerging Integrated Pest Management technique. By using global positioning system (GPS) satellite signals to determine precise locations of insects, diseases, or weeds, growers can practice a technique called "site-specific farming." The advantage of this technique is reduced application of pesticides.

BUSINESS VALUES

The Furman Foods mission is "To continue as a leading supplier of tomato products in the eastern United States by providing high quality products and value-added service built upon solid relationships with our customers, employees, and business partners.

"Furman's will add value to our product line through innovative packaging, the introduction of new products, the use of advanced technologies, and service to niche markets.

"Furman's will look to strengthen and broaden its highly valued customer relationships by "listening," emphasizing convenience and service, and offering value-added solutions.

"Furman Foods is a family-owned, customer-focused, performance-driven corporation that adheres to biblical standards of ethics and morality in dealing with its customers, employees, and business partners."

At left, David Geise, president and CEO, third-generation member of the Furman family, inspects the quality of a crop of peas.

H. J. HEINZ COMPANY

An industry leader with a 130-year history of innovation, H. J. Heinz Company remains committed to its mission of providing superior quality products and wholesome nutrition to consumers around the world.

H. J. Heinz Company products such as these are favorites of customers all over the world.

With more than 5,700 product varieties sold in over 200 countries and territories, H. J. Heinz Company has come a long way from the small backyard garden business it started more than 130 years ago.

In 1869, Henry J. Heinz launched a new company—and helped found a new industry—in a family garden near Pittsburgh. He packed his first product (his mother's fresh horseradish) in clear glass bottles to display its purity. This "pure food" idea was radical for its time and it set a standard for all Heinz products to follow. It also created a lasting bond of consumer trust that enabled Heinz's backyard business to grow into a global food giant with sales now approaching $10 billion.

Today, the H. J. Heinz Company remains a food industry leader, renowned for products of superior quality and wholesome nutrition. Its most popular brand, Heinz tomato ketchup (first served in 1876) is a global icon, and the flagship of a worldwide ketchup, condiments, and sauces business that boasts annual sales exceeding $2 billion. Altogether, Heinz offers more than 150 number-one and number-two ranked brands worldwide. Heinz's exceptional portfolio of powerful brands and businesses includes these other core categories:

- Frozen foods: Ore-Ida frozen potatoes, SmartOnes entrees, Boston Market Homestyle Meals, and the Linda McCartney vegetarian line in the United Kingdom;
- Convenience meals: Beanz Meanz Heinz in the U.K. and Wattie's in New Zealand;
- Infant feeding: Heinz is the leading brand in Canada, the U.K., Australia, and New Zealand; leads in infant cereals in China; and produces Plasmon, the favorite brand in Italy;
- Pet food: 9-Lives and Pounce for cats, Kibbles 'n Bits and Snausages for dogs;
- Tuna: Americans prefer StarKist, Europeans enjoy John West, and Australians like Greenseas; and
- Organic and nutritional: Heinz has an alliance with the Hain Food Group, whose brand leaders include Westsoy, Health Valley, Earth's Best, and Terra Chips.

The growing popularity of away-from-home eating has also been a major opportunity for Heinz, which sells supplies to everything from military bases to finer restaurants to fast-food establishments worldwide.

Under the leadership of Heinz President and CEO William R. Johnson, the company is committed to further global expansion, product innovation, and topline growth in the years ahead. Heinz's recent entries into Indonesia and the Philippines open exciting new growth opportunities for Heinz's Asian sauces business, both in the United States and across the Pacific Rim.

With popular brands, strong markets, and a legacy of quality, Heinz is a company with a proud Pennsylvania history that is poised for continued global growth in the new millennium.

Heinz tomato ketchup, found in almost 47 million U.S. households, is also enjoyed in many countries worldwide.

TASTY BAKING COMPANY

Since 1914 the Tasty Baking Company of Philadelphia has baked its popular Tastykake snack cakes, which have been enjoyed daily by millions of consumers in the mid-Atlantic region and now can be enjoyed throughout the nation.

A baker of individual snack cakes and pies since 1914, Tastykake now produces a variety of mealtime products, including breakfast baked goods and large multiserve cakes, pies, and Danish pastries.

Tastykakes were a success right from the start. The idea of small cakes prewrapped fresh at the bakery and conveniently available at the local grocer, was uniquely appealing to American women in 1914. "The cake that made Mother stop baking" did so because Mother could now buy cakes she could trust to be as fresh and delicious as those she made herself. For the same reasons, Tastykakes are more popular than ever with today's busy families and are enjoyed by millions of consumers who want a wholesome, great-tasting snack.

Back in 1914, a Pittsburgh baker, Philip J. Baur, and a Boston egg salesman, Herbert T. Morris, teamed up and founded the Tasty Baking Company in Philadelphia, which began making a line of small cakes with the catchy name Tastykake. Baur and Morris were determined to use only the finest ingredients, delivered fresh daily to the bakery. They insisted on farm-fresh eggs; Grade A creamery butter; real milk, cocoa, and spices; and natural flavorings from the far ends of the earth.

Their uncompromising standards are adhered to still. In fact, Tastykake secret recipes have remained remarkably the same over the years. Some things are best left unchanged. Special small cakes are ever-popular, including Juniors, first baked in 1917, and Butterscotch Krimpets, made since 1927. The innovative, small rectangular Tasty Pies with fruit and other fillings and cookie-sized KandyKakes (formerly called Tandy Takes), were introduced in the early 1930s.

As for freshness, Tastykakes baked tonight will be on store shelves tomorrow, just as always. In line with changes in health and nutrition recommendations, Tastykake has eliminated tropical oils, reducing the level of saturated fats in its products.

From a single horse-drawn wagon, to early electric cars, to Model T Fords, to today's vast fleet of trucks, Tastykake has moved with the times, continually improving deliveries to ensure the same standards of freshness and service that existed years ago. Distribution has been expanded to New England, the Midwest, and the South, and route owner-operators add new retail sites every day. Tasty Baking Company has become one of the largest independent baking companies in the United States. The most important constant during this extraordinary expansion is that Tastykake is able to maintain the same high standards established so many years ago while producing, every working day, 3.5 million cakes and pies to meet today's market demand. Clearly, Tastykake knows well what can be modified and what must be held sacred. That is why, after all these years, "Nobody bakes a cake as tasty as a Tastykake."

Tastykakes now can be ordered by mail for overnight shipment to any part of the continental United States. Simply call 800-64-TASTY or visit the company's World Wide Web site at www.tastykake.com

Kirbee the Krimpet helped celebrate the 70th birthday of the Butterscotch Krimpet.

CHAPTER FOURTEEN

MONEY MATTERS

FINANCIAL AND INSURANCE SERVICES

At the end of the 18th century, Pennsylvania survived its first economic transformation to what was then a new industrial era in part because of the successful development of its financial institutions. Those financial institutions made 19th-century Philadelphia a major financial center where entrepreneurs could find the capital necessary for ambitious commercial enterprises. • America's oldest bank, the Bank of North America, was founded

in Philadelphia in 1781. As the 19th century progressed and Pennsylvania's economy grew, so did the need for banks. In 1814, legislation authorized the establishment of many other banks in districts throughout Pennsylvania. By 1836, Philadelphia alone had 17 chartered banks, while the rest of Pennsylvania had 32.

As early as 1816, Philadelphians of modest means could deposit their savings with the Philadelphia Savings Fund Society, the nation's first mutual savings bank. At a time when regular banks saw no need to handle small, individual savings accounts, this institution encouraged a whole new segment of the population to begin saving and contributed to the city's growth as a commercial center. Today the society is PSFS, a part of Mellon Financial Corporation. Philadelphia-based Mellon PSFS serves southeastern Pennsylvania and southern New Jersey.

When the mill workers of the Philadelphia suburb of Frankford wished to build or purchase homes, they could apply to the Oxford-Provident Savings and Loan Association. This organization, established in 1831, was the nation's first financial institution to be patterned after Britain's building societies for the financing of homes.

Pennsylvania also played a role in the development of national banking. The First Bank of the United States opened in Philadelphia in 1791. After opposition forced it to close, it was reopened in 1817 as the Second Bank of the United States. Its location in Philadelphia made the city the federal banking capital, and the bank eventually provided the entire nation with uniform currency. President Andrew Jackson in 1832 vetoed legislation to recharter the Second Bank of the United States. The institution remained in business, however, under a state charter. Philadelphia again made financial history in 1863, when First National Bank of Philadelphia, the first federal bank authorized by the National Banking Act of 1863, opened in the city.

The Insurance Company of North America, better known during its long and distinguished history as INA, was America's first stock insurance company, founded in Philadelphia in 1792. In 1807, INA appointed its first independent agent—who operated out of Lexington,

Established in 1790, the Philadelphia Stock Exchange is the nation's oldest stock market. The exchange's first headquarters, seen here ca. 1926, opened in 1834. It was built of Pennsylvania marble.

Kentucky. Thus the insurance agency system was born in America. Because INA's earliest clients were ship owners, the strength of the organization was sorely tested during the War of 1812, when European nations preyed upon neutral American ships. INA survived and grew and was one of only a few insurance companies that honored its obligations to policyholders after the San Francisco earthquake and fire.

When INA combined with Connecticut General in 1982, CIGNA, which employs more than 33,000 people worldwide and has assets of $115 billion, was formed. In 1989, CIGNA moved its headquarters to One Liberty Place in Philadelphia. The company is a leading provider of employee benefits, including health care, group life, and accident and disability policies, as well as retirement and investment products and services. With 1998 revenues of $3.1 billion, CIGNA is one of the largest American insurance companies.

PIONEERS OF FINANCE

Pennsylvania has been home to some of this nation's most successful and influential financiers. Stephen Girard settled in Philadelphia in 1776, where he became a successful merchant with a worldwide trading fleet. In 1812, he arranged for subscriptions for the government war loan issue that saved the U.S. Treasury from bankruptcy. He purchased the controlling interest in the First Bank of the United States after Congress failed to renew its charter and renamed it the Bank of Stephen Girard. He also helped raise the capital for the Second Bank of the United States.

Although the Bank of Stephen Girard was dissolved immediately after his death in 1831, Girard's spirit lives on at Girard College, the educational institution that he founded. Girard's profile can also be seen on the building that was once Girard National Bank (founded by others after his death) and is now the entrance to Philadelphia's Ritz-Carlton Hotel.

Andrew W. Mellon is probably Pennsylvania's most famous financier. Born in Pittsburgh in 1855, he went to work at his family's bank, T. Mellon & Sons, established in 1869. Mellon, who proved to have a unique talent for picking fledgling businesses that were destined for success,

Mellon Financial Corporation, headquartered in Pittsburgh, also has offices in Philadelphia (shown here) and Harrisburg. It boasts $2.7 trillion in assets and is a leading innovator in financial services technology.

nondepository credit institutions, 1,600 security and commodity brokers, 1,700 insurance carriers, 5,200 insurance agents and brokers, 600 holding investment offices, and 1,600 licensed insurance companies. The Commonwealth has seen job gains between 1990 and 1997 among security and commodity brokers (up 36.7 percent), holding and other investment offices (up 15.7 percent), medical services and health insurance carriers (up 66.2 percent), and mortgage bankers and brokers (up 55 percent).

Several of the nation's top banks are situated in Pennsylvania. The PNC Financial Services Group, headquartered in Pittsburgh, is one of the largest diversified financial service providers. Created in 1983 by the merger of Pittsburgh National and Provident National of Philadelphia, its assets total more than $164.5 billion. PNC's services include a full range of financial products and services for business and government as well as regional consumer banking. Mellon Financial Corporation, also headquartered in Pittsburgh, is among the world's largest asset managers. The modern successor to T. Mellon & Sons' Bank, in 1955 it became one of the first banks in America to install its own computer. Today it employs 24,700 people and holds $2.7 trillion in assets. Lincoln Financial Group, a leading provider of individual annuities, life insurance, 401(k) plans, life-health reinsurance, and institutional management and mutual funds, moved its corporate headquarters to Centre Square in Philadelphia from Fort Wayne, Indiana, in 1999 so it could be "in the mainstream of the financial services industry." The company has more than $96 billion in assets and more than $6 billion in annual revenues.

built his own financial empire by backing those businesses. Among the companies Mellon supported were Gulf Oil and Union Steel. (The latter merged with nine other oil companies in 1901 to become United States Steel.) In 1921, Mellon became U.S. Secretary of the Treasury, a position he held through the administrations of Presidents Warren Harding, Calvin Coolidge, and Herbert Hoover.

Today, Pennsylvania has one of America's largest and healthiest financial services sectors. The Commonwealth has more than 4,700 depository institutions, 1,800

John C. Bogle can be called a modern financial pioneer. His company, The Vanguard Group, located outside Philadelphia in Malvern (near Valley Forge), has literally changed the way citizens save and invest while growing into the world's largest no-load mutual fund company, managing assets of $520.9 billion. Bogle has long been a proponent of low-cost index funds over actively managed funds. Vanguard's S&P 500 Index Fund is now among the world's largest mutual funds. Altogether Vanguard serves over 14 million shareholders and offers over 103 domestic funds and 21 additional funds in foreign markets. Vanguard employs over 10,000 people, with over 6,000 employed in Malvern.

A bank customer records a deposit to her account. Pennsylvania is home to some of the nation's oldest and largest banks.

Warren "Pete" Musser left a job as a stockbroker to found a brokerage with a partner. Today, he is chairman of Safeguard Scientifics, which acts like a venture capital firm by investing in promising technology companies. Each year, Safeguard Scientifics chooses its investments from among 6,000 submitted business plans. One of Safeguard's greatest successes is a Utah computer software company called Novell, which grew to dominate the networking market. Safeguard was the original investor in Internet Capital Group of Wayne, which is in the business of helping other businesses use the Internet. Internet Capital Group was among the most successful initial public offerings of 1999, and Safeguard remains its largest stakeholder.

A SUCCESSFUL PARTNERSHIP

Pennsylvania has embarked on a transition to yet another new economy, with government and private institutions working smoothly together to ensure sufficient capital for innovation and growth. Pennsylvania's Department of Community and Economic Development offers a variety of financial and technical assistance programs to expand businesses and develop communities. A business can apply for one or more of its programs with a single application and the assistance of a customer service center. The department also offers low-interest loans for construction,

A young couple discusses insurance needs with an agent. There are 120,000 licensed insurance agents in Pennsylvania.

machinery, and equipment purchases, or for compliance with environmental regulations. The Pennsylvania Economic Development Financing Authority issues tax exempt and taxable bonds. Bond funds are loaned to businesses to finance facilities, equipment, and working capital or for refinancing.

The Commonwealth offers opportunity grants, designed to create or keep jobs in Pennsylvania, and enterprise zone grants, for business development strategies in financially disadvantaged communities. Infrastructure Development Program grants and industrial site reuse grants are also available.

SUPPLY SIDER

In his role as secretary of the treasury, Andrew W. Mellon is sometimes credited with the financial policies that led to the tremendous growth of the 1920s. Other historians blame his policies for the depression. He believed that the taxes of those with high incomes should be reduced so that the savings could be invested by individuals in other enterprises.

THE VANGUARD GROUP

The Vanguard Group, headquartered near historic Valley Forge, Pennsylvania, is the largest pure no-load mutual

fund family in the world, managing more than 100 funds and providing a range of auxiliary financial services.

The Vanguard Group, led by Chairman John J. Brennan, makes its headquarters at a 200-acre campus in Malvern, Pennsylvania.

Mutual funds should exist only to serve their shareholders. This simple, yet radical, concept has been the creed of The Vanguard Group since its beginning in 1975. It has led the firm to become one of the world's largest providers of mutual funds for individuals and institutions.

The typical mutual fund company is owned by outside stockholders, who profit from fees paid by fund shareholders. In contrast, the Vanguard funds are independent investment companies that jointly own The Vanguard Group on behalf of the funds' shareholders. There are no outside stockholders or middlemen. Vanguard's unique corporate structure lets it provide all services *at cost*. The result: The funds' expenses are less than *one-fourth* the industry average, so they can pass on a higher percentage of their investment returns to shareholders.

In 1999, for example, the Vanguard mutual funds had an average expense ratio (the percentage of fund assets used to pay annual operating expenses) of 0.27 percent, or $2.70 for every $1,000 invested. The expense ratio of the average mutual fund was 1.29 percent, or $12.90 per $1,000 invested (source: Lipper Inc.). The 1.02 percent difference, when applied to Vanguard's average 1999 assets of $487 billion, represents annual savings of nearly $5 billion—savings retained by Vanguard shareholders.

Service is crucial to Vanguard, too. *Mutual Funds* and *Worth* magazines both recognized Vanguard's excellence in 1999. In these publications' readers' choice polls, Vanguard was selected as the best overall fund complex and the leader in client service. And serving investors well, on a cost-effective basis, has proven to be a successful business strategy: Vanguard's share of all U.S. mutual fund assets, now approximately 9 percent, has more than doubled since 1988.

STRONG ROOTS
Headquartered near historic Valley Forge, Pennsylvania, Vanguard traces its roots to the inception of the Wellington™ Fund in 1929. The nation's oldest balanced fund, Wellington emphasized diversification and conservatism—holding stocks, bonds, and cash investments—in an era of market speculation. Despite its creation just before the worst years in U.S. financial history, the fund prospered and became one of the largest mutual funds in the nation. In 1975, Vanguard was created to independently serve Wellington and ten other funds then in the stable of Wellington Management Company, LLP, Vanguard's forerunner.

Today Vanguard is the largest pure no-load (or sales commission–free) mutual fund family in the world. It manages more than 100 funds that cover every significant segment of the equity and fixed-income markets.

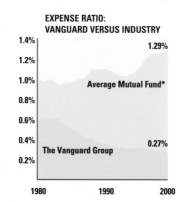

EXPENSE RATIO: VANGUARD VERSUS INDUSTRY

1.4%
1.29%
1.2%
1.0%
Average Mutual Fund*
0.8%
0.6%
0.4%
0.27%
The Vanguard Group
0.2%

1980   1990   2000

*This chart presents the average expense ratios for The Vanguard Group and the mutual fund industry since 1980. *Source: Lipper Inc.*

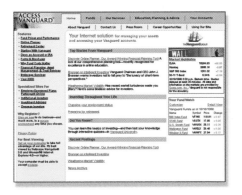
Vanguard 500 Index Fund is its largest fund, with some $100 billion in assets. Moreover, as the nation's first indexed mutual fund, this fund is emblematic of Vanguard's strength in indexing, an investment approach that seeks to outperform the majority of peer mutual funds by matching the return of a market benchmark. Vanguard also offers an array of low-cost stock, bond, and money market mutual funds that are actively managed by experienced investment professionals from around the world.

Because investors have a range of needs, Vanguard also provides auxiliary financial services. Vanguard Brokerage Services® offers investors a means to trade individual securities and non-Vanguard mutual funds. Vanguard Asset Management and Trust Services helps those with large investment portfolios to build and preserve their wealth through ongoing portfolio management. The Vanguard Variable Annuity Plan is a low-cost insurance contract for individuals seeking tax-deferred growth for retirement savings. And Vanguard has taken its low-cost, high quality approach to mutual fund management abroad by establishing subsidiaries in Australia (1996) and Europe (1998).

PUTTING ITS CLIENTS FIRST

Vanguard's client-focused values set it apart. Vanguard manages its funds with prudence and an orientation to the long term. It works to ensure that each portfolio remains true to its stated objective and risk characteristics. Vanguard provides accurate and candid information to inform and educate its shareholders and prospective investors. Vanguard also carefully limits its marketing expenditures. Where other fund groups may spend enormous sums—derived, ultimately, from the assets of investors—on promotional efforts, Vanguard does not.

Nor does Vanguard follow the common practice of advertising past investment performance, which it considers to have limited predictive value.

Today Vanguard has more than 10,000 "crew members" (its nautical nomenclature for employees), most of whom operate from offices in Malvern, Pennsylvania; Scottsdale, Arizona; and Charlotte, North Carolina. This crew serves more than 14 million accounts for clients who have entrusted some $500 billion of their assets to a company they believe offers the industry's best combination of investment performance, service, and value.

A FOCUSED COMPANY

Vanguard bears in mind that every dollar invested in its mutual funds—even in the accounts of large pension plans or endowments—ultimately is destined for the use of individual human beings. In that sense, Vanguard serves only individual investors.

However, to meet the different service and record-keeping needs of individuals who invest on their own as well as those of institutions that are responsible for large sums or for helping their employees invest through retirement plans, Vanguard has two major operating divisions. These divisions—the Individual Investor Group and the Institutional Investor Group—deliver the special services their clients need. Each group is a recognized leader, offering a first-rate array of investment choices and

Vanguard is proud to have started and grown in Pennsylvania, from which it has drawn thousands of superb crew members.

services at costs well below those of the competition.

Both divisions also strive to innovate, continually pursuing ways to use new technology, new processes, or new investment options to better serve clients. And, of course, knowing that it is smart to keep the bosses happy, the crews of both divisions work solely for shareholders.

Vanguard believes that its success ultimately stems from its crew members' focus on the best interests of shareholders. This client-first ethic, one of Vanguard's founding principles, will continue to be the keystone for Vanguard in the new millennium.

THE**Vanguard**GROUP®

JANNEY MONTGOMERY SCOTT LLC

Providing many diversified products and services to more than 300,000 public, corporate, institutional, and individual

customers, Janney Montgomery Scott LLC offers its clients extensive experience, stability, and credibility.

Philadelphia-based Janney Montgomery Scott LLC (JMS) is a full-service brokerage and financial services firm that traces its history back to 1832. With approximately 1,600 employees nationwide, including more than 850 registered representatives, JMS is the largest full service regional brokerage firm headquartered in Pennsylvania.

Since 1982, JMS has been a subsidiary of another Delaware Valley–based institution, the Penn Mutual Life Insurance Company, with more than $10.3 billion in assets. Sturdy Delaware Valley roots continue to be a source of stability and growth for JMS.

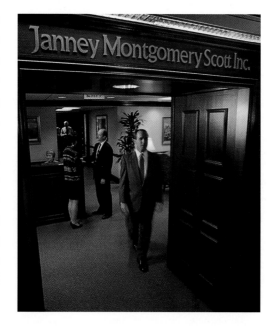

Janney Montgomery Scott is the largest Pennsylvania-based NYSE regional firm. Its Philadelphia headquarters serves as the nucleus of operations for 60 JMS offices that service clients throughout the country.

STATE-OF-THE-ART INVESTMENTS AND SERVICES

"At Janney Montgomery Scott we are very proud of our Pennsylvania heritage," says Rudolph C. Sander, chairman and CEO. "As the oldest New York Stock Exchange member firm headquartered in Philadelphia, we service investors through 60 offices from Massachusetts to

south Florida. Our 25 Pennsylvania offices provide individual clients with state-of-the-art investment services as well as proprietary investment research. Additionally, the JMS Public Finance Department facilitates funding for schools, hospitals, and municipalities throughout the state."

In the 1970s, JMS acquired Hoppin Watson, Inc., along with the second oldest seat on the New York Stock Exchange. JMS also has memberships in the American, Chicago, and Philadelphia Stock Exchanges, affiliated memberships in the Boston, Cincinnati, and Pacific Coast Stock Exchanges, and is active in the Nasdaq Stock Market. The firm's presence in these markets provides extensive block-trading capability, an important JMS function, but just one of the many diversified products and services JMS offers to more than 300,000 public, corporate, institutional, and individual customers.

The Public Finance Department handles everything from municipal underwriting and private placements to financial advisory services and arbitrage rebate reports. With offices in eight states and the District of Columbia, JMS has built a substantial bond distribution network, and its municipal bond department is one of the largest and most active in Pennsylvania.

JMS also ranks among the leading corporate investment banking organizations in its region. Longstanding relationships with major financial institutions have

Every day, more than 120 brokers in Janney Montgomery Scott's bustling boardroom in Philadelphia execute clients' orders in the various marketplaces where the firm trades.

helped make JMS one of the most active regional initial public offering (IPO) and follow-on underwriters.

Institutional services include research and fixed-income trading, as well as execution and block trading. The firm maintains its own highly regarded Investment Research Department, which provides a wealth of in-depth analysis and background material on local, regional, and national companies and industries. The department specializes in providing value-added research on companies headquartered in the mid-Atlantic area. The Institutional Sales Department markets this propri-etary research and investment banking issues to insti-tutional clients throughout the United States and internationally, while the Institutional Trading Desk provides professional execution services to retail as well as institutional customers.

REINVENTING RETAIL

JMS has always been primarily a retail firm, tailoring indi-vidual financial plans to individual investors' goals, and providing all the services and products required to meet those goals. The firm's corporate, institutional, and public finance activities serve to complement the retail category, which includes access to equities, both listed and unlisted; fixed-income vehicles; more than 5,000 mutual funds; insurance products; investment advisory services; and unit investment trusts. Associations with underwriters across the country provide JMS with a constant source of new securities issues for client participation.

JMS support staff are experts in estate and financial planning; equity and fixed-income research; asset management; tax-advantaged investments; participant-

JMS is one of the leading regional investment banking organizations. The codirectors of corporate finance spearhead the firm's services-rich investment banking division, which offers a menu of services including initial public offering (IPO) underwriting and the structuring and placement of private debt or equity securities.

directed IRAs, profit sharing, pension and 401(k) plans; corporate and public finance; and more. The Mutual Fund Department, for example, tracks more than 2,000 mutual funds annually, narrowing them down to the 250 most promising.

Both individual and institutional investors can take advantage of Janney Money Management Services, with its wide array of coordinated investment consulting services, from asset allocations strategies to quarterly performance reports. Janney Retirement Plan Services designs and implements 401(k) and other plans, map-ping out qualified plan options, benefit ideas, cost-saving strategies, and investment alternatives.

Amid a growing tendency toward "go-it-alone" investing, it is reassuring to find a firm like JMS that is still customer- and service-oriented. Whether they want a professional adviser to help design a customized invest-ment profile, or simply prefer to consolidate banking and brokerage activities into one easy-to-manage account, individuals can choose from a wide array of investment options created just for them, from the Keystone Advisory Account to the Janney Central Asset Account.

In a rapidly changing industry, JMS continues to build on a long tradition of stability and leadership, while focusing on one thing: a commitment to provid-ing the best possible financial products and services at competitive prices.

The fixed-income trading room is at the heart of JMS's bond ser-vices. The firm's ability to distribute bonds is extensive, with a substantial retail distribution network of registered representa-tives in its multiple office system covering eight states and the District of Columbia.

Janney Montgomery Scott LLC

A *tradition of excellence since* 1832

Members: New York Stock Exchange and SIPC

HUDSON UNITED BANK

With a friendly spirit, a dedication to customer service, and a commitment to excellence in every aspect of business, Hudson United Bank strives to meet the financial needs of the many communities it serves.

Hudson United Bank welcomes you to banking as it should be. Founded in 1890, Hudson United Bank brings a friendly spirit and a commitment to excellence to everything it does.

Community-oriented, Hudson United Bank strives to deliver superior banking products and services in a friendly, warm environment. Hudson employees greet each and every customer at the door with a warm smile, while delivering unparalleled customer service. Hudson United is a bank

Richard A. Grasso, chairman of The New York Stock Exchange, and Kenneth T. Neilson, president, chairman, and CEO of Hudson United Bank discuss financial strategies.

Hudson United Bank is a community-oriented bank striving to deliver superior banking products and services in a friendly, warm environment.

Rendall Banks, VP-finance of Edwards Engineering; Gerald Werdann, CPA at Werdann DeVito; Luis Nieves, SVP of Hudson United Bank; and Richard Waldrop, president of Edwards Engineering. Edwards Engineering is a client of Hudson United Bank's Commercial Lending division.

that takes the time to get to know its customers, understand their individual needs, and find solutions to help them meet their short- and long-term goals.

"Our difference lies in always delivering our services in a friendly, respectful way. I believe that kind of attention will make us stand out in the marketplace," says Kenneth T. Neilson, president, chairman, and CEO. "And we are committed to delivering on our goal: making our customers' experience a truly superior one—one that separates us from our competition and sets a new standard for community banking."

SUPERIOR SERVICE

Hudson United Bank's excellent customer service has been more than 100 years in the making. With $9.5 billion in assets, Hudson United is the second largest banking company headquartered in New Jersey with branches located throughout New York, New Jersey, Connecticut, and most recently in southeastern Pennsylvania, with the merger of Jefferson Bank. While the bank is continually growing, it currently offers more than 200 branches and employs approximately 2,100 people.

"For all of us, the customer experience defines who we are. It is how a customer feels about us after each contact that decides whether he or she will do business with us again, or recommend us to a friend or colleague," says Neilson. "The way to create this loyalty among our customers is to prove to them every day that we are committed to taking the time to understand their financial needs, and to providing them with the best possible solutions."

INNOVATIVE PRODUCTS

Hudson United Bank offers a full array of innovative products and services to the retail and commercial markets. The bank gladly provides customers with a complete line of personal banking products and services including imaged checking accounts, state-of-the-art 24-hour telephone banking, bilingual ATM networks across the region, loans by phone, alternative investments, insurance products, trust services, mortgages, and a wide variety of consumer loans. And it is all delivered with the kind of personal service and hometown attention that has made Hudson United "a community bank." Its exclusive focus on local markets combined with a closely-knit organization allows customers direct access to senior management and provides the bank with a competitive advantage in attracting customers.

DEDICATION TO BUSINESS COMMUNITIES

Hudson United Bank remains just as dedicated to the growth and success of Philadelphia's business communities. The bank has successfully helped thousands of Philadelphia area businesses grow and has given new ones a chance to get a start and prosper in the community. The bank is able to provide them with a wide variety of commercial loans and services, including international services, cash management, asset-based loans, SBA loans, and private label credit programs.

"Hudson United Bank is an organization with a mission to provide superior financial products and services to its customers throughout the communities it serves," says Neilson.

MELLON FINANCIAL CORPORATION

Headquartered in Pittsburgh since 1869, Mellon Financial Corporation and its 13,000 employees in Pennsylvania

provide a global reach and a range of products to continue meeting the financial needs of each generation.

Like the city and state in which it is headquartered, Mellon Financial Corporation is focused on being the best. With a commitment to providing customer solutions while expanding its leadership in high-growth businesses, Mellon is well positioned to meet the changes that will dominate the financial services industry into the 21st century.

Mellon is proud to have played a significant role in shaping Pennsylvania's past and looks forward to helping to define the state's future. Established in 1869 as T. Mellon & Sons' Bank, Mellon financed the birth of the steel, coke, and aluminum industries in western Pennsylvania and along the East Coast. Over the years Mellon also has fostered the development and growth of companies across the nation and around the world. In addition, as a responsive and responsible corporate citizen, Mellon has long recognized the importance of supporting organizations and activities that drive community development and improve quality of life. It believes strong, ongoing partnerships with its communities foster a positive atmosphere that benefits everyone.

MELLON TODAY
During the late 1980s, with the future of many financial services firms in doubt, innovative thinking along with significant restructuring of Mellon's businesses enabled the corporation to embark upon a renewed strategy designed for growth and return.

Mellon continued its innovative strategic thinking into the 1990s, when it introduced supermarket banking to western Pennsylvania.

Mellon Financial Corporation offers the most choices, convenience, and flexibility for its customers, providing nearly 100 retail stores located in two major grocery chains throughout its operating region.

This program, which has since been expanded to central and eastern Pennsylvania, Delaware, and New Jersey markets, is just one component of a long-term strategic initiative to reconfigure Mellon's retail delivery system. Mellon's goal is to provide customers with greater convenience, service, information, and choice by striking a balance between high-tech and "high-touch" to achieve the right mix of electronic services—telephone, Internet, and video banking—and personal interaction. Mellon expanded its

Mellon recognizes the power of the Internet. The firm continues to focus on technology to meet customer needs and is proud to be a leading technology innovator within the financial services industry.

business banking presence through its 1998 acquisitions of Miami-based United National Bank and the Los Angeles–based 1st Business Bank. Both of these important acquisitions are consistent with Mellon's strategy to expand into geographic areas where there are significant growth opportunities.

A GLOBAL FINANCIAL SERVICES COMPANY

As a major player in the asset management and trust and custody businesses, with more than $2.8 trillion in assets under management, administration, or custody, including more than $500 billion under management, Mellon has a long history of providing investment expertise to consumers, corporations, state and local governments, and other large institutions. Its presence in this arena increased considerably in 1993, following the acquisition of highly regarded The Boston Company, which added substantially to Mellon's institutional trust, investment, and private client businesses.

A year later, Mellon furthered its thrust into the investment business with its landmark merger with The Dreyfus Corporation—the largest combination of a banking firm and a mutual fund company in history. The merger created a trust and money management powerhouse and added a highly respected industry brand name to Mellon's group of businesses. Mellon further expanded this presence with its 1998 acquisitions of Denver-based Founders Asset Management and London-based Newton Management Limited.

Nineteen ninety-nine was a benchmark year for Mellon as a new leadership team, led by chairman and chief executive officer Martin G. McGuinn, sharpened the corporation's strategic focus and set the ambitious goal of becoming the best performing financial services company. Nineteen ninety-nine also saw Mellon successfully and aggressively make the transition to the year 2000. In the *InformationWeek* 500 annual survey of top information technology innovators, Mellon was named one of the five best financial services companies in the United States and overall, with a renewed emphasis on technology as a business tool to continually improve its service to customers, 31st among all companies for innovation and effective application of technology. And in a survey conducted by

the *Financial Times*, Mellon was ranked one of the five most respected global financial services companies. A new E-commerce team was created and works with business line managers to help Mellon provide customers with greater financial choices, control, and convenience via the Internet.

FOCUSED ON BEING THE BEST

As Mellon moves into this new millennium, competition, consolidation, and new products and services are constantly reshaping the global financial services industry. To survive and prosper in this dynamic environment, Mellon follows a strategy of providing a wealth of solutions to all of its customers, expanding its leadership in its high-growth businesses, and delivering superior and sustainable returns for shareholders.

"In short, our goal is to be the best performing financial services company," McGuinn says. "While this statement is simple on its face, it requires serious thought, commitment, and superb execution of our strategy. Becoming the best is an evolutionary process that takes hard work and dedication of all of Mellon's employees who are leading the charge to meet or exceed customer expectations."

Driven by the needs of its customers, Mellon has expanded its geographic reach and its range of financial services and products. Mellon employees, including more than 13,000 strong in Pennsylvania, have maintained a strategic balance that controls risk and provides the flexibility necessary to respond effectively and quickly to an ever-changing business environment. Mellon has prepared to handle well the profound responsibility of meeting the financial services needs of each generation, both in its headquarters city of Pittsburgh and around the globe.

ALLFIRST FINANCIAL INC.

With a heritage of serving central Pennsylvania, Allfirst Financial Inc., a regional, diversified financial services company, offers banking, trust, investment, and insurance to retail, small business, and commercial customers.

Allfirst Bank's South Heidelberg branch, near Reading, Pennsylvania, was one of the first to use the new Allfirst signage, in 1999.

Allfirst Financial Inc. aims to be first by placing its customers first. Allfirst strives to be the most approachable, responsive, and innovative financial services company in the communities it serves—and the company's efforts are paying off. Allfirst is fast developing a reputation as the "human bank."

A regional, diversified financial services company, Allfirst has a strong Pennsylvania presence and deep roots in the region. The company offers a full range of financial services, including banking, trust, investment, and insurance to retail, small business, and commercial customers.

"We seek to instill in our customers the trust and confidence that is so important to deep, enduring relationships," says Paul B. Shannon, president of Allfirst Bank, Pennsylvania, with headquarters in Harrisburg. "By understanding the goals and the challenges of current and potential customers, we can more effectively use our capabilities and resources to help both achieve their goals."

STRONG PENNSYLVANIA ROOTS

Allfirst has a proud heritage of serving central Pennsylvania, tracing its Pennsylvania roots back to 1810 with the York Bank & Trust Company and to 1835 with the Harrisburg Savings Association (HSA). In 1905, HSA became known as Dauphin Deposit Trust Company, one of the strongest banks in central Pennsylvania. Dauphin Deposit survived the Great Depression of 1929

Paul Shannon, president of Allfirst Bank, Pennsylvania, is leading the bank into the new millennium.

and went on to build a sterling reputation as one of the safest banks in the United States.

In 1983, Allied Irish Banks, p.l.c. (AIB), Ireland's leading financial services company, made its initial investment in First Maryland Bancorp and then completed its purchase of 100 percent of the company's shares in 1989. At the time, this was the fifth largest investment ever made in a United States bank by a foreign company.

First Maryland Bancorp acquired York Bank in 1991. During a period of several years, Dauphin acquired Bank of Pennsylvania, Valleybank, and Farmers Bank and then became part of First Maryland Bancorp in 1997.

Throughout the years, AIB's investment has paid off handsomely. The First Maryland franchise has grown into a regional powerhouse that extends from northern Virginia, through Washington, D.C., and Maryland, and into central Pennsylvania.

This company's reputation for resiliency and success during changing times is still evident today. Each addition to its family has enhanced the company's heritage as a bank deeply rooted in this market and committed to the traditional values of trust, security, and loyalty.

The company has grown rapidly in the past decade, and was operating under seven different bank names until mid-1999. To bolster brand identity as a single, unified financial institution, on June 28, 1999, the First Maryland Bancorp family of banks became Allfirst Financial Inc. The new name embodies the strengths and traditions of its heritage as well as its hopes and expectations for the future. A new logo greets customers with a single image of strength, commitment to service, and an unrelenting desire to help customers succeed.

The holding company's banking subsidiary, Allfirst Bank, operates more than 260 bank branches—about half of which are located in Pennsylvania—and more than 575 ATMs. Allfirst Financial Inc.'s assets were $17.5 billion as of December 31, 1999, making it the 43rd largest bank in the United States. Allfirst now accounts for approximately one-third of the assets of AIB, its parent company.

Allfirst employees are involved in numerous community service activities throughout the year, including this volunteer landscaping project, in which employees participated during United Way's Day of Caring.

DIVERSE CAPABILITIES

With nationally renowned cash management systems, small business and middle-market expertise, and the international advantage of AIB, Allfirst is able to meet global needs with a regional presence and a community focus.

Allfirst Financial Inc. includes the following subsidiary companies: Allfirst Bank, Allfirst Financial Center N.A., Allfirst Trust Company N.A., Allfirst Brokerage Company, Zirkin-Cutler Investments Inc., Allied Investment Advisors, Allfirst Life Insurance Corporation, Allfirst Insurance Corporation, Allfirst Annuities Agency Corporation, Allfirst Mortgage Corporation, and Allfirst Leasing Corporation.

Allfirst's commitment to excellence goes beyond the financial services it offers and extends into enhancing the quality of life in the communities it serves. The company's community involvement includes a range of health, education, and civic programs, services, and activities that touch the lives of home owners, businesses, entrepreneurs, neighborhood development organizations, and more. In Pennsylvania, Allfirst actively supports a variety of community organizations, including the Allison Hill Revitalization project in Harrisburg, the Susquehanna Housing Initiative, Lancaster's Inner City Revitalization Group, Drug Free Pennsylvania, the Whitaker Center for Science and the Arts, and many more.

"The men and women of Allfirst are not just bankers, they are caring neighbors who live and work in the communities they serve," Shannon says. "At Allfirst, our commitment to our communities is very strong."

For additional information about Allfirst Financial Inc., visit the company's World Wide Web site at www.allfirst.com.

THE PNC FINANCIAL SERVICES GROUP

A national diversified financial services organization, The PNC Financial Services Group is committed to

delivering insightful thinking and extensive product capabilities.

Internet-based capabilities. These Web products include 30-second responses to on-line auto and home equity loan applications, on-line certificate of deposit auctions, Web bill payment, and more.

Technology has also been a key driver in enabling PNC Mortgage to introduce a breakthrough mortgage origination process. Customers can now receive a mortgage commitment from PNC in as few as 30 minutes, with minimal paperwork.

Innovative products extend to business customers as well. While PNC is among the largest small business lenders in the nation, customers can also expand their marketing capabilities with E-commerce Web site development through iSites@PNC. PNC's Treasury Management

PNC is recognized as a technology leader in financial services. Innovative technologies are utilized to drive efficiency and enhance products, services, and interactions with customers in the new economy.

"The Thinking Behind the Money" is more than a tag line for The PNC Financial Services Group. It is a promise to customers that PNC delivers insightful thinking and proven solutions for every stage of life.

Whether meeting the financial needs of individuals, families, small businesses, or the corporate and institutional sectors, PNC's seven businesses are dedicated to helping each customer realize his or her financial goals.

Commitment to the highest levels of service and profitability has earned PNC a leadership position in a highly competitive industry. A good example of this prominence is consumer banking. PNC Bank, Pennsylvania's largest bank, has built one of the industry's strongest distribution systems, with the largest ATM network in the region, more than 700 branch offices, one of the country's top call centers, and a leading array of

Leadership has long been key to PNC's growth. Pictured from right, Thomas H. O'Brien, chairman; James E. Rohr, president and chief executive officer; and Walter E. Gregg Jr., vice chairman.

business is also distinguished by best-of-class technology—it is a leading national provider of electronic bill presentment and payment.

INVESTMENT EXPERTISE

Larger investors can rely on PNC's reputation, knowledge, and strong foundation when it comes to addressing complex financial situations. PNC Advisors and its Hilliard Lyons subsidiary have grown into one of the nation's 10 largest managers of trusts and assets for high net worth individuals.

With more than $172 billion in assets under management, PNC's BlackRock is among the nation's largest providers of asset and risk management services. The firm offers a full menu of investment products, including 47 mutual funds, and also serves more than 3,000 institutional clients in 16 countries.

PNC has been the presenting sponsor of the world-class Philadelphia Flower Show for the past nine years. Produced by the Pennsylvania Horticultural Society, it is the world's largest indoor flower show and is a testament to PNC's active role in the community. © Robert Ikeler

COMMUNITY SUPPORT

Showing there's a heart behind the thinking, PNC values giving back to the communities it serves. In 1999, the PNC Foundation gave more than $10 million to charities and other nonprofit organizations that help with community development, cultural and artistic endeavors, educational programs, and health and human services programs.

The sponsorship of PNC Park, home of MLB's Pittsburgh Pirates, continues PNC's legacy of supporting the state's businesses, residents, and historic institutions. PNC has also been the proud presenting sponsor of the globally recognized Philadelphia Flower Show and many other Pennsylvania institutions.

Not surprisingly, PNC was ranked among the "100 Best Corporate Citizens" by *Business Ethics*, for its

exceptional commitment to its communities, employees and customers. Additionally, *Fortune* magazine recognized PNC as the fifth "Most Admired" company among super regional banks.

James E. Rohr, PNC president and chief executive officer says, "Our success is founded upon the collective efforts of more than 26,000 members of the PNC family, and I have never been more proud of their achievements. It is my great privilege to lead this company; we have truly transitioned the organization to become a national diversified financial services firm that can make Pennsylvania proud."

PNC's partnership with the Pittsburgh Pirates enhances the team's future and will provide valuable coast-to-coast recognition and exposure for the entire PNC organization.

SOVEREIGN BANK

As a "large full-service bank with a small bank touch," Sovereign Bank appreciates its rich past and remains focused on developing a prosperous future for its customers, its shareholders, and its team members.

Sovereign Bank's corporate headquarters is located in Wyomissing, Pennsylvania.

In this era of unprecedented and turbulent change, the banking industry has been confronting major challenges in regulation, competition, technology, and rising expectations of customers, shareholders, and employees. Communities across the nation remain dependent upon reliable banks for everything financial. To successfully accommodate these wide-ranging demands, it requires imagination, determination, leadership, and sound strategy—qualities that characterize eastern Pennsylvania's Sovereign Bank.

Headquartered in Wyomissing (near Reading), Pennsylvania, Sovereign is the third largest financial institution with home offices in Pennsylvania. With the acquisition of New England's FleetBoston in summer 2000, Sovereign now operates approximately 600 community banking offices and more than 1,000 ATMs in Pennsylvania, Delaware, New Jersey, Connecticut, New Hampshire, Rhode Island, and Massachusetts.

Sovereign Bank's Pennsylvania roots date back to 1875 to the Lancaster County banking community of Union Building and Loan, Industrial Building and Loan, and Home Building and Loan Associations. Its history in Berks County began in 1902 with the Wyomissing Building and Loan Association.

A key component of Sovereign's success has been its program of banking operations acquisitions (approximately two dozen since 1989). Sovereign Bancorp, Inc., a thrift holding company, was formed in 1987 and has expanded through a number of acquisitions from Pennsylvania to Delaware, New Jersey, and New England. Along the way, it has steadily built regional capabilities and strengths.

MAJOR LINES OF BUSINESS

Sovereign provides the full array of commercial products to small and medium-size businesses including traditional loans and lines of credit, asset-based lending, cash management, electronic banking, international banking, and private banking services. A key difference from other banks in its class is the world-class service offered by Sovereign's notably experienced relationship managers, most of whom possess more than 15 years of commercial lending experience. These veteran bankers are able to maintain Sovereign's strong credit quality and to provide superior counsel—and confidence—to staff and customers. Additionally, the bank's business portfolio is appropriately industry-diverse and increasingly protected from local and regional fluctuations by its complementary operations from New England to Delaware.

Complementing Sovereign's commercial framework are its consumer lending and community banking activities, including an alliance with LendingTree.com, a well-respected Internet company whose imaginative marketing has substantially increased Sovereign's loan originations via the Internet.

A STRONG INTERNET PRESENCE

In 1999, Sovereign launched its stand-alone "e-bank"— 1stwebbankdirect. Its primary focus is "affinity marketing"—developing personalized banking relationships with entire organizations.

Sovereign Bank sponsors the Sports Park at Governor Mifflin, Pennsylvania.

Sovereign Bank accepts an award from the Caron Foundation for its outstanding support.

Sovereign first introduced this delivery system to corporations, universities, and not-for-profit organizations in agreements with multiple affinity groups that offer access to eight million potential customers.

Sovereign recognizes that achieving its objectives requires not only sound management but also the consistent performance of a dedicated and competent team. Therefore, it has implemented both a supportive atmosphere for its people as well as concrete programs to ensure its team's success. The company consistently refers to its people not as employees, but as team members. The bank's human resources department is keenly selective in hiring suitable people, and Sovereign's comprehensive training program ensures that every team member is well-informed

and highly skilled. A team member program called "The Sovereign Way" utilizes five, four-week modules to build skills and strategies: customer relationships; listening and communications skills; accuracy and productivity; customized solutions; and customer satisfaction.

Another powerful tool is the SovNet Connection, the bank's internal web site. It encompasses a constantly updated vehicle to provide team members with access to information regarding the bank's products and teams. Team members can order supplies on-line and locate co-workers, as well as view internal newsletters, sales materials, rate sheets, and other useful information at any time.

Continuing its historic dedication to diligence and imagination, Sovereign appreciates its past and remains focused on a productive future for its customers, its shareholders, and its team members. This full-service bank, with a small community touch, strives to fulfill its ambitious mission, "To anticipate the financial needs of our customers and, using the best information systems and financial services available, provide them with customized solutions."

Team members celebrate "The Sovereign Way" at a monthly recognition luncheon.

SOVEREIGN BANCORP, INC. STATISTICS

	1986	2000
Assets	$660 million	$35 billion (pro forma*)
Branches	19	570 (pro forma*)
Operating Income	$4.2 million	$202.3 million
Market Value	$29 million	$1.7 billion
Market Position	20th in PA	Among top 25 in the United States

• As of March 31, 2000

Sovereign Bank

Success is confidence. We can help you get there.™

CHAPTER FIFTEEN

PENNSYLVANIA ON THE MOVE

TRANSPORTATION AND DISTRIBUTION

By 1800, the port city of Philadelphia was shipping more than one-third of the United States' exports, far more than its nearest rivals, New York City and Baltimore. As the century unfolded, Pennsylvania's transportation industry realized spectacular growth, especially as railroads efficiently moved fuel, raw materials, and finished products to factories and consumers throughout the nation. • Today, of course, transportation options in the state are better than ever.

Forty-two urban and rural transit systems are in operation, including Philadelphia-based SEPTA, the nation's fourth largest system, and the Pittsburgh-based Port Authority of Allegheny County, the 13th largest. In 1997–98, originating passengers totalled 287,657,820 and vehicle miles totaled 157,957,525. The industry saw substantial job gains during the 1990s—particularly in local and interurban transit, which grew by 8,887 jobs (37 percent) from 1990 to 1997.

RISE OF THE RAILS

The early-19th-century success of New York's Erie Canal inspired Commonwealth leaders to construct a canal system between Philadelphia and Pittsburgh. The result incorporated both canals and railroads—including the innovative Allegheny Portage Railroad, which employed steam engines to literally lift the canal boats up a series of inclined planes over the formidable Allegheny Ridge east of Pittsburgh. By that time, however, entrepreneurs were already experimenting with short-line railroads to transport natural resources from mines and quarries to canals. A group of Philadelphia businessmen obtained a charter to connect Philadelphia and Pittsburgh by rail, and in 1846 they incorporated the Pennsylvania Railroad. An enormous, gently increasing grade of curved track, the Horseshoe Curve, finally enabled trains to mount the Allegheny Ridge, and by 1854 the entire route was open.

During the 1860s, the now expanded Pennsylvania Railroad and others in the Commonwealth, including the Reading, Lehigh Valley, and Lackawanna and Western, formed a comprehensive network that served all but a few very rural areas by the turn of the century.

As progress continued, a newer form of transportation offering even greater mobility was developed: the automobile. Americans turned to cars, and the golden age of railroads closed. By 1970, many of the country's railroads, including Pennsylvania's, had declared bankruptcy. Recognizing their importance to the economy, Congress created Amtrak that same year and Conrail (a consolidation of the Northeast-Midwest railroads) in 1976, to continue America's passenger and freight rail service. Both were successful, and in 1987 the government returned Philadelphia-based Conrail to the private sector as a for-profit corporation.

A sleek SEPTA commuter train glides into Philadelphia's busy 30th Street Station. The nation's fourth largest transit system, SEPTA is in the process of a five-year, $2 billion capital improvement program.

PHOTOS: THIS PAGE, © *John McGrail;* OPPOSITE PAGE, © *Jim McWilliams Photography*

Today, Amtrak serves Pennsylvania's 4.5 million rail passengers per year, operating about 100 trains per day over 700 route-miles through the state. Philadelphia's 30th Street Station, part of Amtrak's well-traveled Northeast Corridor, is the line's second busiest station in the nation. Ridership between Philadelphia and Harrisburg, the Keystone Corridor, nearly tripled between 1995 and the end of 1999, causing Amtrak and the Pennsylvania Department of Transportation (PennDOT) to allocate $140 million for the creation of the state's first high-speed rail corridor on this route over the next five years.

A new light-rail system, the Schuylkill Valley Metro, is being planned to connect Philadelphia with Reading, not only offering an alternative to busy Route 422 but also spurring development in reemerging, postindustrial communities such as Phoenixville.

SETTING THE PACE: SUPERHIGHWAYS

By the end of the 18th century, Pennsylvania entrepreneurs were determined to improve the rough roads over which Conestoga freight wagons brought foodstuffs to market. Their resolve led to the building of America's first macadam turnpike, completed in 1794, linking Philadelphia and Lancaster. Many other turnpikes followed, both in Pennsylvania and other states.

In 1903, the Pennsylvania General Assembly passed the Sproul-Roberts Act creating the Pennsylvania Department of Public Highways; by 1911 this act had cleared the way for the reconstruction of main highways

Its journey complete, a freighter prepares to dock and unload its cargo. The nation's only state with freshwater, inland, and Great Lakes ports, Pennsylvania is a thriving distribution center.

and had laid the groundwork for the state highway system by dedicating millions of dollars to road improvements. In the 1930s, rural dirt roads were paved.

In the 1930s, too, initial surveys were made for a modern highway that would traverse the state. It was decided to follow the abandoned route of the defunct South Pennsylvania Railroad, from Harrisburg to Pittsburgh. In 1937, the Pennsylvania Turnpike Commission was created to orchestrate it.

When the Pennsylvania Turnpike opened in 1940, it was America's first four-lane, long-distance highway that also was free of intersections, sharp curves, and steep inclines, enabling vehicles to stay in high gear clear across the state. Among the many new concepts incorporated in its design were its layout—on southern exposures, where possible, so the sun could melt the ice and snow on the roads—and its off-turnpike tollbooth positioning on downhill grades, so that drivers might see the booths in time to react rather than be surprised by them. The interstate highway system, begun in the late 1940s, was built on many of the concepts learned and tested on the Pennsylvania Turnpike. From its initial 160 miles of highway, today's turnpike stretches 506 miles across the state, including the Northeast Extension, completed in 1957 between Philadelphia and Scranton. Continuously

Adtranz, of Pittsburgh, developed the world's first totally automated transit system, installed at the new Pittsburgh International Airport in 1992. Today the company's systems loop through city centers around the globe, connecting offices, shops, and hotels.

improved over the years, the Pennsylvania Turnpike has one of the lowest fatality rates in the country.

The state acquired a second east-west highway in the 1950s, as part of the interstate system. Interstate 80, linking New York City with Chicago and the Midwest, went through a relatively undeveloped part of Pennsylvania. Communities along the route took advantage of the opportunity to offer services to truckers and long-distance travelers.

Today, highways remain one of the largest components of Pennsylvania's transportation network. The Commonwealth has the nation's fourth largest state-maintained system of highways, with 119,128 miles of roadway, or 269,435,000 daily vehicle-miles of travel. PennDOT (created in 1970 as the successor to the earlier department of highways) develops and maintains the state highways as well as other transportation services and facilities. In recent years, thanks to additional revenue, commuters and travelers have seen dramatic improvements in maintenance, resulting in smoother rides and better winter road conditions.

WINGING INTO A NEW ERA

Early in the 20th century, daring air shows all over the country fascinated many spectators. But air transportation became more commercial and professional after 1918, when the U.S. Post Office Department began running its Air Mail Service. A new concept, passenger air service, was tested during America's sesquicentennial in 1926 by the Philadelphia Rapid Transit Company, which offered service between Philadelphia, Washington, and Norfolk. The Ludington Line, a passenger

airline owned by the Ludington Exhibition Company, began service in the 1930s from New York City to Washington, D.C., via Philadelphia; the company was the forerunner of Eastern Airlines. In the same period, All American Aviation established airmail service to many small towns in western Pennsylvania, transitioning to a passenger airline in 1949. It later became Allegheny Airlines, eventually expanding into today's US Airways. After World War II, larger and safer planes were being built and more and more people were flying. The jet age came into being, necessitating major improvements at airports throughout the nation, including Pennsylvania.

Today Pennsylvania ranks fourth in the nation in both the number of airports and the number of landing facilities per square mile, with nearly 800 airports, heliports, and private airstrips. Thirty-one foreign and domestic carriers serve the Commonwealth.

Philadelphia International Airport (PIA) is America's fastest growing airport, serving more than 24.2 million passengers per year. Passenger volume increased by 8 percent in 1998 as US Airways developed new service at its Philadelphia hub. PIA is currently undergoing a major capital improvement program; a new 45,000-square-foot retail mall, Philadelphia Marketplace at the Airport, is already in place. An expansion project to be completed by the end of 2001 will add a spacious new $400 million international terminal that is expected to more than double service from Philadelphia. Another regional terminal is being built to accommodate the operations of US Airways Express, a network of nine regional airlines that is part of the US Airways system.

An airliner comes in for a landing at one of the state's 147 public airports. Pennsylvania ranks fourth in the nation in both the number of airports and the number of landing facilities per square mile and is served by 31 carriers.

Pittsburgh International Airport serves more than 20 million passengers annually and is the principal hub for US Airways, which offers 508 daily departures to both domestic and international destinations from this hub.

Among smaller international airports, Harrisburg International handled 1.5 million passengers in 1998. The Lehigh Valley International Airport (LVIA), near Allentown, is seeing increased passenger traffic thanks to affordable nonstop jet service to Orlando, Florida, and an aggressive advertising campaign to make consumers aware that LVIA is a hassle-free alternative for access to eastern Pennsylvania and northern New Jersey.

When it comes to aircraft production, the venerable name of Boeing reverberates throughout Philadelphia. The company's Rotorcraft Program Management Center in the city handles all Boeing helicopter production, including the CH-47 Chinooks the company began with in 1960, as well as new CH-47SD Chinooks with advanced avionics, AH-64 Apaches, and others. Boeing Philadelphia is Pennsylvania's largest manufacturer, providing jobs for more than 5,000 people.

A HEIGHTENED STATE OF DISTRIBUTION

The Commonwealth has an enormous advantage in its location. More than 40 percent of America's population and purchasing power and 60 percent of Canada's lie within a 500-mile radius of the state capital in Harrisburg.

Pennsylvania has three major ports, providing access to the Atlantic Ocean (the Port of Philadelphia and Camden, on the Delaware River), the St. Lawrence Seaway (the Port of Erie, on Lake Erie), and the Ohio and Mississippi Rivers (the Port of Pittsburgh, on the Ohio, Monongahela, and Allegheny Rivers). It is America's only state with freshwater, inland, and Great Lakes ports. The Port of Philadelphia and Camden is directly accessible to more major cities by rail and truck than any other port in the country, permitting next-day or second-day cargo delivery to 65 percent of the United States and 67 percent of Canada. It offers state-of-the-art moving facilities and specialized facilities for perishable cargo. The Port of Pittsburgh is the busiest inland port in the nation. This port moves over 45 million

High-tech mapping and graphics, along with live traffic cams, are tools of the trade for this planner, who is compiling route information at the regional Smartroute Systems Operation Center in Philadelphia.

tons of cargo each year, making it larger in tonnage than the ports of Los Angeles, Baltimore, or Philadelphia.

Pennsylvania's specialized warehousing and distribution firms meet the demands of numerous food-processing and other companies and act as a magnet for international exporters. The Port of Philadelphia and Camden, for example, has over 1,060,000 square feet of on-terminal, temperature-controlled storage and access to more than 125 port-oriented trucking companies. From Pennsylvania, products are easily shipped to every other state in the country and to Canada, Mexico, and South America. The quality and efficiency of warehousing and distribution in Pennsylvania ensure that Commonwealth ports will continue to be a rudder of the nation's commerce in the new millennium.

NEVER SAY DIE

The first cars for Philadelphia's trolleys, or street railways, were drawn by horses. The J. G. Brill Company was one of the first to build horseless trolley cars, and their products were eventually used all over the world. Although very few real trolleys are still running today, Philadelphia has several buses specifically designed to resemble that city's old trolleys.

US AIRWAYS

By supplying its employees with the best technologies available, US Airways leaps into the front ranks of airlines worldwide, serving more than 200 destinations around the globe.

Modern, new airport facilities throughout the US Airways system are welcomed by customers and employees alike. © Cameron Davidson

Since its founding 60 years ago, US Airways has confidently weathered many changes, though few have been as profound as those of the past few years. During that time, US Airways has successfully transformed itself from a regional air carrier to a world-class international competitor, and established a solid, broad-based platform for improved market position.

In addition to being the fifth largest domestic air carrier in the United States (based on passengers flown), US Airways now ranks as a global carrier with more than 200 destinations worldwide, including 38 states and the District of Columbia, Bermuda, Cancun, Grand Cayman, Montego Bay, Nassau, San Juan, St. Thomas, St. Maarten, St. Croix, and the Canadian cities of Toronto, Montreal, Ottawa, Hamilton, and London, Ontario. Transatlantic destinations include Frankfurt, London, Madrid, Manchester, Munich, Paris, and Rome.

US Airways has come a long way from its beginnings in 1939 as an airmail service called All American Aviation. The new company's pilots and flight mechanics, backed by a team of dedicated ground personnel, carried the mail to isolated towns in the Allegheny Mountains of western Pennsylvania. Those skillful flyers who braved severe weather and rugged terrain in the line of duty also brought romance and adventure to the early years of the aviation industry.

The "flying post office" turned out to be profitable as well as exciting, and in 1949 the company moved its headquarters to the Washington, D.C., area, renamed itself All American Airways, and made the transition to passenger service. Changing its name again in 1953 to Allegheny Airlines, Inc., the company commenced a quarter-century of rapid expansion as it forged an innovative network of commuter carriers. To reflect its increasing size and scope, Allegheny became USAir in 1979. Within a decade, USAir acquired first PSA, a major West Coast carrier, and then North Carolina–based Piedmont Aviation—the largest merger in airline history—creating a comprehensive nationwide network, with international service to Canada, Mexico, and the United Kingdom.

Under the new leadership of Stephen M. Wolf and Rakesh Gangwal, the late 1990s saw some of US Airways'

The new international terminal in Philadelphia, scheduled to open in 2002, will more than double space for flights to foreign destinations.

US Airways is the first U.S. carrier to fly the Airbus A330-300 aircraft, which carries 266 passengers in three-class service.

U·S AIRWAYS

most significant challenges and achievements. Since February 1996, when USAir became US Airways, annual revenues have increased 15 percent to $8.6 billion; passenger load factor has increased 8 percent to 70.1 percent. Before 1996, US Airways served two European destinations, now it serves seven; a fleet that was aging is now being rejuvenated; and a once-shrinking route system is expanding both at home and abroad.

US Airways employs some 45,000 workers worldwide, including more than 17,700 in Pennsylvania. Three US Airways hubs, at Pittsburgh and Philadelphia, Pennsylvania, and Charlotte, North Carolina, serve the most heavily populated aviation market in the world. As shown in flights and passengers-carried data provided by the U.S. Department of Transportation and Industry, US Airways is the largest carrier in the Washington-Baltimore area and the first- or second-largest carrier at more than 40 cities in the eastern United States, including most of Pennsylvania's major airports. Through its travel affiliates—US Airways Express, MetroJet, and US Airways Shuttle—and a widening European presence, US Airways is positioned as never before to develop its full potential in the eastern United States, the source of roughly 70 percent of transatlantic traffic.

US Airways Express, a network of nine regional airlines, offers more than 2,600 daily departures at 175 airports throughout the United States, Canada, and the Bahamas. MetroJet, the low-fare, quality all-coach service launched by US Airways in 1998, links major East Coast cities with Florida destinations among other routes. Meanwhile, US Airways' Shuttle is uniquely focused on

the busy Northeast Corridor business markets between Boston and New York; New York and Washington, D.C.; and Boston and Washington, D.C. US Airways' mainline flies to many medium-sized North American cities, and hopes to add places such as Milan, Zurich, Brussels, and Manchester to its current transatlantic destinations. New Airbus A330-300 wide-bodies join the fleet in 2000 and a spacious new $400 million international terminal is under construction at Philadelphia, further enhancing US Airways' service to its burgeoning European network.

US Airways has given its highly dedicated employees two key tools with which to carry out its strategy for the future. The first is fleet revitalization: as many as 400 new Airbus A319s, A320s, and A321s are being added to its fleet, replacing older aircraft. The second is the introduction of the latest computer technology from The SABRE Group in critical areas such as reservations, crew scheduling, yield management, and airport services. In preparation for the new technology and aircraft, 1.5 million hours have been devoted to training more than 24,000 employees throughout the company.

US Airways employees already are using these tools with the positive attitude, excellence, and team spirit necessary to build a world-class global carrier. Working together flight by flight, they have the proven intellect,

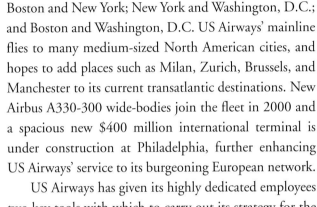

talent, and determination to create a new US Airways—a company dedicated to being the carrier of choice for 70 million passengers on 1.5 million flights a year.

US Airways' Envoy Class service features special menus designed by master chef Georges Perrier of Philadelphia's Le Bec-Fin restaurant. © Cameron Davidson

AMTRAK

With high-speed rail and a commitment to world-class customer service, Amtrak is transforming America's passenger rail service for the new millennium.

Amtrak, America's passenger railroad, is transforming the travel experience for the new millennium. And nowhere is this more evident than in the Commonwealth of Pennsylvania.

It is not surprising that Amtrak and the Commonwealth are working together to redefine transportation. After all, it was the chartering of the Pennsylvania Railroad in the 1840s that launched a transportation revolution that changed the nation. And Pennsylvania was no less important when Amtrak began service, in 1971. The first Amtrak train ran through Philadelphia; Amtrak's first reservation office was located in Pennsylvania; and Amtrak's first state-supported train operated through Erie.

Amtrak's strong presence in Pennsylvania continues today. More than 100 daily trains serve more than 25 stations, including 30th Street Station in Philadelphia, the second busiest station in the Amtrak system. Amtrak customers take more than four million train trips in Pennsylvania each year, traveling not only intrastate, but also on trains headed for cities such as Chicago, New Orleans, Miami, Washington, New York, and Boston. Millions more ride commuter service over tracks maintained by Amtrak personnel. Overall, nearly 400 passenger trains each day travel on Amtrak lines in Pennsylvania.

Amtrak's contribution to the Commonwealth is more than just passenger rail service. Approximately

Improvements to Amtrak facilities throughout Pennsylvania, such as at the Greensburg station, above, are the result of cooperative efforts between Amtrak and the Commonwealth. © Richard Esposito

3,000 Pennsylvania residents are employed by Amtrak, and Amtrak procures goods and services from more than 600 Pennsylvania companies. In direct wages and purchases alone, Amtrak's financial impact on the Commonwealth is more than $250 million annually. Amtrak also supports Pennsylvania's economic competitiveness through the movement of freight service, which uses Amtrak lines between Harrisburg and Philadelphia.

MARKET FOCUS

As impressive as Pennsylvania's railroading past and present is, the future will be even more exciting. Amtrak is redefining the way it does business, both in Pennsylvania and throughout the northeastern United States. Implementing a philosophy that is market focused and customer driven, Amtrak is maximizing ridership and revenue opportunities. Partnerships with freight railroads and companies in the telecommunications, food services, transportation, and hospitality industries are spurring Amtrak's business success.

America's first high-speed rail service, Acela Express, is operated by Amtrak's Pennsylvania-based Northeast Corridor business unit. © Gary Pancavage

The cornerstone of Amtrak's transformation is its Acela[SM] service in the Northeast Corridor. Derived from the words *acceleration* and *excellence, Acela* represents Amtrak's comprehensive approach to customer service. Acela is not just a new train, but a new brand reflecting a whole new way of doing business. And it is a critical part of Amtrak's goal of becoming the preferred mode of transportation in the Northeast.

Amtrak service not only connects travelers to cities throughout the nation, but also highlights Pennsylvania's natural beauty. © Alex Mayes

SERVICES FOR EVERY TRAVELER

Acela includes three service levels that will help define Amtrak's world-class service. Acela Express introduces high-speed rail to the nation. Using new, state-of-the-art trains and traveling at speeds of 150 miles per hour, Acela Express extends frequent, limited-stop premium service to Boston for the first time, and brings southeastern Pennsylvania closer to business centers in Washington, New York, and New England.

Acela Regional service, using newly refurbished trains and reaching speeds of 125 miles per hour, extends Acela's convenient service and its attention to customer satisfaction to Pennsylvania cities such as Harrisburg and Lancaster, and it reduces trip times in the Northeast by up to 20 percent.

Pennsylvanians commuting between the Philadelphia area and New York City benefit from the introduction of Acela Commuter service, which provides rush-hour service between the two cities.

The introduction of Acela service will build upon a flourishing partnership between Amtrak and the Commonwealth. Beginning in 1995, Pennsylvania and Amtrak have worked together to improve service on the Keystone line between Philadelphia and Harrisburg and to market that improved service. This effort has achieved overwhelming success: ridership on the line has nearly

Amtrak®

doubled in less than five years. In 1999, Pennsylvania and Amtrak announced a five-year, $140 million effort to develop the Keystone high-speed rail corridor between Philadelphia and Harrisburg. This joint investment will reduce travel time between the cities from more than two hours to just 90 minutes, with trains traveling at top speeds of 110 miles per hour.

A PROFITABLE PARTNERSHIP

This spirit of cooperation has enabled Amtrak and Pennsylvania to improve service and facilities throughout the Commonwealth. From crew bases in Pittsburgh to platforms in Greensburg, Amtrak and Pennsylvania alike have worked together to make improvements benefiting travelers, the Commonwealth, and employees. Soon to follow will be renovations at the Erie Station and construction of an intermodal station at Harrisburg International Airport. Amtrak and Pennsylvania also are working in partnership with local governments such as in Lancaster, where a rehabilitated station will serve as the linchpin for community redevelopment. Investments from the Commonwealth helped Amtrak locate its new reservation center—and its 575 jobs—in Philadelphia and prepare 30th Street Station for high-speed rail.

New and refurbished trains. Renovated stations. World-class customer service. High-speed rail. At the dawn of a new millennium, passenger rail has a bright future. And Amtrak, working with a committed partner in the Commonwealth of Pennsylvania, is leading the way.

Amtrak and the Commonwealth of Pennsylvania have worked together to create employment opportunities, including at Amtrak's reservation call center in Philadelphia, shown here. © Fran Genovesi

ADTRANZ

An international industry leader and innovator of railway technology, Adtranz provides railway systems, products, and solutions to customers around the world.

With more than 25 locations worldwide including three manufacturing locations in Pittsburgh, and a production facility in California, Adtranz North America has become a world leader in the global transportation industry.

One of the world's largest suppliers of complete railway systems, the company boasts products, systems, and services that seamlessly move large numbers of people around quickly, comfortably, and always reliably. Its product portfolio includes automated guideway transit systems (people movers), traditional rail systems, automatic train control systems, and support services.

Adtranz was formed in 1996 as a result of a merger between Daimler-Benz and ABB. In 1998, Daimler-Benz and Chrysler Corporation merged to become Daimler-Chrysler. Adtranz became a wholly owned subsidiary of DaimlerChrysler in 1999 when DaimlerChrysler acquired ABB's share.

Adtranz North America, established in 1996 when Adtranz was formed, maintains its headquarters in Pittsburgh, while the headquarters for the entire Adtranz group is located in Berlin, Germany.

INNOVATING TRANSIT SYSTEMS

Always at the forefront of innovation, Adtranz North America, through its predecessor company, Westinghouse, developed the world's first totally automated guideway transit (AGT) system in 1966. The experimental Skybus

Adtranz North America serves the global transportation industry with products and services designed to move people reliably to their destinations.

Demonstration Project—an electrically powered, driverless train—began operation in Pittsburgh's South Park on an elevated guideway. While Skybus was not at first accepted in its hometown, it premiered at Tampa International Airport in 1971, and was later installed at the new Pittsburgh International Airport in 1992.

Today, Adtranz is responsible for leading-edge AGT design of 22 systems, including 20 in operation and two currently under construction. From New York to Hong Kong, Los Angeles to Rio, Adtranz's mass transit systems and light rail systems move millions of people in more than 25 major cities around the world.

At the same time, its AGT systems support the smooth flow of pedestrian traffic in 17 international airports, including Gatwick International Airport in London, Pittsburgh International Airport in Pennsylvania, and Changi International Airport in Singapore. In 1996, Adtranz was involved in the complete modernization of Hartsfield International Airport in Atlanta, Georgia, for the Olympic Games. The original people mover, first installed in

The Adtranz AGT system at Tampa International Airport transports passengers between the main landside terminal and five airside satellites.

ADtranz

DaimlerChrysler Rail Systems

1980 and built to link the six terminals of what became the world's largest airport, was refurbished to cope with an estimated two million visitors during two short months of that Olympic year. Controlled by state-of-the-art technology, the driverless people mover trains glide underground, through tunnels beneath the airport's terminals. Today, many airport designs include such systems.

"Our vehicles are electrically powered with rubber tires operating on a dedicated guideway," says Ed Gordon, senior vice president, Adtranz North America. "The guideway can be elevated, at grade or underground; the driverless system is automatically controlled, and offers a smooth ride that belies the sophisticated technology engaged in creating it. This smooth ride is also enhanced by our spacious interiors, which are climate controlled. Our interior design agenda is for passenger comfort and ease of maintenance. Furthermore, our vehicles are able to automatically level themselves to match the floor height of any station platform for ease of entry and exit."

COMPLETE SERVICE SUPPORT

At all AGT sites, Adtranz offers complete operation and support services. The company is dedicated to optimizing system performance, thus its comprehensive maintenance program helps to ensure that potential problems are detected and corrected before they impact the efficiency or availability of the system. As a result, Adtranz's AGT systems demonstrate extremely high reliability levels. To date, they have consistently exceeded a 99-percent availability rate. And since the early 1970s, when the first airport

The innovative Innovia vehicle represents the most advanced AGT technology available today.

system was successfully installed, Adtranz's AGT systems have been known for being environmentally friendly, offering low noise, low vibration, and no pollution.

Adtranz's latest design, Innovia, "the people mover for the new millennium," was launched in 1999 at the North American headquarters. Sleeker, more aerodynamic, and still able to retain passenger comfort and load efficiency, the electrically powered Innovia represents the latest and most advanced engineering technology. Customers appreciate the selection of standard vehicle options without having to consider development costs, since each part is predesigned and ready for implementation. The Innovia prototype is currently being tested in Pittsburgh.

Without question, Adtranz is riding the wave of the booming transportation industry. It recently completed the world's largest circulator system, the Bukit Panjang LRT system in Singapore, and is currently constructing AGT systems at San Francisco and Seattle Tacoma International Airports in the United States. Its latest commissions include Houston International Airport and Leonardo da Vinci International Airport in Rome.

"With the opening of our newest AGT systems in Houston, Rome, and Singapore, Adtranz continues to provide innovative transportation technology to customers worldwide. As always, our aim is to set the standard for excellence," says Raymond T. Betler, president and CEO of Adtranz North America.

Careful maintenance on AGT vehicles optimizes system performance at Hartsfield International Airport in Atlanta.

ALLEGHENY COUNTY AIRPORT AUTHORITY

As the administrating agency for state-of-the-art Pittsburgh International Airport, the Allegheny County Airport

Authority is pursuing a strategic plan to increase the airport's capacity as a cargo hub and a center for business.

Pittsburgh International Airport's landside terminal is a main feature of the airport's efficient, dual-terminal concept. © John A. Wee

Business or leisure travelers tired of the crowded conditions and hustle and bustle at major airports along the East Coast would do well to consider making their flight connections through relatively hasslefree Pittsburgh International Airport. Greater Pittsburgh's major aviation facility is located just 16 miles from downtown Pittsburgh on more than 10,000 acres. It is one of the most modern, efficient airports in the world. In 1999, readers of *Conde Nast Traveler* magazine rated the facility the best airport in the United States and the third best in the world.

ONE OF THE NATION'S MOST EFFICIENT AIRPORTS
Opened in 1992 at a cost of $800 million, Pittsburgh International Airport is acclaimed by passengers and aviation experts as one of the most efficient airports in the world due to its user-friendly design. The airport features a three-million-square-foot landside/airside terminal complex. The airside terminal's user-friendly X-shape design and location between the runways reduces aircraft taxi time and permits easy flight connections.

Other passenger-friendly features of the airport include an underground transit system linking the airport's two terminals; parking for nearly 17,500 automobiles; an automated baggage system capable of sorting up to 400 bags per minute, the second largest in the United States; more than 100 airport shops and boutiques; and moving sidewalks to and from many of the airport's more than 100 gates. The terminals also are connected by a moving walkway to a new, $31.5 million, 330-room Hyatt Hotel and Conference Center.

Served by all the major U.S. air carriers—including U.S. Airways, the airport's primary airline tenant—plus Air Canada and several regional and start-up airlines, Pittsburgh International offers 600 nonstop flights daily to nearly 120 destinations, including Paris, France; Frankfurt, Germany; London, England; and Cancun, Mexico.

And because Pittsburgh International Airport is not constrained by the air congestion or airfield restrictions of most major East Coast airports, its flights generally

Opening in the airport in phases beginning in summer 2000, Airside Business Park, illustrated above, includes offices and flexible space, cargo and fixed-base operation/aviation (FBO) center facilities, and corporate airplane hangars.

2000

Pittsburgh International Airport
Over 40 years of Aviation Excellence

1952

Pittsburgh International Airport, past and present depicted above, is leading the standard for the design of efficient airports.

take off on time and are more likely to arrive on schedule. The airport is operationally efficient and has accumulated numerous awards for its dependability.

Currently, more than 19 million passengers each year avail themselves of the convenience that Pittsburgh International offers. And the number of passengers undoubtedly will grow as the airport's reputation spreads and air carriers increase the number of flights that serve Greater Pittsburgh, an area that has transformed itself from an industrial steel center to a world leader in high technology, medicine, education, and biotechnology.

PLANS FOR ECONOMIC GROWTH

To fulfill Pittsburgh International's potential as one of the nation's top cargo airports, the Allegheny County Airport Authority is in the process of adding cargo capacity and other new cargo-related facilities at the airport. The new development being constructed in 2000 is referred to as the Airside Business Park and Air Cargo Center. The campuslike setting features multiple offices with ample parking surrounding an outdoor plaza and fountain area and allows easy access to Business Route 60.

Also included within the Airside Business Park are three buildings featuring a total of 374,000 square feet of combination high-bay flexible space and office space. In addition, the Air Cargo Center will provide 225,000 square feet of new cargo facilities, constructed on existing airport apron and allowing direct access to the airfield and convenient access to nearby interstate highways. A new Business Aviation Center with a

state-of-the-art executive center and conference facilities will also include three corporate aircraft hangars and aircraft service and maintenance facilities.

Airports increasingly are called upon to serve as catalysts for regional economic development, in line with today's high-tech, time-sensitive economic environment. Pittsburgh International is admirably fulfilling that role. The Airside Business Park/Air Cargo Center and Business Aviation Center projects are already under construction and will be completed in phases in 2001 and 2002. The combined current and projected cargo facilities of Pittsburgh International Airport are expected to add immeasurably to the economy of Pittsburgh, Allegheny County, and, indeed, all of southwestern Pennsylvania. Pittsburgh International Airport is poised to bolster Pittsburgh's new high-tech image and is prepared to open up the world to travelers and businesses that choose to use its leading-edge facilities.

Pittsburgh International Airport's dual-terminal three-million-square-foot complex has a distinctive X-shape midfield terminal.

GE TRANSPORTATION SYSTEMS

GE Transportation Systems, based in Erie, Pennsylvania, is a worldwide leader in rail transportation solutions and services, including freight and passenger locomotives and railway control and communication systems.

Nearly 120 years ago, the great inventor Thomas Edison built the first experimental electric locomotive in his New Jersey laboratory. His invention would mark the beginning of GE Transportation Systems. Headquartered in Erie, Pennsylvania, the company is a major business of General Electric Company and a global leader in the development of surface transportation solutions. GE Transportation Systems is also the largest employer in northwestern Pennsylvania, and together with its employees, is a local leader in community volunteerism and philanthropy.

Right now, thousands of locomotives designed and manufactured by GE Transportation Systems are moving across the landscape of North America and around the world. That includes GE's AC6000 locomotive, which uses alternating current (AC) technology to provide the greatest pulling power available today. The AC6000 is one example of the innovation that typifies the history of GE Transportation Systems. Another example is the company's development of remote monitoring and diagnostics capabilities.

GE Transportation Systems rail service experts in Erie use advanced communications and diagnostics tools, including on-line support, to monitor locomotive fleets around the globe.

GE Transportation Systems, headquartered in Erie, Pennsylvania, is recognized as a global leader in the development of surface transportation products and services. Shown above is the company's innovative AC6000 locomotive, which uses alternating current (AC) technology to provide the greatest pulling power available.

Using a combination of satellite communications, automated diagnostic tools, and GE-based service expertise, GE can monitor the operation of locomotives anywhere in the world in real time.

MOVING FASTER THAN EVER

GE Transportation Systems is a worldwide leader in rail transportation solutions, including freight and passenger locomotives; global services, such as remote monitoring, maintenance, performance upgrades, and parts; railway control and communications systems through GE Harris Railway Electronics; and railcars through GE Capital Rail Services. GE Transportation Systems serves other markets as well, with propulsion and auxiliary power systems for transit vehicles, motorized drive systems for mining trucks, and drilling motors.

GE Transportation Systems

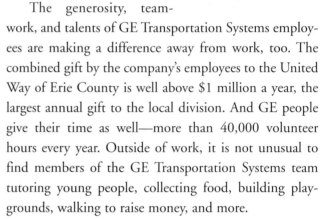

The employees of GE Transportation Systems—at the company's Erie headquarters, at diesel engine manufacturing in Grove City, and at offices and operations around the world—are moving faster than ever to meet customer needs. They have cut the time it takes to build new locomotives by three-quarters. They are developing products like an AC motorized wheel for mining that offers improved productivity. They provide everything from technical support to full maintenance services for customers from the Americas to Asia.

GE Transportation Systems is an ISO-9001 certified company and practices Six Sigma quality principles as the way to do business. Six Sigma is a disciplined approach to process control and improvement that provides a statistically based method of reducing the causes of defects. The term Six Sigma refers to quality at 99.9997 percent or, more practically speaking, just 3.4 defects per million of any product or service.

TALENT AND TEAMWORK

The talents and energies of the people at GE Transportation Systems—their collective ability to stretch and go beyond the boundaries—produces remarkable results. The company is now communicating with customers at electronic speed, using World Wide Web tools to deliver critical information, service solutions, and new business opportunities. This includes an on-line global marketplace that links buyers and sellers of transportation equipment, parts, and supplies.

Shown at right, The Learning Center at GE Transportation Systems is a state-of-the-art educational environment for employees, customers, and the community.

Meanwhile, its combined safety efforts have gained distinction for the company's Erie facility as the largest work site in Pennsylvania to achieve OSHA Voluntary Protection Program (VPP) STAR certification. VPP STAR certification is the highest safety certification in the nation granted by OSHA (Occupational Safety & Health Administration).

The generosity, teamwork, and talents of GE Transportation Systems employees are making a difference away from work, too. The combined gift by the company's employees to the United Way of Erie County is well above $1 million a year, the largest annual gift to the local division. And GE people give their time as well—more than 40,000 volunteer hours every year. Outside of work, it is not unusual to find members of the GE Transportation Systems team tutoring young people, collecting food, building playgrounds, walking to raise money, and more.

In its home state of Pennsylvania and around the world, GE Transportation Systems is dedicated to customer and community success.

IN THE HANDS OF THE PROS
BUSINESS AND PROFESSIONAL SERVICES

Pennsylvania offers a wide range of services that provide the tools and know-how to get a product from the mind of the inventor to the hands of the consumer. Throughout Pennsylvania, legal, accounting, and advertising firms and other specialists and consultants bring solutions, information, and advice to help businesses innovate and grow. Between 1990 and 1997, most of the major industries in the services sector experienced an upswing in

employment, with the greatest job gains seen in recent years in business services (up 33 percent) and engineering and management services (up 10.5 percent).

Law firms in particular have benefited from the booming economy and rapidly changing business scene. According to a 1999 article in the *Philadelphia Business Journal*, large firms providing legal services have grown even larger, expanded geographically, and bolstered strategic areas of practice specifically targeted to the needs of business. Much of this success can be attributed to the increasing need for patent and trademark work in the burgeoning computer and information technology industries.

Pennsylvania is home to some of the country's oldest and most respected law firms. Morgan, Lewis & Bockius L.L.P., established in Philadelphia in 1873, employs more than 1,000 lawyers in virtually every area of law. In 1940, it pioneered the concept of a national law firm when it opened an office in Washington, D.C. It also has offices in Pittsburgh, Harrisburg, and four other U.S. cities as well as overseas. Founded in 1875, Dechert Price & Rhoads employs more than 440 lawyers in seven offices in the United States, including Harrisburg and Philadelphia. A full-service law office, it provides counsel to industrial, financial, commercial, service, and nonprofit enterprises and is ranked among the "most used outside firms" by *National Law Journal*. Kirkpatrick & Lockhart L.L.P., with Pennsylvania offices in Harrisburg and Pittsburgh, opened its doors in 1946 and today employs more than 550 lawyers serving a diverse roster of clients.

Pennsylvania's marketing and advertising industry has also profited from changes in the business world. As the *Philadelphia Business Journal* noted, the Commonwealth's energy deregulation and bank mergers have provided great new opportunities for advertising agencies. Harte-Hanks DiMark, of Langhorne, an expert in regulated and deregulated industries such as utilities and telecommunications, is one of the nation's premier providers of marketing services to the insurance and health care industries. Philadelphia's Brownstein Group is a privately owned, full-service agency

This young shopper makes her selection at one of Pennsylvania's more than 8,000 grocery stores. With so many markets to choose from, shoppers find quality and value at competitive prices.

established in 1964 whose focus today is on building brand identity. Among its clients are some of the world's top names, including Comcast, Foot Locker, the Philadelphia Flyers, and the American Red Cross. Established in 1923, Ketchum is the Pittsburgh region's oldest and largest public relations shop with more than 70 employees; its list of clients includes H. J. Heinz. Jack Horner, a former Ketchum employee, formed his own company in Pittsburgh in 1993; today Jack Horner Communications counts among its clients US Airways and Microsoft.

When it comes to accounting needs, Pennsylvania businesses have no shortage of suppliers to whom they can turn, and among these are some of the giants of the accounting world. Arthur Andersen & Company, with offices in Philadelphia, Pittsburgh, and Lancaster, offers financial statement assurance, consulting, and business process outsourcing. Deloitte & Touche's Pennsylvania offices are in Allentown, Philadelphia, and Pittsburgh. The firm assists clients with assurance and advisory tax, management, and consulting services. Ernst & Young's Philadelphia and Pittsburgh offices provide entrepreneurial growth companies with management, consulting, audits, and tax practice.

For permanent and temporary help, the Commonwealth's personnel services provide skilled, talented workers in an industry that employs nearly 2,000 Pennsylvanians. Accountants On Call, an international company specializing in finance personnel, has offices in King of Prussia, Philadelphia, Pittsburgh, and Oxford Valley. In the Delaware Valley area, Contemporary Staffing Solutions provides permanent, temporary, and on-site management services through offices in Plymouth Meeting, Philadelphia, and Media, while Century Associates of Philadelphia specializes in sales, marketing, and consulting professionals in the Internet, software, and medical fields. Coleman Legal Staffing supplies corporations with permanent and contract lawyers and paralegals through its offices in Philadelphia, Bryn Mawr, and Iselin, New Jersey.

An attorney does research in his firm's library for an upcoming trial. Pennsylvania is home to some of the nation's oldest and most respected law firms.

The new millennium presents ever-growing opportunities for these traditional services as well as for companies offering new kinds of services to high-tech industries such as advanced manufacturing. One such company, Concurrent Technologies Corporation, based in Johnstown, provides government and private organizations with management and technology-based solutions such as business systems consulting, laboratory testing and analysis, information and systems engineering, and modeling and simulation. The company also has offices in Harrisburg, Pittsburgh, West Chester, and in cities throughout the United States.

A BUYER'S MARKET

Wholesale trade is the fifth largest employer among private sectors in Pennsylvania, with more than 270,000 Pennsylvanians working in more than 25,000 businesses.

Slightly more than half are employed in the wholesale trade of durable goods including motor vehicles, parts and supplies; furniture; lumber and construction material; professional and commercial equipment; metals and minerals; electrical goods; hardware, plumbing and heating equipment; and machinery, equipment, and supplies. Distributors of nondurable goods move paper products; drugs; apparel; groceries; farm products; chemicals; petroleum; and beer, wine, and distilled beverages.

A sampling of some of the state's wholesale distributors shows the variety of products available in

Shoppers browse the aisles at Strawbridge's in Philadelphia. Pennsylvania offers bargain hunters everything from country crafts to haute couture—and no state sales tax on clothing.

Pennsylvania. Diamond Lustre, of Lancaster, is a wholesale distributor of products and equipment for the professional auto detailing industry. Scranton's Arley Wholesale specializes in imported tile and stone for building projects, while Moyer & Sons, of Souderton, employs more than 250 people in the wholesale distribution of fuel oil, feed, and grain. The Pennock Company, of Philadelphia, provides jobs for 65 people in wholesale cut flowers, and the Stradler Distribution Company, of Plumsteadville, distributes imported malt beverages.

Retail trade is the second largest employer among Pennsylvania's private sectors. Since 1992, employment in this field has increased every year, and by 1998 more than 960,000 Pennsylvanians were employed in over 64,137 retail trade establishments.

More than 150,000 people are employed in more than 8,000 grocery retail stores throughout the state. Some of the largest among these are Acme Markets, Genuardi's Family Market, Giant Food Stores, and Weis Markets.

General merchandise retailers in Pennsylvania— indeed throughout the world—owe a huge debt to one John Wanamaker of Philadelphia. This visionary saw the possibilities for retail trade in 19th-century Pennsylvania, where the cities were populated with consumers eager to purchase manufactured consumer goods and an expanding rail network could deliver even more customers to the cities. Wanamaker, who began his career as a stock boy in a Philadelphia clothing store, became one of the most successful retail merchants of his era.

PHOTO: © John McGrail

In 1861, Wanamaker went into partnership with his brother-in-law in what would become the largest men's retail clothing store in America. In 1876, the year of America's centennial celebration, Wanamaker moved his operations to a huge freight shed abandoned by the Pennsylvania Railroad and added women's clothing and other goods. Wanamaker's Grand Depot became a tourist destination for visitors to the Centennial Exposition. In the years following, the master retailer transformed the Grand Depot into a warehouse of specialty shops, building one section at a time. Wanamaker's creation, the world's first department store, opened just in time for the company's golden jubilee in 1911.

Wanamaker is also remembered as a pioneer in merchandising for his use of newspaper advertising, seasonal sales, exhibitions, and in-store fashion shows and for his innovative Bargain Room, or what today's shoppers might call a bargain basement. His company thrived for more than a century, but the name was retired in 1995 when Wanamaker's was purchased by the May Department Stores Company. Today, the historic building that housed his original department store is occupied by Lord & Taylor.

For years, thanks in large part to Wanamaker's popularity, people flocked to Philadelphia to shop. But after World War II, more and more people moved to the suburbs, and the retail industry moved with them. In 1959, Kravco began planning a shopping center in the small community of King of Prussia. The town, named after an 18th-century tavern that was still standing, seemed poised for growth due to its location at the junction of the Pennsylvania Turnpike, the Schuylkill Expressway, and Route 202. The King of Prussia Plaza opened in 1963 with three anchor department stores. Soon plans were made for an adjacent mall to be called the Court at King of Prussia, designed to cater to the more affluent and fashion-minded who might otherwise shop in Philadelphia or even New York City.

The success of the two linked malls inspired a total renovation, which was completed in 1998. The refurbished Plaza section is lined with marble and punctuated by domed courts fitted with skylights. The atmosphere is opulent and the setting fit for the upscale shops and anchors. The Court and the Plaza together occupy nearly three million square feet of floor space, are anchored by nine department stores, and feature nearly 400 shops, making King of Prussia home to the second largest retail mall in the United States.

Throughout the Commonwealth are found dozens of malls, many anchored by two of Pennsylvania's own department stores: Boscov's, headquartered in Reading, and the Bon Ton, headquartered in York. Pennsylvania is also well served by outlet shopping destinations. Some of the best-known include Reading, whose 300 factory outlets prompted *Destinations Magazine* to name it the "best shopping destination in North America," Lancaster, and Grove City, 50 miles north of Pittsburgh.

While many Pennsylvanians will travel miles for a good bargain, others prefer to shop from the comfort of their living rooms. They and shoppers across the country can thank Joseph Segal, who established QVC, for this convenience. The virtual mall that shoppers can visit any hour of the day or night simply by turning on the television was set up by Segal, founder of the Franklin Mint—which markets collectibles such as Princess Diana dolls—in 1986 in West Chester. By 1993, QVC was the nation's number one televised shopping service in sales, profit, and reputation, as well as one of the largest purveyors of gold jewelry in the world. QVC is currently the world's premier electronic retailer, reaching 94 percent of U.S. homes with cable. QVC introduces America to over 250 products per week and can accept over 95,000 telephone orders per hour. The company recently added an on-line shopping site called iQVC. In 1999, a Harris Interactive poll rated iQVC first in customer satisfaction out of 180 Internet shopping sites.

According to the Travel Industry Association of America, shopping has become a favorite activity for both domestic and foreign travelers. In 1999, the Shop Pennsylvania task force was created to promote Pennsylvania as a state that has no sales tax on apparel and to boost its stores, malls, and outlet centers to tourists. John Wanamaker would be proud.

'PHILLY LAWYER'

Alexander James Dallas was one of Pennsylvania's most famous lawyers; his reports on decisions by the Pennsylvania and federal courts are an excellent source of scholarly information on the earliest years of the U.S. Supreme Court. Dallas served as secretary of the Commonwealth of Pennsylvania and in 1814 was appointed by President Madison as secretary of the U.S. treasury.

GENUARDI'S FAMILY MARKETS

Proud of its rich heritage as a family-owned and family-operated business, Genuardi's Family Markets

remains committed to its simple traditions of hard work, superior service, and premium quality.

Truly a family-run business, Genuardi's Family Markets is steeped in a strong sense of family pride that dates back to 1920, when Genuardi's first began.

The business first started when Gaspare Genuardi and his wife Josephine began growing vegetables on a small farm in Norristown, Pennsylvania, then delivering them to neighbors by horse and wagon, and later by Model T. They soon developed a reputation for their fine quality produce and superior service. Gaspare's strong sense of customer service continues to be the cornerstone of Genuardi's success.

FAMILY PRIDE

Gaspare and Josephine passed on the family traditions of hard work and customer dedication to their nine children. Five of their sons—Charlie, Frank, Joe, Tom, and Jim—helped with the business throughout the early days and became known to the customers as the Genuardi brothers.

In the 1930s the Genuardis opened a small corner store, and later the Genuardi Superette where the family worked together. This early success helped the business to grow, and in 1954, the Genuardi brothers opened the first Genuardi Market on Main Street in Jeffersonville.

With hard work and customer dedication, Gaspare and Josephine Genuardi laid the cornerstone for a supermarket dynasty.

It was the first independently owned supermarket to open in the Norristown area.

From the time of the first supermarket, and throughout the 1950s, 1960s, and 1970s, the Genuardi brothers built a family of stores which became one of the largest, most respected independent supermarket businesses in the Delaware Valley, spanning Montgomery, Chester, Bucks, and Delaware counties.

As the number of stores grew, the Genuardi brothers envisioned a day when the next generation would lead the business. In the 1980s, they developed a plan for transition so the business could continue to grow at a rapid rate.

The retirement of the Genuardi brothers launched the decade of the 1990s and a third generation of Genuardi family members took charge of the company: Charles A., Skip, Tom Jr., Larry, Anthony, Joe Jr., David, Michael, and Jim. All nine shareholders have worked within the business virtually all of their adult lives.

In 1990, Charles A. Genuardi was elected company president by the board of directors and remains in that position today. He and the other shareholders, along with a team of key executives, have guided Genuardi's Family Markets through significant changes and have achieved many milestones.

In the last few years, the Genuardi family members have turned over the day-to-day operations of the company to a highly skilled and experienced team of executives and managers. This transition has allowed the family members to carry the "family pride" message to

The Genuardi brothers (from left)—Frank, Jim, Charlie, Joe, and Tom—supported and built the business for more than four decades.

customers and employees, and to devote many hours of personal service to food industry associations and a variety of civic organizations.

"Family pride is our legacy and our identity," says President Charles A. Genuardi. "Genuardi's has always succeeded through hard work, dedication to the customer, and a personal commitment to being the best."

With a commitment to steady growth, Genuardi's continues to lead the retail food industry with fresh innovative ideas. One of its main strategies is making major investments in technology and human resources development. Throughout the Delaware Valley, people recognize Genuardi's stores for their charming decor, outstanding amenities, state-of-the-art equipment, superb value, and legendary customer service.

Under the leadership of the third generation (from left)—Jim, Larry, Michael, David, Charles A., Tom Jr., Anthony, Skip, and Joe Jr.— Genuardi's Family Markets has experienced tremendous growth.

DEDICATION TO EMPLOYEES

Throughout all of this growth, Genuardi's continues to be employee-focused regarding work environment, employee compensation, and advancement opportunities. Today, just as in the past, Genuardi's offers superior training programs and actively encourages team members to expand their skills via various educational opportunities. "Genuardi's has always had the best people in the business," says Charles. "Our team is skilled and knowledgeable. We recognize that people are the source of our strength, and the key to our future." And of more than 7,000 employees companywide, 5,500 work within the Pennsylvania borders.

In addition to dedication to employees, Genuardi's Family Markets firmly believes in a key principle instilled by Gaspare Genuardi—dedication and service to the communities where Genuardi's does business. In 1976 Genuardi's established a direct cash rebate program for nonprofit groups called the Community Cash Back program. By the end of 2000, the Community Cash Back program will have awarded more than $20 million to 3,500 nonprofit organizations since its inception. Another program, Genuardi's Children's Charities, was started in 1997 and has donated more than $60,000 to organizations that serve children.

Under the leadership and direction of the third generation, Genuardi's has experienced tremendous growth. In 1997, Genuardi's acquired Zagara's Specialty and Natural Foods, a nationally recognized upscale food emporium. Genuardi's now operates 33 stores in Delaware, Pennsylvania, and New Jersey and three Zagara's stores in Pennsylvania and New Jersey.

In 1999 the Wharton School of Business and the Pennsylvania Small Business Development Council recognized Genuardi's as Pennsylvania's "Family Business of the Year". More than 7,000 team members carry on the company traditions of freshness, superior quality, terrific prices, and family pride—a living legacy to the founders, Gaspare and Josephine Genuardi.

Genuardi's Superette (circa 1940) was located on Main Street in Jeffersonville, Pennsylvania.

MODERN GROUP LTD.

Dedicated to exceeding customers' expectations, Modern Group Ltd. has become one of the nation's largest and most respected distributors of material handling, construction, and maintenance equipment.

A company that has grown from six people to more than 580, from one location to 24, and from annual sales of less than $1 million to more than $154 million, Modern Group Ltd. has emerged as one of the nation's largest distributors of material handling, construction, and maintenance equipment.

Headquartered in Bristol, Pennsylvania, the privately owned Modern Group comprises five operating divisions: Modern Handling Equipment Company; Modern Handling Equipment of N.J., Inc.; Modern Equipment Sales & Rental Co.; Seely Equipment and Supply Co.; and Modern Construction Equipment Co. Collectively they offer a wide variety of services including equipment sales, leasing, short-term rentals, service, parts, training, and financing solutions. Equipment provided includes everything from forklift trucks to aerial work platforms to loading dock equipment, plus items for homeowner and contractor rentals.

A CUSTOMER-FOCUSED REPUTATION

Modern services companies throughout the competitive mid-Atlantic region from New York City to Washington, D.C., and Atlantic City to Harrisburg. In this region, Modern proudly serves more than 10,000 customers who represent a broad range of industries such as shipping, industrial maintenance, distribution, utilities, construction, manufacturing, warehousing, and public works. Known for its ability to retain customers, Modern today services some customers who have been with them for 30 years. Proud to offer a customer-focused reputation,

The corporate headquarters for Modern Group Ltd. is located in Bristol, Pennsylvania.

Modern strictly adheres to its vision statement "To satisfy our customers by exceeding their expectations." The company's number one belief is "Outstanding customer service in everything we do." With this focus in mind, Modern has kept its acquisitions and growth in line with meeting the customer's needs.

"Our interest is based entirely on customer need— what we have to do to respond and how can we best take care of that customer. That's the value of service," says David Griffith, president and CEO.

The history of Modern Group has been about service through strengthening its core business and expanding its offerings. Modern Group began in Philadelphia with the founding of its predecessor, Rapids Handling Equipment Company, a sales outlet for the conveyor manufacturer Rapids-Standard Co. in 1946. Rapids Handling employed six people, among them Joe McEwen, who now serves as chairman of Modern Group. The first expansion came in 1947 when the company became a franchised dealer for Hyster, a major West Coast forklift

Pictured from left are George Wilkinson, CFO; David Griffith, CEO; and Joseph McEwen, chairman of the board.

truck manufacturer. Rapids Handling continued as a conveyor distributor and forklift truck dealer until 1955 when by mutual agreement with Rapids-Standard, the company decided to form a spin-off entity that would focus on the forklift-truck end of the business. The result was Modern Handling Equipment Company, formed by McEwen and partner Jack Grimison (who died in 1960). The company, then 29 people strong, remained at the same location. In 1966, the company acquired a Hyster dealership in northern New Jersey and formed a new division, Modern Handling Equipment of N.J., Inc.

GROWTH AND DIVERSIFICATION

In 1975, Modern began the first of its successful diversification endeavors when it purchased Master Welding of Wilmington, Delaware, forming Modern Equipment Rentals, Inc. The move enabled the company to take in a huge new market with the construction equipment business. In 1977, Modern expanded its product line to include loading dock equipment, shelving, and plant and shipping department products, with the acquisition of Material Handling Equipment Company in Bala Cynwyd, Pennsylvania. The resulting division remained under the original company name.

By 1979 a holding company, Modern Group Ltd., was formed in order to better manage the various divisions. In 1984, Modern started a new company, Modern HiLift Equipment Co. In 1991, the group formed yet another division with the acquisition of Seely Equipment and Supply Co., Inc., of Wall, New Jersey, and in 1995 it surpassed $100 million in sales—a major milestone. In 1998, Modern merged two divisions— Modern HiLift and Modern Equipment Rentals—into a new division called Modern Equipment Sales & Rental Co. In 1999, the group added its fifth division with the start-up of Modern Construction Equipment Co.

Today the company is led by the executive management team of McEwen, Griffith, and George Wilkinson, executive vice president and CFO. Together the team has led Modern to a 10 percent annual growth rate, a net worth of more than $100 million in assets, and sales in excess of $154 million (for fiscal 1999).

The team is quick to credit its employees as major contributors to Modern's prosperity. Since the beginning, McEwen has remained firmly committed to the

Modern Handling Equipment Co. and Modern Handling Equipment of N.J., Inc., divisions of Modern Group Ltd., rent and sell the Hyster forklift.

company's employees, believing that if Modern gives back to the employees "they will constantly do the right thing for the company and for the customer." Accordingly, the company's vision statement includes "maintaining high employee morale." To that end, Modern Group provides an employee stock ownership plan (ESOP), established in 1981, that allows every employee a chance to own part of the company. The ESOP, which was initiated by McEwen as a measure to sell the company back to the employees, offers employees who work more than 1,000 hours a year and who have six consecutive months of employment the option to have a percentage of their salaries put into the plan. As a result, employees now own approximately one-third of the company.

As for the future, Modern's strategy is to develop its Internet presence and to focus on the goals that have helped it prosper. "The keys to our growth are service, the aftermarket, our overall rental opportunity, and just doing our job very, very well," says Griffith. "The Modern of tomorrow is not the Modern of yesterday, but our core beliefs remain. If we stick to those beliefs, our future will be sustained."

The Genie aerial work platform is sold and rented by Modern Equipment Sales & Rental Co.

GIANT FOOD STORES, INC.

The bright, modern supermarkets of Giant Food Stores, Inc., offer customers a one-stop, quality shopping experience, providing wide variety, everyday low prices, and exceptional service.

Giant Food Stores, Inc., began in 1923 when its founder, entrepreneur David Javitch, opened a small meat market in Carlisle, Pennsylvania. His main goal was to provide a living for his family, but ultimately he also built the foundation of one of the most successful grocery store chains in the nation.

In 1936, Javitch purchased a store in Lewistown, Pennsylvania, naming it Giant Shopping Food Center. A marked departure from his original store, Carlisle Meat Market, Giant was a complete grocery store. The concept proved to be successful. Today, Giant Food Stores, Inc., based in Carlisle, operates more than 160 stores, in six states. It operates under the name Giant Food Stores throughout Pennsylvania; under the name Martin's Food Markets in Maryland, Virginia, and West Virginia; and under the name Edwards Super Food Stores in New York and New Jersey. The company employs more than 24,000 people.

Giant's goal is to provide a one-stop, quality shopping experience with "everyday low prices," a retail business

This Giant Food Store, located in Carlisle, Pennsylvania, is an example of the company's state-of-the-art markets.

philosophy it helped launch. Javitch first introduced the concept in 1972. As part of its strategy of everyday low prices, Giant offers double coupons in all its markets, and the stores have even been known to offer triple coupons. Giant cites such merchandising efforts as examples of its strategic procedures, to which it attributes its success with the concept of everyday low prices.

PEAK PERFORMANCE AND EXPANSION

Giant has been a top performer in operating earnings, as well as in return on investment and return on assets. Sales are currently around $3.5 billion, and the firm recently recorded its 27th consecutive year of increased sales and earnings. Much of that success is due to Giant's associates, competitive pricing, and continued expansion efforts.

The wide variety of seafood is always fresh at Giant, where "Only the best will do."

Another key to that growth has been Giant's association with Ahold USA. In 1981, the Javitch family made a significant decision to perpetuate the growth and financial stability of the company. Giant entered into an alliance with Netherlands-based Ahold, an international, multifaceted company involved in manufacturing and retailing food and other consumer goods in Europe and the United States.

Giant continued to operate as an autonomous member of the Ahold group under the direction of the existing Giant management team. At the time of the agreement, Giant was operating 29 supermarkets. Over the next decade, the entire Ahold organization, as well as Giant, grew and prospered. Giant Food Stores was further strengthened when two other grocers joined the Ahold network. Tops, Inc., based in New York, and First National Supermarkets, located throughout Ohio and the New England states, merged with Giant, resulting in one of the largest supermarket conglomerates in the United States. In addition, Giant, Tops, and First National continue to share innovative concepts while working together to create operating efficiencies.

Giant has expanded on its one-stop shopping experience in some stores, with the addition of banks, pharmacies, and Carryout Cafes. Gas stations are the latest convenience addition. So far, 10 Giant stores have installed gas pumps in their parking lots to provide self-service gasoline. Customers may either pay the attendant or pay in the store when they purchase their groceries. Another popular concept is the Kid City Fun Center. The in-store Kid Centers offer entertainment for children while their parents shop.

"Walter" represents the highest quality perishables, which are expected at Giant Food Stores.

LONG-RANGE GROWTH

The Giant plan for the future is optimistic. It calls for continued growth within Pennsylvania and neighboring states. The company's three-year plan includes opening six new stores per year in existing or neighboring areas. Giant also prides itself on keeping its existing stores in tip-top shape. Major remodelings are scheduled for every five years, while minor remodeling projects occur every 12 to 18 months to help keep stores looking as good as new. Stores range in size from 36,000 to 64,000 square feet.

Despite the firm's phenomenal growth, Giant remains loyal to the culture established by its founder more than 70 years ago. Employees continue to adhere to Javitch's original philosophy—providing service and value to the customer, creating a positive work atmosphere, and supporting the community.

WEIS MARKETS, INC.

Since 1912 Weis Markets, Inc., of Sunbury, Pennsylvania, has thrived and prospered by building its grocery stores on principles of value, ingenuity, and hard work.

One of the most consistently profitable supermarket companies in the nation, Weis Markets continues to expand operations in its primary marketing areas: Pennsylvania and Maryland. © The Lewisburg Studio

In 1912, two brothers named Harry and Sigmund Weis opened a modest neighborhood grocery store in Sunbury, Pennsylvania, a town located on the banks of the Susquehanna River. Little did they realize what their hard work would bring. Today, nearly a century later, Weis Markets, Inc., is a multibillion dollar supermarket company operating in six states and is known as an industry leader.

The company's success started with the Weis brothers' innovative ideas, which were continued by generations of loyal employees. Committed to selling groceries at a fair price, the brothers sold their goods on a cash-and-carry basis, rather than credit, which helped customers save money. Customers responded and their business grew. Through the years, the company expanded, opening numerous stores across central Pennsylvania. Eventually these smaller stores gave way for larger supermarkets.

Today, Weis Markets operates stores in six states, employs more than 20,000 people, and is publicly traded (NYSE:WMK). Weis Markets also operates a 1.1 million-square-foot distribution center in Milton, Pennsylvania, and a dairy and meat processing plant as well as an ice-cream plant in Sunbury, Pennsylvania, where the company maintains its corporate office. Weis Markets is now one of the largest purchasers of Pennsylvania produce and dairy products. As a result of its intensive, customer-driven focus, in 1999 Weis Markets generated total sales exceeding $2 billion.

Understanding its customers' changing needs is the driving force behind Weis Markets' success story and its current expansion program. With its new store prototype, the company has implemented many timesaving design features that offer added convenience and value. Under the leadership of its chairman Robert F. Weis and company president Norman S. Rich, Weis Markets began its most ambitious expansion ever in 1995. By the end of the century, Weis Markets had built or opened 38 stores and expanded or remodeled 51 others—more than half its store base. In the years ahead, Weis Markets will match or exceed the pace of its recent expansion program.

Weis Markets is strongly connected to the neighborhoods it serves, supporting local and national charities including the Children's Miracle Network, the Geisinger Medical Center's Children's Hospital in Danville, Pennsylvania, and other pediatric charities across the state. Other beneficiaries of Weis Markets' charitable efforts include the Red Cross, the Salvation Army, Special Olympics, hospitals, food banks, volunteer fire companies, educational facilities, and individual United Way chapters.

"Looking ahead, we will continue to focus on expansion through our store development program and acquisitions, which will help our company compete and succeed in both existing markets and in the new ones we enter. We will also look to continue our tradition of being a good neighbor in the areas where we operate," says Robert F. Weis, chairman of Weis Markets. "Weis Markets has begun the new century with the financial resources, employee base, merchandising expertise, and market share that will contribute to our enduring success in an extremely competitive marketplace in the years to come."

Weis customers enjoy large meat and deli departments with a wide selection of high quality meats and cheeses.

AGGRESSIVE FOOD SALES

One of the leading food brokerage companies in the region, Aggressive Food Sales believes that maintaining

integrity, honesty, and loyalty in every business relationship provides the keys to success.

A combination of old-fashioned work ethics, technical savvy, and more than four decades of hard-earned experience puts Aggressive Food Sales (AFS) in a class of its own among independent sales organizations servicing the food industry.

Norman Weiss, AFS president, attributes his very early exposure to the world of business as the genesis to his becoming the leader of one of the region's top-earning food industry brokerage companies.

"I was nine years old when I first began working in my father's food processing business in Philadelphia," says Weiss. Weiss worked for 20 years in the family business, learning firsthand the many different facets of the food industry. In 1985, Weiss took this knowledge and experience and founded AFS.

AFS specializes in matching the manufacturer's product to end-users in both the food service and retail sales arenas. The company represents an extensive list of products sold to restaurants, government agencies, hospitals, schools, and other institutions nationwide, with a strong emphasis on Italian food distribution. Maintaining a keen interest and understanding of each product line is key when mounting innovative sales campaign programs for new principals.

Unlike its more traditionally structured competitors, AFS develops each business partnership on an individual basis.

"We don't use a cookie-cutter approach," says Weiss. "Each situation is unique and merits its own individualized plan."

Headquartered in Bucks County, Pennsylvania, AFS has dramatically increased its sales growth over the past 15 years and has expanded

A personal approach, combined with modern technology, is key in bringing new products to market.

recently into international markets. The company operates on the belief that integrity, honesty, and loyalty to each business relationship are the cornerstones of success.

With the landscape of food service brokerage changing rapidly into a more technology-based industry, Weiss believes AFS is uniquely positioned to meet the challenges of the next millennium.

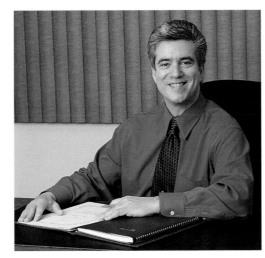

"The Internet plays a large part in the world of sales today, but it still must be combined with face-to-face communications and a personal touch," Weiss says.

Norman Weiss, president and founder of Aggressive Food Sales, is shown here at the company's corporate headquarters in Bucks County, Pennsylvania.

CHAPTER SEVENTEEN

BEYOND WORDS
MEDIA AND TELECOMMUNICATIONS

A new industry began in Pennsylvania with a paper mill constructed outside Philadelphia in the 1690s and a printing press set up in 1686. Pennsylvania's first newspaper, the *American Weekly Mercury,* began publication in 1719, making it one of America's earliest newspapers, and by the mid-18th century, Philadelphia was already a major center for publishing and bookselling. • Benjamin Franklin remains one of Pennsylvania's most famous publishers.

In 1729, he introduced the *Pennsylvania Gazette,* which is today acknowledged to have been one of the best newspapers in the American colonies. He is perhaps more famous for the annual almanac he printed from 1732 to 1757, commonly called *Poor Richard's Almanack.* Franklin also invented improvements for the printing press and manufactured some of America's first good printing ink. His bookstore was one of the best in the colonies.

GETTING THE WORD OUT

During the entire 19th century, Pennsylvania had a printing and publishing industry second only to that of New York. One of the major players was Joshua Ballinger Lippincott, who started as a clerk in a bookstore, purchased the business in 1836, and founded the publishing house called J. B. Lippincott & Co., which was by 1850 a sizeable publisher of Bibles, prayer books, and general literature. Lippincott soon became known for publishing respected reference works, including *Lippincott's Pronouncing Biographical Dictionary,* published in the 1870s and which remained in print for 75 years. Lippincott's publication *The Dispensatory of the United States of America,* first published in 1833, broke a record in 1967 when its 26th edition made it the world's oldest continuously published reference work under private ownership. Lippincott is also known for the medical periodical the *American Journal of Nursing,* first published in 1900.

The name Lippincott lives on in Philadelphia at Lippincott Williams & Wilkins, which was formed by a merger of Lippincott-Raven (the successors to J. B. Lippincott) and Williams & Wilkins, a subsidiary of Wolters Kluwer NV, a publishing company headquartered in Amsterdam and active in 26 countries. Lippincott Williams & Wilkins publishes medical, nursing, and allied health information in both print and electronic formats and may soon become the world leader for electronic delivery of health-science information. Though the company no longer publishes *The Dispensatory of the United States of America,* its 4,000 titles in more than 100 disciplines include a number of books on pharmacology. Its *American Journal of Nursing* is still an indispensable source of information for every practicing nurse.

Ten-year-old Simon Mellitto hawks newspapers on American Street in Philadelphia, in front of F. W. Woolworth. At the time, only New York's publishing industry was greater than Pennsylvania's.

Philadelphia, publishers of the *Catholic Standard & Times.* Both are still located in Philadelphia. W. B. Saunders today upholds Philadelphia's reputation in the health care information industry with over 3,500 titles in the health sciences.

Farther north near Allentown, an entrepreneur who was interested in reforming American eating habits, J. I. Rodale, established a model farm near Emmaus in 1940. In 1942, he published the first issue of *Organic Farming and Gardening.* The publication's successor, *Organic Gardening,* is now the largest gardening magazine in the world, with a circulation of 600,000, and Rodale is a thriving publishing house.

It was also in 1942 that Walter H. Annenberg inherited his father's media conglomerate, Triangle Publications, which included Philadelphia's daily newspaper—the *Philadelphia Inquirer*—and radio and television stations across the country. Annenberg launched *Seventeen* magazine in 1944 and *TV Guide* in 1953. His television station WFIL-TV began airing *Bandstand* in 1952. Renamed *American Bandstand* in 1956, the phenomenon ran on television for another 31 years. Starting in 1969, Annenberg began selling his various properties, and is remembered today primarily for philanthropy.

Printing and publishing remain important in Pennsylvania today, employing over 82,000 people in about 2,500 establishments. Rodale Press, still headquartered in Emmaus, publishes 75 to 100 home and garden and health and fitness titles per year. The Institute for Scientific Information (ISI), founded in 1958 by Dr. Eugene Garfield, is a database publisher headquartered in Philadelphia with more than 800 employees worldwide. ISI's Web-based products provide scholarly research information in the sciences, social sciences, arts, and humanities.

In 1891, Cyrus H. K. Curtis established the Curtis Publishing Company, which became known for its magazines. Two Curtis publications, *Ladies' Home Journal* and *Saturday Evening Post,* had subscribers throughout the nation and attracted submissions from just about every aspiring American writer. *Ladies' Home Journal* is currently published by Meredith Corporation in New York, *Saturday Evening Post* by the Saturday Evening Post Society in Indiana.

The neighborhood around Washington Square was Philadelphia's publishing district during the early 20th century. Both the Lippincott and Curtis houses were located there, as were other well-known publishers such as W. B. Saunders and the Roman Catholic Archdiocese of

Although television was introduced to America in 1939 at the New York World's Fair, this new means of communication was first demonstrated in Pittsburgh in 1929 by Vladimir Zworykin, who worked for Westinghouse Electric. He invented the kinescope and the iconoscope.

Pennsylvania has 84 daily newspapers. The *Pittsburgh Post-Gazette* was founded in 1786 in the village that was then growing up around Fort Pitt, making it the oldest paper in the United States west of the Alleghenies. Its daily circulation is 243,000 and its Sunday circulation is 424,000. The *Allentown Morning Call*, which was founded in 1883 and is now part of the Tribune Company, has a daily circulation of 135,000 and a Sunday circulation of 200,000. Knight Ridder owns both the *Philadelphia Daily News* (daily circulation 166,350) and the *Philadelphia Inquirer.* Founded in 1829, the *Inquirer* is America's oldest surviving daily newspaper. It has been awarded 18 Pulitzer Prizes and has a daily circulation of 425,000 and a Sunday circulation of 871,000. In 1999, the *Inquirer* joined 6ABC Action News in creating an on-line news source. Viewers can log on at any time via their computers for up-to-date weather reports and live news simulcasts.

TO INFORM AND ENTERTAIN

Pittsburgh made broadcasting history on Election Day in 1920. Prior to that year, people waited for the morning paper to find out who had been elected president, or they went to the newspaper office to check the posted returns. But at six o'clock that evening, Leo H. Rosenberg began broadcasting the returns on KDKA Radio. He also mentioned that people listening to the broadcast might want to make themselves known, so that the station could tell how far the signal was reaching and how it was being received. Letters poured in. KDKA had launched the commercial broadcasting industry. KDKA-AM is still on the air today with a news, talk, and sports format.

Telecommunications towers such as this one are appearing throughout Pennsylvania, which bills itself as the State of Technology. There are currently nearly 100 telecommunications providers operating in the Commonwealth.

In 1954, Pittsburgh made history again when WQED debuted as an educational, community-owned television station, an alternative to commercial television. WQED is known today for originating such favorites as *Wonderworks,* National Geographic specials, and *Mister Rogers' Neighborhood.* Other major television broadcasters include KDKA (CBS), WPXI (NBC), WTAE (ABC), and WPGH (Fox) in Pittsburgh; KYW (CBS), WPVI (ABC), WCAU (NBC), WHYY (PBS), and WXTF (Fox) in Philadelphia; and WPHL (WB) in Wilkes-Barre. WSPX, operated by the Pennsylvania State University, is one of the nation's few public stations to be licensed to a university.

More and more movies are being made in Pennsylvania, where production costs are far more economical than in Los Angeles or New York. *The Sixth Sense* and *Silence of the Lambs* were film hits that took full advantage of their Pennsylvania settings. An entertainment complex under way on Philadelphia's Avenue of the Arts, scheduled for completion in 2002, will include, among other amenities, soundstages and recording studios so that producers will have a permanent place for filmmaking in Pennsylvania. Under Governor Tom Ridge, Pennsylvania began trade missions to sell the state as a film location.

The Commonwealth is also served by nine cable providers, including Coudersport's Adelphia Digital Cable, New York–based Time Warner's Time Warner Cable, and Philadelphia's Comcast Cable Communications. Comcast, the nation's third largest cable company with 17,000 employees, develops, manages, and operates broadband cable networks and provides broadcasting content. It is currently the principal owner of the QVC home shopping channel and has a two-thirds interest in Comcast-Spectacor, which owns and operates the Philadelphia 76ers basketball team, the Philadelphia Flyers and Philadelphia Phantoms hockey teams, and the First Union Center and First Union Spectrum arenas (the former is the site of the 2000 Republican National Convention). Its Comcast SportsNet is a 24-hour regional sports television network.

IN TOUCH WITH THE WORLD

The telephone communications industry has seen significant growth and job gains between 1990 and 1997 (up 13.3 percent). Many companies are opening call centers and back-office operations in southeastern Pennsylvania and in the area around Scranton. EchoStar, the owner of DISH Network (which provides 1.4 million customers with direct satellite broadcasting), will assign 2,000 customer service representatives to McKeesport, where they will answer questions about programming and billing.

In order to grow, high-technology businesses demand an advanced telecommunications network capable of supporting methods of communication even more sophisticated than those available today. In 1994, Bell Atlantic–Pennsylvania, one of the Commonwealth's largest telecommunications companies providing the state's majority of residence and business lines, initiated a network modernization plan that includes the installation of hundreds of thousands of miles of fiber-optic cable. The goal is to provide customers with ubiquitous broadband telecommunication capabilities for advanced communications features by 2015. Broadband capabilities deliver all types of data, including video, audio, and film, to one's television, telephone, or computer. Another top Pennsylvania company, Coudersport-based Adelphia Business Solutions (formerly Hyperion Communications), provides local and long-distance service, messaging, high-speed data, and Internet services through fiber-optic networks to business customers in more than 50 cities.

For up-to-date information on Pennsylvania's high-technology communication and information services, individuals and businesses can access Pennsylvania's new Digital Atlas, the nation's first computer database of high-technology infrastructure. Nearly 11,000 Pennsylvania organizations, including utilities and radio and television stations, were surveyed so that the atlas could indicate the location of resources such as fiber-optic lines, microwave towers, and satellite uplinks just as a standard atlas shows roads and highways. Users can even create customized maps of specific resources. The Digital Atlas was developed by the Governor's Office for Information Technology and is available through the Commonwealth's Web site at www.state.pa.us.

A TOUCH EASIER

The first push-button telephone, Touch-Tone, was manufactured by the Western Electric Manufacturing and Supply Unit of Bell System Service and was put into commercial use in Carnegie and Greensburg on November 18, 1963. The service was offered for an extra charge on an optional basis.

ATX TELECOMMUNICATIONS SERVICES

ATX Telecommunications Services provides integrated communications solutions, combining expertise with world-class technologies in local, long-distance, Internet, E-business, network, and wireless services.

ATX's Thomas Gravina and Debra Buruchian (both seated), along with the executive team's four vice presidents, (standing in back) have guided the company since its founding.

ATX Telecommunications Services is a technology company with vision. ATX's ability to understand its customers' current needs while anticipating the products and services that will add value in the future has made ATX one of the nation's premier integrated communications providers.

Founded in Philadelphia in 1985, ATX began by offering long-distance services to local businesses. A decade later, ATX began adding depth to its product portfolio, fostering the company's evolution into a dominating force in the telecommunications industry. Expanding the "capabilities" scope of its business, as well as reaching north and south of its Pennsylvania headquarters, ATX soon became a leading one-stop shop for voice, data, wireless, and Internet services.

The dramatic growth over ATX's 15-year history has seen the company go from five employees to more than 550, adding 20,000 clients and achieving annualized revenues in excess of $160 million. Today, ATX teams operate from headquarters and technical facilities in and around Philadelphia, with sales offices in Allentown, Pennsylvania; New Jersey; Delaware; Maryland; and Washington, D.C. Additional locations in Pennsylvania and throughout the entire eastern corridor of the country are set to open in 2000.

"With a rapidly growing client base and a 99.5 percent customer retention rate, we accomplish what many companies only strive for—continuous and substantial growth in an extremely competitive industry—while maintaining a focus on superior quality and a dedication to excellence," says partner and co-CEO Thomas Gravina. Gravina and Debra Buruchian, also a partner and co-CEO, have been with ATX from its earliest days. Together, they have successfully deployed innovative technologies while building knowledgeable sales and service organizations that learn about a business before custom-tailoring solutions to meet its needs.

Buruchian's and Gravina's emphasis on technical excellence combined with a commitment to service have shaped ATX's corporate culture as well. Among a variety of honors, in April 2000 ATX was chosen from more than 40 companies to receive the "Best New Campaign" award given by the United Way of southeastern Pennsylvania. ATX was also recognized for excellence in leadership by the Greater Philadelphia Chamber of Commerce and the Philadelphia Area Council for Excellence at the Seventh Annual Business and Community Excellence Tribute in June. In addition, ATX is a three-time finalist for Technology Company of the Year at the prestigious Enterprise Awards.

In March 2000, ATX announced its plans to merge with CoreComm Limited, a communications company sharing common values and objectives with ATX, and competing in markets throughout the United States. With ATX preserving its Pennsylvania roots, the combined companies have operations in 30 states as a result of the merger. This step now allows ATX to bring its total-solution communications model to an ever-growing number of customers in the nation and the world, and virtually guarantees the unlimited potential of this visionary company.

ATX's merger with CoreComm strengthens the company's network and technical operations, with a $10 million Technology Management Center anchoring its nationwide infrastructure.

SPRINT

A leading global communications company, Sprint remains committed to offering the latest in telecommunications

products and services with exceptional customer satisfaction.

Celebrating its 100th anniversary in 1999, Sprint, an innovative, cutting-edge telephone company, has made remarkable accomplishments over the past century, with undoubtedly many more to come.

Sprint traces its roots to 1899, when Cleyson L. Brown launched the Brown Telephone Company in Abilene, Kansas. Brown accessed power for the phone service by hooking a generator to his parents' grain grinding mill—a method used to provide electric service in Abilene. The company's name was changed to United Telephone in 1911 when it joined forces with three other Kansas independent phone services. In 1928, the growing phone company bought a majority of the stock in Harrisburg-based Cumberland Valley Telephone Company, which was comprised of five merged companies. A merger with GTE Sprint in 1986 eventually led to United acquiring controlling interest in Sprint in 1989. Shortly thereafter the company adopted the Sprint name.

Today, Sprint serves more than 400,000 customers in 92 Pennsylvania telephone exchanges. Headquartered in Carlisle, Sprint provides local telephone service to all or parts of 25 counties in western and central Pennsylvania.

Sprint is a global communications company that is at the forefront of integrating long distance, local, and wireless communications services. Sprint offers a full portfolio of products and services that includes local, long distance, Internet, paging, and personal communication services (PCS). In addition, Sprint provides video and data products and services to customers inside and outside its operating territories.

The company has become one of the world's largest carriers of Internet traffic. Sprint built and operates the United States' first nationwide all-digital, fiber-optic network, and the firm is considered a leader in advanced data communications services.

Sprint PCS subscribers can now access the Wireless Web on their PCS phone by using their handsets or laptops to connect to the Internet. The Wireless

Sprint offers its customers a world of business solutions.

Web also includes customized information updates sent directly to the handset from the Yahoo! Web site. Sprint PCS serves the majority of the nation's metropolitan areas, including more than 4,000 communities across the country. In addition, Sprint PCS has licensed PCS coverage of nearly 270 million people in all 50 states.

As Sprint begins its second century of service, the company's primary objectives remain the same: offering customers the latest in telecommunications products and services, and providing them with exceptional customer service. For more information, visit Sprint's Web site at www.sprint.com.

Sprint's customers enjoy reliable, affordable, high quality telephone service.

CHERBO PUBLISHING GROUP, INC.

The power of the printed word in an expanding global marketplace cannot be overstated. Cherbo Publishing Group's books combine exciting prose with stunning photography to bring its clients' message to the world.

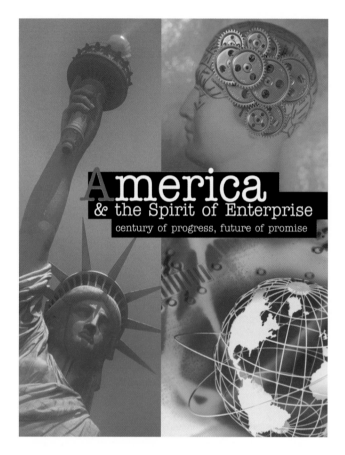

Founded on the premise that fine publications should offer the most persuasive, enduring, and cost-effective medium for publication communication, Cherbo Publishing Group (CPG) has emerged as the dominant publisher of quality books for commercial, historical, civic, and trade associations.

"Cherbo Publishing Group is a growing, privately held corporation with a talented and experienced staff, modern facilities, and state-of-the-art production and fulfillment technology," says company president Jack Cherbo. "These along with our professional sales and marketing organization of proven skill and integrity, our sophisticated network of suppliers and contractors, and our distinguished reputation all add up to CPG's recipe for success."

It was Jack Cherbo, a pioneer in the chamber-of-commerce and association publishing industry, and Elaine Hoffman, Cherbo's executive vice president, who took

Cherbo Publishing Group private in 1993. The company was formerly a division of Jostens Inc., a Fortune 500 company and the world's largest maker of school yearbooks and class rings. Jostens pioneered this specialty print business and became the largest international company in the yearbook and class ring industry. Today, Encino, California– based Cherbo Publishing Group has regional offices in Philadelphia, Minneapolis, Houston, and various marketing facilities throughout the country.

PUBLICATIONS OF QUALITY

CPG's publications—most of which are created in collaboration with a sponsoring agency—promote the economic development of America's cities, counties, and

Among the many publications in production at CPG are America and the Spirit of Enterprise: Century of Progress, Future of Promise, *sponsored by the U.S. Chamber of Commerce, and* California: Golden Past, Shining Future, *sponsored by the California Sesquicentennial Foundation.*

states, both domestically and internationally, and enhance the image and preserve the history of the country's corporations, associations, organizations, and institutions.

CPG books are editorially reliable, lastingly useful, and uncommonly pleasing to the eye and mind. They offer imaginative conception and design, solid and appealing text and illustrations, quality materials and manufacture, followed by energetic promotion. Each publication is developed, after thorough market research, to meet specific needs of and provide concrete advantages for sponsors, corporate participants, and readers. The

written and illustrated with period and modern photography, these books make an ideal commemorative gift.

CPG also publishes annual metro reports for business and industry, incorporating graphics, illustrations, and photographs in a soft-cover format. These books promote economic development by highlighting a city's business and livability advantages for companies or individuals considering a move to the area. Filled with comprehensive information, they include informative demographics, profiles of local companies and organizations, and other essential information.

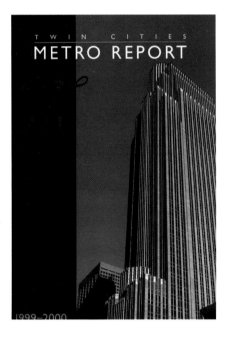 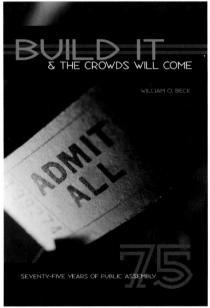 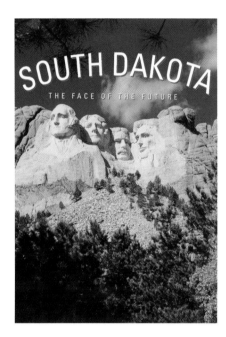

books' uses are many; those often cited by sponsors include economic development promotion, membership development and retention, personnel recruitment and orientation, as well as client and public relations.

A WIDE RANGE OF CHOICES

A glance at the topics covered by CPG gives an idea of the scope and variety of its publications. Among these is the current millennium commemorative series, including the upcoming *California: Golden Past, Shining Future* and *Nebraska: Bringing Our Heritage Into the 21st Century.* Written by award-winning authors, these beautiful, fully illustrated volumes celebrate the past, present, and future of cities and states around the country by chronicling 20th-century inventions and innovations while extolling the city's or state's quality of life and its business environment.

CPG's special interest publications serve to celebrate an anniversary or other special occasion for a corporation, organization, or professional or trade association. Skillfully

CPG produces a variety of publications, including (from left to right) metro reports, special interest books, and the state millennium series.

The international airport histories feature ample illustrations and rich anecdotes that trace the creation and growth of airport facilities and services, and the influence of the airports on the surrounding area's economic growth. These books include fascinating historical vignettes and profiles of airport-related businesses and organizations.

CPG IN THE NEW MILLENNIUM

While CPG pays tribute to the cities it writes about, it also contributes to its own community and many others through various organizations such as the United Way, artistic foundations, and other philanthropic groups.

As the new millennium begins, CPG takes on an expanded role, one that will continue to create stunning publications serving corporate and community entities not only in this country but in marketplaces around the world.

CHAPTER EIGHTEEN

A SOLID BASE
LAND DEVELOPMENT AND UTILITIES

Throughout the 18th century, Pennsylvania probably attracted more immigrants than any other colony. In the years immediately following the American Revolution, it was growing faster than the nation as a whole. Immigrants quickly settled William Penn's three original counties and then moved westward to claim the Susquehanna Valley. Only the Allegheny Ridge and the presence of Native Americans held them in check—for a time.

After 1800, the coal, lumber, and oil industries encouraged the development of the northern part of Pennsylvania. Following the Civil War, Pennsylvania's anthracite coal region, from Carbondale to Shamokin in the northeast, saw further development, as did Pittsburgh, Philadelphia, and the areas surrounding these industrial cities.

The buildings erected during this time proclaim the wealth that the industrial era brought to Pennsylvania. Both Pittsburgh and Philadelphia are graced with elaborate city halls built in the French Renaissance style. Architect Henry Hobson Richardson is remembered for his buildings in the Romanesque Revival style, sometimes referred to as "Richardson Romanesque." Richardson's masterpiece remains the Allegheny County Court House and Jail in Pittsburgh. In the Philadelphia area, architect Frank Furness designed buildings in the neo-Gothic style distinctively decorated with geometric ornamentation. Philadelphia's quintessential Furness structure is the Pennsylvania Academy of the Fine Arts.

The 20th century was an era of suburbanization as Bucks, Delaware, Montgomery, and Chester Counties became increasingly populated and developed. In 1999, Gov. Tom Ridge signed into law Growing Greener—a $650 million plan to preserve farmland and open space, protect watersheds, and make the nation's best state parks better. Lately, Pennsylvania's booming tourism industry has led to development in popular areas such as Pike and Monroe Counties in the Poconos.

GREAT DEVELOPMENTS

Construction is the seventh largest private sector employer in Pennsylvania, providing jobs for more than 200,000 people. In the 1990s, most of the Commonwealth's counties experienced growth in construction jobs, and construction remains one of the highest paying industries in Pennsylvania in terms of hourly and weekly earnings. Statewide there are more than 21,500 people employed in nonresidential building construction and over 34,000 in residential building construction, as well as over 138,000 special trade contractors such as plumbers, masons, and carpenters.

These construction workers are nearing completion of a skyscraper in Philadelphia's Center City. At one time, city laws forbade building anything taller than the hat on City Hall's statue of William Penn.

The related real estate industry employs over 45,000, including more than 4,700 subdividers and developers, 21,000 real estate operators and lessors, and 19,000 real estate agents and managers. Employment in the real estate industry overall grew 6.2 percent from 1990 to 1997.

Pennsylvania's most famous developer may well be Willard G. Rouse III, the man who was bold enough to propose that new buildings in Philadelphia could be taller than the hat on the statue of William Penn on top of City Hall. The towers of Rouse's One Liberty Place and Two Liberty Place changed the city's skyline forever. His Great Valley Corporate Center—built on the site of an old municipal dump, two quarries, and a number of cornfields—inspired other builders to join him in creating the facilities for the service and technology centers that have since swarmed into the Route 202 Corridor in southeastern Pennsylvania. Rouse currently chairs the Regional Performing Arts Center Inc., which manages the construction of this exciting new facility rising on the Avenue of the Arts in Philadelphia. Rouse also established Liberty Property Trust of Malvern, a real estate investment trust that acquires, develops, and manages commercial properties and over 1,000 acres of land.

Monitoring the energy flow at the PECO Energy Company's control center in Philadelphia is a key part of this man's job. Part of the business community since 1881, PECO provides regulated electricity and natural gas service to more than 1.5 million customers in the state.

Pennsylvania has myriad other real estate firms, including Brandywine Realty Trust of Newtown Square, a real estate investment trust also engaged in acquiring, developing, leasing, and managing suburban offices and industrial properties; and CB Richard Ellis, the largest vertically integrated commercial real estate services firm in the world. Ellis's Pennsylvania offices can be found in Philadelphia, Harrisburg, and Pittsburgh.

DESIGNS FOR LIVING

The Commonwealth boasts some of this country's oldest and most well-known design companies. Kling Lindquist, founded in 1946, is one of the nation's top integrated architecture, engineering, and interior design firms. Employing over 400 people in offices in Philadelphia and Washington, D.C., Kling Lindquist has completed more than 4,500 projects worth more than $15 billion in constructed value. Burt Hill Kosar

William Penn could be called Pennsylvania's first urban planner. Having seen how plagues and fires swept through the crowded, winding streets of London, he adopted a grid plan for his capital city of Philadelphia. Individual homes would sit in the center of a sizeable garden plot, and the city would thus become a "greene Countrie Towne." The grid plan prevails to this day, but Philadelphia real estate quickly became too valuable for all those gardens.

With a healthy regard for preserving Pennsylvania's history and green spaces, these architects are among many creating business centers and housing developments that will foster controlled growth in the new millennium.

Rittelmann Associates, whose Pennsylvania office is in Butler, employs more than 350 people in six offices in architecture, engineering, landscape architecture, interior design, and facilities management.

Among Pennsylvania's most famous construction firms is the Wohlsen Construction Company. Founded in 1890 in Lancaster County, Wohlsen is one of the leading construction services companies in the mid-Atlantic states, with projects ranging from warehouses to high-rise offices. Rouse/Chamberlin Homes, another leader, was named by the National Association of Homebuilders and *Builder* magazine in 1997 as America's Best Builder in the 100-to-500-homes category. The firm is known for carefully planned site designs that encourage a spirit of neighborhood. Its president and CEO, Sarah Peck, was recently chosen as one of *Philadelphia Business Journal*'s Women of Distinction.

CLEANING UP THEIR ACT

As land development increases, the amount of land on which to build decreases, raising concerns over environmental issues. Throughout Pennsylvania, abandoned or underutilized factories left over from the industrial revolution dot the landscape. These structures possess the built-in advantages of good access to transportation routes and utilities and a skilled workforce residing nearby. Unfortunately, many of these sites are contaminated by hazardous waste, and companies have been reluctant to build on them. In the past, government policies required that all contaminated sites be restored to pristine conditions, and the government held the current owners of a property responsible for all cleanup, even though the contamination might have been caused by the previous owner or user of the site. The unintended result was that developers and builders bypassed these sites in favor of breaking new ground.

Under the leadership of Governor Ridge, Pennsylvania took action in 1995 by creating the Land Recycling Program. Cited by the Ford Foundation and the John F. Kennedy School of Government as a top government innovation, the Land Recycling Program limits future liability for the new owner once cleanup standards are met. It encourages innovation from the private sector, rather than

Waste sites such as this are being converted into useable land as part of the state's Land Recycling Program, a joint effort by government, corporations, and private organizations to conserve land.

insisting that the government knows best. It also simplifies the approval process and provides grants and loans to help finance environmental assessments and cleanups. Unlike the federal Superfund program that provides funding for the cleanup of the most seriously contaminated sites,

FRANKLIN AND THE KITE

Whether or not Benjamin Franklin was the first to demonstrate that lightning and electrical matter were one in the same, there is no doubt that his experiment to do so is the most famous. One day in 1752, he ventured out in a thunderstorm with a key tied to the string of a kite made from a silk handkerchief. Soon the threads of the kite string began to stand erect, and when he touched the key "he perceived a very evident electric spark," as scientist Joseph Priestley recounts. The experiment was the inspiration for Franklin's most famous invention, the lightning rod.

John D. Rockefeller, who in 1870 founded the nation's first petroleum company, Standard Oil, controlled 90 percent of the industry by the 1880s. For 20 years, politicians and lawmakers fought to break up the monopoly. Rockefeller lost the battle in 1911, when the Supreme Court instructed that the trust be broken up into 34 companies.

Pennsylvania was one of the first states to offer its citizens the choice of an electricity supplier. As of September 1999, more than 450,000 customers have used the Commonwealth's electric choice program.

Pennsylvania's Land Recycling Program covers all contaminated sites in Pennsylvania.

The program puts abandoned industrial sites back into use and back on the tax rolls while expanding manufacturing. It is a boon for the Commonwealth's urban areas, transforming unsightly and hazardous sites near residential areas to bustling centers of commerce. At the same time, it alleviates suburban sprawl and preserves farmland and open space. To date, more than 600 sites have been cleaned up, at which more than 17,000 people now work.

Thanks to the Land Recycling Program, for example, the Shenango Valley Industrial Development Corporation was granted $1.6 million to develop a new

industrial park on part of an old Sharon Steel Corporation facility; and a site in York that had been abandoned for more than 30 years was reborn as the Industrial Plaza of York. The latter resulted in a gain of 500 jobs and won the prestigious Phoenix Award of Distinction for Brownfield Development from the Engineers' Society of Western Pennsylvania.

LIGHTING THE WAY

Long before electricity could be considered a public utility, intellectuals in 18th-century England, France, Germany, and Italy were reading a text called *Experiments and Observations on Electricity* written by Benjamin Franklin and some of his friends who had been investigating electrical phenomena. They concluded that "electrical fire" was attracted by water and metals, prompting Franklin to propose that buildings be protected against lightning with iron lightning rods, one of the many practical innovations for which Franklin is remembered.

In the early 1950s, Pennsylvania entered into a unique public/private partnership with Duquesne Light and Power and the Atomic Energy Commission. With Westinghouse Electric acting as general contractor, construction began in 1955 on the Shippingport Atomic Power Station located north of Pittsburgh. When the plant was ready for operation in 1957, it represented the first attempt to offer nuclear power through a public utility and the first atomic electric power plant used completely for peaceful purposes.

It was during the administration of Gov. John K. Tener (1911–15) that Pennsylvania first began regulating public utilities through a new state public service commission. This agency was transformed during the 1930s into the Pennsylvania Public Utility Commission (PUC). Today, this commission regulates natural gas, transportation, water and wastewater,

In Pennsylvania, as throughout the world, use of the cellular phone is exploding. Here, electrical workers install cellular phone antenna.

electricity, and telecommunications. In 1997, the PUC had under its jurisdiction 17 electric utilities, 38 gas utilities, and 207 water utilities, including more than 45 municipal water companies. Due to growth in the telecommunications market, in the same year there were more than 500 providers of local telephone utilities, resellers, access providers, operator services, and local exchange carriers.

SITE-SEEING

When Bethlehem Steel closed its facility on Bethlehem's south side in 1995, company administrators decided to redevelop the site rather than abandon it. They divided it into two sections: a commerce center and Bethlehem Works, where the Smithsonian's National Museum of Industrial History will be housed.

Most of the state's energy needs are met by 11 major investor-owned utilities; eight of them generate all or a portion of their energy, and three resell wholesale power. In 1996, Pennsylvania's utilities generated 139 billion KWH for sale to customers and other operating systems. Coal-fired units generated 56.7 percent of the state's energy, and nuclear generation accounted for 36.8 percent of the total. Between 1981 and 1996, the state's energy demand grew 1.7 percent annually. A 20-year projection made in 1996 forecasted that net generation by coal would increase by 14.4 percent but gain only .5 of a percentage point of total net generation. Nuclear generation is expected to decrease to 31.5 percent of the total. Energy generated from natural gas and oil-fueled combustion turbine, combined cycle, and steam units was projected to increase from 1.9 percent of the total to 9.6 percent.

Pennsylvania is on the leading edge in energy deregulation. In 1996, Governor Ridge signed into law the Electricity Choice and Competition Act, which resulted in significant savings for consumers and businesses on their utility bills. In 1999, after one of the first, largest, and most successful pilot programs in America, two million customers signed up for the Pennsylvania Electric Choice Program, generating savings of more than $1 billion. This program enables consumers to shop for an electric generation supplier licensed by the Pennsylvania PUC. As of mid-1999, the PUC had licensed more than 50 suppliers to serve industrial, large commercial, small business, and residential customers. This makes Pennsylvania one of the nation's most receptive markets for alternative suppliers, and means that any home owner or business administrator can select an electric generation supplier from anywhere in the nation.

Pennsylvania's PECO Energy Company has announced a merger with Unicom, the Chicago-based parent of Commonwealth Edison, intended to take these companies to the forefront of the deregulated power industry. The combined firm, to be called Excelon, will be the nation's fourth largest electricity generator and the largest nuclear plant operator in the United States. The headquarters will be on a site being developed in Chester County.

All across the state, school districts and municipalities have begun forming electricity consortiums to purchase electricity on a collective basis, the savings passed on to local taxpayers. New companies are forming to broker electricity over the Internet. For example, OnLineChoice.com, a Pittsburgh-based company, pools consumers to drive prices down.

Late in 1999, a decision by the PUC enabled consumers to select their local phone company, which will result in more choices and better prices. The decision also ensures that the same services are offered to all customers in all parts of the state, including the traditionally higher-cost rural areas. The PUC will implement a consumer education program on how to shop for a local telephone service provider.

Also in 1999, Governor Ridge signed into law a bill for natural gas deregulation so that natural gas customers can begin shopping for suppliers too.

The future looks bright for the utilities industry as companies seek alternative energy sources. One such company, Energy Unlimited, of West Conshohocken—a division of the American Refining Group—operates the state's first classified wind farm and is involved in hydro and solar power. Advances in these and other energy areas ensure a powerful Pennsylvania for the 21st century.

CURRENT TECHNOLOGY

George Westinghouse, who founded the Westinghouse Electric Company in Pittsburgh in 1886, developed a transformer that could provide electric lighting through alternating current. The company's first central power station was built in Greensburg in the late 1880s, and within a decade, 95 percent of the world's electric power was generated by alternating current. The company, now headquartered in Monroe, went on to become a producer of nuclear reactors, radar, and military electronic systems.

PHOTO: © Digital Stock

UTILITIES

PECO ENERGY COMPANY

With more than a century of experience in pioneering leadership, PECO Energy Company moves into this new millennium with a three-pronged program for expanding its services to power customers.

Even basic transformers need planned maintenance to continue operating optimally. Here, a PECO Energy technician handles the job at the PECO Energy Company Plymouth Service Building.

PECO Energy Company has played an integral part in shaping economic development in the state of Pennsylvania, and the Philadelphia-based company plans to expand on that role in the 21st century.

Founded in 1881, PECO Energy is a pioneer in the power industry. Ever since the company introduced the first electric lights on Philadelphia's Chestnut Street, more than a century ago, it has been a dynamic industry leader.

PECO Energy was among the first energy companies in the nation to embrace nuclear power when it participated in President Eisenhower's Atoms for Peace program in the 1950s. Today PECO Energy maintains ownership stakes in eight separate nuclear reactors in the United States.

The company also has been a leader in the development of fossil power generation. PECO Energy has built some of the largest fossil plants in Pennsylvania. Today it generates nuclear, fossil, and hydroelectric power.

The energy industry is moving into an exciting new era, and once again PECO Energy is positioning itself at the forefront to capitalize on new opportunities. The company's primary objective is to become the world's leading provider of clean energy, and it is putting the processes and structures in place to make that vision a reality. One long-term goal is to maintain a strong market share in the firm's traditional electricity service area, as well as to establish a significant position in other retail electricity markets in Pennsylvania and across the nation.

CLEAN, EFFICIENT ENERGY

The key to PECO Energy's success in deregulated power-generation markets will be to own or control a significant amount of environmentally clean and efficient generating capacity in targeted regions of the United States. Ultimately, PECO Energy plans to more than double its generation capacity in the first few years of the new century.

A PECO Energy technician performs maintenance tasks for underground energy transmission and distribution.

With safety in mind always, these PECO Energy technicians review their strategy before beginning work at a customer's property.

PECO Energy has responded to industry deregulation by rapidly transforming itself from a regulated power company to a competitive player in diverse markets. The firm has leveraged its strengths to expand through initiatives in power generation, marketing, and distribution, and in telecommunications and infrastructure services. Aggressive business strategies are being carried out in all three of PECO Energy's main business segments to help realize that new growth.

DIVERSIFIED OPPORTUNITIES

Through its power generation and marketing business group, PECO Energy has become one of the largest and most active marketers of energy in Pennsylvania. The 10,000 megawatts of electric generating capacity owned or controlled by PECO Energy, combined with its diverse national portfolio, makes the company one of the largest generators and wholesale deliverers of electricity in the United States. In addition, industry restructuring and deregulation are opening up new markets for wholesale power, as well as new opportunities to acquire generating plants across North America.

A second business unit, PECO Energy Distribution Company, provides regulated electricity and natural gas service to more than 1.5 million customers in southeastern Pennsylvania. PECO Energy Distribution applies its high-performance work culture in its regulated business in order to reduce costs and increase efficiency while sustaining reliability, customer satisfaction, and safety.

PECO Energy is tackling a variety of innovative, unregulated ventures with its third business unit, Exelon Ventures. Some of these efforts include Exelon Energy, which is a competitive energy supplier in Pennsylvania. Exelon Communications offers wireless and fiber optics–based communications services, while Exelon Infrastructure Services provides infrastructure services to utility companies and developers.

Just as PECO Energy was a pioneer in illuminating Chestnut Street in the 19th century, the company is continuing to break new ground in the midst of a rapidly changing industry. Another of PECO Energy's innovative moves is its proposed merger with Chicago-based Unicom Corp. The merger will help to define the way utility companies will evolve in the 21st century. The new holding company will be the nation's largest electricity utility based on its approximately five million customers and revenues of approximately $12.4 billion. It will be the fourth largest power generator in the United States, with a generation portfolio of more than 22,500 megawatts, which helps to position it as a leader in the nation's growing wholesale power marketing business.

PECO Energy continually strives to maximize success and profit through increased cost efficiency, energy service performance, and customer satisfaction. At the PECO Energy Call Center, above, a customer consultant assists callers.

AMERICAN REFINING GROUP, INC.

A successful petroleum refining company, American Refining Group, Inc., of Bradford, Pennsylvania, continues

to expand its product base and to pursue its vision of becoming "A Total Energy Company."

American Refining Group, Inc. (ARG), a petroleum refining company, has been operating within the state of Pennsylvania for approximately 30 years. ARG started its first refinery in McKees Rocks, Pennsylvania. Later the company moved to Indianola, Pennsylvania, and focused on Transmix, a product that results from oil and gasoline commingling in a pipeline. This process takes place on a daily basis within various petroleum pipelines throughout the United States. Transmix refining requires a separation process to render original value to the product, whether it be gasoline or an oil product. The Transportation Fuels Division of American Refining Group first handled the company's Transmix refining.

American Refining Group later purchased a similar refinery in Hartford, Illinois, to perform the same task. This single-minded focus enabled ARG to become the largest Transmix refiner in the world.

The Bradford Refinery maintains a state-of-the-art packaging facility that offers more than 110,000 square feet of packaging and storage capacity under one roof.

REFINERY PURCHASE ENHANCES OPERATIONS

In February of 1997 American Refining Group purchased the Bradford Refinery, located in Bradford, Pennsylvania, from the Witco Corporation. This refinery, which began operations in 1881, is the oldest continuous operating lube oil refinery in the world. It also was the first refinery in the United States to achieve ISO-9002 quality certification, a status reflective of the total quality goal of its employees. The refinery resides on 131 acres and consists of five processing units. It has 375 feedstock and product storage tanks emphasizing the wide diversity of products produced at the site. It also has a large two-story office building and a modern research and development laboratory. Associated with the refinery is a blending plant for finished lubricants and a 110,000-square-foot packaging plant and warehouse.

The Bradford Refinery is one of only a few refineries in the world that can produce hundreds of specialty lube oil products.

The Bradford Refinery consists of five processing units on 131 acres. The refinery exclusively utilizes Penn Grade Crude as its feedstock for production.

THE BRADFORD IMPACT

It is hard to imagine the impact, from a historical perspective, that the Bradford area has had on the rest of the world. Even the name given to the oil production area bears the name Bradford to reflect the heart of all activities. The Bradford Field is comprised of approximately 115,000 contiguous acres of land (100,000 acres are located in Pennsylvania and 15,000 acres are located in western New York). In 1881 this field produced 83 percent of the country's entire oil output and 77 percent of all the oil produced in the world.

The Bradford Refinery offers many strategic and unique products. It is one of the few refineries in the entire world that can produce hundreds of specialty products; hence, the Bradford Refinery bears the name "The Lubricants and Specialty Products Division." Some examples of the unique diversity of the refinery include: Brad Penn™ branded Penn Grade™ passenger car motor oils, Gulf® branded motor oils, private-label motor oils, Gyro oils, Penn Grade resins, quench oils, ink oils, aluminum rolling oils, low sulfur gasoline, low sulfur diesel fuels, shock absorber fluids, and specialty waxes.

OPPORTUNITIES FOR THE NEW MILLENNIUM

As we enter the new millennium, American Refining Group has conducted extensive research identifying the opportunities that lie ahead for the Bradford Refinery. To that end, ARG will be investing over $25 million in new state-of-the-art equipment. This move will position the Bradford Refinery to become one of the leading specialty refineries in the world, producing products that meet or exceed the highest standards set for the industry.

In addition to the refinery operation, American Refining Group consists of two additional entities: American Refining & Exploration Corporation and American Refining and Biochemical Company. In order to focus its resources and maximize all efforts at the Bradford Refinery, American Refining Group sold its Transportation Fuels Division in February of 1999.

A VISION FOR THE FUTURE

American Refining Group's vision goes beyond petroleum products and into the expansive realm of "A Total Energy Company." For example, its chairman and chief executive officer, Harry R. Halloran Jr., holds patents in chemical technology that one day may provide a breakthrough in the development of chemical products. This process would be applied through the use of renewable feedstock, as opposed to carbon-base feedstock that major petroleum and chemical companies use exclusively today. American Refining Group is proud of its past and looks forward to its contributions to the state of Pennsylvania—as well as the country—as it enters the new millennium.

Tom Oliphant is director of research and development for American Refining Group. He constantly reviews product formulas to discover new methods in the refining process that will enhance products and benefit customers.

ENERGY UNLIMITED, INC.

A pioneer in the wind energy industry, Energy Unlimited, Inc., seeks to grow and expand its energy services throughout the world and to build upon its fruitful years of experience.

Weather has not deterred the development of wind technology. As long as wind consistently occurs at a speed in excess of 14 mph, wind farms can be developed throughout the world. © AWEA

Energy Unlimited, Inc., (EUI) of West Conshohoken, Pennsylvania, was formed in 1980 by chairman and chief executive officer, Harry R. Halloran Jr. A visionary in the renewable energy field, Halloran has provided leadership as a past president, and presently, a board member of the American Wind Energy Association (AWEA). Halloran also serves as chief executive officer of American Refining Group, Inc., which is one of only a few manufacturers in the entire world that produces hundreds of specialty oil and lubricating products.

One of Energy Unlimited's first ventures in the renewable arena was a wind development project in San Gorgonio pass near Palm Springs, California. This project originally consisted of 16 megawatts (MWs) of wind energy, and has been expanded to comprise 25 MWs of wind energy owned, and or managed, by Energy Unlimited. There is also an additional 20 MWs of wind energy that EUI developed through a joint venture at an adjoining site. Energy Unlimited's wind development San Gorgonio project, including its joint venture, totals over 400 wind turbines, ranging in size from 65 kilowatts to 1 MW.

In addition to the San Gorgonio, California, project, Energy Unlimited recently developed a 5 MW wind project known as the Ponnequin. The project is located in Weld County, Colorado, which is approximately 75 miles north of Denver, Colorado. EUI's next project will be within the state of Pennsylvania. EUI has developed and is operating the first classified wind farm within the state and is presently performing a series of analyses to determine the best site locations for a series of 10 to 20 MW wind projects.

Energy Unlimited's business relationships include a joint venture agreement with WaterHealth International, a company that holds a technology license agreement to manufacture and sell a patented water purification system developed by Lawrence Berkeley National laboratory. This technology won *Discover* magazine's and *Popular Science* magazine's award for best new technology in 1996. Energy Unlimited provides wind, solar, and hydro equipment as well as the know-how to power the technology for remote application throughout the world.

Energy Unlimited also has entered into a joint venture agreement with Ingersoll-Rand Energy Systems, a subsidiary of Ingersoll-Rand, to distribute cogeneration energy units throughout a six-state region within the northeast section of the United States.

Additionally, EUI has entered into a joint venture with Solera Energy Systems Pvt., Ltd., of India to expand renewable energy technology within India utilizing EUI management expertise and joint venture relationships.

Wind turbines are now manufactured with a kilowatt nameplate capacity of production of more than one megawatt of electric generation. © AWEA

A SOLID BASE

247

PPL CORPORATION

Electricity and natural gas provider PPL Corporation, a Fortune 500 company based in Allentown, is a worldwide organization marketing electricity in Pennsylvania and throughout the United States and other countries.

With roots that extend back to Thomas Edison and the advent of the commercial electricity business in the United States, PPL Corporation is a major player on the world energy stage. At the same time, the company remains a major corporate citizen at home, working to strengthen its communities, create new jobs through economic development, preserve the environment for future generations, and improve the quality of education.

PPL Corporation is a Fortune 500 company based in Allentown, Pennsylvania. It delivers electricity and natural gas to more than 3.5 million customers in Pennsylvania, the United Kingdom, Chile, Bolivia, and El Salvador. PPL also markets wholesale or retail energy in 43 U.S. states and Canada. It provides energy services for businesses in the mid-Atlantic and northeastern United States. And it generates electricity at power plants in Pennsylvania, Montana, and Maine.

Founded in 1920 as a company providing electricity service to most of eastern Pennsylvania, PPL has grown to become a worldwide organization with more than $4.5 billion in annual revenues, through its operations in nine countries and coast-to-coast electricity marketing in the United States.

At the heart of PPL's 80-year success story is a commitment to understanding and meeting customer needs. The exceptional customer service of PPL has been confirmed by independent surveys, both in the United States and

PPL Corporation markets power to wholesale or retail customers in 43 U.S. states and in Canada.

abroad. And, PPL is a leading advocate of customer choice in the new energy market, at both the state and national levels.

Following a corporate realignment scheduled for completion in 2000, PPL Corporation will have four major business lines:
• PPL Utilities will operate PPL's 1.3 million–customer electricity delivery business in Pennsylvania and the company's natural gas delivery operation, which serves 70,000 customers in Pennsylvania and Maryland.
• PPL EnergyPlus, one of the leading suppliers of competitively priced electricity in the mid-Atlantic region, markets wholesale or retail electricity in

At the PPL subsidiary Elfec, in Bolivia, a customer service executive assists customers applying for electricity service.

43 U.S. states and Canada. PPL EnergyPlus also provides energy services for businesses in the mid-Atlantic and northeastern United States through five mechanical contracting companies, with operations in Pennsylvania and New England.

• PPL Generation will operate the company's growing fleet of domestic power plants.

• PPL Global owns electricity delivery companies in the United Kingdom and in Latin America and develops generation projects. PPL Global also owns power plants in Spain and Portugal, and it is building new power plants in Connecticut, Arizona, and Pennsylvania.

Although PPL Corporation is a global company, it remains committed to its communities in Pennsylvania. For example, about 1,500 PPL employees spend 150,000 hours each year in community volunteer activities with the support of the corporation. This is just another example of the ways PPL gives something back to its communities. Because the success of PPL depends

on the prosperity and strength of the cities, towns, and regions where the company operates—throughout Pennsylvania, as well as around the world.

In Pennsylvania, near Hazelton, PPL utility line workers, above, install underground cable to deliver electricity. PPL generates electricity at power plants in Pennsylvania, Montana, and Maine. Shown below is the PPL Martins Creek power plant in Pennsylvania.

GPU ENERGY

Pennsylvania-based GPU Energy, a subsidiary of international energy supplier GPU, Inc., provides expanded electricity services to customers and increasing returns to shareholders in a deregulating utility environment.

Bringing power to businesses and residences, GPU Energy is a leader in providing customer-driven energy services.

Building on its reputation as a customer-driven deliverer of electricity, GPU Energy works to create opportunities for new and existing businesses in Pennsylvania.

To maintain a leadership position in the transmission and distribution of electricity, GPU Energy management has taken steps to operate more efficiently and be more responsive to customers.

BUILDING CUSTOMER SATISFACTION

"Over the past decade we have made significant efforts to reduce costs to benefit our customers and to achieve a higher level of overall customer satisfaction," says Michael Chesser, president and chief executive officer of GPU Energy. "GPU Energy's record of customer service will be what makes the company successful as our industry becomes more competitive." GPU Energy's mission includes providing developmental opportunities for existing and potential businesses in the state. The company's business development staff and other experts assess customers' office, manufacturing, and

warehousing needs and help customers deal with financing issues, technical and training needs, and government regulations. Businesses, in turn, are able to review available commercial and industrial sites through a computer-generated list maintained by the company.

GPU Energy, headquartered in Reading, Pennsylvania, has working partnerships with municipal and state governments, real estate brokers, and

An experienced and skilled workforce supports GPU Energy's core business of transmitting and distributing electricity to more than two million customers in Pennsylvania and New Jersey.

development professionals. Most recently the company has cooperated in projects with companies such as Hershey Foods, Pella Windows, and Elk Shingle.

"We have all the ingredients to serve business and industry: an experienced business development team, a strong international presence, and available skilled labor in a service area that spans two states in the mid-Atlantic region—the heart of the United States marketplace," says Rebecca Wingenroth, GPU Energy director of business development.

GPU Energy has a tradition of supporting the communities it serves as a deliverer of electricity. In addition to supporting charitable organizations, GPU Energy employees volunteer their time for community activities.

INTERNATIONAL OPERATIONS

GPU Energy is the trade name for three electric utility subsidiaries of GPU, Inc., a Fortune 500 company. Domestically, through GPU Energy, GPU, Inc., provides electricity services to two million customers in Pennsylvania and New Jersey. In addition, GPU, Inc.'s International Group has ownership and interests in the electricity distribution and supply business in England, Australia, and South America and in generating facilities in six foreign countries. GPU, Inc., which recorded operating revenues of $4.8 billion in 1999, serves more than 4.3 million customers globally.

GPU Energy's competitive position in the industry has been championed through the business strategy of GPU, Inc., to make the transmission and distribution of electricity the core business of the corporation.

As a responsible corporate citizen, GPU Energy supports the volunteer activities of its staff, who help strengthen the communities in the company's territory. On a court at the Oakbrook Coliseum, above, employee athletes provide coaching for young basketball players.

EXPANDED SERVICES, LOWER COSTS

"GPU Inc.'s goal is to provide expanded utility services to our customers and increasing returns to our shareholders in the rapidly deregulating utility environment," says Fred D. Hafer, GPU, Inc., chairman, president, and chief executive officer. "Our strategy for that goal is to focus our actions on being the best energy delivery company. We intend to be a first quartile performer in our chosen industry. We also have undertaken a major initiative to improve and expand customer service and at the same time reduce the cost of providing that service.

"Our future is bright. GPU Energy will keep functioning as a key element of the GPU, Inc., strategy for success in the new electric utility frontier," Hafer says. "The changes taking place in our industry will benefit the citizens of Pennsylvania. We are excited to do business and have GPU Energy headquartered in the Keystone State."

When Pella Corporation was looking for a manufacturing location, GPU Energy's business development professionals helped the company find this site in Gettysburg, Pennsylvania.

PHILADELPHIA SUBURBAN WATER COMPANY

With a long history of providing exceptional customer service and superior technical expertise, Philadelphia Suburban Water Company supplies water to approximately 1.2 million Pennsylvanians in five counties.

From PSW's distribution control center, operators manage the daily delivery of 110 million gallons of water through 3,500 miles of pipe that span PSW's 488-square-mile service territory.

Among the basics often taken for granted in cities across America is a plentiful and reliable supply of quality water. Such easy confidence is the direct accomplishment of the expertly managed private sector utility, Philadelphia Suburban Water Company (PSW).

As one of the nation's largest investor-owned water utilities, PSW provides drinking water to some 1.2 million people in five Pennsylvania counties. PSW's more than 3,500 miles of pipe supply a 488-square-mile service territory with up to 176 million gallons of water daily from reservoirs holding up to 10 billion gallons.

Headquartered in Bryn Mawr, Pennsylvania, PSW employs a staff of approximately 550 people who work at one of three primary operating divisions or one of nine treatment plants.

PSW was created as Springfield Water Company in 1886 by a group of Swarthmore College professors in an effort to supply water to Springfield Township. The company's service territory quickly grew and by 1925, shareholders decided to change the name to Philadelphia Suburban Water Company. Philadelphia Suburban Corporation (PSC),

a holding company, was created in 1968 and was listed on the New York Stock Exchange in 1971.

With the passing of the federal Safe Drinking Water Act (SDWA) of 1974, numerous U.S. water utilities faced rigorous new water quality standards. Many undercapitalized water providers discovered that SDWA compliance required heavy investments too costly for their customer base, and turned to larger private sector companies as potential buyers for their systems or to provide operations and management services. In such an arena, PSW's aggressive attention to basics—water quality, sound infrastructure, customer service, and astute financial management—ideally positioned the company to use its resources to acquire municipal and private water systems.

PSW's long history of superior technical performance and exceptional customer service provided the foundation for its vigorous growth-through-acquisition strategy employed since 1992. In 1996, PSW entered the wastewater business. By 2000, PSW's growth-through-acquisition strategy resulted in 30 water system acquisitions, four wastewater system acquisitions, and six additional revenue-generating growth ventures.

PSW begins the 21st century with a customer base of nearly 320,000 accounts as well as a growing wastewater business. Philadelphia Suburban Water Company continues to be one of the nation's leading providers of low-cost, high quality public water service.

PHILADELPHIA SUBURBAN
W A T E R   C O M P A N Y

PSW provides quality drinking water to approximately 1.2 million residents in a five-county suburban area outside the city of Philadelphia.

REAL ESTATE AND DEVELOPMENT

A SOLID BASE

INSIGNIA/ESG, INC.

The experienced professionals of Insignia/ESG, an Insignia Financial Group company, provide full-service

commercial real estate services locally, nationally, and abroad.

Since 1876, Philadelphia has been headquarters for leading real estate services through Insignia/ESG, Inc., formerly Jackson-Cross Company. © B&H Photographics

Insignia/ESG has amassed a management and leasing portfolio of 230 million square feet of office, medical, industrial, and retail space. In the United States, the company completes real estate transactions involving more than 178 million square feet annually. The firm's capital advisers complete investment sales and financing transactions valued at more than $4.3 billion per year.

PERFORMANCE STRENGTH

This performance in a period of overall robust economic growth, while not surprising, is attributed by the firm to several factors. One is what Insignia/ESG Philadelphia's executive managing director, J. Richard Jones, terms the company's greatest asset: "Capable people with the knowledge to interpret current market data." This talented group of in-house professionals has extensive experience with property management, leasing, financial services, and more.

Insignia/ESG's ongoing success also can be credited to strong internal, or "organic," growth of the firm's existing institutional client base. In addition, it has

Being innovative, flexible, and the first to embrace new business models and concepts before they become mainstream is the formula that has placed Insignia/ESG, Inc., in the top echelon of commercial and residential real estate services companies in the United States and the United Kingdom.

In Philadelphia, Insignia/ESG was formerly Jackson-Cross Company, a firm that traces its roots back more than 120 years to its founding by Joseph T. Jackson in 1876. Jackson-Cross was one of the oldest commercial real estate services firms in the nation and the market leader in Greater Philadelphia. Today, using state-of-the-art technology, Insignia/ESG provides a broad spectrum of information and services to assist clients in making sound short-term and long-term decisions regarding their real estate and strategic business needs.

Insignia/ESG was formed in 1994 as a wholly owned subsidiary of Insignia Financial Group, Inc. (IFG), a publicly traded company listed on the New York Stock Exchange.

Insignia/ESG generates annual worldwide revenues of more than $678 million in gross volume.

Philadelphia's central business district is home base for the firm's regional headquarters location. © B&H Photographics

pursued a strategic growth policy of acquiring established regional firms that hold a dominant share of their markets. As a result, Insignia/ESG has been ranked as one of the top five management firms in several states, including Arizona, California, Florida, New Jersey, and New York. Rather than imposing its own management practices on its acquired firms, Insignia/ESG applies these firms' own best practices—an integration philosophy that helps to foster entrepreneurial spirit and innovative decision making.

This building complex is 1800/1880 John F. Kennedy Boulevard, the Philadelphia headquarters address of Insignia/ESG, Inc. © B&H Photographics

A FULL RANGE OF SERVICES

Insignia/ESG provides a broad range of services: agency leasing, tenant representation, industrial services, retail services, investment sales, property and facilities management, advisory and consulting, development services, hotel services, energy management, and mortgage brokerage. As a tenant representative as well as a corporate real estate adviser, the company represents a diverse clientele that ranges from Fortune 500 corporations to nonprofit institutions and emerging growth companies.

Insignia/ESG's consulting group provides strategic planning, needs analysis, deal structuring and financial engineering, and transaction management, negotiations, and implementation for its clients. A unique managed brokerage system gives the brokerage team access to the firm's internal market research information and proprietary databases. The ad hoc team approach, which combines business, financial, and transaction management skills, enables the firm to provide sophisticated analyses and solutions for its clients' complex real estate needs.

REAL ESTATE WORLDWIDE

The comprehensive services provided by Insignia/ESG in the real estate market range from the regional level to the national and international arena. IFG acquired Richard Ellis St. Quintin, and formed Insignia Richard Ellis. The venerable 225-year-old London-based firm has 800 employees in eight offices throughout the United Kingdom. The acquisition of the firm, valued at more than $58 million annually, has provided a springboard for European expansion and enables Insignia/ESG to assist its clients in the United States with their real estate needs in the United Kingdom.

Even though Insignia/ESG is a global company, the firm continues to maintain a strong regional presence, remaining actively involved in the community. Insignia Philadelphia's Real Estate Forecast Breakfast, held annually for more than 20 years, now hosts more than 1,800 people at breakfast meetings in Philadelphia, Wilmington, and the Lehigh Valley. Proceeds are donated to the local agencies of United Way. And, in 2001, this successful market breakfast is being rolled out nationally and will be held in Insignia's major markets.

Leadership and teamwork, along with expertise and professionalism, have contributed to where Insignia/ESG is today. Not only is the company ready to meet clients' growing real estate needs in Greater Philadelphia, its suburbs, and the Lehigh Valley; it is well-prepared to meet the challenges of the global real estate marketplace in the 21st century.

Insignia's new logo is designed to denote the firm's unified operations, enhance recognition of its name, and present a contemporary image of its advanced capabilities in the use of state-of-the-art technology.

Intelligent
Innovative
Imaginative
ingenIous
insIghtful
internatIonal
Incomparable
indefatIgable
Intrepid
indIspensable
Industrious
Informed
inquisItive
indomItable
Integrated

Insignia SM
ESG

CHAPTER NINETEEN

THE KEY TO THE FUTURE

EDUCATION

Until the middle of the 18th century, Pennsylvania had neither college nor university. But as the colony prospered, its citizens became increasingly interested in providing their children with an education beyond that being offered on a rudimentary level by the province's church and community schools. Benjamin Franklin agreed, and in the 1740s he published a pamphlet, *Proposals for the Education of Youth in Pennsylvania,* to inspire public interest in an "academy."

In 1749 the trustees of the proposed school met and adopted a constitution embodying the essence of Franklin's proposals. In 1751, the academy held its opening exercises. In 1779, it became known as the University of Pennsylvania—the nation's first university.

Today, Pennsylvania has 217 colleges and universities, the third largest concentration of postsecondary schools in the United States. Each year, the Commonwealth awards more than 62,000 bachelor's degrees. According to the National Center for Education Statistics, Pennsylvania ranks third in attracting the most freshmen from out of state.

While quantity does not necessarily equal quality, the annual ratings published by *U.S. News & World Report* regularly place Pennsylvania colleges and universities among the best in the nation. In 1999, the University of Pennsylvania, in Philadelphia, was among the country's top 10 universities. Swarthmore College, Haverford College, and Villanova University (named for the cities in which they are situated) were rated, respectively, first and fifth among American liberal arts colleges and first in the Northeast among schools with a regional draw.

Franklin's academy, the University of Pennsylvania, was nonsectarian. Since 1791, it has been a privately endowed institution controlled by a board of trustees. In 1810, the trustees organized the university into distinct sections including a college with medical and law departments. Besides giving North America its first medical school, the University of Pennsylvania established the nation's first collegiate business school, journalism program, university teaching hospital, and modern liberal arts curriculum.

DIVERSITY BRINGS CHOICE

Pennsylvania can thank religious and ethnic diversity for many of its other colleges and universities. The Presbyterian faith, for example, required a college-educated clergy. Many Scots-Irish Presbyterians settled the Pennsylvania frontier, where they established colleges

ABOVE: *Delaware County Community College students go by the book in assembling an electrical project for one of their industrial arts classes.* OPPOSITE: *Alexander Calder's sculpture* Jerusalem Stabile, *at the University of Pennsylvania's Blanche Levy Park in front of Meyerson Hall, adds a contemporary accent to the historic campus.*

such as Dickinson, which was founded in Carlisle in 1773 and named for Pennsylvania patriot John Dickinson. The college today continues the liberal arts tradition it was founded on, granting degrees in arts, sciences, and preprofessional programs. Pittsburgh Academy, to the west, got its start in a log cabin in 1787, where it served the Scots-Irish Presbyterians and other settlers who were building their community. Today, this institution is known as the University of Pittsburgh, which comprises not only its 132-acre main campus but also campuses in Johnstown, Greensburg, Titusville, and Bradford. Its 42-story Cathedral of Learning, one of the tallest academic buildings in the world, houses rooms depicting various ethnicities.

Duquesne University, also in Pittsburgh, was founded by the Catholic Holy Ghost Fathers in 1878. It now ranks as one of the top 10 Catholic universities in the United States, providing undergraduate and graduate education of the highest quality in liberal and professional disciplines. The University of Scranton, another Catholic-based institution, was founded as Saint Thomas College in 1888 by the bishop of Scranton. In 1942, its control was transferred to the Jesuits. The university today serves approximately 4,700 students.

Temple University, in Philadelphia, is Pennsylvania's most famous historically Baptist school. It was established in 1887, when Russell H. Conwell, of the Grace Baptist Church, began tutoring young men for the Christian ministry. It has grown into a comprehensive public research university with more than 30,000 students in its 16 schools and colleges. Temple has five campuses in Philadelphia and its suburbs and additional campuses in Harrisburg, Rome, and Tokyo. Bucknell University, in Lewisburg, founded by a Baptist group from Philadelphia, actually predated Temple by 41 years. Bucknell presently enrolls 3,550 students in its programs in liberal arts, engineering, management, education, and music.

Ursinus College, in Collegeville, is one of many institutions founded by Pennsylvania's numerous German sects in the late 19th century. A private liberal arts college with state-of-the-art science facilities, Ursinus counts among its former faculty John Mauchly, coinventor of the computer. Elizabethtown College, founded by the German Baptist Brethren in 1899, is ranked third among regional liberal arts colleges in the North by *U.S. News & World Report.*

Other Pennsylvania colleges and universities were made possible by the philanthropy of some of the Commonwealth's successful 19th-century industrialists. Asa Packer, the self-made millionaire who built the Lehigh Valley Railroad, contributed 50 acres of land and $500,000 in the 1860s to found Lehigh University in Bethlehem. No American to that date had ever offered such a lump sum for an endowment. Because of Packer's generosity, tuition at Lehigh was, for a time, free. In 1900, Andrew Carnegie endowed the Carnegie Technical Schools (comprising the School of Science and Technology, the School of Fine and Applied Arts, the School

Students at the Temple University School of Dentistry in Philadelphia practice their skills on patients in the school's large infirmary, at the same time offering a valuable service to the community.

A Swarthmore physics professor and his students study laboratory equipment that simulates conditions on the surface of the sun. The college is rated number one among American liberal arts colleges.

of Apprentices and Journeymen, and the Margaret Morrison Carnegie School for Women) in Pittsburgh; the institution began granting degrees in 1912. In 1967, the school joined the Mellon Institute to become Carnegie Mellon University, considered one of the finest technical universities in the world.

Philadelphia financier Anthony J. Drexel established the Drexel Institute of Art, Science and Industry in that city in 1891; it became Drexel University in 1970. Drexel was one of the nation's first educational institutions to offer "cooperative education" programs, in which students alternate periods of study with periods of related full-time professional employment. Today more than 2,400 local, national, and global businesses, including Glaxo SmithKline, Lockheed Martin, ARCO Chemical, PECO Energy Company, and E. I. DuPont de Nemours, employ Drexel students as part of the program.

A STATE OF THE ART

At the request of the Pennsylvania State Agricultural Society, the Commonwealth chartered what would become the Pennsylvania State University (Penn State) for the scientific study of farming in 1855. When George W. Atherton became its president in 1882, he revitalized the

school by introducing the study of engineering and founded the Agricultural Experiment Station as a center for scientific research. During the 1930s, Penn State opened branch campuses to accommodate those students who were unable to reside on the main campus at University Park.

THANKS TO BEN AGAIN

A financial contribution from Benjamin Franklin established Franklin College in Lancaster in 1787. Its founders were originally allied with the clergy of the Lutheran and German Reformed Churches, but this religious connection was severed after World War II. In 1853, Marshall College moved to Lancaster and was combined with Franklin College to form Franklin and Marshall College, another one of Pennsylvania's excellent liberal arts colleges and one of the oldest institutions of higher learning in the United States.

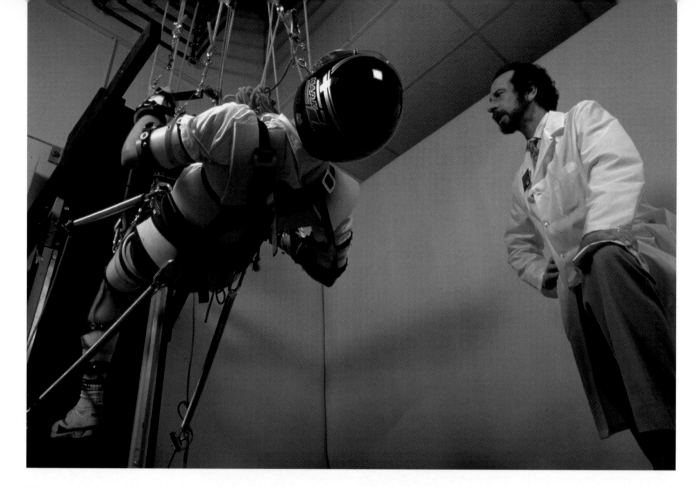

Today Penn State is among the top research universities in the nation and is the largest one in the state. More than 340,000 alumni have received degrees in the university's 11 academic units. Penn State currently has 19 regional campuses and four special-mission campuses, including the Dickinson School of Law in Carlisle and the College of Medicine in Hershey.

In 1857, the Pennsylvania legislature passed the Normal School Act, which guaranteed that teachers would receive a quality education at regional "normal schools" throughout the state. Between 1911 and 1921, the Commonwealth purchased these regional schools and

Researchers at Penn State's Center for Locomotion Studies test a zero-gravity locomotion simulator and gravity replacement load. The system will be used for exercise on the International Space Station.

established the present configuration of 14 state-owned educational institutions. By 1982, it had transformed the 14 into four-year liberal arts colleges and universities, individually known as the (City name) University of Pennsylvania of the State System of Higher Education. The system comprises Bloomsburg, California, Cheyney, Clarion, East Stroudsburg, Edinboro, Indiana, Kutztown, Lock Haven, Mansfield, Millersville, Shippensburg, Slippery Rock, and West Chester. Each offers a range of liberal arts and professional preparation programs.

PAVING THE WAY

William Penn's original constitution for Pennsylvania contained a provision for the education of all children. The one Pennsylvania adopted in 1790 created free schools for the poor, and finally, in 1834, the Commonwealth extended free public education to all children.

Today, more than 1.8 million children attend the state's public schools and more than 330,000 are enrolled in private schools. During the academic year 1997–98, 127,981 students graduated from Pennsylvania's high schools; 90,689 of them, or 70.9 percent, were college bound. The 1997–98 dropout rate was only 2.6 percent.

EDUCATED WOMEN: GOOD FOR SOCIETY

One of America's first proponents of women's education was Pennsylvanian Benjamin Rush. He argued in 1787 that women were required to be the "stewards, guardians of their husbands' property," and the chief educators of children. He therefore advocated that women study practical subjects like the English language, penmanship, and bookkeeping along with history, biography, and travels, subjects that would make a woman "an agreeable companion for a sensible man."

Pennsylvania has 109,691 public school teachers and 21,399 private school teachers. The tradition of local control is strong; each school district maintains its own strategic plan. Within the last decade, however, the state government has taken on a larger role, enacting legislation to allow the creation of charter public schools, establishing rigorous real-world academic standards to prepare students for success in higher education or the workplace, and setting higher standards for teachers.

For more than a quarter of a century, Pennsylvania has offered talented high school students the opportunity to attend the Governor's Schools of Excellence for advanced education. Industry experts at these schools begin preparing students early for careers in fields such as the arts and sciences, health care, teaching, and information technology.

READY FOR THE 21ST CENTURY

Pennsylvania's institutions of higher education are especially responsive to the challenges of the new economy. As businesses became eager to hire candidates knowledgeable in E-commerce, Drexel and Lehigh Universities were among the first in the nation to offer relevant courses, programs, and concentrations, including practical internships in the real business world. Graduates of Pennsylvania colleges and universities are so highly sought after that the governor and the state legislature are encouraging the formation of partnerships and programs designed to encourage them to remain in the state and work for companies and institutions there.

Pennsylvania's commitment to excellence in education today includes the practical goal of preparing an innovative workforce ready to meet and exceed the demands of the 21st century.

These gifted young musicians at the Curtis Institute of Music received full merit scholarships to attend—as do all students at the world-renowned Philadelphia institute.

NEWS FROM THE RESEARCH FRONT

Ian Zagon, Ph.D., professor of neuroscience and anatomy, and Patricia McLaughlin, D. Ed., associate professor of neuroscience and anatomy, discovered a new drug to fight pancreatic cancer during their work at the Pennsylvania State College of Medicine in the late 1980s. The Milton S. Hershey Medical Center at the college is the only site now conducting phase 1 clinical trials of the drug.

TEMPLE UNIVERSITY

With campuses and programs located around the world and ambitious goals for the future, Temple University

offers a comprehensive public research system that is ready to meet the challenges of the 21st century.

Temple University is one of Pennsylvania's three public research universities. With an enrollment of approximately 29,000 students, Temple has a distinguished 115-year-old mission of providing high-quality education at an affordable cost.

With ambitious programs for enhancing academics and expanding its global outreach, Philadelphia-based Temple University is positioned to be one of the leading academic institutions in the 21st century. Two aspects reflect this position: Temple maintains campuses around the world, from Philadelphia to Tokyo to Rome, and it has launched a program of strategic initiatives to meet the requirements of today's complex world.

Temple is one of only 89 Carnegie Research I institutions in the nation. These universities offer a full range of degree programs, from baccalaureate to doctoral; award 50 or more doctoral degrees a year; and give high priority to research. Temple employs 2,600 full-time and part-time faculty, many of whom are drawn by the university's well-deserved reputation for interdisciplinary research. The university has 16 schools and colleges, offering bachelor's degrees in 125 fields, master's degrees in 94, and doctoral degrees in 49. There are four professional schools: law, medicine, dentistry, and podiatric medicine.

The new Liacouras Center is a multipurpose recreation and convocation complex that is home to the renowned Temple basketball teams.

MAINTAINING HIGH ACADEMIC STANDARDS

Temple University has managed to raise the bar academically while keeping tuition costs down. An aggressive recruitment program is yielding major dividends. In the fall of 1999, the number of freshmen enrolled at Temple was 2,902, up 27 percent from the previous year. The average Scholastic Aptitude Test (SAT) scores of entering freshmen saw a 25-point increase. Over a 15-year period (1984–99), the cumulative rate of increase in Temple's tuition was the lowest of any university in Pennsylvania or the region.

Part of Temple's appeal to the best and the brightest students is undoubtedly the rejuvenated Main Campus in north Philadelphia. The $29 million Tuttleman Learning Center, built with matching Commonwealth funds, opened in the fall of 1998. This 128,000-square-foot complex with a soaring atrium

Temple University students celebrate their long-awaited graduation.

lobby, houses 20 cyber-age classrooms and six computer laboratories, along with the Scholars Information Center, the Distance Learning Center, the Library Reading Room, the Temple University Writing Center, and the undergraduate Honors Program.

The Liacouras Center is named for Peter J. Liacouras, Temple's seventh president, who retired June 30, 2000, after 18 years as chief executive. With a maximum seating capacity of 11,000, the multipurpose Liacouras Center—home court for men's and women's basket-

ball—hosts concerts, rodeos, technology expos, theater productions, and commencements. It also has been the economic spark for a revitalization of the neighborhoods surrounding Temple, bringing new housing as well as retail and entertainment projects to the area.

Another part of the Liacouras Center is the IBC Student Recreation Center, which is one of two new recreational facilities for the student body. These and other exciting efforts have attracted more students who want to live on campus. In August 1999, Temple opened a new student residence hall—its third one in recent years—and began construction in early 2000 on a 1,000-bed residence hall.

The new Tuttleman Learning Center features 20 cyber-age classrooms and a computer laboratory building.

STRATEGIES FOR THE FUTURE

In developing its strategic initiatives for the future, Temple focused on four areas—technology, tourism, health care, and the global economy. Temple has responded to the demands of the modern world by establishing new colleges and programs. The College of Science and Technology (CST) and The School of Tourism and Hospitality Management were launched in 1998, and Virtual Temple, an independent, for-profit venture designed to market courses on the Internet, was authorized by the Board of Trustees in 1999.

A RENOWNED HEALTH SCIENCES CENTER

The university is recognized internationally for medical research conducted at its Thrombosis Center and Fels Institute for Cancer Research and Molecular Biology. The Heart Transplantation Center is one of the busiest adult heart transplant programs in America. New facilities include the Children's Medical Center and the affiliated Shriners Hospital for Children. Temple University Hospital is the core of the emerging Temple University Health System, Inc.

Snow-laden pine boughs frame the Bell Tower, a Temple University landmark.

WIDENER UNIVERSITY

With a solid 179-year history of academic excellence and success, the private, nonprofit Widener University

continues to excel as one of the top schools in the northeast region of the United States.

Founded in Wilmington, Delaware, in 1821, Widener University is a comprehensive teaching institution that covers three campuses in Pennsylvania and Delaware. Recognized as one of the top universities in the region, Widener earned a top tier ranking in *U.S. News & World Report*'s annual survey of America's Best Colleges for 2000.

A private, nonprofit university, Widener offers liberal arts and sciences, as well as professional and preprofessional curricula in 147 programs of study leading to associate, baccalaureate, master's, or doctoral degrees.

Widener University is comprehensive. It includes the College of Arts and Sciences, as well as the Schools of Law, Business Administration, Engineering, Nursing, Hospitality Management, and Human Service Professions.

Old Main—originally built in 1868 and rebuilt in 1882 after a fire destroyed much of it—was the home of Pennsylvania Military College, and today is a landmark building of Widener University. The chimes of the Old Main bell tower still mark time for students, faculty, and the academic community.

A HISTORY OF CHANGE

The university was originally founded in 1821 as a Quaker school for young gentlemen. Known as the Bullock School, the college went through numerous institutional changes as well as a relocation change in 1862 to West Chester, Pennsylvania, before becoming the Pennsylvania Military College in 1892.

In the mid-1900s the composition of the student body rapidly changed with the increasing enrollment of civilians. In 1972, the university introduced a more modern structure to reflect its changing demographics. The cadet corps was disbanded, and the academic offerings were organized into the programs that form the foundation of today's university. At the same time as this reorganization, the school decided to change its name to Widener College, after a prominent Philadelphia family, famous for its numerous contributions to higher education, the arts, and charity. And in 1979, the college adopted the name Widener University to better reflect the addition of five graduate schools and colleges, as well as its physical expansion from one campus to two.

Widener opened its Delaware campus in 1976 and its Harrisburg, Pennsylvania, campus in 1988. The main campus remains in Chester, Pennsylvania, 15 minutes from historic Philadelphia, and two hours from Washington D.C., and New York City.

Today approximately 7,000 students, who hail from 30 states and 39 countries, attend Widener University.

At Widener University, classes are small and students are taught by professors, not graduate assistants. With the full attention of dedicated professors, students freely express their views and share ideas.

Out of its 2,100 undergraduates, 48 percent typically rank in the top quarter of their graduating class, 92 percent rank in the top half, and in a 1999 survey conducted by the university, 93 percent of students responding were employed or in graduate school within six months of graduating.

At Widener University all students, including freshmen, are encouraged to work with professors on research.

Widener offers a bit of everything—history, tradition, 179 years of teaching excellence, outstanding professors with national and international reputations, several Hall of Fame athletes, and 18 academic all-Americans in 10 different sports, eight of whom were honored within the last few years. As always, Widener's emphasis is on energizing, motivating, and helping students achieve their maximum potential—academically, socially, culturally, athletically, and charitably within the community.

Widener University is NCAA Division III, offering 22 varsity sports for men and women, and intramural and individual recreation opportunities.

Widener takes technology seriously. For this reason it has joined with Crozer-Keystone Health System, University City Science Center, and others in establishing a technology park located near Widener's main campus. University Technology Park is the result of a shared vision of an environment where creativity, synergy, and new technology flourishes. Park tenants enjoy the full advantage of a 100 percent plug-and-play building, using the wideband fiber-optic network for global communications.

"Our community involvement includes charitable efforts by students, faculty, and administrators alike," says Bruce. "The university is involved in programs such as school literacy, community health, science and engineering education, economic development, and numerous other outreach initiatives. Widener represents a multitude of possibilities both for its students, and the world where those students live."

A PRIORITY ON STUDENTS

In part, Widener's success comes from placing a priority on developing an exceptional environment for its student body. Most undergraduates live on campus in comfortable student housing. Classes are small, with an average 12-to-one student-to-professor ratio, and are taught by the professors themselves, rather than by graduate students. "Our faculty members pride themselves on the personal relationships they build with their students," says Robert J. Bruce, president of the university. "We place strong emphasis on sound education—not just career-preparation—for both undergraduate and graduate students. We seek to prepare students for the futures they will shape."

Widener provides Internet access in every dormitory with free technical support. Additionally, to keep students on track with the academic guidelines for graduation within four years, Widener provides tutoring free of charge, and some 83 percent of its students receive financial aid so monetary issues can be less of a concern throughout their terms on campus.

Widener University is a tier-one institution ranked among the top 40 universities in the region, according to U.S. News & World Report.

DELAWARE COUNTY COMMUNITY COLLEGE

Since its founding in 1967, Delaware County Community College has remained true to its mission of offering students

"educational programs and services that are accessible, comprehensive, community centered and flexible."

The rolling, wooded main campus of Delaware County Community College is located off Route 252 between Media and Newtown Square.

Making higher education available to all who seek it has been a cornerstone of Pennsylvania's state constitution since the 18th century, and for more than 30 years, Delaware County Community College (DCCC) has been carrying out that mandate with distinction for those in the Philadelphia area.

An associate degree-granting institution founded in 1967, DCCC is the ninth largest college in the Philadelphia area. Based in Media, Pennsylvania, DCCC continues to maintain a policy of open admission and to promote a program of academic excellence to every student attending the school.

Accredited by the Middle States Association of Colleges and Schools and funded by the residents of 11 local school districts and the state, DCCC offers more than 60 college and university-level programs that equal the

first two years of a bachelor's degree. In addition, the College also offers career preparation and short-term certificate programs designed to train graduates for specialized occupational fields.

CUSTOMIZED, INDIVIDUAL ATTENTION

As a convenience to students whose busy lifestyles preclude attending traditional classes, DCCC offers distance-learning options including television, independent study and Internet courses. It also offers advanced computer training in programs such as MCSE, MOUS, A+, Cisco and CCNA, as well as a unique series of courses in a one-course, one-credit, one-weekend module.

What truly sets DCCC apart from most other institutions of higher learning, however, is the individual attention its faculty, administrators and staff members give to each student.

"Here at DCCC, each student is important to us," says Dr. Richard D. DeCosmo, president of DCCC. "The College looks forward to helping each student achieve an educational experience that will meet his or her personal needs and goals."

DCCC's average class size of 21 students combined with the fact that instructors and professors, instead of graduate students, teach each class, provides students with a personal, small-school atmosphere where faculty members and staff get to know students by name.

Dr. Richard D. DeCosmo has served as president of Delaware County Community College since 1980.

BRIDGES—NOT BARRIERS

"We provide students at DCCC with bridges instead of barriers," DeCosmo says. "Our concern is not with a student's SAT score or how many A's he or she has obtained, but with how motivated the student is to succeed and how we can help facilitate his or her success."

Today, more than 23,000 students, including more than 200 international students from 38 different nations, attend daytime, evening and/or weekend classes on DCCC's scenic 123-acre main campus located 14 miles west of Philadelphia, and at its six off-campus locations in Delaware and Chester counties. Since its inception, more than 200,000 students have benefited from its credit and non-credit courses.

ACADEMIC PASSPORT

Each year, approximately 1,200 DCCC students transfer to colleges and universities in Pennsylvania under the college's "academic passport program." The College's competency-based curriculum certifies that all graduates possess the skills, attitudes and values needed to succeed in their individual area of study.

"The students who transfer to four-year colleges each year are proof of our students' high level of achievement as well as DCCC's sound reputation," says DeCosmo. "So are the number of employers who clamor for our career program graduates to strengthen their workforce."

DCCC is well prepared to serve the increasingly diverse and changing work environment that students will face in the new millennium. A DCCC education helps to ensure that they will be ready to take on the challenges of life and the working world in the 21st century and beyond.

ABOVE RIGHT: *DCCC offers certificate training programs for MOUS, MCSE, A+, Cisco and CCNA.* ABOVE LEFT: *DCCC students enjoy learning in high-tech graphic design labs.*

In recent years, for example, the College has expanded significantly its technological capabilities, adding 35 new, high-tech computer labs on its main campus. It has equipped these new labs with more than 700 personal computers, a Macintosh platform that supports the latest applications in graphic design and the DCCC Net, which provides campus-wide access to programs and applications, including an ultrafast T1 line to the World Wide Web.

ONE-STOP CAREER RESOURCE CENTER

In addition, the College has created one of the Philadelphia area's largest career and counseling centers, which offers a wide variety of career services and job-related sources designed to help its graduates take the next step in their professional lives. In fact, the center has been so successful that it was selected in 1999 by the Commonwealth of Pennsylvania to feature CareerLink, a unique, one-stop delivery of career services offered to job seekers and employers in the Philadelphia area. An employment center, Delaware County CareerLink connects employers and job opportunities with qualified job seekers. There are two centers in Delaware County, one in Chester and one at DCCC's main campus. The Web site is www.pacareerlink.state.pa.us.

PROGRAMS AND ADMISSIONS

To learn more about DCCC's programs and open admission policy, contact the Admissions Office at 610-359-5050 or visit DCCC on the Web at www.dccc.edu.

Professor Larry Woodward, at left, explains an assignment to DCCC students in his architecture class.

THE UNIVERSITY OF PITTSBURGH

The University of Pittsburgh strives to maintain and further its tradition of offering quality teaching, research, and service to the Commonwealth of Pennsylvania and the world.

Classes were first held in 1787 in a log house, a replica of which now sits on the University of Pittsburgh's campus in the Oakland section of Pittsburgh.

The University of Pittsburgh traces its roots to the chartering of the Pittsburgh Academy in 1787, the year the United States Constitution was written. The academy's founder, Hugh Henry Brackenridge, hoped the school, then consisting of a single log house, would serve as a "candle lite in the forested wilderness." More than 200 years later, the University of Pittsburgh has evolved in extraordinary ways.

As the 21st century begins, the university is an internationally recognized center of learning and research, strong in the arts and sciences and the professions. Fondly known to students and alumni as "Pitt," the university is a major provider of top quality higher education in its region, one of the nation's largest producers of pioneering research, and a leading American institution creatively interacting with the rest of the world.

Mark A. Nordenberg, the university's 17th chancellor, oversees a Pittsburgh campus of 16 undergraduate, graduate, and professional schools, as well as regional campuses in Bradford, Greensburg, Johnstown, and Titusville, Pennsylvania. He is the former dean of Pitt's law school and a member of the university community since 1977. "A community of intellectuals is, by definition, committed to the power of the mind and bound together by its interest in ideas," says Nordenberg. "Certainly, that is one important dimension of life at Pitt. But a university also should be an institution with a heart—an institution that values nothing more than the potential that exists within its people."

FAR-REACHING IMPACT

A private institution for most of its past, the University of Pittsburgh became state-related in 1966, establishing a relationship with the Commonwealth of Pennsylvania that has served both partners. Looking back over the three decades of Pitt's state-related status, Nordenberg sees an era characterized by accomplishment, growth, and a steady rise in intellectual stature for the university, with far-reaching benefits for the citizens of Pennsylvania.

Mark A. Nordenberg is the 17th chancellor of the University of Pittsburgh.

The University of Pittsburgh has approximately 200,000 alumni throughout the world.

During the past three decades, Pittsburgh has conferred more than 200,000 degrees, more than 40 percent of them reflecting the graduate-level learning experience so often essential for success in today's increasingly complex and competitive world.

In recent years, University of Pittsburgh students have achieved high levels of academic attainment. This year, yet another Pitt student was named a Marshall Scholar, and in the past 15 years, Pitt has had more Rhodes and Marshall scholars than any other college or university in Pennsylvania, public or private.

The university continues to attract the best and the brightest students in record numbers. The five-year period from 1995 to 1999 saw not only a 60 percent increase in freshman applications, but superior quality: 55 percent of current freshmen ranked in the top 20 percent of their high school class and 30 percent ranked in the top 10 percent. The combined freshman SAT score for the fall 1999 class was 26 points higher than it was in 1995, and 20 percent of that same class was eligible for the university's prestigious Honors College. In 1999, undergraduate students from the university were awarded four National Science Foundation (NSF) Fellowships, three Goldwater Scholarships, and the only Udall Scholarship in Pennsylvania.

THE UNIVERSITY OF PITTSBURGH'S SCHOOLS

- Arts and Sciences
- Business
- Dental Medicine
- Education
- Engineering
- General Studies
- Health and Rehabilitation Sciences
- Honors College
- Information Sciences
- Law
- Medicine
- Nursing
- Pharmacy
- Public and International Affairs
- Public Health
- Social Work

Pitt has earned international recognition for the world-class quality of its programs in disciplines as diverse as philosophy and transplantation surgery. On average, one transplant is performed at the University of Pittsburgh Medical Center every 18 hours of every day. The university boasts two of the top five philosophy departments in the nation and the world's leading center in the philosophy of science.

Indeed, the university is an acknowledged leader in many different areas. Pitt is among the top 20 universities in the nation in total federal science and engineering dollars attracted, and in the top 10 in terms of federal

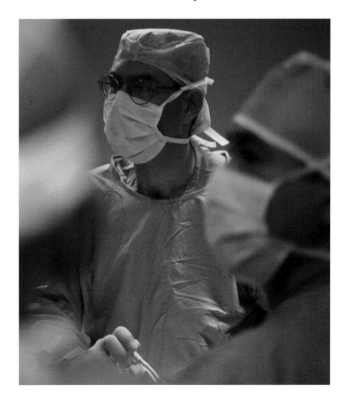

The University of Pittsburgh Medical Center is known worldwide for its pioneering medical research.

Ranked among the top 20 institutions nationally in attracting federal grants, Pitt annually imports $300 million in sponsored research.

support for medical research. In the decade from 1985 to 1995, Pitt claimed the largest market share increase of any U.S. university in funding from the National Institutes of Health. Pitt also ranks first among the nation's universities in funding from the National Institute of Mental Health. The sponsored research conducted by the university annually imports more than $300 million into western Pennsylvania.

Pitt is a member of the Association of American Universities, the top 60 research universities in North America. The university's research breakthroughs in the past few years include the development of environmentally safe "green" steel, discovery of a new planetary system within our galaxy, and the first applications of gene therapy for treating rheumatoid arthritis.

In the 1950s, at the University of Pittsburgh, Jonas Salk developed the vaccine that conquered polio, at that time the most feared disease in the nation.

A VISION FOR THE FUTURE

Recently, Pitt's board of trustees, working closely with Chancellor Nordenberg, adopted as a definition of its mission, "The University of Pittsburgh: 2000–

2005," a document that emphasizes the university's commitment to a continued pursuit of excellence in core academic enterprises—undergraduate education, graduate and professional education, and research. More broadly, the document asserts that "by aggressively supporting the advancement of Pitt's academic mission, we will clearly and consistently demonstrate that this is one of the finest and most productive universities in the world."

Chancellor Nordenberg says, "We must become even stronger and more innovative in these challenging times—true to the work ethic of western Pennsylvania, rich in intellectual rigor, and committed in every respect to effectively preparing students for life and careers in the 21st century."

Already one of the largest employers in the Pittsburgh area, Pitt has a very strong institutional commitment to the people and economy of the region. More than 61,000 Pitt alumni live and work in Allegheny County, enriching the local labor pool and contributing billions to the local economy.

The University of Pittsburgh has approximately 26,000 graduate and undergraduate students at its Pittsburgh campus and 6,000 students at its four regional campuses.

In the past 15 years, the University of Pittsburgh has produced more Rhodes and Marshall scholars than any other college or university in Pennsylvania, public or private.

Nordenberg affirms that "the strength of the university is directly dependent upon the strength of the region. It is also true, more than ever, that the strength of the region requires a strong University of Pittsburgh. We are a major economic force in the region. And by expanding the existing base of knowledge, we help people to lead fuller, healthier, more productive lives."

As Pitt defines its missions for the new century, it remains a place of enduring tradition. "Over the course of the last 213 years, this university has been the site of many high victories—individual and institutional," says Nordenberg. "But if we creatively apply our shared wisdom and have faith in our ability to successfully pursue lofty goals, I have no doubt that our greatest victories are yet to come."

At the heart of the university complex stands a 42-story neo-Gothic tower, the Cathedral of Learning. It contains, among other treasures, 26 international classrooms, each the product of several years of work by artisans from the countries represented—international microcosms of the diverse world cultures that have converged in Pittsburgh, where the "candle lite" of the city's namesake university now shines brighter than ever.

"We are building on a strong foundation," says Nordenberg, "the result of the talent and dedication of others. The university's most prominent characteristic should be an unrelenting commitment to excellence, the successful pursuit of quality in everything we do. This we owe to all who depend on us."

The University of Pittsburgh's 42-story Cathedral of Learning is the tallest school building in the western hemisphere.

University of Pittsburgh

A Leader in Education, A Pioneer in Research, and A Partner in Regional Development

UNIVERSITY OF THE SCIENCES IN PHILADELPHIA

University of the Sciences in Philadelphia upholds its tradition as a pioneer in health science education through

innovative curricula, technologically advanced facilities, and programs that lead to a diversity of professions.

Nestled in an enclave of historic Philadelphia known as University City sits the nation's first, and today one of its largest, schools of pharmacy, University of the Sciences in Philadelphia (USP), a private, coeducational school with an undergraduate enrollment of 2,000. USP continues its tradition of pioneering work in health science education with not only state-of-the-art pharmacy programs, but also expanded curricula leading to diverse health science careers, such as research scientist, biomedical writer, physician assistant, occupational therapist, teacher, and others.

USP can trace its roots back to Carpenters' Hall in the City of Brotherly Love, where in 1821 a group of 68 druggists and apothecaries met to map out the future of training for their profession. Those early visionaries formed the foundation for the institution that would be known first as the

The campus of University of the Sciences in Philadelphia is within a two-hour drive of 75 percent of all U.S. pharmaceutical firms. Shown above is Griffith Hall. © Jason Jones

Philadelphia College of Apothecaries and next as the Philadelphia College of Pharmacy. In 1998, University of the Sciences in Philadelphia was given its current name, a true representation of the breadth of the university.

USP is composed of four separate colleges—Philadelphia College of Pharmacy, the College of Health Sciences, the College of Arts and Sciences, and the College of Graduate Studies. Bachelor's degrees are offered in 16 major courses of study, plus a pre-med track and science teacher certification. Along with science courses, all undergraduate programs include basic studies in the liberal arts. Graduate studies include 11 master's programs and five doctoral programs; schedules can be tailored for working professionals as well as full-time students.

Traditionally a curriculum innovator, USP was the first and only school in the nation to offer a bachelor's degree in pharmaceutical technology and bachelor's and master's degrees in biomedical writing. Other innovative programs range from pharmaceutical marketing and management, to health policy, physician assistant studies, health psychology, and environmental science.

USP
UNIVERSITY OF THE SCIENCES IN PHILADELPHIA

Researchers at University of the Sciences in Philadelphia explore a wide range of topics, from the neurochemical causes of depressive illness to medicinal and natural product chemistry, efficiency and absorption of drugs, and cancer cell invasion and motility. © Jason Jones

STATE-OF-THE-ART FACILITIES

Situated on a 25-acre site in University City, which is home to some 30,000 students attending USP and other institutions, such as Drexel and the University of Pennsylvania, the USP campus consists of classroom buildings and a library surrounding a central courtyard, with a large student center and residence halls nearby. The Joseph W. England Library contains one of the largest collections of pharmaceutical literature in the United States, much of which is on-line for use by health care professionals worldwide. The Marvin Samson Center for the History of Pharmacy is home to USP's extensive collection of more than 10,000 pharmaceutical and medical science objects dating back five centuries. Pharmaceutical artifacts such as mortars and pestles, apothecary jars, weights and balances, patent medicines, signs, and other rare items reflect USP's rich heritage.

The university's more than 80 laboratories include the Center for Advanced Pharmacy Studies (CAPS), the first such laboratory at any pharmacy college nationwide to be so technologically well-equipped for pharmacy studies and research.

USP continues to develop its extensive physical plant. "We are building a new science and technology facility that we think will help our students look beyond the horizon in education and provide them with an opportunity to build a strong base for future problem solving," says Philip P. Gerbino, Pharm.D., president of USP and also a USP alumnus.

Other notable alumni include founders of six of the 10 leading pharmaceutical companies in the United States. William Procter Jr.—known to many as the father of American pharmacy for his role in helping found the American Pharmaceutical Association in 1852—was a USP graduate, as were Eli Lilly, Henry S. Wellcome, Silas Burroughs, Gerald F. Rorer, Robert L. McNeil Jr., and William Warner.

An astonishing collection of 10,000 artifacts, memorabilia, photographs and artwork is housed in the Marvin Samson Center for the History of Pharmacy. © Peter Howard Photographer, Inc.

EDUCATIONAL COMMUNITY OUTREACH

As a longtime leader in health science education, USP was the first in its field to join PRIME (Philadelphia Regional Introduction for Minorities to Engineering), which prepares minority students for science-based professions. USP also has implemented a center for extended and distance learning, in order to meet the needs of the student or working professional on a nontraditional track. In the university's tradition of advancing the American pharmaceutical industry, USP researchers explore issues from AIDS and cancer to new systems for drug delivery.

With technical knowledge expanding exponentially, today's pharmacy and science graduates face an array of challenges not met by yesterday's practitioners. USP is committed to preparing students for critical roles in their professions. This commitment is evident by the number of professional associations the university has created to serve the health science industry, such as:

- The Office of Professional Programs (OPP), providing solutions for pharmaceutical care to the pharmaceutical industry, managed care organizations, and government agencies
- The Institute for Pharmaceutical Economics (IPE), an international research and policy center
- The Geriatric Pharmacy Institute (GPI), researching the effects of pharmaceuticals on elderly patients
- Advanced Concepts, providing education to representatives of the pharmaceutical and other industries.

"We want to bridge education to real-world experiences," says Dr. Gerbino. "We are very much involved with a confluent approach, integrating the pharmacy side with that of patient-centered health care."

At the state-of-the-art Center for Advanced Pharmacy Studies, laboratories are equipped with the latest technology. In this lab, pharmacy students learn to make drug therapy decisions. © Jason Jones

COMMUNITY COLLEGE OF ALLEGHENY COUNTY

Providing affordable, superior quality academic and workforce training programs, the Community College of Allegheny County is doing its part to build a strong, economically sound community.

Community College of Allegheny County (CCAC) students enjoy a small student-to-faculty ratio in all the college's programs.

The Pittsburgh region has successfully made the transition to a more diversified economy. The new regional economy includes the establishment of high-tech computer technology industries whose growth has revitalized a region long dependent on heavy manufacturing and steel. The exceptional educational leadership of the Community College of Allegheny County (CCAC) supports this economic resurgence by providing the educational foundation needed to fuel such an economic transition and by helping to keep a mixed economy supplied with talent.

Working with state-of-the-art medical and research universities, a vibrant high-technology sector, and manufacturing companies looking to expand, CCAC has stepped up to the challenge by providing exceptional educational and workforce development programs to meet the increased demand for highly skilled labor.

"CCAC is playing an important role in the economic resurgence of southwestern Pennsylvania," says Dr. Roy Flores, president of CCAC. "Approximately 94 percent of our graduates remain and work in the local area."

When the Pittsburgh steel industry collapsed, it was CCAC's dislocated workers program that put 10,000 unemployed workers back on their feet. For more than 20 years, CCAC has demonstrated its effectiveness by working closely with area industries, professional organizations, and government agencies to develop and deliver effective educational and workforce training programs.

As the largest provider of workforce training in western Pennsylvania, CCAC is a major player in the region's resurgence. More than 20,000 students either have tuition paid by an employer, or receive training under contract. CCAC's academic and workforce training programs provide expanding businesses with the latest skills and degrees to keep the region globally competitive. The college provides customized contract training for 80 of southwestern Pennsylvania's top employers.

PREPARING AND TRAINING STUDENTS

In the field of computer science, CCAC has nearly 12,000 students enrolled in credit and non-credit computer classes. Health-related careers are also a significant component in the region's resurgence. Pittsburgh is internationally recognized for outstanding medical research and health care. CCAC is the area's largest provider of training for health care professionals.

"A cooperative relationship between higher education and business is the

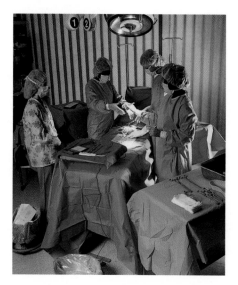

CCAC has one of the largest allied health programs in the country. Students gain hands-on medical experience at some of the area's finest hospitals and clinics.

Students in CCAC's engineering and sciences technology career programs enjoy the benefits of a cutting-edge curriculum. Graduates of these programs enter the field with the skills and knowledge necessary to stay competitive in today's job market.

key ingredient to economic growth," says Dr. Flores. "Increasingly, the success of a business depends on the knowledge, skills, and abilities of all its workers. Human capital is becoming the most difficult asset for companies to acquire."

PROVIDING LEADERSHIP

CCAC recently changed its mission statement to highlight its emphasis on workforce training. The college not only strives to provide superior quality and affordable education, but also "to provide leadership in workforce training and support the economic development of the region."

CCAC accomplishes this mission with the sponsoring help of the state and county governments. The financial assistance provided by these two government bodies helps the college keep the best quality education affordable and accessible to all.

To address the region's critical shortage of computer programs, CCAC partners with CTE, a subsidiary of Carnegie Mellon University. Under the agreement, students earn certificates in software systems development and computer programs based on the latest curriculum developed by CMU's subsidiary. Currently, there are 108 students enrolled in the program.

Collaborating with four-year colleges and universities is a major CCAC initiative. As such, CCAC has established 30 transfer agreements with state and regional

institutions. Students may transfer to many of these schools without losing any credits.

SERVING THE COMMUNITY

Since 1966, the four campus locations of CCAC have fulfilled the educational needs of more than two million students in the Pittsburgh area, offering associate degrees in more than 200 academic disciplines. CCAC is the second largest community college in Pennsylvania and one of the largest multicampus community colleges in the nation. Students can take advantage of modern classroom facilities, state-of-the-art computer labs, a computerized, on-line and connected collegewide library system, and extensive physical education and fitness centers.

The college's value to the community is further highlighted by looking at a profile of the CCAC student. Students at CCAC are working women and men with 51 percent identified as adult learners and 18 percent representing minority groups. The average age of a CCAC student is 29 years old.

People come to CCAC seeking new careers, career advancement, and personal enrichment. Lawyers, accountants, and other professionals count on CCAC to provide them with continuing education credit courses. Students seeking a four-year degree choose CCAC for its academic quality as well as the transfer agreements with regional universities. Continuing education programs also provide residents with classes that enrich a person's quality of life. More than 50,000 Allegheny County residents take advantage of the college's many learning opportunities.

CCAC

Intercollegiate sports teams are present at each campus. The men's baseball team at South Campus was recently ranked ninth in the nation by the National Junior College Athletic Association for Division II. CCAC also offers a wide variety of men's, women's, and co-ed intramural sports teams.

CHAPTER TWENTY

THE FINER THINGS IN LIFE
TOURISM, HOSPITALITY, AND THE ARTS

Tourism is serious business in Pennsylvania. The Commonwealth ranks fourth in the nation for domestic leisure travel—112.4 million people visited Pennsylvania in 1997, the latest date for which figures are available. That same year, Philadelphia marked the first time it welcomed more domestic leisure travelers than New York City. Of all Pennsylvania's regions, Hershey/Dutch Country in central Pennsylvania, with its scenic countryside,

shopping outlets, entertainment options, and increasing number of excellent restaurants, is Pennsylvania's most popular in terms of dollars spent. Following close behind are the Philadelphia and Pittsburgh areas and the Poconos. In all, visitors to Pennsylvania spend approximately $19.4 billion annually on travel-related goods and services, including transportation, accommodations, food, retail purchases, and tours. The industry, which is growing at an annual rate of 5 percent, provided jobs for more than 424,700 people in 1996.

A study conducted by D. K. Shifflet and Associates noted that in 1997, travel spending and its associated economic activity resulted in $4.7 billion in earnings for Pennsylvania residents. In comparison, the 2000 Republican National Convention in Philadelphia is expected to generate, by itself, approximately $100 million in direct economic impact—and $300 million more indirectly—for the Philadelphia area.

Tourism and hospitality constitute the third largest industry in the Philadelphia area as well as one of the region's most significant growth sectors. In 1997 the city was the destination for 30.3 million day-trippers and

10.3 million overnight visitors. An increase in hotel occupancy rates from 63 percent in 1992 to 75 percent in 1996 was the catalyst for expanding accommodations in the area. Since its opening in 1993, the Pennsylvania Convention Center has generated more than $185 million in tax revenues and more than 7,300 new jobs. Plans are now under way to expand the building to accommodate larger groups and simultaneous conventions.

Tourism is a key industry for Pittsburgh as well, ranking as the region's eighth largest economic engine. More than 39 million people visited Allegheny County, of which Pittsburgh is a part, in 1996.

Pennsylvania cities once again are thriving as centers for the arts, culture, and entertainment. Downtown areas are being revitalized and new venues and attractions added all the time.

In Philadelphia, for example, when the venerated Philadelphia Museum of Art held an 11-week Paul Cézanne retrospective in 1995, it worked with 15 hotels

The Pennsylvania Ballet, founded in 1963, brings energy and exuberance to its performance of The Nutcracker. *Critics applaud the company for linking top-notch technique with dazzling artistry.*

PHOTOS: THIS PAGE, © John McGrail; OPPOSITE PAGE, © H. Mark Weidman

276

to create "Cézanne packages" —promotions that resulted in the sale of more than 37,000 room-nights. The Philadelphia Orchestra and Pennsylvania Ballet draw crowds to the Academy of Music and Avenue of the Arts. This year, Independence National Historical Park will add a new home for the Liberty Bell, that internationally revered symbol of freedom, outdoing even the present climate-controlled, glass-walled chamber that features Independence Hall itself as the backdrop. By 2001, the elegant glass roof of the Crystal Palace, a $245 million regional performing arts center on Broad Street, will grace Philadelphia's skyline. The new home of the Philadelphia Orchestra and several other performing arts companies will have state-of-the-art facilities, including a 2,500-seat concert hall and 650-seat recital hall. Also in 2001, the Philadelphia waterfront will become the site of a spacious entertainment complex that will add even more to Philadelphia's already significant allure.

In Pittsburgh, people pack the Benedum Center for the Performing Arts and Heinz Hall downtown for the top-rated Pittsburgh Symphony, Pittsburgh Opera, Civic Light Opera, Pittsburgh Ballet Theatre, and Broadway shows, while appreciative audiences fill theaters and playhouses throughout the area. Even smaller cities such as Erie and Williamsport support symphony orchestras that bring tourists and suburbanites out for a lovely evening on the town.

Three museums in the state were built specifically for children, with hands-on exhibits geared to their interests: the Children's Museum in Pittsburgh, the expERIEnce Children's Museum in Erie, and the Please

Glorious in autumn, Pike County's Shohola Falls tumbles across nine ledges as it pours into an 80-foot-deep gorge. Shohola Creek, known for huge trout, spills another 200 feet under a cover of thick hemlock.

Touch Museum in Philadelphia. The latter was the first museum dedicated to children under seven years of age, and the first allowing them to touch, play in, and explore the exhibits.

One sign of a vibrant city, of course, is its restaurants. New ones are opening constantly in both Philadelphia and Pittsburgh, and the restaurateurs are winning critical acclaim in fine dining circles.

Some say that Philadelphia's celebrated restaurant renaissance began not in the 1990s but rather three

On a wintry day, Independence Hall calls to mind the spirit of the colonists in their struggle for freedom. It was here that they drafted and signed the Declaration of Independence and U.S. Constitution.

decades earlier with the arrival of Georges Perrier, who came from France in 1967 to work with renowned restaurateur Peter von Starck at La Panetière. With von Starck's blessing, Perrier opened Le Bec-Fin on Spruce Street in 1970 and in 1983 moved the restaurant to its present location on Walnut Street. This internationally acclaimed dining establishment, with its Louis XVI décor and classic French cuisine, is now the anchor of Philadelphia's fine dining district on Walnut Street.

One aspect of Philadelphia's ongoing restaurant renaissance has been an explosion of restaurants featuring tasty ethnic European and Asian cuisines. In addition, service and ambience have improved everywhere. Restaurants in historic neighborhoods like Rittenhouse Square now offer al fresco dining in the summer, so that patrons can enjoy the ambience of the neighborhood over fine food or cocktails. Keen competition among restaurants now weeds out the amateurs—although the city still has plenty of unpretentious neighborhood restaurants with their own warmth and charm.

Culture of a different sort entices visitors to other parts of the state. Americans have come to regard this nation's 19th-century industrial past with a certain nostalgia, which has made hot tourist destinations of the workaday towns and industrial sites of that era. Tour boats in Easton ply the Lehigh Canal, the waterway that once provided Philadelphia with coal. Busloads of visitors stop at the old steel mills in southwestern Pennsylvania, where they discover how the steelworkers lived and struggled to organize.

Pennsylvania has capitalized on this new trend in tourism by creating Heritage Regions throughout the

BACK TO THE FUTURE

In 1902, Joseph V. Horn and Frank Hardart opened Horn and Hardart, America's first Automat, on Chestnut Street in Philadelphia. Intended as a kind of self-service cafeteria, the Automat required customers to peer into small compartments containing prepared food and place their orders by dropping coins into the slot next to the items they wanted. Quick and "automatic," it was an early version of fast food. In 1924 the company added "takeout"—prepackaged Automat food.

PHOTO: © John McGrail

Commonwealth—areas dedicated to different aspects of the state's industrial history, such as iron and steel manufacturing, coal mining, canals, railroads, agriculture, and even early highways.

The Commonwealth has always had a wealth of attractions for those who enjoy being outside in the fresh air. Living historical farms such as the Peter Wentz Farmstead in Worcester or Old Economy Village in Ambridge are popular with families. Children, of course, prefer the Commonwealth's 16 amusement parks and water parks. Hersheypark, in south central Pennsylvania's Lebanon Valley, is most popular in terms of attendance, welcoming 2.4 million visitors each year—but Kennywood Park outside Pittsburgh, Dorney Park & Wildwater Kingdom in Allentown, and Knoebel's Amusement Resort in Elysburg all have plenty of character and their own fans. Kennywood and Knoebel's have the flavor of old-time amusement parks, while Dorney has the added attraction of a water park adjacent to its regular amusement park. Country fairs such as the York Fair or the Bloomsburg Fair annually draw more than half a million attendees to each of their exhibitions, competitions, and big-name entertainment.

Nature lovers and sports enthusiasts don't have to look far for suitable activities—starting, perhaps, with Pennsylvania's popular Rail-to-Trails program, the nation's most extensive trail system, made up of the level beds over which railroad tracks once lay. Hikers and bicyclists now can roam the pristine trails for miles through scenic and historic areas without having to dodge cars. Downhill and cross-country ski resorts such as Montage Mountain near Scranton and Jack Frost and Big Boulder Ski Areas in the Poconos offer varied terrain for skiers. More than 2,500 lakes and 54,000 miles of rivers and streams are stocked with brook, brown, and rainbow trout and small-mouth bass for fishers. Eight million acres of state and private game lands—especially the rustically beautiful World's End State Park in Forksville or Parker Dam in Clearfield County, in the heart of the Moshannon State Forest— invite hunters to try for white tailed deer, ruffed grouse, or other wild fowl. Fifty of Pennsylvania's state parks have

facilities for campers, ranging from campsites to basic cabins, and the state department of conservation and natural resources offers a 24-hour toll-free phone reservation system. North of Pottsville, Locust Lake State Park's campsites overlook a scenic lake. Cook Forest— sometimes called Pennsylvania's Black Forest—on the picturesque Clarion River is a beautiful spot to rent a rustic cabin and enjoy miles of trails. Professional outfitters provide all the necessary equipment for exciting white-water rafting trips in locations such as the Lehigh Gorge in northeastern Pennsylvania, the Youghiogheny River in southwestern Pennsylvania, or Pennsylvania's Grand Canyon in the north central part of the state.

Pennsylvania's seven major league teams—the Philadelphia Phillies and Pittsburgh Pirates (baseball), Philadelphia 76ers (basketball), Philadelphia Eagles and Pittsburgh Steelers (football), and Philadelphia Flyers and Pittsburgh Penguins (hockey)—plus a dozen minor league affiliates keep spectator sports aficionados happy, and the Commonwealth's numerous colleges and universities add to the mix with a variety of sports. There are even sporting events one wouldn't expect to find in Pennsylvania, such as Forksville's Winter Dog Sled Races.

The development of tourism is one of the Commonwealth's top priorities. The Governor's Advisory Council on Travel and Tourism, a public/private partnership, was established in 1997 to develop a strategic master plan. In the not so distant future, Pennsylvania will have three new state-of-the-art tourist attractions—the National Constitution Center in Philadelphia, the Museum of the American Revolution in Valley Forge, and the National Museum of Industrial History in Bethlehem—with more on the distant horizon. Of national rather than just local interest, these attractions are certain to raise Pennsylvania's profile for the world to see.

KORMAN COMMUNITIES

Emphasizing quality in construction, landscaping, and services, Korman Communities creates luxury short-term furnished suites that combine the service and amenities of a fine hotel with the comfort of home.

Woodview—apartments, suites, and club—is situated on a hilltop in the Main Line, Pennsylvania, overlooking the Great Valley Corporate Center and Valley Forge National Park. Its community center, at left, features a swimming pool, whirlpool spa, sauna, fitness facility, business/conference center, movie theater, and cappuccino bar.

Korman Communities has been refining the art of providing luxury accommodations for nearly a century. From its origins as one of Pennsylvania's largest home builders to the creation of KormanSuites, the nation's first short-term furnished apartments, the company has ensured that every Korman community reflects its decades of experience—and a new level in apartment living.

A TRUE FAMILY COMPANY

The focus of Korman Communities is on the resident because, like many Pennsylvania businesses, Korman Communities is a family concern.

Hyman Korman began building homes in 1919 with hardwood floors, slate roofs, and brick-on-block construction in northeast Philadelphia. His son, Samuel Korman, moved into developing planned communities, including leasing properties—a relatively novel concept at the time.

Generation three of the family brought Steve Korman, with his forward-thinking, customer-oriented philosophy. He took the company to a new level— a hybrid of rental apartments and hotel/hospitality properties, named Korman Communities.

Korman Communities created the short-term furnished suite, a hotel alternative (a hybrid of apartment and hotel that offers twice the space and half the cost of a standard hotel) in the mid-1960s. The suites were rented on a monthly basis, furnished, and fitted with accessories for business clients. Weekly maid service and morning coffee service were introduced later. Korman Communities blossomed in the mid-1990s, taking the concept, product, locations, amenities, and services to higher levels by offering resortlike services to residents of both the furnished suites and the apartments.

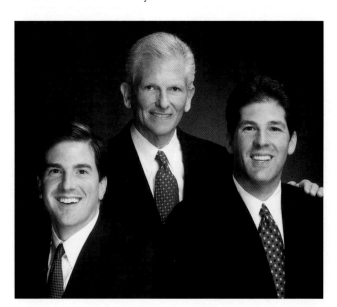

Brad Korman, Steve Korman, and Larry Korman—third and fourth generations of the Korman real estate family started by Hyman Korman in 1909—are the principals of Korman Communities. They were responsible for creating the KormanSuites brand-name corporate suite concept in the 1980s, as well as the company's nationwide expansion in the 1990s.

This fourth-generation team, led by Larry and Brad Korman, has built on the strong foundation established by earlier generations. It has broadened the business both regionally and conceptually. The company is extending its market reach by making nationwide property acquisitions. As a key strategy, Korman Communities acquires the most luxurious apartment communities in the most desirable regions to expand its short-term, furnished-suite program. The company has recently acquired 11 luxury apartment communities, entering new markets in Delaware, North Carolina, and Georgia, and has plans to add to its portfolio of properties in Pennsylvania and New Jersey.

The company's current portfolio consists of more than 20 apartment communities, including locations in Philadelphia, northeast Philadelphia, Bucks County; Montgomery County; Chester County; and the state's capital, Harrisburg.

PIONEERING VISIONARIES WITH SOLID VALUES

The Korman name is associated with quality customer service, first-rate communities, and constant attention to detail. The fourth-generation members, who run Korman Communities, have held the same core values: quality, uniqueness, excellence, service, and teamwork. These values, represented by the acronym QUEST, have helped shape the character and culture of the company.

"The word *quest* also has meaning in terms of our company's vision," says Larry Korman, president of Korman Communities. "We are on a quest not only to manage the best apartment communities in Pennsylvania and on the eastern seaboard, but also to make Korman

Rittenhouse 222, a new renovation of Horace Trumbauer's 1926 landmark high-rise building on prestigious Rittenhouse Square in Philadelphia's Center City, offers corporate suites with park views, full hotel services, 24-hour concierge, grand ballroom, fitness center with Cardio Theater Exercise Entertainment system, coffeehouse, pasta bar, and executive business and conference centers.

Communities part of the new American dream. Because of my great-grandfather Hyman's and grandfather Samuel's upbringing as farmers, our family and company have adopted very basic and solid values. Therefore, the way we got where we are is just as important as where we are going. The word *quest* symbolizes both the values of our first generation and the vision of our current generation."

Dunwoody Place, in Atlanta, Georgia, is a gated community with the features of a luxury resort. One-, two-, and three-bedroom apartment homes and furnished suites with hotel-style appointments are set amid landscaped gardens with a state-of-the-art fitness center, architect-designed pool, lighted tennis courts, coffee bar, complimentary club breakfasts, and an executive business center, library, and conference facilities.

YORK COUNTY AGRICULTURAL SOCIETY
YORK FAIR/YORK EXPO CENTER

The York County Agricultural Society, a nonprofit group of citizens dedicated to preserving the county's agricultural history, operates the York Expo Center rental program and sponsors the vibrant and historic annual York Fair.

Each September York Expo Center is the site of the York Fair, operated by the York County Agricultural Society.

For more than two centuries America's oldest fair has been attracting people young and old with agricultural competitions, educational exhibits, and family entertainment.

The first York Fair took place in 1765—11 years before the signing of the Declaration of Independence. Thomas Penn, son of William Penn, granted a charter for the York Fair in recognition of the "flourishing state to which the town has arrived through their industry." At a time when most colonists were farmers, the first American fair was truly a celebration of agriculture. It showcased the latest techniques, equipment, and accomplishments of York County's pre–Revolutionary War citizens.

Today's annual York Fair, held for 10 days in September, draws hundreds of thousands of people who come to enjoy thrills on the modern midway or to see big-name entertainers. More than 200 years after the York Fair began, people still enjoy the agricultural exhibits, livestock competitions, horticultural displays, and baking and cooking contests. The York Fair is one of south central Pennsylvania's biggest events, and it preserves a vital link to the region's agricultural heritage.

The livestock shows draw participants from among the best and brightest 4-H Club and Future Farmers of America (FFA) members. More than 1,000 animals are entered for Junior Livestock and Open Competition during the fair.

Through the years, the York Fair has hosted a parade of celebrities and leaders, from Bob Hope to pop singer Britney Spears to former presidents Theodore Roosevelt, John F. Kennedy, and George Bush.

Just as important, the fair is a place for the people of York County to move about on foot, walk through the midways, and greet each other socially as people did in cities in earlier eras. For civic groups, the fair is also a fund-raising event, with volunteer members staffing concession stands and selling special foods available only during the fair.

People also delight to see the skills and possessions of their fellow citizens. They come to see exhibits including arts, crafts, furniture making, photography, and antiques.

The York Fair is operated by the York County Agricultural Society, a nonprofit group of citizens dedicated to preserving the county's agricultural heritage. The society also operates the rental program for York Expo Center, which provides year-round exposition and meeting facilities for a growing list of trade shows and other events.

Midway rides are among the exciting attractions at the York Fair, which also features horticultural and agricultural exhibits, livestock competitions, baking and cooking contests, food concessions, and more.

HERSHEY ENTERTAINMENT & RESORTS

Hershey Entertainment & Resorts Company, an amusement-based venture founded by the legendary Milton S. Hershey,

continues to earn substantial profits that in turn help perpetuate the philanthropic efforts of The Hershey Trust.

Having fun is serious business for Hershey, Pennsylvania–based Hershey Entertainment & Resorts Company. The firm operates more than a dozen businesses ranging from an amusement park to hotels to professional sports franchises.

Hershey Entertainment & Resorts was founded in 1927 when Milton S. Hershey separated his chocolate manufacturing operations from his other business interests. All of the non-chocolate-producing divisions were reorganized under the name Hershey Estates, which later became Hershey Entertainment & Resorts.

Over the past 70-plus years, the company has grown to encompass a wide variety of entertainment interests. Hershey Entertainment & Resorts employs approximately 1,200 people year-round, as well as more than 3,200 seasonal and part-time employees. Current operations include the Hersheypark entertainment complex, Hersheypark Arena & Stadium, The Star Pavilion, ZooAmerica North American Wildlife Park, Hershey Bears AHL hockey club, Hershey Wildcats A-League soccer team, the Hotel Hershey, the Hershey Lodge & Convention Center, Hershey Highmeadow Campground, Hershey Nursery, and Hershey Laundry and Textiles.

The sky over the Hotel Hershey is decorated with brilliant colors during the annual Halloween in Hershey balloon festival.

Hersheypark was founded in 1907 as a picnic area for Hershey employees. Today, the 110-acre, world-class theme park known as "the cleanest and greenest theme park in America," features more than 50 rides and attractions, including ZooAmerica, an 11-acre walk-through zoo that is home to more than 200 animals from five regions of North America.

Hersheypark Arena, with 7,256 fixed seats, hosts the American Hockey League's Hershey Bears, as well as a variety of other family performances ranging from *Disney on Ice* to the Harlem Globetrotters.

The 25,000-seat Hersheypark Stadium accommodates a variety of outdoor concerts and sporting events, including games played by the Hershey Wildcats professional outdoor soccer team. Hersheypark Stadium also contains The Star Pavilion, a 7,200-seat open-air amphitheater.

The Hotel Hershey, a historic Mobil 4-Star, AAA 4-Diamond luxury hotel, was built by Milton S. Hershey in 1933, and today the resort features 235 guest rooms; 25,000 square feet of meeting, banquet, and exhibit space; and a 17,000-square-foot European-style spa and fitness center scheduled to be completed in the fall of 2000. The Hershey Lodge and Convention Center is the Northeast's largest convention resort. With 667 guest rooms, 100,000 square feet of meeting space, and a decor that is uniquely Hershey, it's the sweetest place to meet and offers a great family getaway.

Other Hershey Entertainment & Resort business interests include the 55-acre Hershey Highmeadow Campground, Hershey Nursery, a landscape design firm, and Hershey Laundry and Textiles.

Hershey Entertainment & Resorts is privately owned by The Hershey Trust, which acts as trustee for the Milton Hershey School. Milton S. Hershey established the school for orphan boys in 1909, and the profits from Hershey Entertainment & Resorts continue to fund the school.

ABOVE RIGHT: *Great Bear, one of eight world-class roller coasters and Pennsylvania's only steel inverted looping roller coaster, made its debut in Hersheypark in 1998.* RIGHT: *Hershey's product characters appear throughout Hershey's properties and are a favorite attraction for kids of all ages.*

PART THREE

REFLECTIONS AND VISIONS

Leadership and innovation are hallmarks of the Keystone State, a place of not only spectacular educational and natural resources but of partnerships and progress, a place whose leaders have been spearheading change since before the American Revolution. The strong, leading-edge economy that powers Pennsylvania today is the launch pad for its success tomorrow. Pacesetters in both the public and private sectors have set into motion ideas and initiatives to ensure the Commonwealth's continued growth and leadership on the world stage. • In the following pages, representatives in the vanguard of their fields offer visions for Pennsylvania's future, tying the advances of the 20th century to the possibilities of the 21st. Just as the polio vaccine, developed by Jonas Salk at the University of Pittsburgh, dramatically improved our prospects for health, or Plexiglas, developed by Rohm and Haas in Philadelphia, revolutionized manufactured products in the early 20th century, so the human genome project, choices for renewable energy, and the Internet have effected sensational change at its close. • The future, the essayists suggest, will depend on innovators, those who understand the changing needs of the consumer and can turn ideas into revolutionary new products and processes. As globalization and digital technologies continue to define commerce and the quality of life, higher education will play an increasing role in developing a creative, socially responsible workforce. Partnerships forged by government, business, and higher education will provide the infrastructure and expertise needed to meet the challenges and embrace the opportunities of this exciting new era.

READY FOR THE BRAVE NEW WORLD

H. A. WAGNER

Chairman of the Board and Chief Executive Officer, Air Products and Chemicals, Inc.

H. A. Wagner received his bachelor of science degree in mechanical engineering from Stanford University and his master of business administration degree from Harvard. He holds an honorary doctorate in engineering from Lehigh University and an honorary doctorate of laws from Moravian College. Mr. Wagner serves on the board of directors of CIGNA Corporation, PACCAR, United Technologies Corporation, and Daido-Hoxan, Japan's second largest industrial gas company. He is on the policy committee of the National Business Roundtable, the executive committee of the Pennsylvania Business Roundtable, and is a member of the Business Council. He also serves on the board of trustees of Lehigh University and is a member of KidsPeace® National Council for Kids.

In 1950, *Fortune* magazine called the 20th century the "chemical century." With all due respect to our friends in the auto and computer fields, we think the writers at the famous business publication were not far off the mark. Few have had greater and more wide-ranging impact on industry and consumers around the world than the men

and women who have developed, manufactured, and marketed the chemicals used for hundreds of purposes in thousands of products—including, of course, cars and computers. And our state of Pennsylvania has played a proud and essential part in that compelling story.

The chemical industry began in this country just outside Pennsylvania when E. I. DuPont set up his gunpowder plant along the Brandywine River in Delaware in 1802. A century later, when industrialization was in full swing in the United States, enterprising businesspeople of varied backgrounds and talents began establishing chemical companies that turned their innovative ideas into revolutionary new products and technologies. Some of the best known and most successful of those set up shop in Pennsylvania.

A CENTURY OF ACHIEVEMENT

What does it take for a company to succeed, prosper, and grow—in fact, just to survive—for a century? It's more than the ability to stay with your customers and the emerging technologies. It takes the insight to anticipate and the will to change. I think that fairly sums up the leaders in our industry in this state. Time and again, the people who operate the chemical companies in Pennsylvania have shown the foresight and the vision to keep in front of the changing needs of their customers.

And this has kept us strong and growing.

A few highlights from the past century will illustrate the impact our colleagues in Pennsylvania have made.

Rohm and Haas was launched by two forward-looking young men who brought their leather-tanning process here from Germany. It didn't take them long to extend their creative energies to new areas and begin introducing new products. One of their signature successes was Plexiglas®, a product so popular that just protecting its name has presented a challenge to its producers.

Pennwalt showed the inventive spirit that has characterized our industry by moving from basic chemicals to plastics. Famed for the Gibbs Cell, used to produce chlorine and caustic soda, Pennwalt made the strategic transition into new areas, developing exciting products like Kynar® polyvinylidene fluoride, a tough and versatile plastic.

PQ Corporation began as a manufacturer of silicates used primarily in detergents. It broadened that capability into technologies in industrial and specialty chemicals, like glass beads used in reflective materials.

PPG, the country's first commercially successful plate glass manufacturer, reinvented itself as a major producer of chlor-alkali chemicals, industrial coatings, trade paints, and fiberglass.

And, if I may add a note about my own company, we at Air Products and Chemicals have made some significant contributions to industry, too. Our founder, Leonard Pool, introduced a new way to generate low-cost oxygen that had an immediate and lasting impact on the metals industry. From there, our people developed technologies for producing hydrogen (used in every NASA space shot and to make clean-burning fuels) and helium (an essential component in MRI and other medical applications).

Today, the chemical companies in the Keystone State, at more than 500 plants, make more than products; they make a vital contribution to the economy of our commonwealth and our nation. We employ over 70,000 people who earn over $4 billion a year and contribute nearly $12 billion to the gross domestic product—third in the nation for chemical industry output. A record and a role to be proud of.

FROM NOW ON, ALL OF US IN THE INDUSTRY WILL HAVE TO PLAY BY A NEW RULE: ADAPT ON THE RUN

Now, what about the road ahead? Charting the future is never easy. But some aspects of the direction the chemical industry will take are already becoming clear.

MOVING IN A NEW DIRECTION

First, the industry is becoming a truly global enterprise—all the way from supplier to consumer. Our industry has been a key source of trade dollars for the United States, being one of the largest and most consistent trade surplus generators for many years. In the future, supply sources, manufacturing centers, technologies, and even people will become less defined by country and more defined by quality, cost, innovation, and speed. The focus will move toward emerging markets and sources of supply. And we will move with it.

The second trend is electronic commerce. Serving our customers—and being served by our suppliers—now demands not only greater speed, but incredible flexibility. From now on, all of us in the industry will have to play by a new rule: adapt on the run. To do that, we will have to be smarter and faster than we've ever been before. The information revolution is making its presence felt in a big way.

And, of course, innovation. The skill that got us here will continue to be an essential ingredient. I'm not talking just about new processes and new products, but the whole approach to business, every aspect of every system and process we use. We will have to stay ahead of the curve if we expect to be around for another hundred years.

The past century has been an amazing time for the chemical industry. For someone like me, who has been on board for over a third of it, it has been an incredible ride. But buckle up. It's a brand new world out there—again. We'll face challenges and opportunities we can't predict. But one thing I do predict: the chemical industry is ready.

PENNSYLVANIA'S GOT ENERGY!

HARRY R. HALLORAN JR.

Chairman and Chief Executive Officer, American Refining Group, Inc.

Harry R. Halloran Jr. has been the CEO of American Refining Group since 1974. He is also the founder, chairman, and CEO of Energy Unlimited, the founder of Renewable Energy Development Corporation and American Refining & Biochemical, the founding trustee of the Enlightened World Foundation, and chairman of the Global Dialogue Institute. He also serves on the board of visitors for the College of Commerce and Finance and is a member of the board of trustees at Villanova University, the Shipley School, and the Academy of Natural Sciences. Mr. Halloran holds a bachelor of science degree from the University of Pennsylvania and a master's degree in theology from the Augustinian College in Washington, D.C.

Pennsylvania is the nation's leader in energy competition, breaking the old paradigm of electricity and gas monopolies deciding what customers want. Customer choice is not just a theory in Pennsylvania, it's a reality! • Early on, Governor Tom Ridge charged Public Utility Commission Chairman John Quain with the job of bringing electricity competition to Pennsylvania. A collaborative process yielded consensus legislation passed in 1996, and in 1997 Pennsylvania began the country's largest "pilots." By January 1, 2000, 100 percent of customers were able to choose their electricity supplier.

More than half of all electricity supplied to Pennsylvania industry is provided on a competitive basis, and more than 500,000 customers benefit. Last year, electricity customers in Pennsylvania saw prices fall $1 billion, half of the decline resulting from across-the-board rate cuts and half from savings due to competition.

INNOVATIONS AND IMPROVEMENTS

Innovation now characterizes the electricity industry. In 1999, the first retail sale of electricity through the Internet occurred in Pennsylvania, as did the first retail sale of "green" renewable energy in the eastern United States. The largest solar energy array in the region now operates on a retail store outside Philadelphia, and plans have been announced for 25 solar systems on Philadelphia area schools to be installed by Conectiv Energy.

The first commercial wind energy project in the region was started by Energy Unlimited on New Year's Eve of 1999 outside of Hazleton. Another developer has a commercial wind project scheduled for completion in Somerset County during 2000. As technology evolves

and new products such as fuel cells become commercially available, Pennsylvania's open market ensures that new technologies come here first.

Pennsylvania state government hasn't missed out on the action, saving millions of taxpayer dollars through competitive procurement of electricity. Most recently, the government used an Internet auction for cost savings and dedicated 5 percent of its electricity procurement to renewable energy as a boost to that emerging market.

THE BENEFITS OF COMPETITION

Part and parcel of this restructuring has been the ability of the electric utilities to focus on what they do best. Two of Pennsylvania's largest utilities have elected to sell their electricity generation facilities, focusing on their distribution systems and on unregulated businesses. Another utility has decided to leverage its world-class competency in nuclear plant operations by purchasing and operating nuclear plants across the country. Companies from outside Pennsylvania are coming here to buy existing generation facilities, upgrading efficiency and emissions controls in the process. They are also building new "merchant" plants, such as the 700-megawatt natural gas facility under construction outside of Lebanon.

Reliability of electric service is not sacrificed in the process. The central and eastern portions of Pennsylvania are part of the Pennsylvania–New Jersey–Maryland PJM Interconnection, L.L.C., one of the oldest and largest power pools in the world. PJM became the first independent system operator (ISO) in the East in 1997. PJM was originally organized by the traditional electric utility

Pennsylvania is leading the country in delivering real competition in electricity and natural gas to our state's businesses and homes, and that's why we say, "Pennsylvania's got energy!"

MORE THAN HALF OF ALL ELECTRICITY SUPPLIED TO PENNSYLVANIA INDUSTRY IS PROVIDED ON A COMPETITIVE BASIS, AND MORE THAN 500,000 CUSTOMERS BENEFIT

companies that provided electricity to residential, commercial, and industrial users in Maryland, Delaware, New Jersey, and Pennsylvania. Other electricity generators are now party to the PJM transmission and distribution network. Every user in the PJM territories can learn the various charges/rates by referring to the PJM Open Access Tariff.

PJM continues to oversee regional transmission and generation adequacy under competition. Through the transition to competition, Pennsylvania's electric utility companies have remained financially sound, with the two largest announcing record earnings for 1999.

The transition to electricity competition has been accompanied by statewide education programs yielding high public awareness of the new right to shop for electricity. Surveys have shown choice of electricity supplier to be popular, with vast majorities voicing overwhelming approval.

Governor Ridge has also committed to competition in natural gas, through legislation ensuring all gas customers have choice by 2001. Of course, industrial customers in Pennsylvania have had competitive gas choices since the 1980s, and that will not change. But smaller businesses and households now will have these same opportunities. Included in the gas competition legislation is the elimination of the gross receipts tax on natural gas—an $82 million tax cut for Pennsylvania businesses and households that took effect January 1, 2000.

NEW MILLENNIUM, NEW HORIZONS

JEFFREY A. ROMOFF

President, UPMC Health System

A New York City native, Jeffrey A. Romoff received a bachelor of science degree with honors from City College of New York. After completing a master of philosophy degree in political science at Yale University Graduate School of Arts and Sciences, he moved to Pittsburgh in 1973 to head the Regional Education and Programming Division at the Western Psychiatric Institute and Clinic (WPIC). In the ensuing years, Mr. Romoff became the administrator of WPIC, vice president of health sciences at the University of Pittsburgh, president of the University of Pittsburgh Medical Center (appointed in 1992), and senior vice chancellor of health administration at the University of Pittsburgh. In 1997, he assumed his current position as president of UPMC Health System.

In an era of remarkable change, few sectors of our society have undergone as profound a transformation as health care. Within our lifetimes, we have seen astonishing advances in medical science. The human genome project, the gamma knife, advances in the early detection of ovarian, breast, and prostate cancers, and exciting

new approaches to organ transplantation are but a few examples.

Pennsylvania has been at the forefront of some of the most significant developments in this arena, particularly in the transformation of basic research into clinical practice, the advancement of technology, and the evolution of a new framework for the delivery of health services.

Only 50 years ago, polio was a major public health threat, crippling or killing almost 20,000 children annually. Today, this disease has been virtually eradicated in the United States because of work done by Dr. Jonas Salk at the University of Pittsburgh in the 1950s. Other medical advances originating in Pennsylvania's universities and medical centers have led to improved treatments for cancer, cardiac disease, diabetes, and a myriad of other conditions.

At the same time, advances in technology have radically altered the way in which disease is diagnosed and treated. New imaging modalities have been developed that offer definitive diagnostic capabilities that were previously achievable only via invasive procedures, and minimally invasive surgical capabilities have been devised that allow major surgical procedures to be performed through incisions that can be covered with a Band-Aid.

The behavioral health arena has also been transformed. Pharmaceutical developments have provided new treatment strategies for the management of bipolar disorders, depression, and other serious psychiatric conditions and shifted the locus of care from more restrictive institutional settings to community-based partial-hospitalization and outpatient programs.

Along with improved clinical capabilities, new knowledge about the etiology of disease has stimulated the development of preventive care strategies ranging from use of tamoxifen for women at high risk for breast cancer to prophylactic use of aspirin for heart disease. Around the corner are even more dramatic developments as genomics evolves as a clinical discipline and gene therapy is integrated into clinical practice.

CHANGES AND CHALLENGES

Beyond the clinical considerations, health care research and innovation have an enormous economic impact on the Commonwealth. In 1999, Pennsylvania's research centers attracted more than $850 million in funding from the National Institutes of Health and acted as a catalyst for the development of new biotechnology-based businesses regionally, nationally, and internationally.

We have also seen fundamental changes in the delivery system. We have moved from medical treatment

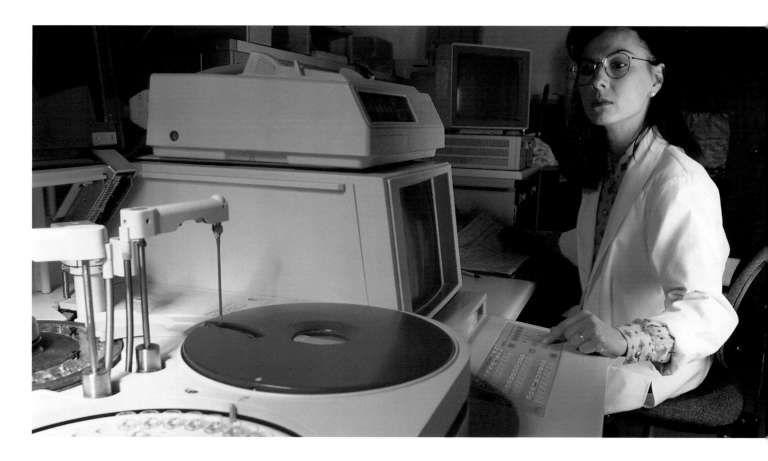

AROUND THE CORNER ARE EVEN MORE DRAMATIC DEVELOPMENTS AS GENOMICS EVOLVES AS A CLINICAL DISCIPLINE

to health care; from a focus on disease to a focus on prevention; and from an institutionally centered inpatient approach to a community-based, outpatient framework.

While we can and should celebrate these accomplishments, we know that there are major challenges ahead. Today, health care costs top $1.3 trillion and consume almost 14 percent of the gross domestic product. At the same time, more than 44 million Americans are uninsured, and enormous disparities exist in access to and use of services along racial, ethnic, and economic lines. Changing population demographics will exacerbate many of the problems that we face today.

The very foundation of health care as a healing discipline has been challenged by the recent Institute of Medicine study that cited medical errors as a major health threat, accounting for as many as 98,000 deaths annually. This study, along with other reports that have documented enormous variability in clinical practice patterns, must act as a call to action for health care providers to adopt evidence-based medical practices and standardize delivery mechanisms to improve outcomes and reduce errors.

HEALTH CARE FOR A NEW CENTURY

Information technology is key to creating tomorrow's delivery system. The development of an effective electronic health record, which brings together information from all clinical settings along with advanced decision support capabilities and "error traps," will enable physicians to become more effective and efficient, and at the same time more patient focused.

Tomorrow's consumer will be more educated, more demanding, and more skeptical. The health care industry, working in collaboration with the communities it serves, must continue to evolve to assure it remains responsive to consumers' needs and wants. At the same time, our industry must adapt to harsh financial realities brought about by changes in governmental and private payment systems, which limit the resources and options that are available.

As an industry, we are more than ready to face these challenges. We have a right to be proud of all that has been accomplished and to look forward to new horizons in the new millennium.

HIGHER EDUCATION

LEADERSHIP THROUGH HIGHER LEARNING

GRAHAM B. SPANIER

President, The Pennsylvania State University

Graham B. Spanier is president of the Pennsylvania State University and professor of human development and family studies, sociology, demography, and family and community medicine. He has served as chair of the National Collegiate Athletic Association (NCAA) Division I Board of Directors and of the Council of Presidents of the National Association of State Universities and Land-Grant Colleges. He is a member of the board of directors of the Pennsylvania Association of Colleges and Universities. Dr. Spanier earned his doctorate in sociology from Northwestern University and his bachelor's and master's degrees from Iowa State University. He previously served as chancellor of the University of Nebraska–Lincoln and has led Penn State since 1995.

The growth of the learning society in the latter half of the 20th century has brought to the fore the role higher education's leadership plays in the progress of our nation. Pennsylvania is fortunate to be able to call upon a diverse higher education community to help meet the challenges of a knowledge economy. The Commonwealth

is home to several of the leading research universities in the nation. More than 140 institutions of higher education serve individuals, communities, and businesses throughout the state and address a wide array of educational needs.

THE CHANGING LANDSCAPE OF HIGHER EDUCATION

Institutions of higher education today open their doors to a vastly increased number of students. During the last 25 years alone, the rate of Pennsylvania's high school graduates who went on to college rose by more than two-thirds, to 71 percent, exceeding the national average. It is projected that from now until 2008, 40 percent of new jobs nationwide will require at least an associate degree, so the demand for higher education is likely to continue to grow. The increasing role of colleges and universities in workforce development is a very significant chapter in the modern history of higher learning.

With greater numbers came greater diversity among learners, a change that also has profoundly affected institutions of higher education. We have opened up our colleges and universities to more adult learners, part-time students, women, and minorities. This transformation, still in process, has made substantial progress in extending the economic and social benefits of higher learning more fully throughout society. The

growing inclusiveness of our campuses is responsive to the challenges of a pluralistic society. It is a vital expression of the opportunity that higher education represents and a plus for the education provided to all students.

Within our commitment to prepare students for life in a diverse world, the confluence of our educational mission and character, citizenship, civility, tolerance, and social responsibility is of increasing importance. Our society has seen an erosion of some traditional social structures and values. Institutions of higher education are in a unique position to provide leadership in understanding this phenomenon.

Another change that is transforming Pennsylvania's colleges and universities is the globalization of higher education. Whether our students are interested in business, environmental studies, journalism, engineering, or art, they will find themselves drawn over time into an international milieu. Employers are eager to hire graduates who speak a foreign language and who understand world geography, international politics, and global economics and have an appreciation for cultural understanding. Institutions of higher education long have promoted international understanding, and our curricula are now permeated with a global perspective. Our schools have scores of international exchange opportunities that provide access to emerging technologies and new markets around the world.

The importance of innovation for Pennsylvania's economic competitiveness, and more generally, for the quality of life in our state, challenges higher education in several ways. Those institutions whose mission includes research are key players in the scientific and technological advancements that underlie the development of new products, the introduction of new efficiencies, improvements in health care, and progress on environmental and other societal concerns. Colleges and universities across the board are equipping students with a new set of active and collaborative learning skills to support critical thinking and creative problem solving. They also are giving greater emphasis to lifelong learning and institutional outreach. More active partnerships with business and industry are a hallmark of all of these developments.

Among the most profound changes higher education has seen is the impact of the new digital technologies that are revolutionizing communications and the processing of information. These advancements facilitate teaching and learning, discovery, and outreach in

ORGANIZATIONS AND COMMUNITIES ARE EAGER TO PARTNER WITH OUR INSTITUTIONS TO ADDRESS EXPANDING KNOWLEDGE NEEDS

ways that could not be imagined just a few decades ago. The added flexibility, enhanced capacity, more intensive involvement, and extended collaboration made possible by these technologies are the perfect complement to the higher learning needs of our changing world. No institution of higher education can afford to leave these technologies behind.

OPPORTUNITIES FOR THE FUTURE

Pennsylvania's colleges and universities have unprecedented opportunities to promote economic, human, and cultural development for the Commonwealth and enhance the quality of life for its citizens. Fields such as the life sciences and information technology are of tremendous importance to the future and require integrated efforts in teaching, research, and service to position our state at their forefront. The increasing emphasis on the value of intellectual capital makes more compelling than ever our role in educating each new generation of Pennsylvania citizens. Continuing and distance education will be an area of substantial growth. Organizations, industries, and communities are eager to partner with our institutions to address expanding knowledge needs. Responding to the challenges of societal change, Pennsylvania higher education can look forward to an active role in the 21st century.

SHINING PAST, BRILLIANT FUTURE

LAWRENCE A. WEINBACH

Chairman, President, and Chief Executive Officer, Unisys Corporation

Lawrence Weinbach joined Unisys in 1997 after a career with Arthur Andersen, including eight years as managing partner and chief executive of Andersen Worldwide. Mr. Weinbach serves on the boards of Avon Products, the University of Pennsylvania and the Wharton School, Carnegie Hall, the Philadelphia Orchestra, the Regional Performing Arts Center in Philadelphia, the Greater Philadelphia First Foundation, the Greater Philadelphia Chamber of Commerce, and Catalyst. He was appointed chairman of the Team Pennsylvania Human Resources Investment Council by Governor Tom Ridge. Mr. Weinbach is a 1961 graduate of the Wharton School of the University of Pennsylvania.

The Commonwealth of Pennsylvania enjoys a long and auspicious history of leadership and innovation. Two hundred years ago it led the American Revolution. One hundred years ago it was a leader in the Industrial Revolution. Fifty years ago it led the computer revolution. And today it is among the leaders of the Internet revolution, as

information technology permeates every aspect of business, government, and our daily lives.

The computer revolution began when electrical engineers J. Presper Eckert and John Mauchly came together at the University of Pennsylvania in 1946 to develop ENIAC, the world's first large-scale, general-purpose digital computer. Could they have imagined then that they were ushering in a new era, one in which technology would revolutionize the way we work, the way we live, the way we interact with fellow citizens?

The innovation at Penn led directly to UNIVAC, the world's first large-scale commercial computer, which was built in Philadelphia and delivered to the U.S. Census Bureau in 1951 by the company that later became Unisys Corporation. It is this rich heritage of technological innovation that inspires our commonwealth to be a leader in the Internet revolution and makes us proud to call Pennsylvania our home as we move forward in the Internet economy.

A HIGH-TECH HOTBED

There's no question that technology will be the driving force in the 21st century, one that offers significant economic potential for all Pennsylvanians. Pennsylvania is already a leader among states that have embraced the Internet revolution and are preparing their citizens and

their economies to address the challenges and opportunities of the new millennium.

Numerous innovative programs are fostering technology development and attracting technology investment to the Commonwealth. For starters, entrepreneurs can use the Internet to access all the government forms they need to start a business, making it easier to start a business here than anywhere else in the nation.

An exciting initiative called Lightning Manufacturing is applying the speed and agility of the Web to business processes such as engineering and development. Lightning Manufacturing provides an electronic community where Pennsylvania companies can collaborate to quickly develop products and attract customers from across the state and the globe.

In the western part of the state, the Pittsburgh Digital Greenhouse is creating a partnership between high-tech companies and educational institutions to provide the infrastructure and expertise needed to accelerate technology development.

Pennsylvania is also driving high-tech progress in other ways, such as offering a research and development tax credit, eliminating state tax on computer services, and convening Tech 21, an advisory group of technology entrepreneurs who are working to make Pennsylvania a technology leader.

ENIAC, the world's first large-scale, general-purpose digital computer, was developed at the University of Pennsylvania by a team led by John Mauchly and J. Presper Eckert.

OUR ON-LINE OPPORTUNITY

But for Pennsylvania to emerge as a true leader in the Internet economy, it must help extend technology to all citizens so that everyone can benefit from the Internet revolution. Ultimately, Pennsylvania's high-tech leadership will come not from a computer or a line of code but from the creativity and hard work of its citizens.

Fortunately, Pennsylvania is taking the steps necessary to prepare its citizens to compete in the Internet economy. Appropriately, these programs start with our children. The nationally acclaimed Link to Learn program is investing hundreds of millions of dollars in computers and technology training for students and their teachers.

The SciTech Scholars program provides scholarships to Pennsylvania students who are studying technology. In return, the students agree to work in Pennsylvania for up to three years after they graduate. As part of the program, technology companies such as Unisys provide internships for students and jobs for graduates.

For those entering or already in the workforce, CareerLink brings together dozens of job-training and education programs into a single Internet service center. Pennsylvania was the first to offer such a resource, and the CareerLink Web site is accessed tens of millions of times by job seekers and employers alike.

Unisys Chairman Larry Weinbach introduces the Unisys e-@ction Enterprise Server ES7000, the first Intel-based mainframe computer designed for high-volume electronic business.

These efforts are part of Pennsylvania's overall strategy to foster growth among local technology companies, attract innovative new companies to the state, and provide citizens with the education and opportunity they need to achieve success in the Internet economy.

The Internet revolution holds great promise for Pennsylvania, building stronger ties between people and government, delivering a greater number of services and a higher level of service to all citizens, strengthening local communities across the state, and enhancing the effectiveness and reach of education, economic expansion, and social progress. Now, Pennsylvania's government, its educational institutions, its entrepreneurs and business leaders, and its citizens must come together to meet the challenges and embrace the opportunities of this exciting era. At Unisys we are prepared to join all Pennsylvanians in making the Commonwealth, in the words of Governor Tom Ridge, "a leader among states and a competitor among nations."

'ENTICING INTELLECTUAL APPETITES'

ARDATH H. RODALE

Chairman and Chief Executive Officer, Rodale Inc.

Ardath H. Rodale is chairman and CEO of Rodale Inc., a global leader in healthy active living information. Its publications include such well-known magazines as *Men's Health, Organic Gardening, Prevention,* and *Runner's World.* Rodale Books publishes nearly 100 new books each year, including *The Doctors Book of Home Remedies.* In 2000, Rodale was named one of *Fortune* magazine's 100 Best Companies to Work For in America. Ms. Rodale is the author of two books, *Climbing Toward the Light* and *Gifts of the Spirit,* and "Reflections," a monthly column in *Prevention* magazine. She was named one of the 50 Leading Women Entrepreneurs in the World by the Star Group in 1999 and a Distinguished Daughter of Pennsylvania by Governor Tom Ridge in 1997.

The publishing industry has deep and strong roots in Pennsylvania. America's first publisher, Benjamin Franklin, printed *Poor Richard's Almanack,* a publication designed to "educate and entice the intellectual appetites of the American people," in 1732. • Franklin and his successors understood that the power of the written word inspires

people to improve their lives and change the world around them. Since the Declaration of Independence was proclaimed in the *Pennsylvania Magazine,* Thomas Paine's powerful voice for revolution, communicating passions and dreams has always been at the core of the publishing industry.

INFORMATION REVOLUTION

The economical and social effects of the industrial revolution were coupled with scientific and technological advances as publishers catered to America's growing interests and needs. Readers wanted the latest recipes and dressmaking patterns, the best short stories, and home handyman advice—in addition to the daily news.

During the last century, an information revolution changed how ideas were created, produced, and disseminated to the public. In the early 1900s, slow printing presses literally stamped out editions of popular titles like *Harper's, Popular Mechanics,* and *Philadelphia Magazine,* and only 1,943 magazines were published in the United States. Today's computer-driven presses print at speeds of

over 3,000 feet per minute, producing over 150,000 U.S. magazines that fill newsstands and mailboxes around the world. Plus, more than 850 new magazines are published in this country each year.

The computer also has transformed the way in which we deliver information to readers. Publishers routinely update and improve stories at the eleventh hour, and add breathtaking photos to enrich the written word. The Internet expands the sharing of ideas across worldwide boundaries in milliseconds. So, whether readers are interested in calculating the calories burned by walking, tracking the leaders of the Tour de France, or solving a bug problem in the garden, they get the information they need and want faster—and better—than ever.

Most national magazines have an on-line version and use it to interact with readers beyond their printed pages. The Internet enhances stories by integrating text, sound, video, computer graphics, and animation. It creates instantaneous public access to vast resources of information, and expands the reach of printed ideas to new readers. E-communication provides instant feedback on

COMMUNICATING PASSIONS AND DREAMS HAS ALWAYS BEEN AT THE CORE OF THE PUBLISHING INDUSTRY

articles in current issues, and it helps to quickly test new ideas and conduct market research with existing and potential subscribers.

The magazine Web site is a personal, instantaneous interaction between publisher and reader, a community of geographically dispersed individuals with a common interest. For example, Rodale's *Runner's World* magazine, in conjunction with its Web site www.runnersworld.com, coaches readers on training for a race, connects these readers on-line with other would-be marathoners, and literally runs the race with them—26.2 miles to success! Connectivity with readers is how magazines stay vibrant. A magazine thrives when it understands and fosters that unique relationship between its editorial product and its readers and the trust that results.

MEDIAMELD

The new century offers readers new ideas, insights, information, and inspiration on an interactive, personal basis through a seamless blend of media. Unlike *Poor Richard's Almanack,* my own company's *Backpacker* brand properties include a magazine, two Web sites, a book series, and a public television show, reaching its community and spreading its message across all media. "Mediameld," we call it.

We are living in a time of dynamic change—one that the innovative Franklin would have certainly found most enticing.

PENNSYLVANIA—KEY PLAYER IN THE INFORMATION REVOLUTION

Many of the pivotal events of the media industry that occurred during the 20th century took place in the Commonwealth. Here are just a few that have changed the way the world is informed and entertained.

- The world's first commercial radio station, KDKA, broadcast the presidential election returns from Pittsburgh. (1920)
- The first use of the postal zip code took place in Pittsburgh. (1943)
- The first electronic computer—ENIAC (Electrical Numerical Integrator and Computer)—was designed at the University of Pennsylvania. (1946)
- The nation's first community antenna television system, later known as "cable," was constructed in Mahanoy City. (1948)
- *TV Guide,* the largest selling weekly magazine in the United States, published its first edition in Philadelphia. (1953)
- The world's first community-owned television station, WQED-TV, began public broadcasting in Pittsburgh. (1954)
- The first newspaper vending machine was manufactured and leased in Columbia. (1954)
- The first Internet "emoticon"—the smiley :-)—was created at Carnegie Mellon in Pittsburgh. (1980)
- The first live broadcast of the home shopping network QVC took place in West Chester. (1986)

THE EVOLVING WORLD OF TRAVEL

KIMBERLY K. SCHALLER

Vice President, Sales and Marketing, Hershey Entertainment & Resorts

Kim Schaller is one of the top marketing professionals in central Pennsylvania. A recipient of both *Central Pennsylvania Business Journal's* Top 40 Under 40 award and the YWCA's Tribute to Women in Industry award, Schaller is the first and only female vice president of Hershey Entertainment & Resorts. Previously, she was director of marketing and sales at Space Center Houston and prior to that was employed by PPO&S Advertising and Public Relations in Harrisburg. A graduate of the Pennsylvania State University, Schaller is a member of the Governor's Travel and Tourism Committee, the International Association of Amusement Parks and Attractions' Marketing and Public Relations Committee, and the Pennsylvania Hospitality Association.

I have had the privilege of being involved in the travel industry my entire career and have loved every minute of it. It is constantly changing; it is vibrant and it is dynamic. For the most part, people love to travel. It changes their perspective, their outlook, and, in many ways, it changes them. There is a big world out there, and the prospect of exploring it is incredibly exciting to many, including me.

I feel very fortunate to live in a state where tourism is so highly regarded: as a viable industry with significant economic impact. We are blessed with a wide variety of tour and travel options within our borders and a huge population base in neighboring states from which to attract visitors. I've lived in Texas and Florida—two states with outstanding travel destinations to market—but I keep coming back to Pennsylvania.

THE POWER OF THE CONSUMER

The most significant changes I've seen in the industry are not limited to changes in technology; they extend to changes in the travel consumer.

People are traveling in record numbers; it's actually staggering. Whether for business or recreational purposes, people are taking to the air, the rails, and the roads in droves. Las Vegas, Orlando, Nashville, Branson—all inventing and reinventing themselves, evolving in what they have to offer and whom they offer it to.

When visiting a destination like Orlando, you have to admit that you look around and say, "When is this going to end? How much stimuli can I take on a family vacation?" *Simple* is the operative word. Life is remarkably complicated, and simple choices have become very complex decisions. The options for travel are overwhelming, and today's consumers expect more than they ever have before.

Leisure time is a precious commodity with an incredible value. The traveler of today lays the responsibility of "good times for all" squarely on our shoulders. It's up to *us* to ensure that not a moment of this precious time is wasted—and we are up to the challenge. Those of us who have answered the call have survived, and those who have not are out of business.

I have been so impressed watching the hospitality industry respond to this educated, evolving, insistent consumer with changes such as an airline bill of rights, the reinvention of the travel agent, customized packaging, the "customer comes first" orientation, frequent traveler programs—all developed to meet the needs of the user.

Technology and a healthy economy have played a huge role in this process. We have the ability to welcome a repeat guest to a restaurant or hotel and simultaneously pull up a guest history file that will tell us exactly what the guest likes and dislikes, and we jump to accommodate him or her. That's a true sign of the times.

The World Wide Web is a tremendous tool in seeking out travel information, but the statistics continue to support the fact that with their actual booking, users still prefer assistance from a *live* person.

As a member of the Governor's Council on Travel and Tourism, I have been very encouraged regarding the future of travel in Pennsylvania. We have set forth over a dozen initiatives in a strategic master plan designed to coming back again and again. They are loyal and generous, if we treat them well. As an industry, we can never let up on this pursuit—an unwavering commitment to our customer.

AN AIRLINE BILL OF RIGHTS, CUSTOMIZED PACKAGING, FREQUENT TRAVELER PROGRAMS—ALL WERE DEVELOPED FOR THE USER

take Pennsylvania into the new century. We benchmarked travel efforts in certain key states, analyzed national and international trends, did a complete review of our existing travel products statewide, and came up with a very exciting vision for the future. It involves a commitment at the highest levels to travel as a viable economic driver, the development of tourist-friendly amenities, the marriage of private- and public-sector efforts and resources, and a consistent image for the state of Pennsylvania.

We represent an economic force that is all about the right things in life: camaraderie, adventure, relaxation, education, and renewal.

AN OPEN CHANNEL OF COMMUNICATION

We know that it's all about listening to our customers, which is not a unique concept. As an industry, we have been remarkably successful in hearing what they have to say; travel products today are truly incredible. Today's customers reward us by

A life-sized Hershey's Kiss poses with a young visitor at Hersheypark, in Hershey, Pennsylvania. Honored in 1999 by the International Association of Amusement Parks for its outstanding efforts to develop people in the amusement industry, the 110-acre theme park is one of Pennsylvania's top tourist attractions. It boasts more than 55 rides, plus restaurants, live entertainment, and gift shops.

THE PROMISE AND THE CHALLENGE

STEPHEN M. WOLF
Chairman, US Airways Group

A graduate of San Francisco State University, Stephen M. Wolf joined Arlington, Virginia–based US Airways Group, Inc., in 1996 after a long career in leading positions at other airlines, the most recent as chairman and CEO of United Airlines. In addition to memberships on the board of directors of R. R. Donnelley & Sons Company, Philip Morris USA, Georgetown University, and the Alzheimer's Disease and Related Disorders Association, Wolf is a trustee of the Brookings Institution. He also has been named an Officer of the Legion of Honor by President Jacques Chirac of France, a country in which Wolf and his wife, Delores, have had a longstanding interest.

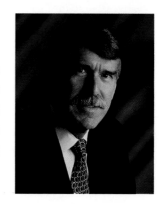

In an era of remarkable change, few sectors of our society have witnessed greater revolution in the past century than transportation, our ability to move people and goods from one place to another with efficiency and ease. As a result, mobility has been increased, underscoring in the most dramatic fashion the American penchant for experimentation

and change in our lives, and commerce has expanded exponentially, with the marriage of computers and air, rail, and road cargo producing the phenomenon and efficiencies of on-time production.

In short, the quality of life has been enhanced in once unimaginable ways as innovation after innovation has made travel both accessible and comfortable.

There is a tendency to forget that just two or three generations ago, a trip from Harrisburg or Erie to Los Angeles was undertaken only with very complex planning and might have taken many rather uncomfortable days by train or car. Today, a resident of Harrisburg or Erie can reach Los Angeles with ease, having the choice of several airlines for a trip that lasts a few hours and involves perhaps one change of plane. Or, if the preference is auto or rail, a vastly improved infrastructure makes these options more feasible for the average family or business as well. And all can be planned easily with a few clicks of a computer keyboard.

CHOICES FOR TRAVEL

As a society, we have choices—remarkable choices—and few states have done as good a job as Pennsylvania has at making those choices available to all its citizens. Allow me to use air travel, the sector I know best, as an example.

In the 1940s, when Philadelphia Municipal Airport became Philadelphia International Airport, approximately 40,000 passengers were carried in the first year of operations. The airlines serving the airport mainly flew twin-engine DC-3 passenger aircraft.

WHAT IS THE PICTURE TODAY?

In 1999, more than 25 million passengers passed through Philadelphia International—more passengers in a day than were served in a full year just half a century ago. The most modern passenger jets carry customers nonstop to more than 100 destinations throughout the United States, the Caribbean, and Europe. Terminal facilities have been modernized and new international and regional aircraft facilities are under construction. Interstate highways and passenger rail facilities bring travelers to the terminal doors.

Across the state, in Pittsburgh, the picture is the same. In the 1940s, fewer than a million air travelers passed through Pittsburgh International annually, a number that grew to the 20 million level in the 1990s, as the airport grew dramatically after it became a US Airways hub. Today, there is nonstop service not only throughout the United States, but to key European destinations as well. Again, an efficient highway system brings passengers to the airport. As in Philadelphia, a

network of regional aircraft flights complements access to the large airports by road and rail.

In short, whether one lives in Philadelphia or Pittsburgh, in Harrisburg or Erie, in Wilkes-Barre or Altoona, the option of air travel is available today where it was not 60 years ago.

But airports alone do not tell the story. First a passenger or cargo must get to the airplane. Today, a remarkably complex system of highways, including an interstate system that did not exist a few decades ago, and rail marshalling yards makes the connection of road, rail, and air part of everyday commerce.

our new Airbus aircraft not only are quieter and more environmentally friendly, but they bring unparalleled passenger comfort inside the cabins, with laptop ports and telephones available at every seat.

But what will happen as the number of people traveling increases? If we use Pittsburgh International as an example, we see that the number of passengers passing through the airport is expected to grow by at least 50 percent in the next 20 years to more than 30 million annually. Philadelphia can expect equal or greater growth. Air freight, too, is projected to grow at a similar rate. Will we have the roadways to carry passengers and

THE MARRIAGE OF COMPUTERS AND AIR, RAIL, AND ROAD CARGO PRODUCES THE EFFICIENCIES OF ON-TIME PRODUCTION

INFRASTRUCTURE IS KEY

And it is this connectivity that is our biggest challenge for the future. The great airlines, railroads, and road freight companies that play so much a part of Pennsylvania's life today will undoubtedly continue to innovate, making the movement of people and goods simpler and more inviting. If I may use my own company as an example,

freight efficiently? Will there be sufficient groundside facilities? Will our air traffic control system keep pace?

This is our promise and our challenge, and just as the transportation industry has met both in decades past, I am confident we will do so in the decades to come. Pennsylvania is poised for continued leadership in this quest.

BIBLIOGRAPHY

Adams, Carolyn et al. *Philadelphia: Neighborhoods, Division, and Conflict in a Postindustrial City.* Philadelphia: Temple University Press, 1993.

Alberts, Robert C. "The Good Provider." *American Heritage* 23, no. 2 (1972): 26–47.

American City Business Journals. <www.bizjournals.com> (1999–2000).

Bishop, Todd. "Review Preview: Marketing and Media," and "Review Preview: Law." *Philadelphia Business Journal,* Jan. 1–7, 1999.

Bomberger, Bruce, and William Sisson. *Made in Pennsylvania: An Overview of the Major Historical Industries of the Commonwealth.* Harrisburg: Pennsylvania Historical and Museum Commission, 1991.

Bulkeley, William M. "Tech IPO's Put Unsung Backer in the Limelight." *Wall Street Journal,* Oct. 14, 1999.

Butko, Brian A. "Larger than Life Along the Lincoln Highway." *Pennsylvania Heritage* 21, no. 3 (1995): 20–29.

Clark, William H. "Bedford County: From Indian Trails to Tourist Resorts." *Pennsylvania Heritage* 12, no. 2 (1986): 12–17.

Cochran, Thomas C. *Pennsylvania: A Bicentennial History.* New York: Norton, 1978.

Davis, Christopher R. "Tourism and Civic Boosterism in Punxsutawney, PA, 1899–1909." *Western Pennsylvania Historical Magazine* 68, no. 2 (1985): 101–130.

"Editor's Interview: Agricultural Exports Poised to Grow." *Central Penn Business Journal,* July 30, 1999.

Erdman, Timothy M. "Hershey: The Sweet Smell of Success." *American History Illustrated* 29, no. 1 (1994): 64–69.

Farmerie, Samuel A. "The Call of the Clarion." *Pennsylvania Heritage* 11, no. 2 (1985): 32–37.

Freeman, Sabina Shields. "The Northwest's Vintners." *Pennsylvania Heritage* 14, no. 2 (1988): 4–9.

Fuller, Theodore, Kathleen Miller, and Stephen Smith. *Road to 2000: Update on Pennsylvania.* University Park, Pa.: The Pennsylvania State University Center for Economic and Community Development, September 1998.

Gorenstein, Nathan. "SAP Announces Plans for $150 Mil Headquarters Complex in Pennsylvania." *Philadelphia Inquirer,* Sept. 12, 1997.

Hanson, Joyce. "Harrisburg is High Tech Growth Spot." *Central Penn Business Journal,* July 30, 1999.

Harris Pennsylvania Industrial Directory. Twinsburg, Ohio: Harris Publishing Company, 1997.

Hays, Samuel P., ed. *City at the Point: Essays on the Social History of Pittsburgh.* Pittsburgh: University of Pittsburgh Press, 1989.

Heath, Tracy. "Destination Pennsylvania: Building the Perfect Location." *Site Selection* 44, no. 4 (1999): 651–663.

Hill, Miriam. "Index Funds Impossible to Ignore." *Wall Street Journal,* November 9, 1999.

Hoover's Online: The Business Network. <www.hoovers.com> (2000).

Klein, Maury. "John Wanamaker." *American History Illustrated* 15, no. 8 (1980): 8–15.

Klein, Philip Shriver, and Ari Hoogenboom. *A History of Pennsylvania.* New York: McGraw-Hill, 1973.

Lincoln Financial Group. "Lincoln Financial Group Signs Lease for Headquarters in Philadelphia" (press release). April 29, 1999.

Lubove, Roy. *Twentieth-Century Pittsburgh.* Pittsburgh: University of Pittsburgh Press, 1996.

Miller, E. Willard. *A Geography of Pennsylvania.* University Park, Pa.: The Pennsylvania State University Press, 1995.

——. *Pennsylvania: Keystone to Progress: An Illustrated History.* Northridge, Calif.: Windsor Publications, 1986.

Mumma, Laura Sickel. "Eagles Mere: Of Cottages and Kings." *Pennsylvania Heritage* 12, no. 3 (1986): 18–25.

Myers, Albert Cook. *Narratives of Early Pennsylvania, West New Jersey, and Delaware, 1630–1707.* New York: Charles Scribner's Sons, 1912.

Ockershausen, Jane. "The Valley That Changed the World." *Pennsylvania Heritage* 21, no. 3 (1995): 12–19.

Pennsylvania Agricultural Statistics Service. *1997–1998 Statistical Summary and Pennsylvania Department of Agriculture Annual Report.* Harrisburg: Commonwealth of Pennsylvania, 1999.

Pennsylvania Public Utility Commission. *Electric Power Outlook for Pennsylvania, 1996–2016.* Harrisburg: Commonwealth of Pennsylvania, n.d.

——. *1997 Utility Consumer Activities Report and Evaluation,* Harrisburg: Commonwealth of Pennsylvania, 1997.

Pennsylvania State Data Center. *Pennsylvania County Industry Trends, 1994–1998.* Harrisburg: Commonwealth of Pennsylvania, 1999.

Pennsylvania State University, College of Agricultural Sciences. "Survey on Logging Opens Up Opportunities for Change" (press release). April 14, 1999.

Pennsylvania State University, College of Agricultural Sciences, Agricultural Information Services. <www.aginfo.psu.edu> (1999–2000).

Risse, Guenter B. *Mending Bodies, Saving Souls: A History of Hospitals.* New York: Oxford University Press, 1999.

Sack, Saul. *History of Higher Education in Pennsylvania.* Harrisburg: Pennsylvania Historical and Museum Commission, 1963.

Scranton, Philip, and Walter Licht. *Work Sights: Industrial Philadelphia 1890–1950.* Philadelphia: Temple University Press, 1986.

Sexton, Sean. "Consumers Rate iQVC Highest Among On-line Shopping Sites." *IMarketing News* 1#5 (1999): 8.

Stevens, Sylvester Kirby. *Pennsylvania: Birthplace of a Nation.* New York: Random House, 1964.

——. *Pennsylvania History in Outline.* Harrisburg.: Pennsylvania Historical and Museum Commission, 1976.

Tascarella, Patty. "Communicating Success." *Pittsburgh Business Times,* May 3, 1999.

Tebbel, John William. *A History of Book Publishing in the United States.* 4 vols. New York: R.R. Bowker Co., 1972–1981.

Venable, Tim. "Ready for the Twenty-First Century: Today's High-Tech Pennsylvania." *Site Selection* 43, no. 3 (1998): 521–539.

Vogel, Morris J. *Cultural Connections: Museums and Libraries of Philadelphia and the Delaware Valley.* Philadelphia: Temple University Press, 1991.

Wall, John. "Mushrooms on the Move." *Penn State Agriculture* (1999): 9–21.

——. "Putting More on the Plate." *Penn State Agriculture* (1996): 19–23.

Wilson, Erasmus. *Standard History of Pittsburgh, Pennsylvania.* Chicago: H.R. Cornell, 1898.

Wilson, Martin W. "Delaware Water Gap: Birth and Death of a Resort Town." *Pennsylvania Folklife* 35, no. 2 (1985-86): 80–92.

Wright, Nancy Allison. Airmail Pioneers. <www.airmailpioneers.org> (1999).

In addition to the sources listed above, Web site postings by the following entities provided information used in this publication: Accountants on Call, Adelphia Business Solutions, Alcoa, Allegheny Particleboard, Allegheny Technologies, Allentown Morning Call, Amtrak, Arthur Andersen, Bethlehem Steel, Brandywine Realty Trust, Brownstein Group, Bucknell University, Calgon, Carnegie Mellon University, CB Richard Ellis, CB Technologies, Century Associates, Cigna Corporation, Coleman Legal Staffing, Comcast, Concurrent Technologies, Connaught Laboratories, Contemporary Staffing Solutions, Dechert Price & Rhoads, DecisionOne, Deloitte & Touche, Diamond Lustre, Dickinson University, Drexel University, Duquesne University, Eastern America Transportation Warehousing Logistics, Eastern Wood Products, Ernst & Young, GAI Consultants, Harrisburg International Airport, Harte-Hanks DiMark, Hazelton Environmental, Hershey Foods, H. J. Heinz, Institute for Scientific Information, Jefferson Health System, Kennametal, Keystone Powdered Metals, Kirkpatrick & Lockhart, Kling Lindquist, Knouse Foods Cooperative, Lancaster Laboratories, Lehigh Valley International Airport, Liberty Property Trust, Lincoln Financial Group, Lippincott Williams & Wilkins, Lucent Technologies, Mack Trucks, Mellon Bank, Microbac Laboratories, Morgan Lewis & Bockius, Norton Pakco Industrial Ceramics, Pennsylvania House, Pennsylvania State University, Pfaltzgraff, Philadelphia Daily News, Philadelphia Inquirer, Philadelphia International Airport, Philadelphia Museum of Art, Pittsburgh Children's Museum, Pittsburgh International Airport, Pittsburgh Mercy Health System, Pittsburgh Post–Gazette, PNC Bank, Port of Philadelphia and Camden, Port of Pittsburgh, QVC, Respironics, Rodale, Roy F. Weston, St. Christopher's Hospital for Children, SAP America, Shared Medical Systems, Sunoco, Systems and Computer Technology (SCT), Tasty Baking, Temple University, Tenet Health, Turkey Hill Dairy, Unisys, University of Pennsylvania, University of Pittsburgh, UPMC Health System, University of Scranton, Ursinus College, U.S. News & World Report, Vanguard Group, Western Pennsylvania Hospital in Pittsburgh, WQED, Zippo Manufacturing.

INDEX